TOWARDS A BETTER ASSESSMENT (
DAMAGES FOR PERSON

TOWARDS A BETTER ASSESSMENT OF PAIN AND SUFFERING DAMAGES FOR PERSONAL INJURIES

A Proposal Based on Quality Adjusted Life Years

Vaia KARAPANOU

intersentia

Cambridge – Antwerp – Portland

Intersentia Publishing Ltd.
Sheraton House | Castle Park
Cambridge | CB3 0AX | United Kingdom
Tel.: +44 1223 370 170 | Email: mail@intersentia.co.uk

Distribution for the UK:
NBN International
Airport Business Centre, 10 Thornbury Road
Plymouth, PL6 7 PP
United Kingdom
Tel.: +44 1752 202 301 | Fax: +44 1752 202 331
Email: orders@nbninternational.com

Distribution for the USA and Canada:
International Specialized Book Services
920 NE 58th Ave. Suite 300
Portland, OR 97213
USA
Tel.: +1 800 944 6190 (toll free)
Email: info@isbs.com

Distribution for Austria:
Neuer Wissenschaftlicher Verlag
Argentinierstraße 42/6
1040 Wien
Austria
Tel.: +43 1 535 61 03 24
Email: office@nwv.at

Distribution for other countries:
Intersentia Publishing nv
Groenstraat 31
2640 Mortsel
Belgium
Tel.: +32 3 680 15 50
Email: mail@intersentia.be

Towards a Better Assessment of Pain and Suffering Damages for Personal Injuries.
A Proposal Based on Quality Adjusted Life Years
Vaia Karapanou

© 2014 Intersentia
Cambridge – Antwerp – Portland
www.intersentia.com | www.intersentia.co.uk

ISBN 978-1-78068-230-3
D/2014/7849/75
NUR 820

British Library Cataloguing in Publication Data. A catalogue record for this book is available from the British Library.

ACKNOWLEDGEMENTS

Writing this book would not have been possible without the help, support and good advice of numerous people. If it weren't for Roger van den Bergh and Louis Visscher, I would have never started this PhD in the first place. Roger, I am grateful to you for your support and for giving me the opportunity to research on my own ideas. Louis, your excellent supervision has been a decisive factor for the completion of this book. Thank you for the insightful suggestions, the continuous guidance, the inspiration, the intellectual stimuli and the endless hours of discussion. I owe you my deepest gratitude. A special thank you goes to Anthony Ogus for providing invaluable advice and comments, which critically improved my research, as well as support before and after the defence of the dissertation on which this book is based. I am truly grateful for your help. I would also like to thank Michael Faure for providing resourceful comments and suggestions throughout the writing of this book but most importantly for his attentiveness in the crucial final stage. I am grateful for your help.

Spending three years in the Erasmus School of Law allowed me to test empirically the hypothesis that being in the proximity of incredibly smart people is beneficial for one's research and personal development. For that positive influence I would also like to thank the rest of the amazing RILE group: Ann-Sophie Vandenberghe, Wicher Schreuders, Alessio Pacces, Marianne Breijer, Alessandra Arcuri, Sharon Oded, Franziska Weber, Pieter Desmet, Weiqiang Hu and Klaus Heine. I am more than grateful to Jennifer Arlen, Thomas Ulen, Neil Rickman, Gerhard Wagner, Werner Brouwer, Siewert Lindenbergh and Stefan Weishaar for insightful comments and suggestions during presentations and/or private discussions on parts of this book. The remaining mistakes are my own.

Even though one doesn't wish to be reminded of this after finishing it, the truth is that writing a PhD is a demanding task that involves stressful deadlines, long working hours and makes scarce the time spend with family and friends. I want to apologize to all of those who had to bear with me and cope with time scarcity. An enormous thanks goes to my brother for his inexhaustible humour. Christo, you gave me a reason to smile even in the face of the most absurd circumstances. Stefane, I know you don't like to be thanked but I wouldn't have gone through this without you. You are my sunshine and breath of fresh air. Finally, I would like to thank my parents, Dimitri and Antigone for their unconditional love, patience and support. The example you have set is my driving force. I love you with all my heart and I dedicate this book to you.

CONTENTS

TABLE OF CASES

ENGLAND AND WALES

Cook v. J.L. Kier and Co. [1970] WLR 774
Wise v. Kaye [1962] 1 QB 638
H. West & Son Ltd v. Shepard [1964] AC 326
Lim Poh Choo v. Camden and Islington Area Health Authority [1980] AC 174
Heil v. Rankin [2001] QB 272
Alan Roger Plater v. Sonatrach [2004] EWHC 146 (Qb)
Simmons v. Castle [2012] EWCA Civ 1288

FRANCE

François vs. Monsanto T.G.I. Lyon, 13 fév. 2012, n° 2012/144

GERMANY

LG Bonn 02.05.1994 9 O 323/93
LG München I 23.08.2004 17 O 1089/03 SP 2005, 52
LG Baden-Baden 24.10.2006 1 O 374/04
LG München I 11.01.2007 19 O 12070/04
LG Münster 17.04.2009 16 O 532/07, NJW 2010, 86
OLG Saarbrücken 16.05.1986, NJW-RR 1987, 984
OLG Hamburg 20.04.1990 zfs 1990, 260; NJW 1990, 2322
OLG Frankfurt a. M. 01.12.2001 1 U 35/03
OLG Stuttgart 18.03.2003 1 U 81/02 NJOZ 2003, 3064
OLG Frankfurt 23.12.2003 8 U 140/99
OLG Koblenz 18.03.2004 5U 1134/03 NJW-RR 2004, 1025
OLG Hamm 09.03.2006 6 U 62/05, NJW-RR 2006, 1251
OLG München 24.09.2010 10 U 2671/10, BeckRS 2010, 23467
OLG Schleswig 09.10.2009 4 U 149/08
BGH 16.02.1993 NJW 1993, 1531
BGH 13.10.1992 NJW 1993, 781

GREECE

MonProtLeukadas 472/2004
EfAth 7146/1992, [1995] HellDni, 647, No. 11
EfThes 2717/2002
EfLarisis 919/2005, [2006] ESigD, 283
EfAth 6009/2005
EfDod 307/2005
EfThes 1328/2006, Armenopoulos, 8/2008
EfThes 2601/2006
EfPatron 151/2009
EfPatron 672/2009
EfAth 2591/2010, NV 61/2013, 2695
EfPirea 102/2011, Piraiki Nomologia 23/2011, 156
EfPirea 24/2012
EfPirea 278/2013
DPrAth 3441/2006
DEfThes 1876/2012
AP 526/2006
AP 433/2008, [2008] ESigD, 150
AP 605/2008, [2008] ESigD, 165
AP 1216/2008, [2008] ESigD, 428
AP 1174/2009, [2009] ESigD, 429
AP 525/2011
AP 72/2012
AP 924/2013

ITALY

Repetto v. A.M.T. di Genova, Corte cost., 14/07/1986, no. 184
Valentini v. Castaldini, Trib. Verona, 15/10/1990
Tribunale di Savona, 29/07/2005
Tribunale di Roma, sez. XIII, 24/11/2005
Tribunale di Roma, sez. II, 16/01/2009, n. 908
Tribunale di Pisa, 01/08/2009, n.189/2002 R.G
Tribunale di Modena, sez. Lav., 30/11/2011, n. 287
Tribunale di Roma, XIII sez. Civ., 22/02/2012 n. 36620
Corte d'Appello di Roma, 23/02/2009
Corte di Appello di Bari, sez. II nr. 737, 23/05/2011
Cass. Civ., sez. III 04/03/2008 n. 5795
Cass. Civ., sez. III 12/12/2008 n. 29191
Cass. Civ., sez. III 13/05/2009 n. 11059
Cass. Civ., sez. III 07/06/2011 n. 12408
Cass. Civ., sez. III 13/07/2011 n. 15373

Cass. Civ., sez. III 10/03/2012 n. 5770
Cass. Civ., sez. III 21/04/2012 n. 9147
Cass. Civ., sez. III 26/10/2012 n. 18484
Cass. Civ., sez. III 03/10/2013 n. 22585
Cass. Civ., sez. III 14/01/2014 n. 531
Cass. Civ., sez. III 23/01/2014 n. 1361
Cass. Civ., sez. III 28/01/2014 n. 1762
Cass., 24/10/2008 n. 25751
Cass., UU. sez. Civ., 11/11/2008 n. 26972
Cass., UU. sez. Civ., 14/01/2009 n. 557

THE NETHERLANDS

Rb. Groningen, 24–03–2000, rolnr. 98–1028
Rb. Den Haag, 19–06–2002, rolnr. 99–791
Rb. Zwolle, 02–10–2002, rolnr. 01–1113
Rb. Utrecht, 31–03–2004, rolnr. 03–155
Rb. Alkmaar, 24–12–2008, VR 2009/60
Rb. Rotterdam, 20–10–2010, VR 2011/135
Rb. Midden-Nederland, 06–02–2013, RAV 2013/47
Hof Den Haag, 19–03–1996, VR 1999/149
Hof Arnhem, 30–11–2004, VK 2005/73, 381
Hof Den Bosch, 17–10–2006, VR 2007/11
Hof Leeuwarden, 08–02–2011, JA 2011/87
HR 08–07–1992, nr. 14852, NJ 1992/714
HR 20–09–2002, NJ 2004/112

UNITED STATES

Xavier vs. Philip Morris USA Inc., 787 F. Supp. 2d, 1075 (N.D. Cal. 2011)

LIST OF ABBREVIATIONS

CBA	Cost-Benefit Analysis
CEA	Cost-Effectiveness Analysis
CUA	Cost-Utility Analysis
DALY	Disability Adjusted Life Year
EU	European Union
HUI	Health Utilities Index
QALY	Quality Adjusted Life Year
SG	Standard Gamble
TTO	Time Trade-Off
UK	United Kingdom
USA	United States of America
VAS	Visual Analogue Scale
VSL	Value of Statistical Life
VSLY	Value of Statistical Life Year
WTP	Willingness To Pay
WTA	Willingness To Accept
NICE	National Institute for Health and Clinical Excellence

LIST OF TABLES AND FIGURES

TABLES

FIGURES

CHAPTER 1

INTRODUCTION

The assessment of noneconomic damages associated with personal physical injuries remains a daunting task for courts and is the subject of a longstanding and unresolved debate in legal scholarship. Personal physical injuries are closely related to human activity and may hence occur in a multitude of contexts, for instance as a result of defective products, medical errors, traffic or work-related accidents. The consequences of such injuries can be very detrimental to the lives of the victims, especially when they involve permanent disability. The numbers are quite revealing. According to the latest statistical data from the European Commission, traffic accidents occurring on the roads of the European Union in 2012 resulted in more than 28,000 fatalities. For every death it was estimated that four permanently disabling injuries, such as brain damage or spinal cord lesion, and eight serious injuries occurred.[1] A similar situation is observed in the workplace where, based on the most recent statistical data, more than 2.8 million serious accidents occurred in 2009, resulting in 3,806 fatalities.[2] The way in which courts assess pain and suffering damages in cases of personal physical injuries does therefore not only concern legal theory and practice, but can also potentially directly affect a large number of people. Improving the way pain and suffering damages are currently assessed in the context of tort law lies at the heart of this book.

1.1. AIM OF THE RESEARCH

On the occurrence of wrongful behavior that results in personal injury, the injured party can claim pain and suffering damages for the immaterial loss incurred. Assessing this loss is not straightforward and there are different approaches to guide the assessment across the European legal jurisdictions. In

---

[1] European Commission, Mobility and Transport, "Statistics – Accidents Data," http://ec.europa.eu/transport/road_safety/specialist/statistics/index_en.htm (accessed 31.03.2014). See also European Road Safety Observatory, *Annual Statistical Report 2011,* European Road Safety Observatory, [2011].

[2] Eurostat, "Health and Safety at Work Statistics," European Commission, http://epp.eurostat.ec.europa.eu/statistics_explained/index.php/Health_and_safety_at_work_statistics (accessed 31.03.2014).

some countries, for instance, courts are assisted in their assessment by the existence of systematized tables, which report the amounts that have been awarded for specific injuries in previously adjudicated cases.[3] In others, ranges of injury-specific amounts are stipulated, based again on awards that have been granted by courts in the past.[4] Instead of using ranges, courts in some countries are guided by tables that include amounts corresponding to points of invalidity.[5] In other countries where no system of rationalizing pain and suffering damages is in place, judges may enjoy full discretion in deciding the magnitude of the award.[6] However, despite the different ways employed to assess damages for personal injuries, legal literature in most of these European legal systems recognizes that the paramount goal aimed at through awarding pain and suffering damages is to compensate the victim for the harm she has incurred.[7] Satisfaction of the victim is also frequently mentioned as a secondary goal. The extent to which these goals can be reached is greatly determined by the calculation of damages. However, given that there are different approaches to assessment, which is likely to result in diverging amounts, the question emerges as to which approach can generate pain and suffering damages that best fulfill the goals of tort law.

Besides reaching amounts that fulfill the goals stipulated by legal theory, a further improvement in the assessment approach and the resulting pain and suffering damages may be possible if insights from the economic analysis of tort law are taken into consideration. According to law and economics, tort law aims to reach the goals of deterrence, loss spreading and reduction of the administrative costs of the legal system.[8] To induce potential tortfeasors to abstain from careless or excessive activities, damages should fully reflect the immaterial loss incurred due to the injury. On the other hand, the attainment of the goal of loss spreading is directly influenced by which losses are reflected in the awards, as losses that are not included in the damage awards remain with the victim. Finally, reducing the

[3] See for instance Susanne Hacks, Ameli Ring and Peter Böhm, *Schmerzensgeldbeträge 2009* (Bonn: Deutscher Anwaltverlag, 2009); ANWB, *Verkeersrecht: Smartengeld* (The Hague: ANWB, 2014) for Germany and the Netherlands respectively. These publications provide an overview of the amounts that have been awarded in the past for specific injuries.

[4] See Judicial College, *Guidelines for the Assessment of General Damages in Personal Injury Cases*, 12th ed. (Oxford: Oxford University Press, 2013). These guidelines, which are published biennially, include amounts that have been awarded in England in the past.

[5] Francesco D. Busnelli and Giovanni Comandé, "Italy," in *Damages for Non-Pecuniary Loss in a Comparative Perspective*, ed. W. V. Horton Rogers (Wien, New York: Springer, 2001); Francesco D. Busnelli and Giovanni Comandé, "Italy," in *Compensation for Personal Injury in a Comparative Perspective*, eds. Bernhard A. Koch and Helmut Koziol (Wien, New York: Springer, 2003); Basil Markesinis et al., *Compensation for Personal Injury in English, German and Italian Law* (Cambridge: Cambridge University Press, 2005), p. 238.

[6] Konstantinos D. Kerameus, "Greece," in *Damages for Non-Pecuniary Loss in a Comparative Perspective*, ed. W. V. Horton Rogers (Wien, New York: Springer, 2001), pp. 129–134.

[7] Cees van Dam, *European Tort Law* (Oxford, New York: Oxford University Press, 2006), pp. 301–303.

[8] Guido Calabresi, *The Costs of Accidents. A Legal and Economic Analysis*, 5th ed. (New Haven: Yale University Press, 1977), p. 24.

costs of the legal system with respect to immaterial losses suggests that the fewest resources possible should be allocated to assess the corresponding pain and suffering damages. Damages are thus regarded as the instrument with which these goals can be attained. The overall aim is to minimize the total costs of accidents.[9] An assessment approach that is capable of minimizing the total accident costs can therefore reasonably be expected to generate significant benefits for the tort system in general, e.g. through the more efficient use of resources. Hence, it is desirable that pain and suffering damages are also calculated so as to fulfill the goals of tort law as stipulated by law and economics.

It follows that the aim of this study is to improve the assessment of pain and suffering damages awarded for non-fatal personal injuries by translating insights from legal theory and law and economics into practical recommendations for assessing damage amounts. However, the assessment of damages for personal injuries involves an evaluation of the impact of the immaterial loss incurred, which falls outside the competence of tort law and the economic analysis of tort law. The tools to evaluate this impact should therefore be sought in specialized disciplines dealing exactly with how personal injuries and other health conditions affect individuals.

Health economics is one such discipline. In the context of health economics, the Quality Adjusted Life Year (QALY) is a measure used to evaluate different health care programs and medical interventions in terms of the benefits they generate for quality of life and the costs they require for their implementation.[10] The QALY can express how different health conditions may affect quality of life. Given that pain and suffering damages are also intended to compensate for a decrease in quality of life, it is meaningful to investigate whether the QALY could be used for assessing pain and suffering damages in the way recommended by legal theory and by law and economics. Answering this question will make clear whether there is the possibility for further improvement of pain and suffering damages using insights from health economics.

1.2. RESEARCH QUESTIONS

The study addresses two main questions: *How should pain and suffering damages in cases of personal physical injuries be assessed in order to fulfill the goals of tort law as these are stipulated by traditional legal theory and by law and economics?*

---

[9]   Ibid., p. 24.
[10]   John Brazier et al., "A Review of the Use of Health Status Measures in Economic Evaluation," *Health Technology Assessment* 3, no. 9 (1999), pp. 3–4; Paul Dolan, "The Measurement of Health-Related Quality of Life for use in Resource Allocation Decisions in Health Care," in *Handbook of Health Economics*, ed. Anthony J. Culyer and Joseph P. Newhouse, Vol. 1, Part 2 (Elsevier, 2000), p. 1723; Sherman Folland, Allen C. Goodman and Miron Stano, *The Economics of Health and Health Care*, 5th ed. (Upper Saddler River (NJ): Prentice Hall, 2007).

How can insights from health economics research involving the impact of different health conditions on the quality of life be used to this end?

As explained in the previous section, the aim of this study is to explore the possibility of an improvement in the current assessment of pain and suffering damages. Besides reaching amounts that fulfill the goals stipulated by legal theory, it is suggested that the approach used to assess pain and suffering damages should also strive to generate amounts that fulfill the goal of the economic analysis of tort law, i.e. the minimization of total accident costs. Given that the assessment of pain and suffering damages involves evaluating the impact of the immaterial loss incurred due to the injury, this study will explore whether insights from a research field specializing on the impact of different health conditions on the quality of life, can be used to attain the stipulated goals. The QALY, a measure that has been used so far in the context of health economics, will be considered as a potential metric to achieve this aim. To address the main research questions, several subquestions are formulated that correspond to the chapter structure of the dissertation.

The first question is: *what goals does tort law aim to achieve with respect to pain and suffering damages and what criteria do these goals imply that should be taken into consideration in the assessment of pain and suffering damages?* Answering this question is important because in order to improve the amounts currently awarded, the goals aimed at through pain and suffering damages should be clear. A subsequent question is whether court practice in certain European countries for assessing these amounts takes into account the stipulated criteria.

Moving on to the economic analysis of tort law, the second question tackled in the study is: *what are the goals of tort law aimed at through pain and suffering damages according to law and economics and how should pain and suffering damages be assessed in order to attain them?* The goals of tort law, as accepted by economic analysis, are presented to provide the underlying rationale that should permeate the assessment of damages for immaterial losses.

Having clarified which goals are aimed at through pain and suffering damages and how should these damages be assessed in order to attain them, the next series of questions refers to the QALY. More specifically, *what is the QALY and for what purpose has it been used so far in the context of health economics? How is it calculated? How can it be monetized? What are the advantages and limitations arising from its use in the context of health economics?* Answering these questions paves the way for the next part of the analysis, which explores whether the QALY could be used in a tort context for assessing pain and suffering damages.

The subsequent questions therefore look at the potential of using the QALY in a different context than what it was initially intended for. More specifically they ask: *what steps should be taken to use QALYs for the assessment of pain and suffering damages arising from personal physical injuries in a tort law context? What are the implications (advantages/disadvantages) of using a measure which was initially devised for cost-effectiveness analyses in the domain of health economics, to assess tort damages?* And lastly, *can a QALY-based framework for the assessment of damage awards facilitate the attainment of the goals of tort law with respect to pain and suffering damages, as those are stipulated in law and economics and traditional legal theory?* The first two questions imply that some adjustments would be necessary if the QALY were actually to be employed in assessing pain and suffering damages. The last question focuses on whether a QALY-based framework could improve the current assessment of pain and suffering damages hence promoting the goals of compensation, satisfaction and minimization of total accident costs.

After the main analysis of the possibility of using QALYs in the context of tort damage assessment, the next questions aim to explore the extent to which the results of the analysis may change, if insights from cognitive psychology are taken into account. These insights suggest that victims (i.e. plaintiffs) as well as judges may make false predictions about the victims' future well-being after a personal injury, which may influence the calculation of pain and suffering damages accordingly. It is therefore important to ask: *do insights from cognitive psychology affect the analysis with respect to implementing QALYs for the assessment of pain and suffering damages? If yes, could QALYs deal with the arising implications?*

The last question posed is: *how can the results from the QALY analysis be used in practice in the calculation of damages for non-pecuniary losses in cases of personal injuries?* Analyzing proposals for the improvement of the assessment of pain and suffering damages at a theoretical level is of little value if these proposals cannot be practically implemented. Therefore, answering this last question aims to show whether and how it could be feasible to use QALYs for assessing pain and suffering damages in actual personal injury cases.

To provide answers to the above research questions the dissertation uses insights not only from legal theory, but also from law and economics and health economics. Insights from legal and law and economics scholarship with respect to achieving tort law goals are combined and translated to practical recommendations for assessing pain and suffering damages. With respect to the QALY measure from the domain of health economics, the dissertation offers a toolkit for its potential utilization in non-pecuniary damage assessment and makes explicit the cost savings and other advantages emerging from such utilization.

1.3. METHODOLOGY

The study adopts a multifaceted analytical approach. A comparative methodology is followed with respect to the legal treatment of pain and suffering damages. The legal provisions of five different countries pertaining to the assessment of damage awards are discussed and the assessment approaches used in these countries are compared. The benchmark for the comparison is the competence of the assessment approaches to reach the goals aimed at through pain and suffering damages. The countries investigated are: England, Germany, Greece, Italy and the Netherlands. The reason for the selection is that these countries enable the examination of a variety of assessment approaches. With the exception of Germany and the Netherlands, where damages are assessed in a similar way, i.e. with the assistance of tables including previously awarded amounts, each of the countries follows a different approach for assessing damage awards.[11] England has additionally been selected because it is interesting to explore how a common law country treats pain and suffering damages. A number of court cases from the selected jurisdictions are reviewed and the pain and suffering damages that have been awarded are juxtaposed with the amounts that would result from the application of an improved assessment approach.

To investigate which approach for assessing pain and suffering damages would improve the current amounts, the study relies on law and economics methodology.[12] The rational choice theory is thus applied to answer the research questions together with methodological individualism, as the basic unit of analysis is individual action. This implies that the approaches for assessing pain and suffering damages are evaluated on the basis of the incentives they can provide to prospective accident parties in order to optimize their behavior before and after the accident. The point of departure for the law and economics analysis is the seminal book by Guido Calabresi entitled *The Costs of Accidents*,[13] which has been accepted in law and economics scholarship as setting forth the basic theory of the economic analysis of tort law and laying the path for its more formal exploration.[14] Law and economics literature (both theoretical and empirical) pertaining to the effect of pain and suffering damages on deterrence, insurance and the costs of administering the tort system, as well as related topics, are studied to spell out how a different determination of pain and suffering damages could contribute to the minimization of total accident costs.

In light of the findings from law and economics literature, it is subsequently investigated whether (and which) information from health economics research regarding the impact of different health conditions could be used to build a framework that enables a better assessment of noneconomic damages. Theoretical foundations as well as methodological issues of cost-effectiveness

---

11   See *infra* chapter 2.

12   Heico Kerkmeester, "Methodology: General," in *Encyclopedia of Law and Economics: The History and Methodology of Law and Economics*, eds. Boudewijn Bouckaert and Gerrit de Geest, Vol. 1 (Cheltenham: Edward Elgar, 2000), pp. 348 ff.

13   Calabresi, *The Costs of Accidents. A Legal and Economic Analysis*.

14   To name a few important scholarly publications that followed: Richard A. Posner, "A Theory of Negligence," *The Journal of Legal Studies* 1, no. 1 (1972), pp. 29–96; John Prather Brown, "Toward an Economic Theory of Liability," *The Journal of Legal Studies* 2, no. 2 (1973), pp. 323–349; William M. Landes and Richard A. Posner, *The Economic Structure of Tort Law* (Cambridge, Massachussets; London, England: Harvard University Press, 1987); Steven Shavell, *Economic Analysis of Accident Law* (Cambridge, MA: Harvard University Press, 1987).

analysis are discussed to the extent they are necessary to illustrate how the QALY works in the context of health economics and which adjustments should in turn be made so that the QALY can facilitate the assessment of pain and suffering damages in a tort law context. Research results from cost-effectiveness analyses, in which different health conditions are evaluated, are taken into account as they provide necessary information for a potential application of a QALY-based approach.

After the mainstream analysis, insights from cognitive psychology are considered, which are relevant for the topic of pain and suffering damages. It is examined whether these insights can influence the assessment of pain and suffering damages and to what extent, if at all, they should be taken into account.

1.4. SCIENTIFIC AND SOCIETAL RELEVANCE

This research is highly relevant both from a scientific and a societal perspective. The question of how to assess pain and suffering damages related to physical injury is a recurring one in legal scholarship. Current assessment approaches are criticized on a multitude of grounds including that they lack an instrument to evaluate the immaterial loss incurred due to different types of injuries and translate it to monetary awards. The assessment of pain and suffering damages has also given rise to a longstanding debate in the context of the economic analysis of tort law where the emphasis lies on efficiency and more specifically on the efficient use of resources by way of minimizing the total costs of accidents. The proposition to use insights from health economics to facilitate the assessment of pain and suffering damages is a novel idea with a great deal of potential since it can incorporate both legal and economic considerations and has not yet been (adequately) investigated in legal and law and economics scholarship. More specifically, the QALY measure from the domain of health economics can provide an instrument, which is currently lacking, to reflect the impact of different types of injuries as well as to help minimize the total costs of accidents. This research also investigates another scientifically relevant question, namely whether psychological phenomena such as hedonic adaptation and focusing illusion may affect the assessment of pain and suffering damages.

From a societal perspective, how pain and suffering damages are assessed is important because personal physical injuries are very common in different contexts. Improving the way in which courts assess pain and suffering damages does therefore not only contribute to the ongoing scientific discussion, but can also potentially influence in a positive manner the lives of a large number of people. Discussions with respect to improving the way pain and suffering damages are assessed are currently taking place in some European countries.[15]

---

[15] See *infra* chapter 2.

The present research not only explores the possibility of an improvement but also goes one step further by building a framework based on the results of the analysis and providing examples of how it could be practically implemented. In light of the relevant discussions, the results of the analysis could therefore be of significant practical value, as they could inform (and potentially reform) policy and judicial practice, especially in the countries already considering a change in the way pain and suffering damages are assessed.

1.5. CONTENT STRUCTURE

Following this introduction, Chapter 2 investigates pain and suffering damages from a legal perspective. Focusing mostly on legal systems of European countries, the chapter initially explores the goals of the award of pain and suffering damages in tort law. Compensation stands out as the principal goal of awarding damages for immaterial losses, followed by satisfaction, which is of secondary importance. The analysis then turns to how pain and suffering damages for physical injuries are dealt with more specifically in five European countries: England, Germany, Greece, Italy and the Netherlands. A review is made of the law of each country (in the case of England, the precedent too) that stipulates for which immaterial losses pain and suffering damages are awarded and what criteria play a role in the assessment. In light of this information, the current judicial practice in these countries with respect to the assessment of pain and suffering damages is discussed. These practices are evaluated on the basis of their ability to reach the stipulated tort law goals.

Chapter 3 investigates pain and suffering damages from a law and economics point of view. The analysis starts off by identifying what the goals of tort law are according to the economic analysis. These goals – deterrence, loss spreading and reduction of the administrative costs of the legal system – provide the underlying rationale that should permeate the assessment of pain and suffering damages. It is explained that for deterrence reasons, damages awarded should fully reflect, in a consistent and predictable manner, the total extent of the immaterial loss incurred. On the other hand, it is shown that to achieve optimal loss spreading, the victims should not be (fully) compensated for immaterial losses because people are generally not willing to purchase insurance against such losses and therefore receiving pain and suffering damages would result in insurance against their will. Finally, it is demonstrated that in order to minimize administrative costs, pain and suffering damages which are correct on average are preferred to an accurate evaluation in every individual case. It follows from the analysis that a discrepancy exists between the goals of deterrence and loss spreading regarding the treatment of immaterial losses that influences the award of pain and suffering damages. The chapter discusses the solutions that have been proposed thus far to strike a balance between the two goals. One of the solutions involves awarding an amount that corresponds to the 'ex ante determined damages', namely to the amount an individual would be willing to spend on accident avoidance. Nevertheless, the chapter concludes that there is no methodology that would be able to assess the 'ex ante determined damages' for non-fatal injuries.

So far, the analysis has stipulated that a set of criteria should be incorporated into the assessment of pain and suffering damages in order to effectively achieve the goals of tort law. Improving pain and suffering damages would therefore include using an assessment approach that is capable of taking these criteria into account. Given that legal as well as law and economics scholarship lack the competence to evaluate the impact of immaterial losses incurred due to personal injuries, it is worthwhile to explore whether other disciplines dealing with different health conditions and impairments could contribute to this end. Chapter 4 introduces the QALY, a measure that has been used in cost-effectiveness analyses to evaluate health treatments and medical interventions. By discussing its characteristics and the most important issues pertaining to its use, the chapter aims to make clear that apart from the purpose for which it was initially intended, the QALY possesses many elements that make it an appropriate measure to be employed in alternative contexts involving assessments of health and life. More specifically, the QALY combines in a single metric an evaluation of quality of life and duration of a health impairment as it expresses the value of living one year with a certain health condition. The chapter stresses the fact that QALYs enable the relative ranking of different health conditions based on evaluations of individuals regarding the quality of life experienced with a specific condition. By attaching a monetary value to the QALY, this relative ranking can also be expressed in monetary terms. The detailed analysis aims to show that the QALY is a reliable measure for the quality and duration of life that has resulted from thorough scientific research.

Taking into consideration the preceding analysis, Chapter 5 shows how QALYs could be applied to assist courts in the assessment of pain and suffering damages in cases of personal injuries. The information that can be found in QALY research regarding the severity and relative ranking of different health conditions is highly relevant in the context of assessing pain and suffering damages. Nevertheless, given that the QALY is a measure that was initially intended for use in health economics and not in the context of tort law, significant attention is paid to potential necessary adjustments that would facilitate this novel use. The chapter shows how, by combining elements from QALY research, amounts for pain and suffering can be generated that fulfill the criteria set for the assessment of damages in previous chapters. The resulting amounts can reflect the gravity and relative ranking of different health conditions in a consistent and meaningful way, thus promoting compensation and satisfaction. Moreover, as they are based on the preexisting evaluations of individuals with respect to the impact of different health conditions, the amounts can provide the measure of the ex ante determined damages that was missing for personal injuries, therefore facilitating deterrence and loss spreading. In addition to the aforementioned benefits, the chapter explains why the proposed framework is expected to result in significant reductions in the costs of the tort system. The concrete case of deafness serves as an example to illustrate the suggested approach. Besides the positive implications that the QALY application would entail with respect to the goals of tort law, it is shown that the approach has related positive consequences with respect to dealing with strategic behavior and inducing victim mitigation of losses. Finally, the chapter discusses the challenge of assessing pain and suffering damages for multiple injuries.

In Chapter 6 the analysis turns to a different issue. The chapter discusses the relevance of psychological insights for pain and suffering damages and more specifically the impact that hedonic adaptation neglect and focusing illusion have on the subjective well-being of the victim. According to these insights, the assessment of pain and suffering damages may be systematically flawed because victims (and judges) disregard the gradual improvement in life satisfaction after an injury and claim for (award) a higher amount than that which would correspond to the actual losses. In view of these insights, several scholars have proposed that the amounts awarded for loss of enjoyment of life should be decreased or even abolished, thus reducing the overall amount of pain and suffering damages. The chapter reviews a large amount of empirical research regarding the phenomena of hedonic adaptation and focusing illusion and shows that they do not occur for all types of injuries, and also that the time and extent of occurrence differs per injury and/or individual. The adoption of a patient-elicited QALY framework would be able to accommodate hedonic adaptation and focusing illusion to the extent that they occur. However, in light of the current inconclusive empirical evidence and normative considerations that may require investigation, it would be reasonable to abstain from incorporating psychological insights into damages assessment.

Chapter 7 shows how the results of the preceding analysis can be used in practice for the assessment of pain and suffering damages in cases of personal injuries. Four cases, namely paralysis due to spinal cord injury, amputation of lower limb (below and above knee), loss of sight in one eye (and loss of one eye), and contraction of HIV, serve as examples to illustrate how applying the QALY framework can generate pain and suffering damages for these physical harms. The resulting amounts are juxtaposed with the amounts that have been awarded in England, Germany, Greece, Italy and the Netherlands for these types of injuries. The chapter concludes with recommendations regarding how the envisaged approach could presently be introduced into the judicial system.

Finally, Chapter 8 summarizes the findings, provides some concluding remarks and identifies avenues for future research.

CHAPTER 2

HOW SHOULD PAIN AND SUFFERING DAMAGES BE ASSESSED?

A Legal Perspective

This book is concerned with personal physical injuries that occur in a tort law context. This implies that in case of an illicit act resulting in injury, the rules of tort law apply in affirming liability and awarding damages. Thus, a party may be liable for inflicting a personal physical injury if she has acted illegally intentionally or through negligence. In certain cases she may even be strictly liable irrespective of her culpability. To found liability, a causal link must exist between the unlawful behavior and the injury inflicted in all three cases and additionally, only in cases of negligence, a duty of care and a breach of this duty are required, the definition of which may differ per country. The tort law context further implies that the parties involved in the dispute arising due to the infliction of injury may be perfect strangers, such as the parties to automobile accidents, or may previously have had a consensual/contractual or market relationship such as the parties involved in medical malpractice cases (doctor–patient), cases of product liability (manufacturer/seller–consumer) and cases of work-related accidents (employee–employer).[16] In the latter cases, if a contractual agreement already exists before the injury was inflicted, the injured party may be able to claim for damages both on the basis of a tort and on the basis of a breach of contract, provided of course that this is allowed by the legal system at hand.[17]

Personal physical injuries may generate two types of losses: monetary losses and immaterial losses. Monetary losses, frequently also referred to as pecuniary, may for instance consist of the loss of future earnings, the costs of hospitalization or doctor visits at home, the costs of paying a maid to clean the house, the costs of taking a taxi instead of driving to work, as well as any other cost incurred after the injury in order to sustain the injured person. With the exception of loss of future income, which is more challenging to assess, these losses are relatively

---

16   Jennifer H. Arlen, "Compensation Systems and Efficient Deterrence," *Maryland Law Review* 52 (1993), pp. 1115–1116.

17   Hans-Bernd Schäfer and Claus Ott, *The Economic Analysis of Civil Law* [Lehrbuch der ökonomischen Analyse des Zivilrechts], trans. Matthew Braham (Cheltenham, UK: Edward Elgar, 2004), p. 223.

easy to ascertain and compensate as they are incurred as a result of spending money on goods and services exchanged in markets, refunding the price of which will mend the loss.

On the contrary, immaterial losses incurred due to personal physical injuries cannot be easily assessed in monetary terms. The difficulty faced by courts in evaluating their extent and calculating the corresponding pain and suffering damages lies in the non-pecuniary nature of these losses. A personal physical injury will primarily involve a physical reduction of health. This reduction may materialize as an impairment of (one of) the five senses of smell, sight, touch, hearing and taste. It may also materialize as loss or diminution of physical ability, such as for instance the loss of sexual function or the ability to walk, and can even involve loss of a body part or disfigurement. Apart from the physical reduction of health, a personal injury may also inflict pain, suffering, anxiety, fear, emotional strain, psychological reduction of health and loss of enjoyment of life. All these negative effects may occur temporarily or indefinitely and lead to a diminution of what could generally be described as quality of life.

This chapter sets forth to investigate from a purely legal perspective the goals of tort law with respect to pain and suffering damages. These goals provide guidance on how immaterial losses arising from personal physical injuries should be treated and which criteria should play a role in assessing the corresponding pain and suffering damages. The existing ways of assessing pain and suffering damages in different countries will be sketched to ascertain whether they take into account the stipulated criteria and subsequently manage to fulfill tort law's goals.

2.1. GOALS OF TORT LAW REGARDING PAIN AND SUFFERING DAMAGES

In the legal literature tort law is designated to pursue several goals and functions. This section lists and analyses in particular the goals of tort law with respect to pain and suffering damages that are accepted by most European legal systems. In doing so it aims to provide an overview of the meaning and essence of these goals in general, i.e. without examining in detail how each goal is perceived separately in each and every country. The discussion of the goals provides guidance as to how the assessment of pain and suffering damages should be performed in order to attain them. Several criteria are subsequently derived for assessing pain and suffering damages.

Two goals of tort law are particularly emphasized in the legal literature with respect to pain and suffering damages: compensation and satisfaction.[18]

---

[18] Van Dam, *European Tort Law*, pp. 301–303. See *infra* sections 2.1.1, 2.1.2 and accompanying notes.

Corrective justice is an objective that is inherent in these goals, but is also sometimes regarded as a separate goal. Other goals that are relevant for pain and suffering damages but are considered as much less significant in most European legal systems are deterrence, loss distribution and punishment. Although the goals of tort law are separately described in theory, their boundaries are rather indistinguishable. This holds true especially for the most important goals of tort law with respect to pain and suffering damages, namely for compensation and satisfaction.

2.1.1. COMPENSATION

First and foremost, compensating the victim is often considered to be the main objective of damages awarded for non-pecuniary losses.[19] These damages aim to offer some counterweight to the victim against the losses she has suffered and restore her, as far as possible, to the *status quo ante,* i.e. to the position she would have had, had the tort not taken place. In this respect, they serve the same goal as damages for pecuniary losses. Yet the goal of compensation is certainly easier to fulfill with respect to pecuniary losses. In these cases, compensation *in natura,* namely a replacement or a repair of the destroyed or damaged object, or an equivalent amount of money to the loss in wealth (*damnum emergens*) and foregone profits (*lucrum cessans*), would achieve the goal of making the victim whole.[20]

Thus, although *restitutio in integrum* is the guiding principle for pecuniary losses such as loss of earnings, medical expenses, etc. resulting from a personal physical injury, full restoration cannot be accomplished with respect to immaterial losses, as a monetary installment would not mend the harm inflicted.[21] Personal physical injury, as already explained, primarily involves a reduction in health, which comprises immaterial elements that are not exchanged in markets and consequently do not have a monetary value readily available. Since the actual loss cannot be accurately evaluated but only approximated, the principle of full compensation for pecuniary losses shifts to

---

[19]   W. V. Horton Rogers, *The Law of Tort,* 2nd ed. (London: Sweet & Maxwell, 1994), p. 244; Walter van Gerven, Jeremy Lever and Pierre Larouche, *Tort Law* (Oxford, Portland, Oregon: Hart Publishing, 2000), p. 19; Basil S. Markesinis and Hannes Unberath, *The German Law of Torts. A Comparative Treatise,* 4th ed. (Oxford, Portland: Hart Publishing, 2002), p. 920; Peter Cane and Patrick Atiyah, *Atiyah's Accidents, Compensation and the Law,* 7th ed. (Cambridge: Cambridge University Press, 2006), p. 458; Van Dam, *European Tort Law,* p. 302.

[20]   Van Dam, *European Tort Law,* p. 302.

[21]   Anthony I. Ogus, *The Law of Damages* (London: Butterworths, 1973), pp. 19, 194; Basil S. Markesinis and Simon F. Deakin, *Tort Law,* 4th ed. (Oxford, New York: Oxford University Press, 1999), pp. 731, 751; Kenneth S. Abraham, *The Forms and Functions of Tort Law,* 2nd ed. (New York: Foundation Press, 2002), pp. 14, 210; Markesinis and Unberath, *The German Law of Torts. A Comparative Treatise,* pp. 916, 918, 919.

'fair compensation' for non-pecuniary losses.[22] Fair compensation means that even if precision in the assessment of damages is not possible, the damages awarded for pain and suffering still ought to take into consideration all the immaterial consequences of the injury, in other words ought to be as full and adequate as possible.[23] The assessment of pain and suffering damages should hence take into account factors like severity and duration of the injury so as to be able to amply reflect its negative impact on the quality of life of the victim. Therefore, fair compensation does not mean that the effort to provide full compensation is abandoned in the case of personal physical injury. After all, several authors argue that even with immaterial losses one should in principle strive for full compensation, however difficult.[24] In practice, the monetary awards granted for personal physical injury allow the injured person to afford an alternative source of pleasure, a compensatory comfort or an activity that draws her attention away from her loss and thus reduces the negative consequences of the tort.[25] In doing so, compensation for immaterial losses is frequently regarded as providing solace for the harm incurred and in that sense it is difficult to differentiate from the goal of satisfaction.[26]

Fair compensation is also closely intertwined with the objective of corrective justice. Although corrective justice is a notion that supposedly permeates tort law and all other branches of law, some commentators regard it as a separate goal of pain and suffering damages under tort law.[27] The idea is that even though monetary installments may actually not succeed in accomplishing full compensation in a literal sense, they should nevertheless be awarded to restore the moral balance between the tortfeasor and the injured, and reinstate the

---

[22]   Markesinis and Deakin, *Tort Law*, pp. 731, 751; Markesinis and Unberath, *The German Law of Torts. A Comparative Treatise*, pp. 916, 918, 919. See also Cane and Atiyah, *Atiyah's Accidents, Compensation and the Law*, p. 165 referring to the guidelines set by the Court of Appeal for the assessment of damages for non-pecuniary loss according to which the awards for non-pecuniary loss should be 'fair, reasonable and just'.

[23]   Markesinis and Deakin, *Tort Law*, p. 731.

[24]   Siewert D. Lindenbergh, *Smartengeld* (Deventer: Kluwer, 1998), p. 60 and Gerda Müller, "Zum Ausgleich Des Immateriellen Schadens Nach §847 BGB," *Versicherungsrecht* (1993), p. 911 who strongly emphasizes the difficulties in measuring immaterial losses.

[25]   Ogus, *The Law of Damages*, pp. 19, 194; Abraham, *The Forms and Functions of Tort Law*, p. 210. See also Herman Cousy and Dimitri Droshout, "Belgium," in *Damages for Non-Pecuniary Loss in a Comparative Perspective*, ed. W. V. Horton Rogers (Wien and New York: Springer, 2001), p. 37; Suzanne Galand-Carval, "France," in *Damages for Non-Pecuniary Loss in a Comparative Perspective*, ed. W. V. Horton Rogers (Wien, New York: Springer, 2001), p. 94; Miguel Martín-Casals, Jordi Ribot and Josep Solé, "Spain," in *Damages for Non-Pecuniary Loss in a Comparative Perspective*, ed. W. V. Horton Rogers (Wien, New York: Springer, 2001), p. 197 expressing this view with respect to damages awarded for pain and suffering in Belgium, France and Spain respectively.

[26]   Ogus, *The Law of Damages*, p. 19; Cane and Atiyah, *Atiyah's Accidents, Compensation and the Law*, pp. 413–414; Van Dam, *European Tort Law*, pp. 302–303.

[27]   Abraham, *The Forms and Functions of Tort Law*, pp. 14–15; Cane and Atiyah, *Atiyah's Accidents, Compensation and the Law*, pp. 421–422.

disturbed fairness or justice.[28] This interpretation may explain why legal theory frequently refers to compensation granted to victims of tort as 'corrective compensation'. More importantly, however, this interpretation implies that the assessment of pain and suffering damages should meet certain criteria to fulfill the goal of fair compensation. It should namely yield similar amounts of pain and suffering damages for comparable injuries in a consistent manner. Consistency can be achieved by basing the assessment on factors such as severity and duration of injury, which are relatively objectively ascertainable and can convey the seriousness of the personal physical injury. Basing the assessment on such factors is more likely to generate pain and suffering amounts that promote horizontal fairness and equal treatment of comparably injured parties, thus coming closer to fulfilling the goal of fair compensation.

The goal of compensation is considered an important, if not the principal, goal with respect to pain and suffering damages in most European countries as comparative analysis clearly shows.[29]

2.1.2. SATISFACTION

The second most important goal of tort law that is relevant for pain and suffering damages is satisfaction.[30] Satisfaction is a rather unclear and vague concept.[31] The definitions of satisfaction offered by legal literature are numerous and not all of them converge to the same meaning. It is not an exaggeration to claim that almost every country that accepts satisfaction as a goal of tort law with respect to pain and suffering damages adopts a slightly different interpretation.

According to one such interpretation, satisfaction has the meaning of acknowledging the harm suffered.[32] In that sense, pain and suffering damages

---

[28]   Rogers, *The Law of Tort*, p. 252; Markesinis and Deakin, *Tort Law*, pp. 36–37; Abraham, *The Forms and Functions of Tort Law*, pp. 14–15; Cane and Atiyah, *Atiyah's Accidents, Compensation and the Law*, pp. 421–422.

[29]   W. V. Horton Rogers, ed., *Damages for Non-Pecuniary Loss in a Comparative Perspective* (Wien, New York: Springer, 2001). Greece is an exception as compensation is not considered as a goal with respect to immaterial losses, see Athanasios Kritikos, *Αποζημίωση από αυτοκινητικά ατυχήματα (Compensation for Traffic Accidents)*, 4th ed. (Athens, 2004), pp. 395–396. See also *infra* sections 2.1.2 and 2.2.1. Compare with the view presented in an American tort textbook, in which compensation is not considered as a goal of tort law but as a means to serve other goals, Abraham, *The Forms and Functions of Tort Law*, pp. 18–19. This function of compensation as a means to serve other goals is recognized by law and economics. See *infra* sections 3.1.1, 3.1.2.

[30]   Cane and Atiyah, *Atiyah's Accidents, Compensation and the Law*, pp. 422–423; Van Dam, *European Tort Law*, pp. 302–303.

[31]   See for instance W. V. Horton Rogers, "England," in *Damages for Non-Pecuniary Losses in a Comparative Perspective*, ed. W. V. Horton Rogers (Wien, New York: Springer, 2001a), p. 60 and Martín-Casals, Ribot and Solé, *Spain*, p. 197 explaining how the notion of satisfaction is perceived in England and Spain respectively.

[32]   Van Dam, *European Tort Law*, pp. 302–303.

serve as recognition of the suffering of the victim and of the fact that her personal condition has deteriorated due to the wrongful act. This interpretation of satisfaction as acknowledgement of suffering and sorrow is adopted in the Netherlands.[33]

Another view explains satisfaction as making up for the injustice done to the victim. Receiving pain and suffering damages soothes the victim's feelings of grievance and resentment and contributes to the restoration of peace that was disturbed by the infliction of harm. 'Appeasement' is an alternative term used to denote satisfaction in this sense.[34] This interpretation of satisfaction makes it indistinguishable from the idea of corrective justice and also implies that in order to attain it, the amount of damages awarded for pain and suffering should bear a relationship to the extent of the immaterial loss inflicted. Criteria such as the duration and severity of the injury, which can reflect the extent of the loss, should therefore be taken into consideration in the assessment. This interpretation of satisfaction also requires that subjective circumstances of the injured are taken into account. The goal of satisfaction therefore provides the necessary justification to incorporate personal characteristics of the victim into the assessment. According to other commentators, this interpretation of satisfaction also encompasses a retributive function.[35] They concede that a necessary step for the correction of injustice is the exposure of the wrongdoer in an open procedure in court. Making the injurer 'suffer' a day in court, where she will accept responsibility for the harm she inflicted and will bear the consequences, is considered to provide a further source of satisfaction for the victim.[36] This retributive function of satisfaction is obviously not fulfilled when a monetary installment is offered to the victim through settlement.[37] The interpretation of satisfaction as retaliation involves modest punitive considerations, which are considered by most European legal academics as having no role to play in civil law.[38] This proximity of satisfaction to punishment has led some countries to reject satisfaction as a goal of tort law with respect to pain and suffering damages.[39]

---

[33]   This is how the Dutch Supreme Court has expressed it, see R.-J. Tjittes, "Smartengeld Voor Bewustelozen (Pain and Suffering Damages for the Unconscious)," *Nederlands Tijdschrift Voor Burgerlijk Recht* (2003), p. 50. See also Siewert D. Lindenbergh, *Smartengeld 10 jaar later* (Deventer: Kluwer, 2008).

[34]   Markesinis and Deakin, *Tort Law*, pp. 36–37; van Gerven, Lever and Larouche, *Tort Law*, p. 19.

[35]   Cane and Atiyah, *Atiyah's Accidents, Compensation and the Law*, pp. 422–423.

[36]   Rogers, *The Law of Tort*, p. 252; Cane and Atiyah, *Atiyah's Accidents, Compensation and the Law*, pp. 422–423.

[37]   Cane and Atiyah, *Atiyah's Accidents, Compensation and the Law*, p. 423.

[38]   See for instance Markesinis and Deakin, *Tort Law*, p. 36; Galand-Carval, *France*, p. 94; Markesinis and Unberath, *The German Law of Torts. A Comparative Treatise*, p. 919.

[39]   See Ernst Karner and Helmut Koziol, "Austria," in *Damages for Non-Pecuniary Loss in a Comparative Perspective*, ed. W. V. Horton Rogers (Wien, New York: Springer, 2001), pp. 7–9; Cousy and Droshout, *Belgium*, p. 37 for Austria and Belgium respectively.

Many countries recognize the goal of satisfaction as being the second most important goal of tort law relevant for pain and suffering damages.[40] In Germany, for instance, satisfaction (*Genugtuung*) is explicitly recognized as an important goal separate from 'fair compensation' (*Ausgleich*), although its alleged modest connection with punishment is heavily criticized.[41] In Italy, satisfaction is perceived as a secondary goal of tort law with respect to pain and suffering damages.[42] In the Netherlands, as mentioned above, satisfaction is interpreted as acknowledgement of the injustice and as such it is considered to be a goal of tort law.[43] In England, satisfaction is understood as soothing the resentment of the victim and is considered to be a goal of tort law especially with respect to cases of intentional tort.[44] A notable case is Greece, where the goal of satisfaction is not of secondary importance but is rather considered to be the sole goal of tort law with respect to pain and suffering damages.[45]

The goal of satisfaction, in the countries that accept it, is emphasized almost exclusively with respect to pain and suffering damages. It further justifies why damages are awarded even in cases of immaterial losses where monetary installments cannot literally compensate for the loss. In that sense it complements and is strongly related to the goal of compensation.

2.1.3.   DETERRENCE

The legal literature on the goals of tort law in general, and pain and suffering damages in particular, sometimes refers to deterrence as a separate goal.[46] The idea is that the prospect of being held liable may induce the tortfeasor to avoid

---

[40]   However, it is not in every legal system that satisfaction is regarded as a goal of tort law with respect to pain and suffering damages. See for instance Karner and Koziol, *Austria*, pp. 7–9; Cousy and Droshout, *Belgium*, p. 37; Martín-Casals, Ribot and Solé, *Spain*, p. 197 for Austria, Belgium and Spain respectively.

[41]   Ulrich Magnus and Jörg Fedtke, "Germany," in *Damages for Non-Pecuniary Loss in a Comparative Perspective*, ed. W. V. Horton Rogers (Wien, New York: Springer, 2001), pp. 112–113; Markesinis and Unberath, *The German Law of Torts. A Comparative Treatise*, pp. 916 ff. In addition, the Federal Court of Germany (BGH) has in several rulings denied the punitive component of satisfaction; see Markesinis et al., *Compensation for Personal Injury in English, German and Italian Law*, pp. 62–64.

[42]   Busnelli and Comandé, *Italy*, p. 178.

[43]   Mark H. Wissink and Willem H. van Boom, "The Netherlands," in *Unification of Tort Law: Damages*, ed. U. Magnus (The Hague: Kluwer Law International, 2001), pp. 158–160.

[44]   Rogers, *England* (2001a), p. 60.

[45]   K. D. Kerameus, "Greece. Damages Under Greek Law," in *Unification of Tort Law: Damages*, ed. U. Magnus (The Hague: Kluwer Law International, 2001), p. 130; Kritikos, *Αποζημίωση από αυτοκινητικά ατυχήματα (Compensation for Traffic Accidents)*, pp. 395–396.

[46]   W. Page Keeton et al., *Prosser and Keeton on Torts*, 5th student ed. (St. Paul, Minnesota: West Publishing Co., 1984), p. 25; Rogers, *The Law of Tort*, p. 247; Van Gerven, Lever and Larouche, *Tort Law*, pp. 25–32; Hein Kötz, *Deliktsrecht*, 9th ed. (Neuwied: Luchterhand, 2001), pp. 18 ff.; Abraham, *The Forms and Functions of Tort Law*, pp. 15–16; Cane and Atiyah, *Atiyah's Accidents, Compensation and the Law*, pp. 424 ff.

causing harm. In law and economics literature, deterrence is regarded as being one of the most important goals of tort law with respect to pain and suffering damages.[47] In the USA, where the law and economics literature has immensely influenced legal scholarship, deterrence is one of the principal goals of tort law.[48] In most European legal systems, however, deterrence is considered to be of minor importance. An exception is England, where deterrence is regarded as one of the main goals of tort law with respect to pain and suffering damages.[49] In other countries, as for instance in Germany, deterrence is sometimes mentioned as a goal but it is certainly not decisive when it comes to awarding damages.[50] The implication for the assessment of pain and suffering damages, if deterrence were considered an important goal of tort law, would be that it should yield predictable and consistent amounts to allow potential injurers to take into account the magnitude of expected liability.

2.1.4. LOSS DISTRIBUTION

Loss distribution is barely mentioned in European legal literature as a goal of tort law. It is mostly textbooks on English law that refer to loss distribution as a function of modern tort law while recognizing that it is of secondary importance especially with respect to immaterial losses.[51] Loss distribution refers to the spreading of losses from a person to a group of people over a long period of time. This occurs for instance when the victim is insured against losses arising from a tortious act, which are then covered by the insurance company and consequently are spread between the other insured individuals within the same insurance pool. Apart from first-party insurance, loss distribution may take place through third-party insurance, health or disability insurance, social insurance and possibly other alternative schemes.[52] Although legal literature in Europe does not regard loss distribution as an important goal of tort law with respect to pain and suffering damages, in law and economics literature it is of paramount significance.[53] In the USA, where law and economics have influenced legal literature, loss distribution is one of the main goals of tort law with respect to pain and suffering damages.

---

[47]   The other important goal is insurance. See *infra* section 3.1.2.
[48]   See *infra* section 3.1.
[49]   Rogers, *The Law of Tort*, pp. 244 ff.; Cane and Atiyah, *Atiyah's Accidents, Compensation and the Law*, pp. 424 ff. However see Markesinis and Deakin, *Tort Law*, pp. 37–38 who assert that deterrence has a plain, subsidiary role in tort law.
[50]   Markesinis and Unberath, *The German Law of Torts. A Comparative Treatise*, p. 903.
[51]   See e.g. Cane and Atiyah, *Atiyah's Accidents, Compensation and the Law*, pp. 416–418.
[52]   Van Gerven, Lever and Larouche, *Tort Law*, p. 22; Cane and Atiyah, *Atiyah's Accidents, Compensation and the Law*, p. 417.
[53]   Calabresi, *The Costs of Accidents. A Legal and Economic Analysis*, pp. 27–28, 39 ff.

2.1.5. PUNISHMENT

The goal of punishment is almost exclusively mentioned in European legal literature with respect to criminal law rather than tort law. Punitive damages express disapproval for the injurer's reprehensible behavior by making her pay an amount of money that exceeds regular compensation levels.[54] In doing so they depart from the goal of compensation, according to which damages must correspond to the inflicted loss rather than the wrongful conduct of the injurer. For this reason, punishment is not explicitly regarded as a goal of tort law in Europe with respect to pain and suffering damages. Punitive damages may be awarded in England in strictly enumerated cases, but these do not include cases of personal physical injury.[55] The availability of punitive damages in cases of personal physical injury in the USA is a striking difference between USA and European tort systems.[56] All American states accept the punishment function of tort law except Louisiana, Massachusetts, Nebraska, New Hampshire and Washington, which either do not allow punitive damages or significantly limit their award.[57]

In sum, it becomes obvious that in European legal systems compensation is generally regarded as the principal goal of tort law with respect to pain and suffering damages while satisfaction is recognized as a goal of secondary importance in many countries. The preceding analysis also showed that depending on their interpretation, compensation and satisfaction are interrelated to a greater or a lesser extent. Moreover, corrective justice is an objective that is inherent in both goals. On the other hand, deterrence, loss distribution and punishment are not generally accepted in European legal systems as goals of tort law with respect to pain and suffering damages.

Taking these facts into consideration and in view of the general acceptance of compensation and satisfaction, the two goals will be considered as a benchmark for the assessment of pain and suffering damages in the forthcoming analysis. The foregoing discussion of compensation and satisfaction clarified the necessary criteria that should be taken into consideration in the assessment of pain and suffering damages in order to attain the goals of compensation and satisfaction. The interrelation of these two goals implies that these criteria may coincide. To fulfill the goal of compensation, the assessment of damages should incorporate all the negative consequences arising from the personal physical injury. To do so, certain criteria should be taken into account that can convey the overall loss and at the same time treat comparable injuries similarly and yield consistent results. Reflecting the extent of the immaterial loss in the

---

[54] Tony Weir, "Damages," in *Tort Law* (Oxford, New York: Oxford University Press, 2002), pp. 200–202.

[55] Markesinis et al., *Compensation for Personal Injury in English, German and Italian Law*, p. 45.

[56] Ibid., pp. 209–211.

[57] John Y. Gotanda, "Punitive Damages: A Comparative Analysis," *Columbia Journal of Transnational Law* 42, no. 2 (2004), pp. 421–422.

amount of pain and suffering damages awarded is also important to attain the goal of satisfaction. Therefore, the starting point for the assessment of pain and suffering damages should lie in the severity of the losses. Factors such as the nature, duration and intensity of the pain, the seriousness of the injury, the extent of the physical and psychological diminution in health, pain, grief and lost enjoyment of life, decreased life expectancy, residual impairments, etc. are hence of paramount importance and should be taken into consideration. Personal circumstances of the victim should also be taken into account in a subsequent stage of the assessment. Issues such as the behavior of the injurer may subsequently lead to slight corrections of the initially assessed amount but will generally have a limited impact.

2.2. PAIN AND SUFFERING DAMAGES IN CASES OF PERSONAL INJURIES

To attain the aforementioned goals, it is evident that court awards for pain and suffering damages should correspond to the harm incurred. In personal injury cases, harm will mostly pertain to permanent or temporary reductions in health which may materialize as diminution in the senses, reduction in life expectancy, loss of body parts, disfigurement or psychological harm, as well as pain, anxiety, fear, suffering, anguish and emotional distress resulting from the injury. It may also involve loss of enjoyment of life if the injury restricts the victim from living a 'normal' life and engaging in 'ordinary' activities. In other words, any health-related consequence arising from the injury that can reduce the quality and duration of life of the victim has to be awarded pain and suffering damages.

So far the term 'pain and suffering damages' has been used here to designate an amount that reflects all immaterial losses incurred. It is however an issue whether courts take into account all non-pecuniary losses when awarding pain and suffering damages. After all, the term 'pain and suffering damages' in a literal sense has a very restricted meaning and only includes damages that are awarded for pain, fear, anxiety, suffering, anguish and emotional distress. Hence, in the following section it remains to be seen which the non-pecuniary losses are for which pain and suffering damages are awarded in different countries. Furthermore, it should be clarified whether courts award pain and suffering damages under a single head or under several heads that correspond to different types of immaterial losses. If damages for immaterial losses are awarded under different heads it will be interesting to look at what factors are taken into account in the assessment of each amount.

Clarifying which losses are incorporated in the damages and what criteria are used for their assessment is important to appreciate whether the assessment methods currently used are capable of achieving the goals of tort law.

2.2.1. 'PAIN AND SUFFERING DAMAGES' IN DIFFERENT COUNTRIES

In England, non-pecuniary losses resulting from personal injuries are compensated by '*pain and suffering damages*' and so-called '*damages for loss of amenity*'.[58] Pain and suffering damages cover pain, distress, anxiety and suffering experienced by the victim, but not sorrow or grief.[59] The injured can only recover these losses provided she is aware of the pain, suffering, distress, etc. that she experiences. Pain and suffering damages are not awarded to victims who are comatose, because pain cannot be experienced while unconscious. Loss of amenity on the other hand is considered an objective loss. The mere fact of the deprivation of the victim from the capacity to use her senses and enjoy her life suffices to receive damages for loss of amenity. Thus, damages for loss of amenity have been so far awarded for the objective fact of loss in cases of impairment or loss in one of the five senses,[60] inability to engage in usual activities, loss or impairment of sexual function[61] and for many others. The victim's awareness of the losses incurred is not a prerequisite for receiving this type of damages. For this reason, damages for loss of amenity have even been awarded in cases of people who were in a complete coma, with the justification that unconsciousness cannot downgrade the fact that the victim suffers a substantial loss.[62] Although described under two headings in legal literature, these damages are in practice indistinguishable as they are compensated in a single amount by courts, referred to as '*general damages*', when both pain and suffering and loss of amenity are experienced.[63]

---

[58]   Markesinis and Deakin, *Tort Law*, pp. 764–766; Rogers, *England*, (2001a), p. 59; Markesinis et al., *Compensation for Personal Injury in English, German and Italian Law*, pp. 46–50. For a conceptual analysis of damages for loss of amenity and their quantification see Anthony I. Ogus, "Damages for Lost Amenities: For a Foot, a Feeling Or a Function?," *Modern Law Review* 35, no. 1 (1972), pp. 1–17.

[59]   Markesinis and Deakin, *Tort Law*, p. 764.

[60]   See the case of Cook v. J.L. Kier and Co. [1970] WLR 774 where damages for loss of amenity were awarded for impairment in taste and smell.

[61]   Ibid. In the same case damages for loss of amenity were awarded for impairment of sexual life.

[62]   See Wise v. Kaye [1962] 1 QB 638 where the idea was first expressed that damages for loss of amenity should be awarded even in cases of unconsciousness. The later case of H. West & Son Ltd v. Shepard [1964] AC 326 affirmed this view "The fact of unconsciousness does not, however, eliminate the actuality of the deprivation of the ordinary experiences and amenities of life which may be the inevitable result of some physical injury". This view was reaffirmed in Lim Poh Choo v. Camden and Islington Area Health Authority [1980] AC 174 where a clear distinction was also made between pain and suffering damages and damages for loss of amenity.

[63]   W. V. Horton Rogers, "England," in *Compensation for Personal Injury in a Comparative Perspective*, eds. Bernhard A. Koch and Helmut Koziol (Wien, New York: Springer, 2003), p. 91; Markesinis et al., *Compensation for Personal Injury in English, German and Italian Law*, p. 46; Van Dam, *European Tort Law*, p. 322.

In Germany, non-pecuniary losses resulting from personal injury are compensated by awarding 'Schmerzensgeld', which literally means 'money for pain'.[64] The new article 253 part 2 of the German Civil Code which entered into force in 2002 states that damages should be awarded for injury to the body, health, freedom and sexual self-determination.[65] The description is quite broad and courts have thus far awarded damages for amputation, loss of sexual function, impairment or loss of senses, severe shock, nervous damage and many other injuries.[66] Therefore, the amount awarded as Schmerzensgeld in Germany actually encompasses both pain and suffering and loss of amenity, as they are considered in England, and even includes damages for lost life expectancy.[67] Regarding comatose victims, a seminal case of 1992 changed the long practice of awarding to the injured only a symbolic amount.[68] The court ruled that the victim is entitled to receive damages even if, due to her permanent unconsciousness, the amount cannot actually fulfill either of the goals of compensation (Ausgleichsfunktion) or satisfaction (Genugtuungsfunktion).[69] In these cases, the court conceded, damages are founded on article 1 of the German Constitution and are thus awarded to express the importance German law attaches to human dignity.[70] Damages for non-pecuniary loss are awarded in a single amount by German courts.[71]

In the Netherlands, the amount awarded to compensate for non-pecuniary losses in cases of personal injury is referred to as 'Smartengeld', which literally translates as 'money for sorrow'.[72] Article 6:95 of the Dutch Civil Code stipulates that a tortfeasor is obliged to provide damages if she inflicted pecuniary loss or

---

[64] Markesinis and Unberath, *The German Law of Torts. A Comparative Treatise*, pp. 915–925; Markesinis et al., *Compensation for Personal Injury in English, German and Italian Law*, pp. 4–5.

[65] Article 253 CC Intangible Losses (2): "If damages are to be paid for an injury to body, health, freedom or sexual self-determination, reasonable compensation in money may also be demanded for any damage that is not pecuniary loss."

[66] For an overview of the conditions for which *Schmerzensgeld* has been awarded see Hacks, Ring and Böhm, *Schmerzensgeldbeträge 2009*.

[67] Markesinis et al., *Compensation for Personal Injury in English, German and Italian Law*, pp. 4–5; Van Dam, *European Tort Law*, p. 322.

[68] BGH 13.10.1992 NJW 1993, 781 followed by BGH 16.02.1993 NJW 1993, 1531. For a more recent case regarding pain and suffering damages for comatose victims see LG Münster 17.04.2009 16 O 532/07, NJW 2010, 86.

[69] Translated excerpt from BGH 13.10.1992 NJW 1993: "the loss of personality, the loss of personal quality due to severe brain injury is in itself a non-pecuniary damage to be compensated, regardless of whether the person feels the impact."

[70] Constitution, article 1 Human dignity – Human rights – Legally binding force of basic rights (1): "Human dignity shall be inviolable. To respect and protect it shall be the duty of all state authority."

[71] Magnus and Fedtke, *Germany*, p. 113.

[72] Wissink and van Boom, *The Netherlands*, pp. 143 ff; Mark H. Wissink and Willem H. van Boom, "The Netherlands," in *Damages for Non-Pecuniary Loss in a Comparative Perspective*, ed. W. V. Horton Rogers (Wien, New York: Springer, 2001), pp. 155–171; Willem H. van Boom, "The Netherlands," in *Compensation for Personal Injury in a Comparative Perspective*,

'other disadvantages'.[73] These 'other disadvantages' are made concrete in article 6:106, according to which an injured party is entitled to damages if she has suffered (among other things) physical injury.[74] On the basis of these provisions, Dutch courts have awarded damages for loss of limbs, scarring, loss of taste and smell, pain, impairment of sexual function, loss of enjoyment of life, suffering, psychiatric illness and other health related immaterial losses. However, it still remains controversial whether a comatose victim should receive pain and suffering damages. The prevalent opinion for many years had been that a permanently unconscious victim is not entitled to damages for immaterial losses because she cannot experience loss.[75] In 2002, the Supreme Court ruled that a victim who was in a coma but regained relative consciousness some weeks before his death was entitled to damages for non-pecuniary loss.[76] The decision provided an ambivalent answer to whether permanently unconscious victims should be compensated, giving rise to different interpretations in the literature.[77] However, in 2013 the District Court of Central Netherlands awarded pain and suffering damages to a comatose victim on the grounds that it is against the right to human dignity and the principle of equality to discriminate between comatose victims and victims who are conscious of their loss.[78] It remains to be seen whether the Supreme Court will endorse this line of reasoning in the future. Damages for immaterial losses in the Netherlands are awarded in a single amount.[79]

A notable peculiarity with respect to damages awarded for non-pecuniary losses after personal physical injury can be found in Italy. Damages awarded in personal injury cases are divided between damages to health, so-called '*danno*

---

[73] eds. Bernhard A. Koch and Helmut Koziol (Wien, New York: Springer, 2003), p. 230. See also the website of ANWB for *Smartengeld* (in Dutch) available at: www.smartengeld.nl/.

[73] Article 6:95 CC: "The damage that has to be compensated by virtue of a statutory obligation to repair damages (due by virtue of law), consists of material loss and other disadvantages, the latter as far as the law implies that there is an additional entitlement to a compensation for such damage."

[74] Article 6:106 CC: "The injured person has a right of compensation for damage that does not consist of material loss, assessed in conformity with the standards of reasonableness and fairness: [...] b. if the injured person sustained physical injuries or if his honour or reputation is injured or if he is harmed otherwise in person".

[75] Lindenbergh, *Smartengeld*, pp. 52–55.

[76] HR 20–09–2002, NJ 2004/112.

[77] See for instance Ton Hartlief, "Privaatrecht actueel. Smartengeld bij bewusteloos-heid," *WPNR* (2003), pp. 111–112 who interpreted this judgment as not allowing courts to award pain and suffering damages to permanently comatose victims while on the other hand Lindenbergh, *Smartengeld 10 jaar later* supported that according to the decision this is possible, permanently unconscious victims can also be entitled to pain and suffering damages.

[78] Rb. Midden-Nederland 06–02–2013, RAV 2013/47. See also Cees van Dam, "Een effectief rechtsmiddel voor een bewusteloos slachtoffer," *Verkeersrecht* (2013), pp. 442–448.

[79] Siewert D. Lindenbergh and Robert Verburg, "Personal Injury Compensation in the Netherlands," in *Personal Injury Compensation in Europe*, eds. Marco Bona and Philip Mead (Deventer: Kluwer, 2003), p. 374.

biologico', and damages for moral suffering, referred to as '*danno morale*'.[80] *Danno biologico* is awarded for injuries that cause temporary or permanent reduction in the mental and physical integrity of the person such as loss of limb, psychiatric injury, disfigurement, loss or impairment of sexual function, etc. This head of damages also covers loss of life expectancy. On the other hand, *danno morale* is awarded for losses such as mental distress, shock, grief, fear, pain and suffering. In recent years, some courts have recognized a third category of damages defined as '*danno esistenziale*' that is intended to compensate for the adverse effects of the injury to the 'dynamic-relational' aspects of everyday life, such as emotional, family and social relationships, cultural and leisure activities etc.[81] It is closely intertwined with *danno biologico* and some courts regard it as its subcategory.[82] However, the Supreme Court has not yet decided whether to admit *danno esistenziale* as a distinct category of damages for non-pecuniary loss.[83] *Danno biologico* and *danno morale* are grounded on different legal provisions. The right to claim damages for *danno biologico* is founded on the combination of the general article 2043 of the Italian Civil Code as well as on article 32 of the Italian Constitution, which protects the right to health.[84] According to the constitutional provision, the right to health is an absolute right so the mere fact of incurring a health-related loss suffices to establish the right of the victim to claim damages. Although *danno biologico* covers losses that in most other countries are considered as non-pecuniary, for Italian law, damages to health form a distinct head of damages that does not exactly coincide with damages for pecuniary or non-pecuniary loss.[85] Damages to health are viewed as a *tertium genus*; even though they are awarded to compensate for a non-pecuniary loss, i.e. the loss of health, according to Italian law they can be

---

[80]   Busnelli and Comandé, *Italy*, (2001), pp. 135–154; Marco Bona, "Personal Injury Compensation in Italy," in *Personal Injury Compensation in Europe*, eds. Marco Bona and Philip Mead (Deventer: Kluwer, 2003), pp. 305–325; Busnelli and Comandé, *Italy*, (2003), pp. 177–180; Markesinis et al., *Compensation for Personal Injury in English, German and Italian Law*, pp. 82–96.

[81]   See Cass. Civ., sez. III 03/10/2013 n. 22585. See also Paolo Russo, *I Danni Esistenziali* (Utet Giuridica, 2014).

[82]   Cass. Civ., sez. III 14.01.2014 n. 531 has accepted this view.

[83]   *Danno esistenziale* has prompted a heated discussion on doctrine and has caused serious conceptual confusion even at the level of the Supreme Court. Characteristic of the current situation is the fact that within few days the Supreme Court has issued contradictory decisions on the topic. See Cass. Civ., sez. III 23/01/2014 n. 1361 and Cass. Civ., sez. III 28/01/2014 n. 1762.

[84]   Article 2043 CC: "A deliberate or negligent event of any sort, which causes harm to another, imposes on the person who committed it an obligation to compensate for the harm done". Article 32 (1) Italian Constitution: "The Republic safeguards health as a fundamental right of the individual and as a collective interest, and guarantees free medical care to the indigent."

[85]   *Danno biologico* was recognized as a distinct head of damages, independent from damages awarded for pecuniary and non-pecuniary losses, by the seminal case of Repetto v. A.M.T. di Genova, Corte cost., 14 July 1986, no. 184, [1986, I] Foro it., p. 2053. See also Bona, *Personal Injury Compensation in Italy*, pp. 306–307; Markesinis et al., *Compensation for Personal Injury in English, German and Italian Law*, pp. 83–87.

objectively assessed in economic terms.[86] *Danno morale* on the other hand refers to damages that are awarded clearly for non-pecuniary losses. *Danno morale* is based on article 2059 of the Italian Civil Code, which for many years has been interpreted as awarding damages for mental suffering only in cases of committed crime.[87] Nevertheless, in recent years it is invoked also for physical injuries resulting from tort.[88] In personal injury cases both heads of damages are awarded, with *danno biologico* being considered to mainly serve the goal of compensation while *danno morale* being thought to fulfill the goal of satisfaction.[89] The two heads of damages are frequently awarded separate amounts while a different method is used to assess each head as will be further explained in section 2.3.1. In cases of comatose victims, *danno biologico* is awarded because in order to receive this head of damages the victim is not expected to be able to perceive the loss.[90] *Danno morale* on the other hand should not be awarded according to theory, because pain and suffering cannot be experienced while unconscious.[91]

In Greece, damages for non-pecuniary losses are referred to as '*monetary satisfaction for moral harm*'.[92] The expression in article 932 of the Greek Civil Code has been chosen carefully to indicate that satisfaction is the primary goal of tort law with respect to non-pecuniary losses since compensation of these losses is not considered possible in a literal sense.[93] Damages for moral harm are awarded in cases of physical impairment, loss of limb, loss or impairment of senses, loss of sexual function, aesthetic damage, severe pain, etc. Experiencing suffering has to be demonstrated because the mere fact of the injury does not suffice to receive damages.[94] Although damages for non-pecuniary losses are

---

[86]   Markesinis et al., *Compensation for Personal Injury in English, German and Italian Law*, p. 86.

[87]   Article 2059 CC Non-patrimonial damages: "The non-pecuniary damage should be compensated only in cases determined by law".

[88]   Busnelli and Comandé, *Italy* (2001), pp. 136–137. In cases where the requirements to claim *danno morale* according to article 2059 CC are not fulfilled, the plaintiff may claim for *danno esistenziale*, for which the restrictions of article 2059 CC do not apply. This head of damages is awarded for loss of quality in daily life, but in practice it is rarely claimed for in cases of personal injury. See Bona, *Personal Injury Compensation in Italy*, pp. 308–309.

[89]   Busnelli and Comandé, *Italy* (2003), p. 178.

[90]   Busnelli and Comandé, *Italy* (2001), p. 143; Bona, *Personal Injury Compensation in Italy*, p. 318.

[91]   However, see the case of Valentini v. Castaldini, Trib. Verona, 15 October 1990 [1991, I, 2] Giur. It., 1991, p. 697, in which the court ruled in favor of awarding damages for moral suffering to a victim in comatose condition.

[92]   Article 932 CC: "In case of tort, apart from compensation of pecuniary loss, the court may award reasonable, according to its discretion, monetary satisfaction for moral harm. This applies especially for those who suffered an offense to health, honour or ignorance or were deprived of their liberty."

[93]   Kritikos, *Αποζημίωση από αυτοκινητικά ατυχήματα (Compensation for Traffic Accidents)*, pp. 395–396.

[94]   Sotirios Manolkidis, "Personal Injury Compensation in Greece," in *Personal Injury Compensation in Europe*, eds. Marco Bona and Philip Mead (Deventer: Kluwer, 2003), pp. 253–254.

supposed to be exclusively awarded on the basis of article 932 CC, another article of the Greek Civil Code has given rise to some controversy in court rulings with respect to damages for personal injury. According to article 931 CC, which entered into force in 1983, if disability and disfigurement affect the victim's future they should particularly be taken into account.[95] This unclear provision, which established a new head of damages, has been interpreted and implemented in different ways by courts. According to one opinion, it provides the legal basis to claim damages for pecuniary loss, which will be incurred in the future, because disability and disfigurement are likely to hinder the social and economic development of the person.[96] Another opinion, however, holds that the provision provides the legal basis for damages, which are awarded for the fact of experiencing disability or disfigurement or damage to health, without the requirement to demonstrate pecuniary loss.[97] The second interpretation, which is supported by the most recent rulings of the Supreme Court,[98] seems to bring this head of damages closer to non-pecuniary losses. In Greece, damages for pain and suffering were in principle not awarded in cases of comatose victims, on the grounds that experiencing moral suffering requires the victim to be able to perceive the loss.[99] However, late court decisions have accepted that pain and suffering damages should be awarded even in cases where the recipient cannot communicate with her environment and is not aware of her condition.[100] Damages for non-pecuniary losses are awarded in a single amount. If, however, the victim is entitled to receive damages under the heads of both articles 932 and 931 of the Civil Code, then the courts may award distinct amounts for each head of damages.

The legal systems reviewed all proclaim to award damages for almost any possible type of immaterial loss arising from personal physical injury. Using different legal justifications, their aim is allegedly to award damages which reflect all the non-pecuniary losses incurred, so as to achieve the goals of compensation and satisfaction.[101] With the notable exception of Italy however, none of the countries analyzed above stipulate a separate head of damages for the reduction of health *per se* due to the injury. Yet this might in fact be the decisive factor to assess the negative consequences of the injury to the quality of

---

[95] Article 931 CC: "The disability or disfigurement inflicted to the victim is taken especially into account for the award of damages if it affects the victim's future."

[96] See for instance the cases AP 526/2006; EfPatron 672/2009; EfPatron 151/2009.

[97] See for instance the decisions of the Supreme Court: AP 433/2008, [2008] ESigD, p. 150; AP 605/2008, [2008] ESigD, p. 165; AP 1216/2008, [2008] ESigD, p. 428; AP 1174/2009, [2009] ESigD, p. 429.

[98] See AP 525/2011; AP 72/2012; AP 924/2013. Both retrieved from the Isokratis Case Law Database, Athens Bar Association.

[99] See EfAth 7146/1992, [1995] HellDni, p. 647, No. 11. Case cited in Kerameus, *Greece*, p. 130.

[100] EfLarisis 919/2005, [2006] ESigD, p. 283; EfPirea 102/2011, Piraiki Nomologia 23/2011, p. 156.

[101] With the exception of Greece that accepts satisfaction as the sole goal with respect to pain and suffering damages.

life of the victim. Even so, if countries manage to otherwise reflect the quality of life decrease in their assessment of pain and suffering damages, then this omission does not hinder the attainment of tort law goals. Therefore, the crucial point becomes whether the ways used to assess damages actually allow courts to account for all the negative consequences of the injury, as they proclaim to do. The previous section clarified which criteria should be taken into consideration in the assessment of pain and suffering damages in order to reflect all the negative consequences of the injury and consequently attain the goals of compensation and satisfaction. Section 2.3 will examine to what extent, if at all, the ways used to assess pain and suffering damages in England, Germany, Greece, Italy and the Netherlands actually take these criteria into account.

It should be noted that the term 'pain and suffering damages' continues to be used here neither in a literal sense, nor in the restrictive way that is interpreted by some countries. Pain and suffering damages here denotes all damages awarded to compensate for the immaterial loss resulting from personal physical injury.

2.2.2. THE INTERPLAY BETWEEN TORT LAW AND THE LAW OF DAMAGES

Before delving into the methods of pain and suffering damage assessment, it is important to clarify a frequently occurring confusion, arising with respect to the difference between tort law and the law of damages. Evidently, the fulfillment of tort law goals is dependent on which losses are to be compensated as such, as well as on the size of the awards that are granted for their compensation. The set of rules that designate both what types of losses are compensated as well as the magnitude of damages awarded for their compensation is frequently referred to as 'the law of damages'. These rules are in some countries systematized as part of tort law, while in others they are found in different parts of the civil code providing guidance for the determination of damages arising not only from tort but also from contractual breach. This for instance is the case in Italy and the Netherlands where the general provisions of the law of obligations regarding damages apply for damages inflicted for both contractual and tortious actions.[102] The importance of the law of damages for the accomplishment of the goals of tort law is self-evident. The fulfillment of tort law goals is dependent on which losses are incorporated in the damages and to what extent they are compensated. Therefore, the law of damages, by designating which losses are to be compensated as well as the size of the amounts to be awarded, actually determines the extent to which tort law goals will be fulfilled.

---

[102]   See Bona, *Personal Injury Compensation in Italy*, pp. 279–280 and Wissink and van Boom, *The Netherlands*, p. 155 for Italy and the Netherlands respectively.

2.3. CURRENT COURT PRACTICE IN PERSONAL INJURY CASES

In the previous paragraphs, it was established that compensation and satisfaction, both complemented with an inherent notion of corrective justice, are the most relevant goals of tort law as far as immaterial losses are concerned. Compensation more specifically, when awarded for non-pecuniary losses incurred due to a personal injury, ought to be as complete as possible, trying to bring the victim back to the situation that would have been the case but for the wrongful act, in so far as that can be achieved. However, the immaterial nature of this type of loss renders it difficult to accurately assess such losses and restore them by monetary means. Therefore, compensation with respect to non-pecuniary losses becomes more flexible, in that damages awarded for these losses have to be fair rather than exhaustively complete. Fair compensation in turn implies that there should be some kind of internal consistency of the awards, in the sense that similar amounts should be awarded for comparable injuries to insure fairness and equal treatment. The notion of corrective justice, which is inherent in the goal of satisfaction, implies that internal consistency of the awards is also important for satisfaction purposes. The demand of fairness, however, does not underplay the importance of an evaluation of the loss that comes as close as possible to the true loss incurred. Thus, the award should reflect all the consequences of a personal injury. The goal of satisfaction also points in that direction. In order for the victim's need for justice to be appeased, the amount awarded should reflect all the losses incurred as a result of the personal physical injury by also incorporating certain subjective circumstances of the victim.

To reflect the full impact of the injury on the general health and the quality of life of the victim, damages should be calculated in light of criteria such as the duration and intensity of the pain, the severity of the injury, the reduction in physical and psychological aspects of health, as well as the loss of enjoyment of life and emotional strain normally associated with the specific injury. The previous section explained that countries recognize these criteria explicitly or implicitly as determinants for the evaluation of pain and suffering damages. It remains to be seen how these criteria figure in their assessment.

2.3.1. HOW DO COURTS ASSESS PAIN AND SUFFERING DAMAGES?

In England, the amounts of pain and suffering damages are set on the basis of precedents.[103] Judges, taking into consideration previous cases, set an amount of

---

[103] Clive Garner et al., "Personal Injury Compensation in England and Wales," in *Personal Injury Compensation in Europe* (Deventer: Kluwer, 2003), pp. 122–123.

pain and suffering damages for the most serious injury conceivable, which is considered as the point of reference for all other injuries.[104] Scaling down from that amount, tariffs for other injuries are created, by making assumptions regarding their relative severity.[105] The tariffs do not consist of concrete amounts for each injury but of a range of amounts. It is at the judges' discretion to grant an amount from within that range, taking into consideration criteria such as the severity of the injury, the age of the victim and other particular circumstances pertaining to the case at hand. With respect to the particular circumstances, one could for instance imagine that a leg amputation would have a more negative impact on an amateur cyclist or an athlete, while it could be less of a loss for a person whose hobby is to play the violin. The judge ought to incorporate these particular circumstances into the amounts awarded. In any case, however, the amounts cannot considerably diverge from those previously awarded for similar injuries as the Court of Appeal controls the level of awards and may interfere in the event of excessive or insufficient amounts for pain and suffering.[106] The size of the current awards is largely a result of the Court of Appeal's decision in the case of *Heil v. Rankin*, to significantly increase the amounts granted for serious injuries.[107] A further 10% rise in general damages has been recently endorsed by the Court of Appeal in the case of *Simmons v. Castle*.[108] Since 1992, the ranges of amounts awarded for different types of injuries, have been gathered and published biennially in the *Judicial College Guidelines for the Assessment of General Damages in Personal Injury Cases.* Currently, the highest amount that can be awarded is for the health condition quadriplegia and is £326,700, or approximately €384,700.[109]

Obviously, the assessment method followed in England for pain and suffering damages can achieve a great deal of consistency and predictability, thus

---

[104] W. V. Horton Rogers, "England. Damages Under English Law," in *Unification of Tort Law: Damages,* ed. Ulrich Magnus (The Hague: Kluwer Law International, 2001b), pp. 61–62; Rogers, *England* (2003), pp. 95–96.

[105] Rogers, *England. Damages Under English Law* (2001b), p. 61.

[106] Rogers, *England* (2001a), pp. 66–67; Rogers, *England* (2003), pp. 95–96; van Dam, *European Tort Law,* pp. 322–323.

[107] Heil v. Rankin [2001] QB 272. See also Markesinis et al., *Compensation for Personal Injury in English, German and Italian Law,* pp. 46–51.

[108] Simmons v. Castle [2012] EWCA Civ 1288. According to the decision, the increase would take effect for judgments granted from April 1, 2013 onwards and should only apply to cases where the claimant's funding arrangements had been agreed after that date.

[109] Judicial College, *Guidelines for the Assessment of General Damages in Personal Injury Cases,* p. 3. The amount is converted to euro by using the annual average exchange rate of 2013 published by European Central Bank. See European Central Bank, "Annual Average Exchange Rate UK Pound Sterling to Euro," European Central Bank, http://sdw.ecb.europa. eu/quickview.do;jsessionid=3B7684CC6E9FC6A5CC6643B99E2E596C?node=2018794&SER IES_KEY=120.EXR.A.GBP.EUR.SP00.A (accessed 31.03.2014). UK pound sterling/euro = 0.84926.

promoting legal certainty.[110] It can also foster equal treatment by ensuring that people with comparable injuries will receive similar amounts. However, basing the currently used tariffs on previously awarded amounts does not necessarily mean that the crucial factors for the assessment, such as the nature and extent of the injury, the age of the victim, the loss of enjoyment of life, etc., figure in the amount finally awarded. It is therefore doubtful that pain and suffering damages granted on the basis of precedent will incorporate the impact of the specific injury on the quality of life of the victim. Moreover, it is also questionable whether injury tariffs that have been created on the basis of past amounts can reflect the seriousness of the injuries and their relative severity. Yet knowing how much more negative influence an injury exerts on the quality of life of the victim, in comparison to others, is critical in awarding damages that promote fair compensation. Another objection to the ability of this assessment method to attain the goals of compensation and satisfaction concerns the size of the amounts granted. The awards are based on the court's perception of the injuries and there is no reason why pain and suffering damages for the gravest injury, used as the reference point for all other awards, should be assessed at current levels instead of an order of magnitude higher or lower. A remark by Rogers on the issue is quite revealing: 'damages for non-pecuniary losses are certainly arbitrary in the sense that it is difficult to find a logical basis on which damages for quadriplegia should be €300,000 rather than, say, €30,000 or €3,000,000'.[111] In the same line of reasoning Cane submits that: 'all such damages awards could be multiplied or divided by two overnight and they would be just as defensible or indefensible as they are today'.[112] It follows that important factors, such as the nature and extent of injury, age of the victim, etc., which have been identified as necessary to be included in the assessment, are employed under this system in a way that does not promote the attainment of the goals of tort law with respect to pain and suffering damages.

In Germany, judges allegedly award pain and suffering damages taking into consideration factors such as the nature and extent of the injury, the age of the victim,[113] the pain and suffering, the emotional impairment, etc. The personal circumstances of the victim are also important. Although judges enjoy a wide

---

[110]   Predictability of the magnitude of the awards combined with other characteristics of the awards could also potentially promote deterrence, which is a goal aimed at in English tort law with respect to pain and suffering damages. See *infra* section 3.1 and accompanying notes.

[111]   Rogers, *Damages for Non-Pecuniary Loss in a Comparative Perspective*, p. 248.

[112]   Cane and Atiyah, *Atiyah's Accidents, Compensation and the Law*, pp. 162–166.

[113]   The age of the victim has been used in a rather ambiguous way by the German courts. Whereas the young age of the victim was considered in most cases as a factor that increases the pain and suffering damages, there have been a few cases where the age of the victim generated a decrease in the award, on the grounds that being young the victim would be able to adapt more easily to her condition. See OLG Saarbrücken 16 May 1986, NJW-RR 1987, 984 in Markesinis et al., *Compensation for Personal Injury in English, German and Italian Law*, p. 68.

discretion, the amounts awarded are expected to be comparable to what was previously awarded for similar injuries.[114] To assist courts in determining damages, the material facts and amounts awarded in previously adjudicated personal injury cases are recorded in systematized tables, where case law is categorized on the basis of the injury suffered. These so-called '*Schmerzens-geldtabellen*' 'should be considered as providing only a suggestion with respect to the magnitude of the damages and should not replace the judge's responsibility to search for the appropriate amount on the merits of the case'.[115] In practice, however, if a judge decides to award a grossly diverging amount from the one indicated in the tables, she has to provide adequate reasons to justify her decision.

A similar way of assessing pain and suffering damages is followed in the Netherlands. Judges have the discretion to award the amount they consider appropriate for the case at hand by taking into consideration factors such as the nature, extent and duration of the harm, specific circumstances of the victim, etc.[116] In practice, however, judges are guided in their assessment by the amounts awarded for similar types of harm in the past. An overview of damages awarded for pain and suffering in previous cases published by the journal *Verkeersrecht* serves as guideline, while courts may also take into consideration amounts awarded in other countries.[117] Although typically unrestricted, their judgments will usually not depart from other court decisions involving similar cases. The resulting awards of pain and suffering damages are considered to be quite modest compared to other legal systems.[118]

The use of tables, both in Germany and in the Netherlands, to facilitate the assessment of pain and suffering damages may generate consistency in the awards and equal treatment of comparable injury cases. However, it does not necessarily result in amounts that reflect the impact of the injury on the quality of life of the victim. Reliance on past rulings gives no information on the factors that influenced the decision. Moreover, reliance does not necessarily mean that the initial rulings were correct to start with. Although the extent, nature and duration of the injury are allegedly given particular attention, it is not clear how they are assimilated by the judge and incorporated into the assessment. In other words, the combination of reliance on past rulings and judicial discretion does not necessarily mean that the crucial criteria for the attainment of compensation

---

[114]   Ibid., pp. 65–68. Discretion of the judge with respect to the amount of damages is explicitly provided for in article 287 (1) of the German Code of Civil Procedure (ZPO): "Should the issue of whether or not damages have occurred, and the amount of the damage or of the equivalent in money to be reimbursed, be in dispute among the parties, the court shall rule on this issue at its discretion and conviction, based on its evaluation of all circumstances".

[115]   Hacks, Ring and Böhm, *Schmerzensgeldbeträge 2009*, p. 15.

[116]   Wissink and van Boom, *The Netherlands*, pp. 155–160; van Boom, *The Netherlands*, p. 230.

[117]   Lindenbergh and Verburg, *Personal Injury Compensation in the Netherlands*, p. 373.

[118]   Wissink and van Boom, *The Netherlands*, p. 159; van Boom, *The Netherlands*, p. 230.

and satisfaction are taken into consideration in the assessment of pain and suffering damages. Moreover, basing pain and suffering damages for each injury on previously awarded damages and the discretion of the judge does not mean with certainty that the relative seriousness of the injuries is reflected in the amounts. Under these circumstances it is doubtful whether the assessment of pain and suffering damages as performed in Germany and the Netherlands takes into consideration the actual decrease in quality of life arising from the injury and consequently whether it achieves the goals of compensation and satisfaction. In recognition of these problems, a working group has been recently set up in the Netherlands to investigate different options for improving the current assessment of pain and suffering damages.[119]

In Italy, a very different method from the ones described so far is used to assess damages for immaterial losses. A distinction has to be made between the two heads of damages, namely damages to health (*danno biologico*) and moral damages (*danno morale*), because a different method is used for their assessment. To assess damages to health in cases of permanent impairment, the judge consults a table, which in Italy's case does not consist of the amounts in previously decided cases, but of amounts corresponding to so-called *invalidity points*. The invalidity points range from 1 to 100, with one indicating 1% of permanent impairment and 100 signifying complete permanent impairment (100%). Each invalidity point corresponds to a pecuniary value, depending on the age of the victim. The younger a victim is, the larger the pecuniary value that is assigned to one point of invalidity. The pecuniary value corresponding to the age and the invalidity of the victim yields the amount awarded as damages to health. The invalidity tables are drafted with the help of medical experts and statistical data, aiming to incorporate and reflect the objective harm to health due to the injury.[120] However, if every court possesses its own table, then it is possible that different pecuniary values for the same point of invalidity will be awarded in each jurisdiction. To avoid the different tables generating systematically divergent amounts for damages to health between jurisdictions, the legislator has intervened with a law that fixed uniform damage tables for the first nine points of invalidity, leaving damages for more serious cases to be determined by courts.[121] By doing so, the legislator in fact only partially dealt

---

[119]   The Workgroup for Pain and Suffering Damages consisting of personal injury lawyers, medical advisors, liability insurers as well as editors and contributors of the Traffic Law Journal (ANWB) has been set up by the Dutch Injury Board (De Letselschade Raad).

[120]   Busnelli and Comandé, *Italy* (2003), pp. 205–207; Markesinis et al., *Compensation for Personal Injury in English, German and Italian Law*, pp. 82–96.

[121]   The law that fixed uniform prices for the first 9% of invalidity, referred to as *micropermanenti* was Law no. 57, 5 March 2001. See Markesinis et al., *Compensation for Personal Injury in English, German and Italian Law*, p. 19. See also www.altalex.com/index.php?idnot=3970 for the currently nationally set amounts of damages to health up to 9% points of invalidity as updated by Decree of the Ministry of Economic Development on 6 June 2013, GU n. 138, 14/06/2013.

with the problem. For more serious cases of invalidity each court would continue to use its own damage table, thus causing a systematic divergence in the amounts awarded between different jurisdictions.[122] However, in recent years some courts have started to make use of the tables compiled by the court of Milan. These tables, updated periodically, start from an amount of €1,452 which corresponds to the amount that is awarded to a one-year-old who incurs 1% of permanent invalidity, up to an amount of €1,198,132 which is granted for total permanent invalidity for a child of that age.[123] The practice was recently formally accepted by the Court of Cassation, which additionally ruled that the assessment of damages to health for the whole country should be performed on the basis of the tables of the court of Milan.[124] However, the ruling has been openly challenged by the court of Rome, which moved on to issue its own tables for damages to health, hence manifesting its intention not to comply with the decision.[125]

The assessment of the other head of damages, namely of moral damages, is performed in a different way than that of damages to health. In fact, there is no clear method stipulated to assess moral damages arising from personal injury.[126] The calculation of damages for moral suffering is left to the wide discretion of the court, which however in every case has to provide an explanation with respect to its decision on the magnitude of the amount.[127] In practice, courts award an amount for moral damages that is roughly half or less than half of the amount awarded for damages to health.[128] This practice has recently been the subject of a significant number of decisions by the Court of Cassation. Several judgments have stipulated that moral damages should not be compensated as a proportion of damages to health; they should rather be judged independently taking into account subjective circumstances of the victim and the gravity of the injury.[129] On the other hand, a number of rulings have supported the ongoing

---

[122]   It is characteristic that during this time, 54 invalidity tables were available, each corresponding to a different court. See www.lider-lab.sssup.it/lider/it/component/tabelle/.

[123]   See Tribunale di Milano, *Liquidazione del Danno Non Patrimoniale*, Tabelle 2013.

[124]   Cass. Civ., sez. III 07/06/2011 n. 12408. Following this decision, in August 2011, the Council of Ministers submitted a draft decree which proposed a national application of uniform damage tables for assessing damages to health for permanent impairments ranging between 10% and 100% of invalidity. The aim of the decree was to handle the unjustified variation of damages to health between different court jurisdictions and set uniform damage tables that would be implemented throughout the country. However, the decree did finally not materialize into legislation as it was criticized on several grounds.

[125]   Tribunale di Roma, XIII sez. Civ., 22/02/2012 n. 36620. See Tribunale di Roma, Tabella Danno Biologico, 2013.

[126]   Busnelli and Comandé, *Italy* (2001), pp. 145–147; Busnelli and Comandé, *Italy* (2003), pp. 205–207.

[127]   Markesinis et al., *Compensation for Personal Injury in English, German and Italian Law*, pp. 94–96.

[128]   Bona, *Personal Injury Compensation in Italy*, p. 323; Markesinis et al., *Compensation for Personal Injury in English, German and Italian Law*, pp. 94–96.

[129]   Cass. Civ., sez. III 04/03/2008 n. 5795; Cass. Civ., sez. III 12/12/2008 n. 29191; Cass. Civ., sez. UU. 14/01/2009 n. 557; Cass. Civ., sez. III 13/05/2009 n. 11059; Cass. Civ., sez. III 10/03/2012 n. 5770.

practice of basing the assessment of moral damages on damages to health while at the same time warning against potential duplication of damages.[130]

Obviously, in comparison to the other assessment methods explored above, Italy is a very special case. The exceptional nature of its system lies in the fact that the decrease in health due to the injury as such is actually taken into consideration. Therefore, the damages awarded reflect more closely not only the immaterial loss incurred due to the injury, but also the relative magnitude of different injuries. Moreover, the assessment method takes into consideration factors which have been considered necessary to include in the assessment in order to accomplish the goals of compensation and satisfaction. However, despite moving in the right direction to achieve the goals of tort law with respect to pain and suffering damages, this method of assessment still suffers from some significant shortcomings. An obvious criticism is that the multitude of existing tables causes systematic differences in amounts within the country's jurisdictions. Although after the ruling of the Court of Cassation many courts award damages to health with reference to the tables of the court of Milan, there are still some courts that implement their own damage tables. Thus, for an identical injury a person may receive a different amount depending on which court she files the claim for pain and suffering damages. However, awarding different amounts for the same loss is a practice that obviously undermines fair compensation and equal treatment. Another problem is the lack of clarity regarding the treatment of moral damages. If moral damages are supposed to mainly serve the goal of satisfaction,[131] then besides reflecting the impact of the injury on the life of the victim they should more importantly take into account personal circumstances of the victim. However, it is not clear how compensating moral damages, as a proportion of damages to health would actually achieve this. The overall impression from the Italian system of assessment is that it is moving in the correct direction to accomplish the goals of compensation and satisfaction. Nevertheless, the above-mentioned problems remain unresolved, undermining its potential to actually attain these goals.

In Greece, the assessment of pain and suffering damages is characterized by wide judicial discretion as there are no systematized tables or tariffs to facilitate and guide the assessment. The judge is supposed to incorporate into her decision factors such as the degree of the injury, the pain experienced, potential aesthetic loss, personal circumstances of the victim, etc.[132] She is also expected to take past rulings into consideration, yet the lack of systematized tables or tariffs does not facilitate awarding amounts in line with existing case law. In practice, the judge has to search herself for relevant case law and the parties involved in the claim

---

[130]   Cass. Civ., sez. UU. 11/11/2008 n. 26972; Cass. Civ., sez. III 07/06/2011 n. 12408; Cass. Civ., sez. III 13/07/2011 n. 15373; Cass. Civ., sez. III 26/10/2012 n. 18484.

[131]   See *supra* section 2.2.1.

[132]   Manolkidis, *Personal Injury Compensation in Greece*, pp. 253–256.

may also provide pertinent information in support of their case. In many cases, the resulting awards for pain and suffering damages are rather low.[133]

It need not be said that this completely unsystematic way of assessing pain and suffering damages has serious consequences for the attainment of the goal of satisfaction.[134] The wide judicial discretion creates reasonable doubt about the criteria used to evaluate losses and the resulting magnitude of pain and suffering damages. It is hence questionable whether the impact of the injury can be reflected in the amounts. Moreover, under the current system it is unlikely that similar amounts are awarded for comparable injuries. In fact, the way in which the judge takes into account (if at all) in her decision the factors identified as being necessary to include in the assessment cannot be ascertained. Therefore, the assessment method of pain and suffering damages in Greece does not have the potential to achieve the goals of tort law with respect to pain and suffering damages.

Table 1. Damages awarded for immaterial losses in England, Germany, Greece, Italy and the Netherlands

Countries	Damages awarded for immaterial losses	Indicative list of losses that receive damages	Damages for comatose victims	Assessment aids
England	Pain and suffering	Pain, distress, anxiety, suffering	✗	Guidelines for the Assessment of General Damages in Personal Injury Cases
	Loss of amenity	Impairment or loss in one of the five senses, incapability to engage in usual activities, loss or impairment of sexual life	✓	
Germany	*Schmerzensgeld* – damages for pain	Amputation, loss of sexual function, impairment or loss of senses, severe shock, nervous damage	✓	*Schmerzensgeldtabellen*
The Netherlands	*Smartengeld* – damages for sorrow	Loss of limbs, scarring, loss of taste and smell, pain, impairment of sexual function, loss of enjoyment of life, suffering, psychiatric illness	Undecided	*Smartengeld gids*

---

[133]   Kerameus, *Greece*, p. 130.
[134]   Remember that in Greece, the only goal with respect to pain and suffering damages is satisfaction because compensation is considered to be unattainable. See *supra* section 2.2.1.

Countries	Damages awarded for immaterial losses	Indicative list of losses that receive damages	Damages for comatose victims	Assessment aids
Italy	*Danno biologico* – damages to health	Loss of limb, psychiatric injury, disfigurement, loss or impairment of sexual function, loss of life expectancy, loss of amenity	✓	Tables with points of invalidity
	Danno esistenziale – existential damages	Adverse effect on lifestyle and usual activities, social, emotional and family relationships		As part of damages to health or independently
	Danno morale – moral damages	Mental distress, shock, grief, fear, pain, suffering	In principle no but have been awarded in few cases	Usually fraction of damages to health
Greece	Monetary satisfaction for moral harm	Physical impairment, loss of limb, loss or impairment of senses, loss of sexual function, aesthetic damage, severe pain	✓	No formal guidance – full judicial discretion
	Damages for disability and disfigurement (?)	Disability, disfigurement		

2.3.2. CAN THE GOALS OF THE LAW OF TORTS (AND DAMAGES) BE REACHED?

In all the legal systems described above, the intensity of the pain, the type, severity and duration of the injury, the loss of life expectancy, the personal characteristics of the victim, and so on, are supposed to play a major role in the calculation of pain and suffering damages. However, the methods used in practice to assess pain and suffering damages have been shown to be incapable of taking these factors into consideration. The most common practice of awarding amounts in line with those awarded in the past for similar injuries does not necessarily mean that the crucial factors were taken into consideration in the initial assessment. Thus, it cannot be assumed that those amounts are correct to start with. Only the Italian method of assessment may reflect the negative consequences of the injury, yet it does so in a way that may eventually undermine fair compensation and equal treatment of identical cases.

It follows that there is a large scope for improving the methods of assessing pain and suffering damages in all the countries analyzed above. An alternative method of calculating damages is needed, one that will be able to achieve compensation and satisfaction. This method should finally realize the countries' claim that they take into account factors such as the nature and extent of the injury, the age of the victim, the loss of enjoyment of life, etc. Incorporating these factors in the assessment will allow the general reduction in quality of life due to the injury to be reflected in the awards.

CHAPTER 3

HOW SHOULD PAIN AND SUFFERING DAMAGES BE ASSESSED?

A Law and Economics Perspective

Identifying the goals of a branch of law is an important task. Clear and coherent goals allow the content of both legal rules and court judgments to be formulated in a way that facilitates their attainment. The previous chapter illustrated that, according to traditional legal theory, tort law serves a plurality of goals. Of these, compensation and satisfaction are widely accepted as being most relevant when the result of a tort is personal injury. They provide guidance as to how losses arising from personal injury should be treated and, particularly with respect to immaterial losses, how pain and suffering damages should be set in order to achieve these goals.

The conclusion drawn from the preceding analysis is that in order to attain compensation and satisfaction, the damages awarded for pain and suffering in cases of personal injury should be determined on the basis of criteria pertaining to the resulting immaterial effects of the injury, namely the reduction in health and quality of life. To assess these effects, the severity and duration of the injury in combination with the age as well as other special characteristics of the victim at hand, should be taken into consideration. Unfortunately, as noted previously, despite being accepted by legal systems as the main elements for determining pain and suffering damages, these criteria are not always explicitly incorporated as such and subsequently not clearly reflected in court decisions. To the extent that judicial adjudication on damages fails to take into consideration the reduction in health and quality of life resulting from a personal injury, it may also be unsuccessful in accomplishing the goals of compensation and satisfaction.

Having investigated the goals of tort law and the subsequently emerging criteria for assessing pain and suffering damages, as these are stipulated by traditional legal theory, the analysis now turns to law and economics. The following sections present the goals of tort law as accepted by economic analysis, in order to provide the underlying rationale that should permeate the assessment of damages for immaterial losses. These goals provide a measure of judgment regarding the competence of current and hereafter proposed methods of damage assessment to attain them. In order to effectively achieve these goals, a set of criteria is proposed that the assessment of immaterial losses and subsequently of pain and suffering damages should fulfill. It remains to be seen whether economic analysis concurs with the goals of tort law and the subsequent criteria for assessing pain and suffering damages as stipulated by traditional legal theory.

3.1. GOALS OF TORT LAW ACCORDING TO LAW AND ECONOMICS: MINIMIZATION OF TOTAL ACCIDENT COSTS

The economic analysis of law has significantly influenced legal scholarship in the USA.[135] In particular the economic analysis of tort law has been so far-reaching that today even mainstream American legal scholars embrace its basic ideas.[136] The publication in the early 1970s of a seminal book by Guido Calabresi entitled *The Costs of Accidents*,[137] in combination with the subsequent booming scholarship on the subject,[138] set forth the basic theory of the economic analysis of tort law and changed, without exaggeration, the way American legal scholarship and justice look at tort law.

In *The Costs of Accidents* Calabresi holds that the principal goals of tort law are justice and the *minimization of total accident costs*.[139] Justice is explained as being the underlying rationale that permeates all areas of law, viewed by Calabresi not literally as a goal but as a prerequisite that a system of legal rules must fulfill.[140] Thus, justice acts as a constraint in the sense that all rules and methods employed to achieve the minimization of total accident costs should be fair. Minimization of total accident costs is unanimously accepted in economic analysis today as the principal objective of tort law. Total accident costs consist of primary, secondary and tertiary costs; hence the objective is broken down into three sub-goals.[141] Primary accident costs involve the costs of precautionary measures as well as the losses that are expected to still occur. To reduce them, potential tortfeasors should be deterred from careless or excessive behavior so as to lower the frequency of accident occurrence and the size of expected accident losses. Secondary accident costs comprise the costs of loss spreading resulting from an accident. They are reduced when losses are allocated in the least

---

135 Ugo Mattei, *Comparative Law and Economics* (Ann Arbor, MI: University of Michigan Press 1997), pp. 3, 223.
136 Gary T. Schwartz, "Reality in the Economic Analysis of Tort Law: Does Tort Law really Deter?," *UCLA Law Review* 42 (1994), pp. 377–378.
137 Calabresi, *The Costs of Accidents. A Legal and Economic Analysis.*
138 To name a few important scholarly publications of the time Posner, *A Theory of Negligence*, pp. 29–96; Brown, *Toward an Economic Theory of Liability*, pp. 323–349, and later on Landes and Posner, *The Economic Structure of Tort Law*; Shavell, *Economic Analysis of Accident Law.*
139 Calabresi, *The Costs of Accidents. A Legal and Economic Analysis*, pp. 24, 31.
140 Ibid., pp. 24–26.
141 Ibid., pp. 37 ff.

expensive way to a larger group of people that is in a better position to bear them. Finally, tertiary accident costs are the costs incurred by the legal system to achieve the previous two goals and are consequently reduced when deterrence and loss spreading are attained with the least cost. By achieving these three sub-goals the principal goal of tort law, namely minimization of total accident costs, can be accomplished.

The following sections analyze the three sub-goals separately and point out the importance of pain and suffering awards for their attainment. Each of the sub-goals stipulates which characteristics are important to take into consideration in the process of the assessment in order to ensure that both the process followed as well as the resulting amounts are consistent with and further promote each goal. More specifically it will be shown that the size and predictability of pain and suffering damages are crucial as they can generate incentives for precautions, hence reducing primary costs, as well as incentives to insure against immaterial losses, hence lowering the costs of spreading the loss. On top of this cost reduction, performing the assessment of pain and suffering damages in court with the least possible resources will further reduce overall tertiary costs.

3.1.1.   THE GOAL OF DETERRENCE

Primary cost reduction, which is most frequently referred to as the goal of deterrence, is achieved when individuals are induced to take optimal precautions that reduce the probability of accident occurrence and/or the magnitude of the losses. Taking precautions involves making decisions on how much care to take and how often to engage in the activity. Optimal precautions, the marginal cost of which equals the marginal benefit arising from the resulting decrease in expected accident losses, minimize the costs of deterrence.[142] Precautionary measures may include, among others, adhering to the speed limits, abstaining from driving when drunk, keeping a safety distance from the preceding vehicle, refraining from crossing against red lights, performing additional diagnostic tests to patients, engaging in more product research, improving safety of products and of production lines, creating more articulate product warnings, etc.

According to economic analysis, tort law induces individuals to take such precautionary measures by threatening them with liability.[143] Every individual whose behavior imposes externalities by way of increasing the risk for others to

---

[142]   Robert Cooter and Thomas Ulen, *Law and Economics*, 5th ed. (USA: Pearson Addison Wesley, 2008), pp. 335–338.

[143]   Ibid., pp. 322 ff.; Schäfer and Ott, *The Economic Analysis of Civil Law*, pp. 113 ff.; Steven Shavell, *Foundations of Economic Analysis of Law* (Cambridge, MA: The Belknap Press of Harvard University Press, 2004), pp. 177 ff.; Louis T. Visscher, "Tort Damages," in *Tort Law and Economics*, ed. Michael Faure, 2nd ed., Vol. 1 (Cheltenham: Edward Elgar, 2009), pp. 153 ff.

suffer losses will be held liable to pay damages if the risk materializes. Individuals will take this prospect into consideration and compare the costs of taking precautions and the benefits arising therefrom in the form of a reduction in expected accident losses.[144] Subsequently, they will ideally choose to take optimal precautions engaging in the level of care and of activity that minimizes expected accident losses. Since the decision to take precautions in the first place largely depends on the amount of damages the individual will have to pay in the event of an accident, assessment of damages becomes very important. Tort damages should generally include both material and immaterial losses to their full extent in order to provide the correct deterrent incentives. Thus, the magnitude of pain and suffering damages awarded should reflect the extent of immaterial loss incurred due to the personal injury to compel the wrongdoer to internalize the negative consequences her behavior imposed on others.[145] Moreover, pain and suffering damages should be assessed in a consistent manner and be based on criteria that yield predictable amounts, so as to allow potential tortfeasors to compare the costs of precaution and of expected liability.[146]

Yet, despite its widespread acceptance, some commentators contest the deterrent potential of tort law.[147] One argument against the ability of tort law to create behavioral incentives for precaution is that many accidents take place due to momentary lapses of attention that cannot be deterred by the threat of liability.[148] However, while some lapses can indeed not be avoided, many of the accidents that are caused because the actor was not paying attention relate to a habitual behavior that can be consciously corrected by the individual. Thus, a driver who leans to switch the radio channel can certainly revise his behavior to reduce risk of accidents. Moreover, inattention can even be corrected in a later stage as in the case of a crack in a bottle that goes unnoticed by factory workers but is detected later in the assembly line.[149]

---

[144] Mark Geistfeld, "Placing a Price on Pain and Suffering: A Method for Helping Juries Determine Tort Damages for Nonmonetary Injuries," *California Law Review* 83 (1995), p. 786; Visscher, *Tort Damages*, pp. 153–154.

[145] Robert Cooter, "Towards a Market in Unmatured Tort Claims," *Virginia Law Review* 75 (1989), p. 396; Richard A. Posner, *Economic Analysis of Law*, 6th ed. (New York, NY: Aspen Publishers, 2003), p. 192; Shavell, *Foundations of Economic Analysis of Law*, p. 236.

[146] Geistfeld, *Placing a Price on Pain and Suffering: A Method for Helping Juries Determine Tort Damages for Nonmonetary Injuries*, p. 786.

[147] Stephen D. Sugarman, "Doing Away with Tort Law," *California Law Review* 73 (1985), pp. 558–664; Joseph H. King Jr, "Pain and Suffering, Noneconomic Damages, and the Goals of Tort Law," *SMU Law Review* 57 (2004), pp. 185–191, 209.

[148] Schwartz, *Reality in the Economic Analysis of Tort Law: Does Tort Law really Deter*, pp. 383–385; King, *Pain and Suffering, Noneconomic Damages, and the Goals of Tort Law*, p. 188. See also Robert Cooter and Ariel Porat, "Liability for Lapses: First Or Second Order Negligence?," *American Law and Economics Association Annual Meetings Working Paper 70* (2008), pp. 1–39 for a theory of liability for lapses.

[149] Schwartz, *Reality in the Economic Analysis of Tort Law: Does Tort Law really Deter*, p. 386.

Another line of criticism argues that any effort to create deterrent incentives is futile due to the amounts awarded for pain and suffering damages. According to this view, pain and suffering damages, which constitute a significant amount of the total awards,[150] are so unpredictable and arbitrary that they cannot possibly provide any guidance towards the end of reducing accidents.[151] The criticism is therefore actually directed against the lack of a framework to assess pain and suffering damages and does not oppose deterrence in essence. Nevertheless, true as it may be that pain and suffering damages are often arbitrary and unpredictable, there is empirical evidence demonstrating that tort law actually deters despite the shortcomings that exist.[152] The evidence on the deterrent effect of tort law seems to be stronger for automobile accidents and somewhat weaker for medical malpractice and product liability cases.[153] Many of the existing empirical studies investigate the effect on deterrence of no-fault automobile insurance systems that were implemented from 1970 onwards in the USA, Canada, New Zealand and Australia. Under no-fault insurance systems, liability for personal injuries is removed or restricted, which implies that the deterrent effect of tort law may be weakened, potentially leading to increased accident rates. In Quebec, Canada, for instance, the replacement of tort liability with a

---

[150]   W. Kip Viscusi, "Pain and Suffering in Product Liability Cases: Systematic Compensation Or Capricious Awards?," *International Review of Law and Economics* 8, no. 2 (1988), p. 208 finds that pain and suffering damages for injury in product liability cases constitute approximately two thirds of the total amount awarded. In a more recent paper he reports that non-monetary damages cover 40% of the total amount awarded in product liability cases and about 75% of the total amount granted in medical malpractice cases, see W. Kip Viscusi, "The Flawed Hedonic Damages Measure of Compensation for Wrongful Death and Personal Injury," *Journal of Forensic Economics* 20, no. 2 (2008), pp. 120–121.

[151]   King, *Pain and Suffering, Noneconomic Damages, and the Goals of Tort Law*, pp. 185–191, 209: "Deterrence and incentive goals of tort law are corrupted when the assessment of damages is arbitrary and lacks any objective referent". For a milder assertion of the same argument see Geistfeld, *Placing a Price on Pain and Suffering: A Method for Helping Juries Determine Tort Damages for Nonmonetary Injuries*, p. 786: "the element of arbitrariness and resultant unpredictability of pain-and-suffering awards undermine the deterrence function of the tort system"; and Schäfer and Ott, *The Economic Analysis of Civil Law*, p. 131.

[152]   For extensive reviews of empirical evidence on the deterrent effect of tort law see Don Dewees and Michael Trebilcock, "The Efficacy of the Tort System and its Alternatives: A Review of Empirical Evidence," *Osgoode Hall Law Journal* 30, no. 1 (1992), pp. 57–138; Schwartz, *Reality in the Economic Analysis of Tort Law: Does Tort Law really Deter*, pp. 390–422; Don Dewees, David Duff and Michael Trebilcock, *Exploring the Domain of Accident Law. Taking the Facts Seriously* (New York, Oxford: Oxford University Press, 1996); Ben C. J. van Velthoven, "Empirics of Tort," in *Tort Law and Economics*, ed. Michael Faure, 2nd ed. (Cheltenham, UK; Northampton, MA, USA: Edward Elgar, 2009), pp. 453–498.

[153]   Dewees and Trebilcock, *The Efficacy of the Tort System and its Alternatives: A Review of Empirical Evidence*, pp. 64–67, 79–83, 95–99 for automobile accidents, medical malpractice and product related accidents respectively; Schwartz, *Reality in the Economic Analysis of Tort Law: Does Tort Law really Deter*, pp. 394–413. The two papers seem to agree about the deterrent effect of tort law on automobile accidents but not on the extent of deterrence with respect to medical malpractice cases. Dewees and Trebilcock conclude conservatively that the results are mixed for medical malpractice while Schwartz finds a decrease of medical malpractice incidents in the range of about 30% in the reviewed studies.

no-fault system resulted in a significant increase in the number of fatal and bodily injury accidents.[154] More specifically, a study by Gaudry found an increase of 24% for bodily injury, while Devlin reported an annual increase of fatal and bodily injury accidents of 6% and 17% respectively.[155] In the USA, tort liability for personal injury accidents was not completely abolished as in Canada but was restricted only to severe injuries and fatal accidents. An early study by Landes investigating the effect of this limited application of no-fault reported an increase in fatal accidents of approximately 4% when the threshold for tort recovery was low and an increase of more than 10% when the threshold for tort recovery was high.[156] Landes' results were also corroborated by other studies confirming that restriction of liability may be responsible for eroding incentives for safe driving.[157] However, these empirical results have also been contested, as some studies found no relationship between introduction of no-fault liability in the USA and the rate of fatal accidents.[158] More recent evidence however also showed a rise in road fatalities due to the switch to no-fault.[159] An increase in fatal accidents was also reported in New Zealand and northern Australia after the implementation of no-fault.[160] The overall evidence indicates that tort law can deter risky behavior in different settings, confirming the view of scholars

154   Marc Gaudry, "The Effects on Road Safety of the Compulsory Insurance, Flat Premium Rating and No-Fault Features of the 1978 Quebec Automobile Act," in *Report of Inquiry into Motor Vehicle Accident Compensation in Ontario*, ed. Coulter A. Osborne, Vol. II (Ontario, Toronto: Queen's Printer, 1988), pp. 1–28; Rose Anne Devlin, "Some Welfare Implications of no-Fault Automobile Insurance," *International Review of Law and Economics* 10, no. 2 (1990), pp. 193–205.

155   Gaudry, *The Effects on Road Safety of the Compulsory Insurance, Flat Premium Rating and No-Fault Features of the 1978 Quebec Automobile Act*, p. 20; Devlin, *Some Welfare Implications of No-Fault Automobile Insurance*, p. 197.

156   Elisabeth M. Landes, "Insurance, Liability, and Accidents: A Theoretical and Empirical Investigation of the Effect of No-Fault Accidents," *Journal of Law and Economics* 25 (1982), p. 62.

157   Marshall H. Medoff and Joseph P. Magaddino, "An Empirical Analysis of No-Fault Insurance," *Evaluation Review* 6, no. 3 (1982), pp. 373–392; Frank A. Sloan, Bridget A. Reilly and Christoph M. Schenzler, "Tort Liability Versus Other Approaches for Deterring Careless Driving," *International Review of Law and Economics* 14, no. 1 (1994), pp. 53–71.

158   Paul S. Kochanowski and Madelyn V. Young, "Deterrent Aspects of No-Fault Automobile Insurance: Some Empirical Findings," *Journal of Risk and Insurance* 52, no. 2 (1985); Paul Zador and Adrian Lund, "Re-Analyses of the Effects of No-Fault Auto Insurance on Fatal Crashes," *Journal of Risk and Insurance* 53, no. 2 (1986), pp. 236–241.

159   See J. David Cummins, Richard D. Phillips and Mary A. Weiss, "The Incentive Effects of No-Fault Automobile Insurance," *Journal of Law and Economics* 44, no. 2 (2001), pp. 427–464.

160   R. Ian McEwin, "No-Fault and Road Accidents: Some Australasian Evidence," *International Review of Law and Economics* 9, no. 1 (1989), pp. 13–24; P. L. Swan, "The Economics of Law: Economic Imperialism in Negligence Law, No-Fault Insurance, Occupational Licensing and Criminology," *Australian Economic Review* 17, no. 3 (1984), pp. 92–108. See however also Craig Brown, "Deterrence in Tort and No-Fault: The New Zealand Experience," *California Law Review* 73 (1985), pp. 976–1002 who found that fatalities in New Zealand actually declined after implementation of no-fault.

who maintain that the threat of liability can influence both individuals and firms.[161]

More specifically, under a rule of strict liability, the injurer will be liable for the total accident costs, namely the costs of precaution and the losses that are still expected to occur. Therefore she will consider what level of care to take and how often to engage in the activity and will make optimal choices so as to minimize her costs. Under this rule, damages should obviously be based on the full losses incurred in order to induce the potential injurer to take optimal care and engage in optimal activity levels.[162] Under a negligence rule, the injurer will have to pay for the total accident costs only if she did not meet the due care level set by courts.[163] As long as the costs of taking optimal care are lower than the total accident costs with less than optimal care, the injurer will choose to take optimal care. Hence, under the negligence rule the damages need not reflect the total loss incurred but rather be high enough to make taking optimal care more attractive than taking lower care. However, under the negligence rule the injurer will just need to adhere to the due care level to escape liability so that she will probably choose a too high, non-optimal level of activity.

In bilateral risk accidents, where both actors can influence the occurrence of the accident, the analysis is somewhat different, as the liability rule should create deterrent incentives for both actors. Under a rule of strict liability with a defense of contributory negligence the injurer will make optimal decisions for the level of care and activity, but the victim will just need to take due care to avoid liability. Thus, she may engage in the activity too often. Under a negligence rule (with or without a defense of contributory negligence) the opposite will occur; the victim will engage both in the optimal level of care and activity to minimize her losses, while the injurer will just take due care that will allow her to escape liability. Thus, she is likely to engage in the activity too often. To give the injurer incentives to take the correct level of care in this case, damages need not fully reflect all the losses but rather be high enough to make taking due care a better choice than taking lower or no care.[164] Therefore, irrespective of the rule chosen,

---

[161]   Landes and Posner, *The Economic Structure of Tort Law*, pp. 10–13; Ted R. Miller, "Willingness to Pay Comes of Age: Will the System Survive," *Northwestern University Law Review* 83, no. 4 (1989), p. 902; Schwartz, *Reality in the Economic Analysis of Tort Law: Does Tort Law really Deter*, p. 443.

[162]   Visscher, *Tort Damages*, pp. 154 ff.; Michael G. Faure, "Compensation of Non-Pecuniary Loss: An Economic Perspective," in *European Tort Law, Liber Amicorum for Helmut Koziol*, eds. Ulrich Magnus and Jaap Spier (Frankfurt am Main: Peter Lang, 2000), pp. 148–149.

[163]   It is assumed here that the due care level set by courts is actually the optimal care level.

[164]   For an analysis of liability rules see Steven Shavell, "Strict Liability Versus Negligence," *The Journal of Legal Studies* 9, no. 1 (1980), pp. 1–25; Landes and Posner, *The Economic Structure of Tort Law*, pp. 54 ff.; Cooter and Ulen, *Law and Economics*, pp. 336 ff.; Shavell, *Foundations of Economic Analysis of Law*, pp. 178–223; Hans-Bernd Schäfer and Frank Müller-Langer, "Strict Liabilty Versus Negligence," in *Tort Law and Economics*, ed. Michael Faure, 2nd ed., Vol. 1 (Cheltenham: Edward Elgar, 2009), pp. 3–45. See also Jennifer H. Arlen, "Re-Examining Liability Rules when Injurers as well as Victims Suffer Losses," *International Review of Law*

in bilateral risk accidents it is not possible to provide both actors with the proper activity incentives because only the residual risk bearer will compare his utility from the activity with the total accident costs; the other actor will compare his utility from the activity with the cost of taking due care.[165]

The same analysis of liability rules, albeit with some variations, also holds for product-related accidents where parties have a preexisting market relationship. A critical factor is whether consumers are aware of the risk level of the product.[166] If they have perfect knowledge of product risk, all liability rules (including no liability) lead to optimal care levels because the knowledge of the risk will induce consumers to take optimal care and market forces will drive firms to take optimal care so as to be able to offer their product at the lowest full price, consisting of the market price and the expected accident losses.[167] If however consumers are not aware of the risk, then only strict liability with a defense of contributory negligence creates optimal care incentives, as in this case the consumers will take due care to avoid having to bear their losses irrespective of their perception of the risk, and firms will take optimal care to reduce accident losses.[168]

The analysis of liability rules becomes relevant for non-pecuniary losses in so far as it has been held that the fraction of losses which does not have to be fully compensated in order to provide actors with the correct behavioral incentives should come precisely from non-pecuniary losses. Adams maintains that in

---

and Economics 10, no. 3 (1990), p. 233; Jennifer H. Arlen, "Liability for Physical Injury when Injurers as Well as Victims Suffer Losses," *Journal of Law, Economics, & Organization* 8, no. 2 (1992), pp. 411–426; Arlen, *Compensation Systems and Efficient Deterrence*, pp. 1108–1111.

[165] It follows that in bilateral accident settings, the choice between the rules of strict liability with defense of contributory negligence and negligence with or without the defense of contributory negligence depends on whose activity level one wants to control, the injurer's or the victim's.

[166] An additional factor that influences the analysis of liability rules is whether the product is a durable, a service or a nondurable. In the case of durables, where it is important how often the consumer engages in the activity, negligence rule induces consumers to take optimal levels of care when they have knowledge of the product risk, while there is no liability rule that induces consumers to take optimal levels of care when they misperceive the risk. For an analysis of liability rules incorporating the factors of consumer knowledge of risk and type of product see Shavell, *Strict Liability Versus Negligence*, pp. 8–9; Shavell, *Foundations of Economic Analysis of Law*, pp. 212–217.

[167] If risks are correctly perceived by the consumers, under a negligence rule, consumers will regard as full price, the price offered by the producer plus the expected accident losses they expect to bear themselves. Under a rule of strict liability, the price offered by the producer will already be the full price, namely it will incorporate expected accident losses. In both cases the producer's costs of care will be included in the offered price. See Shavell, *Strict Liability Versus Negligence*, pp. 3–6, 8–9.

[168] Calfee and Rubin disagree with Shavell at this point. They claim that in cases involving non-pecuniary losses, strict liability leads consumers to involuntary overinsure and distorts product prices. They instead suggest that a negligence rule would be more efficient as "the cost to consumers of underinsurance under a negligence regime is less than the cost of overinsurance and excessive precautions induced by strict liability". John E. Calfee and Paul H. Rubin, "Some Implications of Damage Payments for Nonpecuniary Losses," *Journal of Legal Studies* 21, no. 2 (1992), p. 399. See *infra* section 3.1.2.

bilateral accidents where the victim should also receive behavioral incentives, immaterial losses should not be compensated. The victim would in this way receive behavioral incentives to take precautions to reduce the probability of an accident and/or magnitude of the losses.[169] This line of reasoning is, however, problematic with respect to personal injuries. In accidents resulting in personal injuries, it is highly likely that the total loss inflicted may consist almost fully of non-pecuniary losses or at least be mostly of a non-pecuniary nature. As a result, if in personal injury cases immaterial losses are not incorporated into the damages payment, the deterrent incentives for the injurer will dramatically diminish. Although Adams suggests the elimination of damages for immaterial losses in order to provide deterrent incentives to victims, he acknowledges this problem for accidents involving merely immaterial losses.[170] An additional counterargument against this idea of abolishing damages for immaterial losses relates to the fact that serious injuries leave the victim with a residual loss even after pain and suffering damages have been awarded. Save for temporary injuries that can fully heal, for more serious injuries the reduction in health and quality of life are losses that cannot be fully restored. Therefore, just the prospect of a permanent residual loss in the case of a severe personal injury accident may induce the victim to take care, rendering unnecessary potential cuts in damages for immaterial losses. Besides, there may be much simpler ways to create optimal deterrent incentives to victims that do not affect pain and suffering damages. For instance, according to the preceding analysis of liability rules, the victim would be induced to take due care under any liability rule with a defense of contributory negligence.

It becomes clear that for the economic analysis of tort law, compensation is not a goal in itself but a means to achieve the goal of deterrence. The amount of damages awarded influences the decision of potential tortfeasors to take precautions.[171] The attainment of the goal of deterrence therefore depends on which losses are reflected in the damages awards and to what extent they are compensated. Especially in cases of personal injury, pain and suffering damages should fully reflect the immaterial losses inflicted to provide optimal deterrent incentives. This means that total health reduction and the decrease in quality of life experienced as a result of the injury should be taken into consideration in the assessment of damages. However, apart from incorporating all immaterial losses incurred in the amounts awarded, it is equally important to assess losses in a way that generates predictable and consistent damage awards. Predictable and consistent damage awards are essential to achieve the goal of deterrence, as they allow potential injurers to incorporate liability costs into their choices of care

---

[169]   See Michael Adams, "Warum Kein Ersatz Von Nichtvermögensschäden?," in *Allokationseffizienz in Der Rechtsordnung*, eds. Claus Ott and Hans-Bernd Schäfer (Berlin: Springer Verlag, 1989), pp. 209–217.

[170]   See ibid., p. 217.

[171]   Visscher, *Tort Damages*, p. 153.

and activity. In order to attain the goal of deterrence an assessment method should therefore evaluate the immaterial losses incurred due to the injury by taking into consideration criteria which can reflect the total immaterial loss incurred and result in predictable and consistent damage awards. However, an accepted framework that provides criteria for measuring the reduction in health and quality of life and subsequently translates them in a predictable and systematic manner in pain and suffering damages is lacking in law and economics.[172]

3.1.2. THE GOAL OF INSURANCE/LOSS SPREADING

The second important goal of tort law, according to economic analysis, is secondary cost reduction, which is most frequently referred to as the goal of insurance or loss spreading. Secondary costs are the costs arising after an accident has occurred as a result of a failure to deter it or the fact that it could not have been cost-justifiably prevented.[173] Secondary costs comprise the costs of having to bear the losses that materialize in the event of an accident, which may be reduced by a better spread. The goal of insurance is therefore achieved when tort law induces individuals to optimally spread the accident losses, using the least possible resources. A better spread than the one originally imposed by the harmful event on the parties involved in the accident means the allocation of the losses over time to the larger group of people that is in a better position to bear them.[174] Loss spreading occurs as an implication of risk aversion as people prefer to convert an uncertain loss in the event of an accident into a certain one by paying money in advance. This can be performed in a number of ways.

Buying insurance coverage is one of them. Rational risk-averse individuals prefer a given lower income now, rather than the risk of incurring a loss in the future that will result in an income with the same expected value.[175] Thus, they are willing to forego an amount of money that reduces their current income instead of having to incur losses when the accident materializes. For this reason, individuals are ready to pay a premium to the insurer, who promises in return to

---

[172] The US scholarship on pain and suffering damages, which has been heavily influenced by the economic analysis of tort law and accepts its main findings, confirms this. See David W. Leebron, "Final Moments: Damages for Pain and Suffering Prior to Death," *New York University Law Review* 64, no. 2 (1989), pp. 263–265; Geistfeld, *Placing a Price on Pain and Suffering: A Method for Helping Juries Determine Tort Damages for Nonmonetary Injuries,* p. 811; King, *Pain and Suffering, Noneconomic Damages, and the Goals of Tort Law,* p. 166.

[173] See Calabresi, *The Costs of Accidents. A Legal and Economic Analysis,* pp. 27–29. The term 'secondary' refers exactly to the fact that they arise only after an accident has occurred.

[174] Ibid., pp. 21 ff.

[175] Cooter and Ulen, *Law and Economics,* pp. 49–55; Robert S. Pindyck and Daniel Rubinfeld, *Microeconomics,* 6th ed. (Upper Sadle River, New Jersey: Pearson Prentice Hall, 2005), pp. 161–167.

grant them an amount of money covering the losses, in case they occur.[176] Insurers separate the individuals requesting insurance into different risk pools depending on their risk potential. Subsequently, they take advantage of the law of large numbers, according to which if the number of insured individuals within a risk pool is increased, the expected loss for each individual can be more accurately anticipated.[177] By predicting the expected loss for individuals of a specific risk pool, insurers operating in competitive insurance markets set the premium equal to that loss[178] in order to attract more insureds, or at a slightly higher amount in order to be able to cover the administrative costs of providing insurance.[179] Eventually, the premiums paid by insureds finance the payout amounts for individuals in the same pool, for whom the losses have already materialized.[180] This description illustrates how accident losses in general can be spread via the insurance mechanism. However, it is maintained, not without criticism, that people are not willing to insure, and hence do not actually insure, against immaterial losses. Therefore, the above description may not apply to immaterial losses. This issue will be thoroughly examined below. In any case, the assessment of damages is crucial to achieve loss spreading. By generating consistent and predictable amounts it can allow the insurer to incorporate the expected accident losses into the premium offered, thus influencing the conditions of insurance supply and subsequently of loss spreading.

In addition to purchasing insurance coverage, another way to convert an uncertain loss into a certain one is to pay an increased price for safer products or services. This occurs in cases where parties have a preexisting market or contractual relationship, such as for instance in producer/seller-consumer or in doctor-patient relationships. In these cases, tort damages are considered to function as compulsory insurance.[181] The seller of a product or service incorporates the expected costs of liability into the offered price so as to pass on to the consumers the amount of damages she will be required to pay in the event of an accident.[182] The result is that, on the one hand, consumers benefit from

---

[176]   George L. Priest, "The Current Insurance Crisis and Modern Tort Law," *Yale Law Journal* 96, no. 7 (1987), p. 1539.
[177]   Ibid., p. 1540; Cooter and Ulen, *Law and Economics*, p. 52; Pindyck and Rubinfeld, *Microeconomics*, pp. 166–167.
[178]   When the insurance premium equals the expected accident loss, then the insurance is 'actuarially fair'. See Pindyck and Rubinfeld, *Microeconomics*, p. 167.
[179]   For an excellent analysis of how insurance works see Priest, *The Current Insurance Crisis and Modern Tort Law*, pp. 1521–1590.
[180]   Siewert D. Lindenbergh and Peter P. M. van Kippersluis, "Non Pecuniary Losses," in *Tort Law and Economics, Encyclopedia of Law and Economics*, ed. Michael Faure, Vol. 1 (Cheltenham: Edward Elgar, 2009), p. 220.
[181]   Arlen, *Compensation Systems and Efficient Deterrence*, p. 1117; Geistfeld, *Placing a Price on Pain and Suffering: A Method for Helping Juries Determine Tort Damages for Nonmonetary Injuries*, pp. 793 ff.; King, *Pain and Suffering, Noneconomic Damages, and the Goals of Tort Law*, p. 184.
[182]   Geistfeld, *Placing a Price on Pain and Suffering: A Method for Helping Juries Determine Tort Damages for Nonmonetary Injuries*, pp. 793, 826.

damage awards, but on the other hand they are disadvantaged by the increased product/service prices.[183] This happens especially when damage awards reflect all losses inflicted, namely both pecuniary and non-pecuniary losses to their full extent, as in that case prices have to be significantly increased to pass on the costs of liability. Again, the assessment of pain and suffering damages also plays an important role in this setting. The more predictable and consistent the damages awarded for immaterial losses, the easier it is for sellers to incorporate the liability costs in the product price. Otherwise, in the event of ambiguous and fluctuating damages, sellers will be forced to large price increases, just as insurers would be forced to increase the insurance premium if expected losses were to escalate.[184] This mandatory insurance in the form of increased prices may not be desirable for consumers, however. If that is the case, consumers would prefer to remain 'uninsured' in return for a lower product price, and should therefore not receive damages. In other words, the amount of damages an individual should receive depends on the amount of losses against which a rational individual would purchase insurance.[185] If she would not, then tort law should not force such coverage upon her.[186]

A third way to spread accident losses also involves an advanced, but this time less formal, type of payment. Instead of buying insurance coverage or paying an increased price for goods and services, an individual may choose to spend resources to reduce the probability of an accident and/or the magnitude of the losses if the accident materializes. She may also choose to save an amount of money, which she will use in the event of a loss.[187] Again, also in this case, consistent and predictable damages amounts will allow the individual to decide correctly how many resources to spend or set aside in prospect of a loss.

Optimal insurance is the insurance that equalizes the marginal utility of wealth between the pre-accident and post-accident state of the world.[188] The important question therefore is which losses would people purchase insurance against and to what extent would they choose to insure against them. The answer

---

[183] Paul H. Rubin and John E. Calfee, "Consequences of Damage Awards for Hedonic and Other Nonpecuniary Losses," *Journal of Forensic Economics* 5, no. 3 (1992), p. 250; Geistfeld, *Placing a Price on Pain and Suffering: A Method for Helping Juries Determine Tort Damages for Nonmonetary Injuries*, p. 793.

[184] See Geistfeld, *Placing a Price on Pain and Suffering: A Method for Helping Juries Determine Tort Damages for Nonmonetary Injuries*, p. 788; King, *Pain and Suffering, Noneconomic Damages, and the Goals of Tort Law*, p. 186 "awarding damages for noneconomic pain and suffering, with all their unpredictability and incalculableness, seriously distorts and destabilizes the process of loss allocation".

[185] Shavell, *Foundations of Economic Analysis of Law*, pp. 269–271; Cooter and Ulen, *Law and Economics*, p. 376.

[186] Claus Ott and Hans-Bernd Schäfer, "Schmerzensgeld Bei Körperverletzungen. Eine Ökonomische Analyse," *Juristenzeitung* (1990), p. 568.

[187] Cooter and Ulen, *Law and Economics*, p. 53.

[188] Steven P. Croley and Jon D. Hanson, "The Nonpecuniary Costs of Accidents: Pain-and-Suffering Damages in Tort Law," *Harvard Law Review* 108, no. 8 (1995), p. 1795.

is important for attaining the goal of loss spreading because only the losses for which people would purchase insurance could eventually be spread. Rational risk-averse individuals choose to insure in order to transfer wealth to a state of the world where the need for money is higher. This undoubtedly happens after accidents that inflict pecuniary losses. Due to the decreasing marginal utility of wealth, extra money is of greater significance when one has a little than when one has a lot. Therefore, rational individuals would choose to self-insure against pecuniary losses because after these losses materialize, they have less money left. The utility they would derive from insurance coverage would offset the lost utility from paying the insurance premium. Since individuals would be willing to insure themselves against pecuniary losses they should also receive compensation for such losses. In the same line of reasoning, individuals would not be willing to purchase insurance for losses that do not affect their marginal utility of wealth. This may happen for instance if a unique object with emotional value for the individual, such as an heirloom with no market value, is damaged or lost.[189] In these cases the need for money does not increase after the accident. Hence, people would not purchase insurance and consequently they should also not be awarded damages. Optimal insurance is difficult to attain, however, for accidents that result in a decrease in marginal utility of wealth. In these cases, in order to equalize the marginal utility of money before and after the accident, an individual would prefer to shift money back to the state of the world before the accident occurred, when money was more valuable. An example of a loss that results to a decrease in marginal utility of wealth is the case of death, for which a 'reversed' insurance would be optimal, since less utility, if any at all, can be derived from money after the individual has died.[190]

Coming back to the question of which losses people would purchase insurance against, while it is easy to realize that people would take out insurance against pecuniary losses, it is difficult to ascertain whether insurance would be desirable for immaterial losses arising from personal injuries. After such losses one cannot establish with certainty how the evaluation of money is affected. Nevertheless, the question is important, because, as was explained previously, only if people are willing to purchase insurance against immaterial losses, should they be awarded damages. Otherwise tort law should not force such coverage upon them. However, with immaterial losses, the victim does not lose wealth; as a result she may value money more or less than she did before the accident occurred, or have the same evaluation of money as she did prior to the

---

[189] Shavell, *Foundations of Economic Analysis of Law*, p. 270.
[190] It is perhaps possible to regard as utility from wealth after death, the utility one derives knowing that her money will be given as a bequest to her children and family. However, even in that case it is plausible to assume that the marginal utility of wealth will be less than what the individual would have experienced by using that money before her death. See also Calfee and Rubin, *Some Implications of Damage Payments for Nonpecuniary Losses*, p. 378; Shavell, *Foundations of Economic Analysis of Law*, p. 270; Visscher, *Tort Damages*, p. 163.

accident.[191] If the marginal utility of money increases after the accident so that the victim values money more, then she would purchase insurance. This could happen if the victim were compelled to spend more money by engaging in substitute, more expensive activities in order to balance her life pleasure before and after incurring an injury.[192] That would for instance be the case if a paralyzed victim were to substitute jogging with going to the opera. If the marginal utility of money remains the same after the accident, then she wouldn't purchase any insurance against immaterial losses. This could happen in cases of minor temporary injuries that create no additional need for money. Finally, if the marginal utility of money decreased after the injury, then the individual would again not purchase insurance and would actually prefer to shift money to the pre-injury state, as mentioned previously. Very serious injuries that eliminate ways in which the victim could spend her wealth may be included in this category.[193]

It has been held that marginal utility of wealth cannot increase after a personal injury irrespective of the substitute activities available, and therefore, no damages should be awarded in these cases. Friedman argues that if the victim allocates her wealth to different activities after the accident, then these activities necessarily yield less pleasure, because otherwise she would have spent more on them already before the accident occurred.[194] Nevertheless, it is possible that while healthy, an individual could choose between two activities yielding equal pleasure on the basis of which one was cheaper. If for instance an individual used to rent a boat and sail in the weekends, then having her leg amputated, may force her to replace the activity of sailing with traveling, which is equally enjoyable for the individual but is more expensive, so that her marginal utility of wealth after the accident will increase.

However, apart from Friedman, in law and economics literature, many other commentators support the view that immaterial losses arising from personal injuries belong in the last two categories of losses, namely they cause the marginal utility of wealth to decrease or to remain the same.[195] Cook and Graham provide a formal illustration supporting this view.[196] According to their analysis, there is an amount of money the individual would be willing to receive in order

---

[191] Geistfeld, *Placing a Price on Pain and Suffering: A Method for Helping Juries Determine Tort Damages for Nonmonetary Injuries*, p. 794; Shavell, *Foundations of Economic Analysis of Law*, pp. 269–271.

[192] Alan Schwartz, "Proposals for Product Liability Reform: A Theoretical Synthesis," *Yale Law Journal* 97, no. 3 (1988), pp. 364–366.

[193] David Friedman, "What is 'Fair Compensation' for Death or Injury?," *International Review of Law and Economics* 2, no. 1 (1982), p. 82; Shavell, *Foundations of Economic Analysis of Law*, p. 270.

[194] Friedman, *What is 'Fair Compensation' for Death or Injury?*, p. 82.

[195] Ibid., pp. 82 ff.; Cooter, *Towards a Market in Unmatured Tort Claims*, p. 392; Shavell, *Foundations of Economic Analysis of Law*, pp. 270–275.

[196] Philip J. Cook and Daniel A. Graham, "The Demand for Insurance and Protection: The Case of Irreplaceable Commodities," *The Quarterly Journal of Economics* 91, no. 1 (1977), pp. 143–156.

to forego an irreplaceable commodity, and an amount, referred to as 'ransom', that the individual would be willing to pay to hold on to an irreplaceable commodity. For normal irreplaceable commodities, people are willing to pay more if their income increases. Cook and Graham show that for a normal irreplaceable commodity, the marginal utility of wealth is lower when the individual loses the commodity than the marginal utility of wealth in the state where she holds on to it, even if she has already paid the ransom (so her remaining wealth has already decreased). This result indicates that an individual would not buy full coverage for an irreplaceable commodity because then she would be transferring money from a state with high marginal utility of wealth in order to receive it in a state where it is worth less.[197] Thus, according to their analysis, accident victims should not be fully compensated for non-pecuniary losses caused by injuries.[198]

To explore empirically how marginal utility of wealth is affected after personal injury, Evans and Viscusi surveyed chemical workers on how much more money they would require to work with a dangerous chemical.[199] Using the information on workers' wage-risk differentials they first estimated the utility functions for health and injury and then found that the marginal utility of wealth is higher when one is healthy rather than injured.[200] In a subsequent study exploring marginal utility of wealth for minor injuries, they arrived at the result that minor injuries have the same effect as pecuniary losses, namely that they increase the marginal utility of wealth.[201] These findings are in line with the analysis of Cook and Graham as they imply that, save for minor injuries, people would not be willing to take out insurance against personal injury and consequently should not receive damages for immaterial losses arising thereof. However, this line of research has been heavily criticized on the grounds that conclusions have been drawn by asking people to make judgments regarding circumstances they have not experienced, such as what it would be like to be disabled. Therefore, the argument continues that, relying on the viewpoint of nondisabled persons is problematic because they may underestimate marginal utility of wealth of disabled persons due to their informational problems.[202]

---

[197]   Ibid., pp. 146–149.
[198]   See ibid., p. 151: "the goal of full compensation to victims of violent crime or accidents that result in injury or death is not compatible with economic efficiency", and p. 155 "full compensation is an inefficient policy for tort settlements that involve irreplaceable commodities".
[199]   W. Kip Viscusi and William N. Evans, "Utility Functions that Depend on Health Status: Estimates and Economic Implications," *American Economic Review* 80 (1990), pp. 353–374.
[200]   W. Kip Viscusi, "The Value of Life: Has Voodoo Economics Come to the Courts?," *Journal of Forensic Economics* 3, no. 3 (1990), pp. 353, 371.
[201]   William N. Evans and W. Kip Viscusi, "Estimation of State-Dependent Utility Functions using Survey Data," *The Review of Economics and Statistics* 73, no. 1 (1991), pp. 95, 102–103.
[202]   Ellen Smith Pryor, "The Tort Law Debate, Efficiency, and the Kingdom of the Ill: A Critique of the Insurance Theory of Compensation," *Virginia Law Review* 79 (1993), pp. 110 ff. See also *infra* chapter 6.

Contrary to the scholars supporting the idea that marginal utility of wealth decreases in case of immaterial losses and therefore people are not willing to insure themselves for such losses, Croley and Hanson hold that people are willing to self-insure against immaterial losses because such losses lower their baseline utility.[203] They argue that even though the wealth of an individual may remain intact after an accident, in the post-accident state the individual may still value money more highly than before. The authors provide an illustrative example: if an individual is an opera fan, she will enjoy a ticket to the opera more than an individual who is not so fond of it. Nevertheless if the second individual has recently suffered misfortune, it is likely that a ticket (to the opera or somewhere else) will cheer her up and give her much utility, given that her baseline utility is so low. Therefore, it could be that the second individual derives more utility from the ticket, even though the first likes opera better. Even if immaterial losses may not affect the marginal utility of wealth, they lower the baseline utility. Therefore, individuals might choose to purchase insurance against these losses not because they value money more after incurring the personal injury, but because money can help increase the baseline utility in the post-accident state.[204] The conclusion that follows is that if individuals are willing to buy coverage against immaterial losses, they should also receive damages in the event that they occur.

Besides making theoretical inferences and relying on empirical data on wage-risk differentials, another way to tackle the question of whether people would purchase insurance for immaterial losses is by looking directly at whether they do so in reality. Danzon investigates the actual choices people make regarding public and private disability insurance and arrives at the result that most people are not willing to insure against pain and suffering, which implies that they should also not be compensated for such losses.[205] It is noted, however, that the evidence might be inconclusive because of various constraints that might exist with respect to consumers.[206] Indeed, the position that since people do not demand such insurance in real life, they should also not be compensated for these losses has been heavily criticized. The main argument is that evidence of people's demand should not be seriously taken into consideration, as there are problems that prevent consumers from purchasing insurance for personal injury. More specifically, imperfect information on the range of non-pecuniary losses and the probability of their occurrence is likely to limit insurance demand for

---

[203] Croley and Hanson, *The Nonpecuniary Costs of Accidents: Pain-and-Suffering Damages in Tort Law*, pp. 1813–1822.
[204] Ibid., pp. 1813–1822.
[205] See Patricia M. Danzon, "Tort Reform and the Role of Government in Private Insurance Markets," *Journal of Legal Studies* 13 (1984), pp. 522–524. "This evidence from private and collective choices suggests that the tort norm of full coverage of full of all pecuniary loss plus pain and suffering far exceeds the coverage people are prepared to pay for given the choice".
[206] Ibid., pp. 524–526.

such losses.[207] Moreover, healthy individuals' lack of information on the life of a disabled person and the extent of the need for money following a disability may lead them to underestimate the consequences of personal injury and thus to not demand insurance coverage.[208] The argument according to which one can draw conclusions regarding the desirability of insurance for immaterial losses just by looking at the insurance coverage demanded is also refuted by one more reason. In a world where tort coverage already exists, the choice for insurance coverage is affected by the fact that the tortfeasor is likely to compensate at least some of the losses.[209] This realization might lower the desire to take out full coverage, implying that current insurance demand for immaterial losses is not indicative of the extent of protection individuals wish to have.[210] Nevertheless, despite the counterarguments, the observation that people do not purchase insurance for immaterial losses has led many scholars to claim that there is actually no demand for such insurance.[211]

Other commentators maintain that, in addition to the demand-side problems, supply-side complications may be hindering the supply of insurance for immaterial losses.[212] Just like consumers may lack information regarding the probability and extent of immaterial losses, insurers, on top of that, face the additional problem of not knowing in advance how sensitive insureds are to such losses. The asymmetric information on the side of insurers may result in adverse selection. Individuals who are more prone to accidents or are likely to incur a higher immaterial loss in case of an accident will purchase insurance. Offering coverage to these individuals will increase premiums, forcing low-risk individuals to withdraw from the risk pool, and thus rendering supply of insurance for immaterial losses unsustainable.[213] Apart from adverse selection, asymmetric information may additionally instigate

---

[207]   Croley and Hanson, *The Nonpecuniary Costs of Accidents: Pain-and-Suffering Damages in Tort Law*, pp. 1845–1848.

[208]   Smith Pryor, *The Tort Law Debate, Efficiency, and the Kingdom of the Ill: A Critique of the Insurance Theory of Compensation*, pp. 111–114; Croley and Hanson, *The Nonpecuniary Costs of Accidents: Pain-and-Suffering Damages in Tort Law*, pp. 1845–1848.

[209]   Ronen Avraham, "Should Pain-and-Suffering Damages be Abolished from Tort Law? More Experimental Evidence," *University of Toronto Law Journal* 55 (2005), pp. 947–948.

[210]   Ibid., pp. 947–948.

[211]   Stanley Ingber, "Rethinking Intangible Injuries: A Focus on Remedy," *California Law Review* 73, no. 3, Symposium: Alternative Compensation Schemes and Tort Theory (May, 1985), p. 785; Priest, *The Current Insurance Crisis and Modern Tort Law*, pp. 1546–1547; King, *Pain and Suffering, Noneconomic Damages, and the Goals of Tort Law*, p. 184.

[212]   Schwartz, *Proposals for Products Liability Reform: A Theoretical Synthesis*, p. 365; Croley and Hanson, *The Nonpecuniary Costs of Accidents: Pain-and-Suffering Damages in Tort Law*, pp. 1848–1857.

[213]   Richard A. Epstein, "Products Liability as an Insurance Market," *The Journal of Legal Studies* 14, no. 3 (1985), pp. 650–652; Priest, *The Current Insurance Crisis and Modern Tort Law*, pp. 1547–1548; Croley and Hanson, *The Nonpecuniary Costs of Accidents: Pain-and-Suffering Damages in Tort Law*, pp. 1850–1851.

moral hazard.[214] Insureds may take fewer precautions after they have purchased insurance for immaterial losses or may behave strategically and exaggerate the magnitude of their losses in order to receive higher amounts after the accident happens.[215] This will again affect insurance premiums; however, insurers may be able to reduce moral hazard by making the size of the premiums and payments conditional on the insured's history of accidents or by using deductibles, coinsurance, etc.[216] Last but not least, countervailing social norms in the form of societal rejection of pricing pain and suffering, as well as legal restrictions, may prevent manifestation of both demand and supply of such insurance.[217]

In a recent experiment, Avraham tried to investigate the true willingness of individuals to purchase insurance against immaterial losses by circumventing the aforementioned problems that hinder demand and supply of insurance for such losses. More specifically, in his setting participants were informed of potential injury risks associated with the purchase of certain products to alleviate demand-side problems related to lack of relevant information, and were consequently asked to choose whether and to what extent they would buy insurance against monetary and immaterial losses.[218] Moreover, it was assumed that insurance coverage was offered for all of these losses, so there was no problem in supply. According to his results, people actually demand insurance for both monetary and immaterial losses and in fact they are willing to spend approximately the same amount of money for both types of coverage.[219] Thus, his experimental evidence refutes the idea that damages for pain and suffering should not be awarded because people do not want to self-insure against immaterial losses.

It becomes evident from the foregoing discussion that law and economics has not yet reached a definite conclusion on the question of whether people would self-insure against immaterial losses arising from personal injury, although the idea that people do not (want to) insure themselves seems to have been more influential in scholarship. Therefore, the question remains. As illustrated in the previous section, for the economic analysis of tort law, compensation is not a

---

[214] Epstein, *Products Liability as an Insurance Market*, p. 653; Priest, *The Current Insurance Crisis and Modern Tort Law*, pp. 1547–1548; Croley and Hanson, *The Nonpecuniary Costs of Accidents: Pain-and-Suffering Damages in Tort Law*, pp. 1848–1850.

[215] Priest, *The Current Insurance Crisis and Modern Tort Law*, pp. 1547–1548; Croley and Hanson, *The Nonpecuniary Costs of Accidents: Pain-and-Suffering Damages in Tort Law*, pp. 1848–1850.

[216] See Sloan, Reilly and Schenzler, *Tort Liability Versus Other Approaches for Deterring Careless Driving*, p. 55; Geistfeld, *Placing a Price on Pain and Suffering: A Method for Helping Juries Determine Tort Damages for Nonmonetary Injuries*, p. 787.

[217] Croley and Hanson, *The Nonpecuniary Costs of Accidents: Pain-and-Suffering Damages in Tort Law*, pp. 1851–1856.

[218] Avraham, *Should Pain-and-Suffering Damages be Abolished from Tort Law? More Experimental Evidence*, pp. 957–958, 964–965.

[219] Ibid., p. 977.

goal in itself but rather a means to achieve the goal of deterrence. This section further adds to the earlier conclusions the notion that compensation is additionally a means to achieve the goal of insurance. The amount of damages awarded influences the decisions of insurers as to how high they should set the insurance premiums, as well as the decisions of firms and professionals on how high they should set their product/service prices. Their choices in turn affect the decisions of individuals and consumers regarding the extent of insurance coverage or the amount of product they will purchase. The attainment of the goal of insurance therefore depends on which losses are reflected in the damages awards and to what extent they are compensated. The assessment of damages should thus generate consistent and predictable awards so as to allow the insurer to incorporate the expected accident losses into the premium offered, as well as allow firms and professionals to incorporate the liability costs into their product/ service prices. Nevertheless, especially for cases of personal injury, the prevailing opinion so far suggests that immaterial losses should not be (fully) compensated because people are not willing to purchase insurance against such losses and therefore receiving pain and suffering damages would result in insurance against their will. This conclusion contrasts with the conclusion of the previous section that in order to attain the goal of deterrence, damages awarded for personal injuries should fully reflect immaterial losses. Hence, a discrepancy arises between the goal of deterrence and the goal of insurance with respect to the treatment of immaterial losses. According to the deterrence goal, these losses should be fully compensated, but according to the insurance goal these losses should not be compensated or should be compensated only in part, because otherwise individuals would be insured against their will.

However, while this argument about compulsory insurance makes sense for product- and service-related accidents involving preexisting contractual or market relationships, it is not convincing for automobile accidents and other accidents that occur between perfect strangers.[220] In automobile accident settings, where no prior relationship between injurers and victims exists, the cost of pain and suffering damages is not passed on from the injurers to the victims in the same way it would be passed on from producers to consumers through the price of products or services. Therefore, victims would wish to be fully compensated for both pecuniary and immaterial losses since that would not make their activity more expensive. The argument of undesirable compulsory insurance is thus not adequate to justify the abolishment or reduction of amounts awarded for pain and suffering in accident settings between strangers. Only if the same individuals were both prospective injurers and victims, would it be conceivable that pain and suffering damages would be undesirable. In that case individuals could choose to

---

[220]   Arlen, *Compensation Systems and Efficient Deterrence*, pp. 1115–1116; Geistfeld, *Placing a Price on Pain and Suffering: A Method for Helping Juries Determine Tort Damages for Nonmonetary Injuries*, pp. 818, 826–827.

forego pain and suffering damages as victims, so as to avoid having to incur the cost of compensating for pain and suffering if they were the injurers.[221] In other words, in accident settings between strangers an analogous argument to the argument of undesirable compulsory insurance can be made (to forego pain and suffering insurance provided through tort damages) only if individuals are equally likely to be prospective injurers and victims. However, this is not always the case. Therefore, for this type of accident the alleged discrepancy between the goals of deterrence and insurance seems to be exaggerated. Nevertheless, since the discrepancy is important overall to determine whether and how pain and suffering damages should be awarded, section 3.2 will discuss it more thoroughly and will outline proposals made to overcome it.

3.1.3. THE GOAL OF REDUCING TERTIARY (ADMINISTRATIVE) COSTS

Tertiary costs are frequently also referred to as administrative costs because they involve the costs of using the tort system in order to achieve deterrence and insurance. A workable tort system would imply that its administrative costs should not exceed the cost savings arising from deterrence and insurance. Therefore, reducing tertiary costs actually entails allocating the least possible resources that may yet enable to reach these ends. In essence, this third sub-goal of tort law is about optimizing the tort system so that spending an additional euro in administrative costs would reduce primary and secondary costs by at least one euro. In this respect administrative costs act as a balancing mechanism between the resources spent to achieve deterrence and insurance and the benefits arising therefrom.[222]

One cause of increase of the tort system's administrative costs is the evaluation of damages after an accident has occurred. Evaluating these damages *ad hoc,* namely for each and every individual accident case and in a very precise way, may prove to be too costly especially when non-pecuniary losses are involved. To determine this type of damages as accurately as possible, courts have to devote a significant amount of time and intelligence and consider a lot of information. None of these resources are infinite. Courts are required to deliver decisions within specific time limits. Apart from the procedural demand for speed, timely decisions also benefit victims by awarding damages sooner. Moreover, information required to precisely assess damages for immaterial losses arising from personal injury may not even be readily available. Therefore, for this type of damages the assessment need not be as accurate as possible in each and every case, otherwise that would entail large administrative costs. The

---

[221]   Geistfeld, *Placing a Price on Pain and Suffering: A Method for Helping Juries Determine Tort Damages for Nonmonetary Injuries,* pp. 818, 826–827.

[222]   Calabresi, *The Costs of Accidents. A Legal and Economic Analysis,* p. 28.

right amount of accuracy is achieved when the costs of additional accuracy in the assessment of damages are offset by the benefits that accuracy entails for deterrence and loss spreading.[223]

Especially as far as deterrence is concerned, to improve the incentives of the tortfeasor with respect to engaging in risky behavior, an accurate ex post assessment of the damages is not important as long as the tortfeasor does not have this assessment ex ante at her disposal. Therefore, as long as the assessment of damage awards is correct on average, it will allow the tortfeasor to know in advance the magnitude of the average losses she can cause and enable her to incorporate this information in her care and activity decisions.[224] Evaluating pain and suffering damages correctly on average implies that these damages should not be systematically over- or underestimated, otherwise the tortfeasor will receive excessive or inadequate behavioral incentives. Likewise, for insurance purposes, it is more important that the assessment of damages for immaterial losses is correct on average rather than accurate ex post. If the assessment is correct on average and thus available ex ante, it will enable insurers, product manufacturers and service providers to incorporate this information in their pricing decisions. Premiums and prices set according to the average expected accident losses may induce potential insureds to buy the correct level of insurance and potential consumers to purchase the correct amount of products or services.

Thus, assessing damages correctly on average lowers the cost of trial and may also significantly lower the costs of deterrence and insurance, hence further reducing overall administrative costs. In their analysis, Kaplow and Shavell further argue that it is not even necessary for courts to know in advance the average loss. They suggest that a simple physical description of the injury, which is already available to courts, should be the basis for the damages awarded. Therefore, if for instance an accident involved a 60-year-old woman who incurred hand amputation, damages should be evaluated on the basis of the expected average losses conditional on that physical description.[225] In other words they suggest that damages awarded should be dependent on the easily verifiable immaterial effects of the injury, in combination with the objective characteristic of the victim's age. Average health reduction experienced due to the injury should therefore be taken into consideration in the assessment of damages.

It becomes clear that awarding damages for immaterial losses is very important to achieve the goals of the economic analysis of tort law in cases of personal injuries. Compensation has been shown in the previous sections to be a

---

223   Louis Kaplow and Steven Shavell, "Accuracy in the Assessment of Damages," *Journal of Law and Economics* 39, no. 1 (1996), pp. 202–204; Vaia Karapanou and Louis T. Visscher, "The Magnitude of Pain and Suffering Damages from a Law and Economics and Health Economics Point of View," *Rotterdam Institute of Law and Economics Working Paper Series* (2009), pp. 2–3.

224   Louis Kaplow, "The Value of Accuracy in Adjudication: An Economic Analysis," *The Journal of Legal Studies* 23, no. 1, Economic Analysis of Civil Procedure (1994), pp. 309 ff.

225   Kaplow and Shavell, *Accuracy in the Assessment of Damages*, pp. 202–204.

means to attain the goals of deterrence and insurance. More specifically, the magnitude of the damages awarded and the extent to which they reflect the immaterial losses inflicted influences the fulfillment of the two goals. This section has illustrated that compensation is also a determinant factor for tertiary cost reduction. Nevertheless, to reduce the administrative costs of justice, the most important aspect is not the magnitude of damages, but rather the correctness on average of the awarded amounts. If pain and suffering damages are correct on average, they can inform in advance the decisions of individuals and induce them to reach optimal deterrence and insurance levels, hence contributing to the decrease of primary, secondary and tertiary costs. A proposal made in this direction is to assess damages for immaterial losses taking into account the average losses usually incurred after the specific injury as well as the age of the victim. This will allow courts to estimate damages using minimal resources. Reducing tertiary costs requires the calculation of pain and suffering damages to be accurate to a certain extent so as not to compromise incentives, but also to be as accurate as necessary so as not to waste available resources.

3.2. DAMAGES FOR IMMATERIAL LOSSES: HOW SHOULD THEY BE TREATED?

The foregoing analysis illustrated that compensation of immaterial losses plays an important role in the attainment of the goals of deterrence, insurance and the reduction of the administrative costs of the legal system. However, it also made clear that the goals of deterrence and insurance do not reach the same conclusions with respect to how immaterial losses should be treated in order to attain them. The previous sections explained that compensation of immaterial losses is important for deterrence purposes, but at the same time clarified that according to the prevailing opinion in law and economics scholarship, such losses should not be (entirely) compensated to achieve optimal loss spreading. The question therefore is whether and how pain and suffering damages for personal injuries could strike a balance between the goals of deterrence and of loss spreading. The following sections present solutions to that problem.

3.2.1. DEALING WITH THE DISCREPANCY: PROPOSALS SO FAR

Several law and economics scholars have tried to overcome the discrepancy between the goals of deterrence and insurance with respect to compensating immaterial losses by devising a way to award pain and suffering damages that promotes both goals. Their efforts have been focused on the structure of damage awards, a proper design of which could potentially achieve this objective. A solution that has been widely supported is to compensate immaterial losses by *decoupling liability*. Decoupling liability means that the injurer is liable for a different amount of money than the amount actually awarded to the victim. The victim thus receives an amount equivalent to the amount she would have spent to buy insurance coverage, whereas the injurer pays an amount that reflects all the losses caused by her behavior. The extra amount that the injurer has to pay for deterrence purposes is paid to the state in the form of a fine. The sum of all fines collected may be used to finance the tort system,[226] substitute tax revenues[227] or be returned to the consumers of the product that caused the loss in the form of a subsidy.[228] The idea of using a fine to attain optimal loss spreading and deterrence in case of immaterial losses was first suggested and formalized by Spence and since then it has also been advanced and maintained by other scholars.[229] However, it should be noted that a system of decoupling liability would be disadvantageous for victims in product liability and medical malpractice cases. If an accident occurs and liability is decoupled, the producer or service provider will raise her prices to incorporate the full amount of damages she will have to pay. The victim, on the other hand, will be forced to pay the increased prices but will not receive the corresponding damages. Furthermore, it is always possible in any accident setting that the injurer will seek to settle out of court to avoid paying the extra amount, in which case the deterrent effect of decoupling liability will be eroded for the injurer.[230] Apart from the aforementioned problems, the idea is also criticized as being difficult to implement because it would involve very high administrative costs.[231] The fact that it has so far not been put in practice could be regarded as confirming the criticism expressed against it.

Another suggestion that allegedly has the potential of achieving the goals of insurance and deterrence involves a return to contract. Cooter proposes that potential tort victims could sell their future tort claims to third parties.[232] If the tortfeasor or her insurer were to buy the future tort claim, then in the event of an

---

[226]   Arlen, *Compensation Systems and Efficient Deterrence*, p. 1102.

[227]   Shavell, *Foundations of Economic Analysis of Law*, pp. 272–275.

[228]   Danzon, *Tort Reform and the Role of Government in Private Insurance Markets*, p. 521.

[229]   Michael Spence, "Consumer Misperceptions, Product Failure and Producer Liability," *The Review of Economic Studies* 44, no. 3 (1977), pp. 561–571. See also Danzon, *Tort Reform and the Role of Government in Private Insurance Markets*, pp. 517–550; Shavell, *Economic Analysis of Accident Law*, pp. 233–235; Schwartz, *Proposals for Products Liability Reform: A Theoretical Synthesis*, p. 411; Mitchell A. Polinsky and Yeon-Koo Che, "Decoupling Liability: Optimal Incentives for Care and Litigation," *RAND Journal of Economics* 22, no. 4 (1991), pp. 562–570; Jennifer H. Arlen, "Tort Damages," in *Encyclopedia of Law and Economics, Volume II. Civil Law and Economics*, eds. Boudewijn Bouckaert and Gerrit De Geest (Cheltenham: Edward Elgar, 2000), p. 706; Visscher, *Tort Damages*, pp. 164–165.

[230]   W. Kip Viscusi, "Empirical Analysis of Tort Damages," in *Research Handbook on the Economics of Torts*, ed. Jennifer Arlen (Cheltenham: Edward Elgar, 2013), pp. 461–462.

[231]   Calfee and Rubin, *Some Implications of Damage Payments for Nonpecuniary Losses*, p. 380.

[232]   Cooter, *Towards a Market in Unmatured Tort Claims*, pp. 383–412.

accident, the case would be settled before it went to court. The insurance goal would be reached because every potential victim would be required to purchase insurance to cover the loss from the sold future tort claim.[233] Accordingly, the deterrence goal would be fulfilled because in a competitive market for future tort claims, the bargain between the parties would ensure that the price of the claim would be equivalent to the costs incurred in the event of an accident. The tortfeasor would thus prefer to buy the future tort claim and take the optimal precaution that would lower the cost of the claim, instead of taking no precaution and being exposed to the possibility of litigation.[234] The idea of returning to contract has also been supported by other scholars.[235] Nevertheless, it could be criticized on the grounds that it may involve problems typically arising in the process of concluding a contract, such as bargaining and informational problems, which may impede parties from setting the price of the claim correctly to achieve both deterrence and insurance. Moreover, this proposal of a return to contract could potentially apply in tort cases where the parties are specified, such as in product liability cases, but would not be possible for accidents where the parties are perfect strangers, as in the case of automobile accidents.

Other suggestions that have been put forward for compensating immaterial losses do not necessarily involve pursuing both goals. Depending on the goals one aims at regarding immaterial losses, namely the deterrence or insurance goal, different designs for damages awards have been proposed. Those who prioritize the goal of insurance maintain that pain and suffering damages should be totally abolished, because their current arbitrariness and unpredictability undermine the fulfillment of the goal.[236] On the other hand, commentators who also recognize deterrence as an important goal maintain that pain and suffering damages should be awarded, but that certain criteria should apply in their assessment to enhance their predictability. They suggest using schedules and tables based on previous damages awards or on the severity of the injury and age of the victim, to improve the predictability of the awards.[237] The use of caps or ceilings has also been proposed as a way to make liability costs more predictable and thus ensure the provision of liability insurance.[238]

It should be stressed here that even if insurance were the sole goal of the tort system, awarding pain and suffering damages for personal injury would not necessarily undermine its attainment. Providing pain and suffering coverage

---

[233] Ibid., p. 387.

[234] Ibid., p. 387.

[235] Calfee and Rubin, *Some Implications of Damage Payments for Nonpecuniary Losses*, pp. 402–403.

[236] King, *Pain and Suffering, Noneconomic Damages, and the Goals of Tort Law*, pp. 182–185, 201, 209.

[237] Randall R. Bovbjerg, Frank A. Sloan and James F. Blumstein, "Valuing Life and Limb in Tort: Scheduling "Pain and Suffering", *Northwestern University Law Review* 83, no. 4 (1989), pp. 938 ff.

[238] Geistfeld, *Placing a Price on Pain and Suffering: A Method for Helping Juries Determine Tort Damages for Nonmonetary Injuries*, p. 790.

would probably lead to an increase in insurance premiums, but that would not inevitably generate uninsurability. If pain and suffering awards are assessed in a consistent manner, allowing insurers, producers and service providers to predict the expected personal injury losses and incorporate these losses in the offered premiums, they may continue to provide liability insurance.[239]

Yet insurance is neither the sole nor the primary goal of tort law according to economic analysis.[240] On the contrary, especially with respect to losses arising from personal injury, one would prefer to diminish the probability of incurring or inflicting such losses rather than being able to bear them after the harm occurs.[241] Therefore, inevitably, the deterrence consideration comes first. After all, tort law was not intended as being merely an insurance system. Deterring risky behavior that could otherwise lead to injury is of principal importance and compensating immaterial losses is the way to achieve it.[242] The former suggests that if the proposals for overcoming the discrepancy between the deterrence and the insurance goals with respect to the treatment of immaterial losses are not persuasive enough to be endorsed by law and economics scholarship, it may be worthwhile to give an advantage to deterrence considerations.

So far, the most important law and economics proposals to attain both deterrence and insurance are decoupling liability and returning to contract. The first proposed solution necessitates the interference of the state as it involves collecting fines from injurers. The second proposal suggests putting aside tort law and arranging damages through contract. However, if one wants to solve the problem under the auspices of tort law through court adjudication or settlement and without the intervention of the state, there may be another way to treat immaterial losses that can promote the goals of both deterrence and insurance.

3.2.2. STRIKING A BALANCE BETWEEN DETERRENCE AND INSURANCE: EX ANTE DETERMINED PAIN AND SUFFERING DAMAGES

The argument that tort damages are a form of compulsory insurance and therefore only individuals who would be inclined to insure themselves against

---

[239] Miller, *Willingness to Pay Comes of Age: Will the System Survive*, p. 906: "In setting insurance rates, actuaries are often influenced more by the predictability and spread of damage awards than by the mean award payout."

[240] See Tom Baker and Peter Siegelman, "The Law and Economics of Liability Insurance: A Theoretical and Empirical Review," in *Research Handbook on the Economics of Torts*, ed. Jennifer Arlen (Cheltenham: Edward Elgar, 2013), pp. 185–187.

[241] Avraham, *Should Pain-and-Suffering Damages be Abolished from Tort Law? More Experimental Evidence*, p. 953: "When people need to allocate their money between prevention and insurance, their first priority is always to pay for prevention and then to purchase insurance".

[242] See Landes and Posner, *The Economic Structure of Tort Law*, pp. 186–187.

immaterial losses should receive pain and suffering damages has influenced law and economics scholarship. The implication of the argument is that a single pain and suffering damages award that corresponds to the immaterial loss incurred will promote deterrence but will not simultaneously promote insurance, unless the victim had wanted to insure herself in the first place. However, existing empirical evidence does not reach definite conclusions on people's desire to take out insurance against immaterial losses. The preceding analysis also suggests that while the argument may be valid for accidents where victims have a contractual/consensual relationship, such as in product liability or medical malpractice cases, it does not apply with regard to accidents occurring between perfect strangers. Hence, the discrepancy that pain and suffering damages allegedly create with respect to the promotion of deterrence and insurance is actually less significant than it may appear at first sight.

Nevertheless, as explained previously in section 3.1.2, even if people do not want to insure themselves against immaterial losses or pay a higher price for safer products or services, they may still be willing to spend resources on reducing the probability of their occurrence.[243] These resources can form the basis of pain and suffering damages awards that strike a balance between the goals of deterrence and insurance by promoting both goals. The idea is as follows. In principle, the injurer should pay every person the amount this person was willing to spend to avoid the risk, whether or not the risk has materialized. In this way, victims would in theory be indifferent towards not running the risk or running the risk but receiving the amount they were willing to spend on accident avoidance. Victims would then be ex ante compensated for the risk they run, and injurers would receive adequate behavioral incentives because they would pay for the expected harm caused by their activities. However, given that under tort law the injurer can only be held liable if she has indeed caused losses, only those persons for whom the risk has actually materialized can receive damages. If this damages award can still be based on the amount of resources that people are willing to forego ex ante to reduce expected immaterial losses, it will be correct from both the deterrence and the insurance point of view. The injurer would then correctly internalize the costs the victim would be willing to spend, thus

---

[243] Danzon, *Tort Reform and the Role of Government in Private Insurance Markets*, p. 526; Miller, *Willingness to Pay Comes of Age: Will the System Survive*; Ott and Schäfer, *Schmerzensgeld Bei Körperverletzungen. Eine Ökonomische Analyse*, p. 568; Rubin and Calfee, *Consequences of Damage Awards for Hedonic and Other Nonpecuniary Losses*, p. 249; Geistfeld, *Placing a Price on Pain and Suffering: A Method for Helping Juries Determine Tort Damages for Nonmonetary Injuries*, p. 825. See also Friedman, *What is 'Fair Compensation' for Death or Injury?*, pp. 83, 85, who talks about the willingness of a potential victim to *accept* resources in order to reduce the probability of incurring immaterial losses. There is an issue with respect to whether willingness to pay (WTP) or willingness to accept (WTA) values should be used to calculate damages because research suggests that a disparity exists between these values, see Arlen, *Tort Damages*, pp. 709–710. It should be noted however that WTP values are most commonly used.

receiving incentives to take optimal precautions. Accordingly, the victim would not be 'over-insured' against her will, because the resulting increase in prices or premiums, due to the inclusion in the damages award of immaterial losses, would correspond to the amount she would have spent herself in taking precautions.

To illustrate how pain and suffering damages can be based on this ex ante amount, consider the following: if an individual would have spent €1,000 on precautionary measures that reduce by 0.5% the probability of having an accident in which she gets paralyzed, statistically this implies that the value of avoiding paralysis amounts to €2 million (€1,000 / 0.0005). Hence, the pain and suffering damages that the injurer should pay for inflicting paralysis should also amount to €2 million.[244] Assessed in this manner, pain and suffering damages reach the same result as if amounts are paid before the risk materializes: the injurer ends up paying the amount that the victim was willing to spend on accident avoidance divided by the expected number of accidents since the accident has now materialized. Therefore, according to the proposed approach, it is possible to strike a balance between the goals of deterrence and insurance if *ex ante determined damages*, which are based on the resources the victim would have spent herself on reducing the expected accident losses, are awarded to compensate for immaterial losses. By setting pain and suffering damages on the basis of the amounts that victims would be willing to pay to avoid incurring the accident, the goal of deterrence is promoted, as the injurer receives correct deterrent incentives, while the victim is not over-insured, as she receives damages corresponding to the amount she would have spent herself to avoid the accident. The next section presents a measure that is based on the concept of ex ante determined damages and has been suggested in law and economics scholarship with respect to compensating immaterial losses arising from fatal accidents. However, an equivalent measure is not yet available that would allow the assessment of pain and suffering damages for non-fatal personal injuries based on the cost of precautions that potential victims would be willing to take to avoid the injury.

3.2.3. THE VALUE OF STATISTICAL LIFE (YEAR) FOR FATALITIES

A measure that exactly reflects how many resources people are willing to spend on reducing the probability and/or magnitude of fatal accidents is the *Value of Statistical Life* (VSL). It has been used in the context of *cost-benefit analysis* (CBA) to estimate the costs and benefits to life arising from regulatory

---

[244]   Schäfer and Ott, *The Economic Analysis of Civil Law*, p. 246. See also Friedman, *What is 'Fair Compensation' for Death or Injury?*, pp. 85, 91.

policies.[245] The extensive literature on the VSL investigates how many resources people are willing to spend on reducing the probability of fatal accidents.[246] In everyday life, people are required to take decisions as consumers that involve their health and safety, such as for instance paying a higher price for a new car with more safety features,[247] buying a bicycle helmet for a child,[248] installing smoke detectors to take precautions for a potential fire,[249] or changing one's smoking habits from regular to light cigarettes. Furthermore, some people may choose to undertake dangerous activities in order to receive a risk premium in return, as is the case for individuals engaging in risky jobs. If for instance an individual accepts a wage differential of €700 to incur an extra fatal risk of 1/10,000 then the implicit value of her statistical life would be €7,000,000 (€700/0.0001).

Another measure that is closely related to the VSL and has been used in the contexts of CBA is the *Value of Statistical Life Year* (VSLY), which is derived from VSL estimates. The main difference of the two measures is that the VSLY contains a time factor – more specifically, a life year. To illustrate, if the VSL is calculated at €6,000,000 for a 50-year-old individual with a remaining life expectancy of 30 years, then the VSLY would be 6,000,000 / 30= €200,000. The VSL(Y) is thus derived from the trade-offs people make between wealth and the probability of death.[250] The resulting amounts differ greatly, but according to Sunstein, the VSL is set at about €5.8 million.[251] This amount encompasses both pecuniary and non-pecuniary losses. Nevertheless it has been argued that approximately 50–75% of the VSL consists of immaterial losses.[252]

---

[245] Cass R. Sunstein, "Lives, Life-Years and Willingness to Pay," *Columbia Law Review* 104, no. 205 (2004), pp. 205–252; Eric A. Posner and Cass R. Sunstein, "Dollars and Death," *University of Chicago Law Review* 72, no. 2 (2005), pp. 537–598. For a review article see W. Kip Viscusi and Joseph E. Aldy, "The Value of a Statistical Life: A Critical Review of Market Estimates Throughout the World," *Journal of Risk and Uncertainty* 27, no. 1 (2003), pp. 5–76.

[246] Ibid.

[247] For estimates of VSL derived from the price of new automobiles, see Scott E. Atkinson and Robert Halvorsen, "The Valuation of Risks to Life: Evidence from the Market for Automobiles," *Review of Economics and Statistics* 72, no. 1 (1990), pp. 133–136.

[248] For estimates of VSL for children derived from the market of bicycle safety helmets, see Robin R. Jenkins, Nicole Owens and Lanelle Bembenek Wiggins, "Valuing Reduced Risks to Children: The Case of Bicycle Safety Helmets," *Contemporary Economic Policy* 19, no. 4 (2001), pp. 397–408.

[249] For estimates of VSL derived from fire detectors' costs, see Rachel Dardis, "The Value of a Life: New Evidence from the Marketplace," *American Economic Review* 70, no. 5 (1980), pp. 1077–1082.

[250] Orley Ashenfelter, "Measuring the Value of a Statistical Life: Problems and Prospects," *The Economic Journal* 116, no. 510 (2006), pp. C10–C11.

[251] Sunstein, *Lives, Life-Years and Willingness to Pay*, p. 205 refers to an amount of $6,100,000. This amount was first expressed in dollars from 2013 (see www.bls.gov/data/inflation_calculator.htm) and then calculated in euros on the basis of the 2013 Purchasing Power Parity (PPP) of the euro area as published by the OECD: 0.773 (see http://stats.oecd.org/Index.aspx?DataSetCode=PPPGDP).

[252] Miller, *Willingness to Pay Comes of Age: Will the System Survive*, pp. 893–894.

Due to these characteristics, Posner and Sunstein have proposed that as well as its utilization in CBA, the VSL(Y) has the potential to also be employed in a tort context to assess damages for fatal injuries.[253] Their proposal is in line with the idea of ex ante determined damages that could strike a balance between the goals of deterrence and insurance and enable attaining both goals. However, since the VSL(Y) relates to the resources spent to avoid fatal accidents, it is only appropriate for the assessment of immaterial losses resulting from fatal accidents and cannot be utilized to assess pain and suffering damages arising from nonfatal injuries. Only in case of very severe injuries where it could plausibly be assumed that an individual would be willing to devote the same amount of resources to prevent the injury as she would devote to prevent death, could the VSL(Y) be used.[254] Schäfer and Ott have argued that pain and suffering damages for less severe injuries should be some fraction of the value attached to the willingness to pay to prevent death.[255] However, no suggestion has been put forward as to how these fractions can be determined.

It is evident that, although the VSL is an example of a measure that can be used to arrive at the ex ante determined damages, it lies outside of the scope of this book as it concerns the compensation of immaterial loss arising from fatal injury. A measure analogous to the VSL(Y) that would allow assessing pain and suffering damages for non-fatal personal injury based on the ex ante determined damages is still lacking. The following chapters aim to fill this gap.

---

[253]   Posner and Sunstein, *Dollars and Death*, pp. 537–598.

[254]   See for instance Paul Kind, Rachel Rosser and Alan Williams, eds., *Valuation of Quality of Life: Some Psychometric Evidence* (Amsterdam, New York, Oxford: Holland Publishing Company, 1982). They find that an injury which confines people in bed is considered as detrimental as death. See also Schäfer and Ott, *The Economic Analysis of Civil Law*, pp. 249–250.

[255]   Hans-Bernd Schäfer and Claus Ott, *Lehrbuch Der Ökonomischen Analyse Des Zivilrechts*, 4th ed. (Berlin: Springer, 2005), p. 377. See also Miller, *Willingness to Pay Comes of Age: Will the System Survive*, pp. 896 ff.

CHAPTER 4

QUALITY ADJUSTED LIFE YEARS

A Measure for the Economic Evaluation of Health Care

The method used to assess pain and suffering damages should, according to the previous chapters, take into consideration many different factors to be able to attain the goals of tort law as stipulated both by traditional legal theory and by law and economics. On the one hand, to achieve fair compensation and satisfaction, pain and suffering damages should reflect the total health reduction resulting from the personal physical injury. Therefore, factors such as the type, severity and duration of the injury, the pain and emotional strain incurred, as well as the loss in life expectancy, should figure in the assessment. On the other hand, to strike a balance between the goals of deterrence and insurance and promote both goals through the treatment of immaterial losses, pain and suffering damages should be based on the ex ante determined damages, namely the amount that a victim would be willing to forego before an accident occurs to reduce her expected immaterial losses.

Besides the ability to incorporate these features, the assessment should also generate consistent and predictable amounts. Consistency and predictability of the amounts will facilitate deterrence by allowing potential tortfeasors to take into consideration the prospect of having to pay a certain amount of damages if they inflict harm. Furthermore, it may also promote loss spreading by allowing insurers, product manufacturers and service providers to better predict the expected injury damages and incorporate them into the premiums offered. The analysis in the previous chapter showed that the assessment of pain and suffering damages should additionally be as accurate as necessary to reduce the administrative costs of justice. A proposal in this direction is to assess pain and suffering damages by taking into account the average losses resulting from a certain type of injury as well as the age of the victim. In any case, the assessment method implemented should strike a balance between the costs of additional accuracy and the benefits of that accuracy for the attainment of the aforementioned goals.

Can all these characteristics be accommodated in a single method of assessment? Before answering this question, the current chapter presents the Quality Adjusted Life Year (QALY), a measure that is 'state of the art' in the domain of health economics, commonly used to evaluate the cost-effectiveness of medical interventions and inform the allocation of health care budgets. The following sections explain the origin and the characteristics of the QALY, describe how it is calculated and illustrate the way it is currently used in the context of health economics. However, they do not aim to provide an exhaustive account of the QALY and related topics.[256] Instead, the analysis focuses on its characteristics and the most important issues pertaining to its use to make clear that apart from the purpose for which it was initially intended, the QALY possesses certain elements that render it an appropriate measure for use in alternative contexts, which nevertheless still involve assessments about health and life. More specifically, being able to provide an evaluation of both health condition and length of life, the QALY may constitute an attractive framework for the evaluation of immaterial losses arising from personal physical injuries. The presentation of the QALY and the familiarization with its characteristics therefore paves the way for the forthcoming analysis. However, the extent to which the characteristics of the QALY coincide with the characteristics required of an assessment method for immaterial losses and whether the QALY can actually be used as a method for assessing pain and suffering damages in a tort law setting are issues that will be discussed thoroughly in chapter 5. The current chapter pertains exclusively to the description and the use of the QALY in the context of health economics.

4.1. CONTEXT AND ORIGIN OF THE QALY

The QALY originated as a response to the need of a measure to evaluate and compare the effects resulting from different health care programs.[257] Until the late 1960s and early 1970s, there were two main ways to perform the task: *cost-benefit analysis* (CBA) and *cost-effectiveness analysis* (CEA).

CBA is still used today as a decision tool for resource allocation in a number of contexts related to public policy.[258] It is founded in the tradition of welfare

---

[256]   The interested reader is referred to Michael F. Drummond et al., *Methods for the Economic Evaluation of Health Care Programmes*, 3rd ed. (Oxford; New York: Oxford University Press, 2005); John Brazier et al., *Measuring and Valuing Health Benefits for Economic Evaluation* (Oxford; New York: Oxford University Press, 2007) for exhaustive analyses of the QALY and its use in economic appraisal.

[257]   Here it is taken for granted that the health care market should be regulated to avoid the serious inefficiencies occurring due to the asymmetric information between consumers of health care and insurers, patients and doctors as well as the externalities associated with the generation and the consumption of health care. See Brazier et al., *Measuring and Valuing Health Benefits for Economic Evaluation*, pp. 37–41. Therefore, the evaluation of different health care programs, treatments, interventions et cetera is necessary for the allocation of health.

[258]   The most notable use of CBA is in the context of Regulatory Impact Assessment (RIA). See Andrea Renda, *Impact Assessment in the EU: The State of the Art and the Art of the State* (Brussels: Centre for European Policy Studies, 2006) and John F. III Morral, "An Assessment of the US Regulatory Impact Analysis Program," in *Regulatory Impact Analysis, Best Practices*

economics in which individuals are considered as being the best judges of their own welfare. In CBA, costs and benefits of proposed interventions are compared to reach a decision regarding the desirability of the intervention. The Kaldor-Hicks criterion is used as the guiding principle implying that the proposed intervention is implemented only if the benefits generated exceed the costs ($\Delta B - \Delta C > 0$).[259] However, not all benefits and costs generated by an intervention are readily quantified in monetary terms. For interventions that are expected to affect human life, benefits and costs to life first need to be assigned a monetary value before their comparison can take place. *Revealed preference* and *stated preference* methods elicit individual preferences regarding trade-offs between wealth and the risk of death.[260] In these trade-offs people indicate their *willingness-to-pay* (WTP) a specific amount of money to avoid a certain fatality risk or their *willingness-to-accept* (WTA) an amount of money to incur a certain fatality risk. Using this information the *Value of Statistical Life* (VSL) and the *Value of a Statistical Life Year* (VSLY) are estimated, which are utilized to account for the benefits and costs to life generated by different interventions, in the context of CBA.[261]

The ability to express different types of costs and benefits in a common metric by also pricing non-market goods facilitates the comparison of different effects that would otherwise be incomparable, and is thus viewed by many commentators as an important advantage of CBA over other methodologies for the evaluation of different policies and interventions. This alleged virtue of CBA, however, has been heavily criticized by many social science scholars and particularly so in the context of evaluating interventions that affect human lives. The critique challenges the correctness of pricing non-market goods, such as health and life, on normative and ethical grounds. According to the main argument, some goods are so valuable that they cannot and should not be commodified and exchanged in markets.[262] The idea of 'incommensurability' is further supported by the argument that putting a price on such goods results in reducing their value.[263] Other commentators accept the pricing of life and of

---

[259]   *in OECD Countries*, ed. OECD (Paris: OECD, 1997), pp. 71–87 for the use of CBA in RIAs in Europe and the USA respectively.

[259]   Aki Tsuchiya and Alan Williams, "Welfare Economics and Economic Evaluation," in *Economic Evaluation in Health Care: Merging Theory with Practice*, eds. Michael F. Drummond and Alistair McGuire (Oxford, New York: Oxford University Press, 2001), pp. 34–37; Drummond et al., *Methods for the Economic Evaluation of Health Care Programmes*, pp. 15–17, 212–214; Brazier et al., *Measuring and Valuing Health Benefits for Economic Evaluation*, pp. 37–44, 287.

[260]   Revealed preference methods that are used for the evaluation of non-market goods such as life are the consumer market behavior method and the hedonic wage method. The most frequently used stated preference method for the evaluation of non-market goods is the contingent valuation method. See Alessandra Arcuri, "Risk Regulation," in *Regulation and Economics*, eds. Alessio M. Pacces and Roger J. Van den Bergh (Cheltenham: Edward Elgar, 2012), pp. 314–319.

[261]   For information regarding the VSL and the VSLY see also chapter 3 at section 3.2.3.

[262]   Margaret Jane Radin, "Market-Inalienability," *Harvard Law Review* 100, no. 8 (1987), pp. 1849–1937 refers to the market inalienability of some goods.

[263]   See Arcuri, *Risk Regulation*, pp. 326–328.

other non-marketed goods in the context of CBA, yet they question the methods utilized to produce monetary estimates of these goods and put the emphasis on the issue of how such an evaluation should be performed.[264]

One of the main problems of CBAs conducted in the late 1960s to evaluate proposed health care programs pertained precisely to the restrictive approach used to account for the benefits of the programs. The so-called *human capital approach* used the productivity increase as the sole measure of benefit realized by the proposed program,[265] estimating it on the basis of the present value of increased lifetime earnings.[266] The approach was heavily criticized because it implied that the (only) important result of a health care program generating benefits to health was the increase in productivity. By doing so, it neglected individual preferences regarding health improvements, thus moving away from the theoretical foundations of welfare economics.[267] In addition, it failed to reflect the value of good health and quality of life and assigned small values for improvements in the health of unemployed, poor, retired and other people not receiving wages (e.g. housewives, etc.).[268] Another approach was therefore necessary; one that could express the benefit accrued by health care programs in terms of health improvement and extension of life.

4.1.1. COST-EFFECTIVENESS ANALYSIS FOR THE ECONOMIC EVALUATION OF HEALTH CARE

The technique of *cost-effectiveness analysis* (CEA) was developed to address these concerns.[269] CEA is a method used for the economic evaluation of health care programs in which costs are estimated in monetary terms and benefits accrued to health are expressed in 'natural' units.[270] The term 'natural' indicates that the

---

264   Cass R. Sunstein, *The Cost-Benefit State: The Future of Regulatory Protection* (Chicago: American Bar Association, 2002), p. xi refers to the question whether to perform CBA, as the 'first generation debate' over cost-benefit analysis and differentiates it from what he calls the 'second generation debate' dealing with the question of how to perform CBA.

265   Mark Sculpher, "The Role and Estimation of Productivity Costs in Economic Evaluation," in *Economic Evaluation in Health Care: Merging Theory with Practice*, eds. Michael Drummond and Alistair McGuire (Oxford, New York: Oxford University Press, 2001), p. 99.

266   Dorothy P. Rice and Barbara S. Cooper, "The Economic Value of Human Life," *American Journal of Public Health* 57, no. 11 (1967), pp. 1954–1966.

267   Ezra J. Mishan, "Evaluation of Life and Limb: A Theoretical Approach," *Journal of Political Economy* 79, no. 4 (1971), pp. 691 ff.; Drummond et al., *Methods for the Economic Evaluation of Health Care Programmes*, pp. 217–218. For more information on the theoretical foundations of CBA and CEA, see *infra* section 4.1.1.

268   George W. Torrance, Warren H. Thomas and David L. Sackett, "A Utility Maximization Model for Evaluation of Health Care Programs," *Health Services Research* 7 (1972), pp. 118–119; George W. Torrance, "Measurement of Health State Utilities for Economic Appraisal: A Review," *Journal of Health Economics* 5, no. 1 (3, 1986), p. 4; Magnus Johannesson, *Theory and Methods of Economic Evaluation of Health Care* (Dordrecht, the Netherlands: Kluwer, 1996), pp. 1–2.

269   Johannesson, *Theory and Methods of Economic Evaluation of Health Care*, p. 135.

270   Ibid., pp. 135 ff.; Drummond et al., *Methods for the Economic Evaluation of Health Care Programmes*, pp. 12–14.

benefits generated are not valued in monetary terms.[271] They may for instance include life-years extended, cases of disease averted, number of cancer cases detected, etc. Health care programs, interventions and medical techniques are compared on the basis of the costs and the health outcome generated by using an *incremental cost-effectiveness ratio* (ICER). The ratio expresses the difference in costs divided by the difference in outcome between the programs (ΔC / ΔE).[272] The program that can achieve a predetermined level of outcome in the least cost or the highest level of outcome within a fixed budget will be implemented.[273] CEA thus focuses on the incremental health outcome that can be achieved if one intervention is implemented, in comparison to other interventions or no intervention at all. By expressing the health outcome in natural units rather than monetary terms, CEA cannot evaluate whether the benefits of the proposed intervention exceed its costs and therefore it cannot assess whether a single program is worthwhile to implement, like CBA does.[274] On the other hand, using natural units instead of money allows CEA to escape being criticized for pricing goods such as life and health, which are considered by many as being incommensurable. However, an important shortcoming of using natural units instead of money as the measure of benefit is that CEA can only evaluate and compare health care programs, treatments, interventions, etc. that yield the same type of outcome.[275] Therefore, it would be possible to compare, for instance, two health care programs generating asthma episode-free days, but not possible to compare a program generating asthma episode-free days and a program resulting in a gain of life years.[276] Another disadvantage of CEA is that it cannot evaluate and compare programs, treatments, interventions, etc. that

---

[271] Brazier et al., *A Review of the Use of Health Status Measures in Economic Evaluation*, p. 3.

[272] However, if the health care program is proposed to deal with a health care problem that has not yet been addressed by any other program, then CEA is conducted on the basis of a simple ratio expressing the costs over the health outcome yielded by the proposed program (C/E). In other words the evaluation does not involve any incremental costs and effects since the comparison regards the cost effectiveness of the proposed program against *'doing nothing'*. See Johannesson, *Theory and Methods of Economic Evaluation of Health Care*, pp. 135–136.

[273] Milton C. Weinstein and William B. Stason, "Foundations of Cost-Effectiveness Analysis for Health and Medical Practices," *The New England Journal of Medicine* 296, no. 13 (1977), p. 717; Alan M. Garber et al., "Theoretical Foundations of Cost-Effectiveness Analysis," in *Cost-Effectiveness in Health and Medicine*, eds. Marthe R. Gold and others (New York, Oxford: Oxford University Press, 1996), p. 27. See Magnus M. Johannesson and Milton C. Weinstein, "On the Decision Rules of Cost-Effectiveness Analysis," *Journal of Health Economics* 12 (1993), pp. 460–462 for a detailed explanation of how incremental cost-effectiveness ratio is used to facilitate a decision between competing independent programs and between mutually exclusive programs.

[274] Torrance, *Measurement of Health State Utilities for Economic Appraisal: A Review*, p. 3.

[275] Brazier et al., *Measuring and Valuing Health Benefits for Economic Evaluation*, pp. 9–10.

[276] See for instance the cost-effectiveness analyses performed by Mark J. Sculpher and Martin J. Buxton, "The Episode-Free Day as a Composite Measure of Effectiveness: An Illustrative Economic Evaluation of Formoterol Versus Salbutamol in Asthma Therapy," *PharmacoEconomics* 4, no. 5 (1993), pp. 345–352 and by Daniel B. Mark et al., "Cost Effectiveness of Thrombolytic Therapy with Tissue Plasminogen Activator as Compared with Streptokinase for Acute Myocardial Infarction," *The New England Journal of Medicine* 332,

yield more than one type of outcome. It can therefore not assist decision-making when the choice involves health care programs that affect both health and life duration. These effects cannot be simultaneously captured by CEA and yet they are crucial as it is very plausible that a proposed program may simultaneously improve quality of life and increase life expectancy.

The incompetence of CEA, which uses natural units as the measure of effect, to provide information and subsequently guide decision-making with respect to interventions that influence both mortality and morbidity, generated in the late 1960s the demand to devise a method of evaluation that can simultaneously reflect those elements. Klarman and colleagues were the first to implement the idea to evaluate and compare the cost-effectiveness of kidney transplantation and dialysis on the basis of the life years gained by each intervention with an adjustment for quality.[277] Several publications followed using the same concept of taking into account both health improvement and life extension to evaluate interventions.[278] Nevertheless, it was actually some years later, in a very influential article by Weinstein and Stason explaining how a quality adjusted life year could be used as a measure of effect in CEA, that the concept of QALYs became broadly known in the policy-maker and medical world.[279] Later on, in 1985, in another important piece of work on the economic appraisal of health policy, Williams illustrated the usefulness of QALYs by explaining how he used cost per QALY to evaluate the cost-effectiveness of coronary artery bypass grafting.[280]

Since then, for the last 20 years and more, the QALY has been extensively used in the context of CEA to inform resource allocation with respect to health care at the societal level, to measure and compare population health and to evaluate the effectiveness of medical interventions in patient groups in clinical trial settings.[281] It is a widely endorsed measure for health care decision-making, considered 'state

no. 21 (1995), pp. 1418–1424 where the effectiveness measures are respectively asthma episode-free days and years of life gained.

[277] Herbert E. Klarman, John O'S. Francis and Gerald D. Rosenthal, "Cost Effectiveness Analysis Applied to the Treatment of Chronic Renal Disease," *Medical Care* 6, no. 1 (1968), p. 50.

[278] S. Fanshel and J. W. Bush, "A Health-Status Index and its Application to Health-Services Outcomes," *Operations Research* 18, no. 6 (1970), pp. 1021–1066 proposing as a measure of outcome the 'function years'; J. W. Bush, S. Fanshel and M. M. Chen, "Analysis of a Tuberculin Testing Program using a Health Status Index," *Socio-Economic Planning Sciences* 6, no. 1 (1972), pp. 49–68 using the 'function years' to evaluate a tuberculin testing program; Torrance, Thomas and Sackett, *A Utility Maximization Model for Evaluation of Health Care Programs*, pp. 118–133 proposing the 'health index day' as the measure of outcome; Milton C. Weinstein and William B. Stason, *Hypertension: A Policy Perspective* (Cambridge, MA: Harvard University Press, 1976), p. 243, proposing QALY as a way to measure the benefits accruing after the application of various hypertension treatment programs; Richard Zeckhauser and Donald Shepard, "Where Now for Saving Lives?," *Law and Contemporary Problems* 40, no. 4 (1976), pp. 11 ff., proposing the use of QALYs as a unit of output for lifesaving and health improving policies.

[279] Weinstein and Stason, *Foundations of Cost-Effectiveness Analysis for Health and Medical Practices*, pp. 716–721.

[280] Alan Williams, "Economics of Coronary Artery Bypass Grafting." *British Medical Journal* 291, no. 6491 (1985), pp. 326–329.

[281] Brazier et al., *Measuring and Valuing Health Benefits for Economic Evaluation*, p. 29.

of the art' in the domain of health economics.[282] CEA that uses QALYs as the measure of effect instead of natural units and reports the results in cost per QALY gained, is considered a special form of CEA and referred to by many scholars as *cost-utility analysis* (CUA).[283] To avoid complexity, the use of abbreviated terms is kept to a minimum in the following text, so the term CEA will be used henceforth to indicate cost-effectiveness analyses that use QALYs as the measure of effect.

CEA does not have a strict theoretical economic foundation. Many scholars have tried to embed cost-effectiveness analysis into welfare economics by stipulating the assumptions under which that would be possible.[284] Others support an *extra-welfarist* foundation of CEA, according to which, apart from individual welfare, other aspects such as health are important and should be maximized.[285] Some scholars view the extra-welfarist foundation of CEA more broadly, referring to it as the *decision-maker approach* of the CEA and maintaining that CEA should be utilized in a pragmatic way, adopting elements that would allow the decision-maker to allocate the resources in a way that maximizes the desired outcome, which includes but may not be limited to health.[286] The decision regarding which theoretical foundation CEA adheres to is important, as it has methodological implications for the economic evaluation of health care, including, but not limited to, the choice of whose preferences are going to be considered and the way in which the health outcome will be valued.

4.1.2. THEORETICAL FOUNDATIONS OF QALY-BASED CEA

The welfare economics approach implies that the aim of CEA is to improve social welfare, which is considered to be a function of individual preferences.[287] To

---

[282]   Patrick Hofstetter and James K. Hammitt, *Human Health Metrics for Environmental Decision Support Tools: Lessons from Health Economics and Decision Analysis* (Washington: U.S. EPA, Office of Research and Development, [2001]); Marilyn Dix Smith, Michael Drummond and Diana Brixner, "Moving the QALY Forward: Rationale for Change," *Value in Health* 12, no. 1 (2009), pp. S1-S4.

[283]   Marthe R. Gold et al., *Cost-Effectiveness in Health and Medicine* (New York, Oxford: Oxford University Press, 1996), p. xviii.; Johannesson, *Theory and Methods of Economic Evaluation of Health Care*, p. 151; Drummond et al., *Methods for the Economic Evaluation of Health Care Programmes*, pp. 137 ff.

[284]   Johannesson, *Theory and Methods of Economic Evaluation of Health Care*, pp. 151–153 and Garber et al., *Theoretical Foundations of Cost-Effectiveness Analysis*, pp. 25–37 support that CEA should be embedded in welfare economics.

[285]   Anthony J. Culyer, "The Normative Economics of Health Care Finance and Provision," *Oxford Review of Economic Policy* 5, no. 1 (1989), pp. 34–58.

[286]   Robert Sugden and Alan Williams, *The Principles of Practical Cost-Benefit Analysis* (Oxford: Oxford University Press, 1978), pp. 181–197; Werner B. F. Brouwer and Marc A. Koopmanschap, "On the Economic Foundations of CEA. Ladies and Gentlemen, Take Your Positions!" *Journal of Health Economics* 19, no. 4 (2000), pp. 444 ff.; Drummond et al., *Methods for the Economic Evaluation of Health Care Programmes*, pp. 358–359.

[287]   Garber et al., *Theoretical Foundations of Cost-Effectiveness Analysis*, p. 29.

---

evaluate whether social welfare improves, the Kaldor-Hicks criterion is applied, according to which an intervention brings forth an improvement in social welfare if the people who benefit can pay to compensate those who lose and still be better off than before the intervention, without requiring compensation to actually take place.[288] Therefore, individual preferences with respect to the gains generated from an intervention have to be first expressed and accounted for before an intervention can be considered to increase overall welfare. Health care programs, interventions and so on do not always lead to pre-specified improvements in health conditions, but may also have higher or lower improvements, as well as inflict milder or more severe adverse effects. This implies that the preference of individuals for an intervention should be elicited in such a way that it takes into account the possibility that different health outcomes may occur. Expected utility theory, developed by von Neumann and Morgenstern, shows that, if individual behavior satisfies some specific axioms, the strength of individual preferences over uncertain outcomes can be elicited.[289] According to the theory, a rational individual will choose between different interventions, on the basis of the utility of their outcomes. The probability of each outcome is multiplied by its utility and the sum of these probability-weighted utilities yields the expected utility of the intervention. This calculation is performed for all interventions compared, so that in the end, individuals are able to rank interventions on the basis of the expected utility they generate.

Under a welfarist approach for CEA, QALYs are supposed to represent the individual utility associated with a particular health outcome.[290] However, in order for QALYs to actually represent utility, their calculation should be based on expected utility theory, while a number of additional conditions for utility and individual preferences must also hold.[291] Some of the conditions are rather

---

[288]   Ibid., pp. 32–34; Brazier et al., *Measuring and Valuing Health Benefits for Economic Evaluation*, pp. 41–44.

[289]   Drummond et al., *Methods for the Economic Evaluation of Health Care Programmes*, pp. 139–143; Matthew D. Adler, "QALY's and Policy Evaluation: A New Perspective," *Yale Journal of Health Policy, Law, and Ethics* 6 (2006), p. 21. For the original publication see John Von Neumann and Oskar Morgenstern, *Theory of Games and Economic Behavior* (Princeton: Princeton University Press, 1944).

[290]   Brazier et al., *Measuring and Valuing Health Benefits for Economic Evaluation*, pp. 46–51. This explains why the term cost-utility analysis is frequently used to denote QALY-based CEA. See also Drummond et al., *Methods for the Economic Evaluation of Health Care Programmes*, p. 139.

[291]   For the calculation of QALYs in cases of chronic health states Joseph S. Pliskin, Donald S. Shepard and Milton C. Weinstein, "Utility Functions for Life Years and Health Status," *Operations Research* 28, no. 1 (1980), pp. 206–224 have identified three conditions. The first condition is '*mutual utility independence*', which stipulates that quality of life should be utility independent of life duration and life duration should also be utility independent from quality of life. In other words, the preference of an individual for a gamble over quality of life should not be affected by life duration and vice versa. If, for instance, an individual is indifferent between living the rest of her life with back pain or undergoing a treatment which may lead to full health for the rest of her life with a two-thirds probability and to death with a

restrictive and therefore are usually only approximately satisfied.[292] Moreover, many studies have shown that people in real life do not follow the model suggested by expected utility theory, to make decisions.[293] Although expected utility theory has not been intended to describe reality but rather to yield normative predictions, the fact that its axioms are frequently violated has led some scholars to propose alternative theories, with the most prominent one being suggested by Tversky and Kahneman.[294] Their '*prospect theory*' takes into consideration insights from psychology and proposes a more realistic framework for individual decision-making. Some important scholars in the domain of health economics are strongly advocating a descriptive use of prospect theory to measure the relative desirability of health outcomes.[295] Nevertheless, despite the

---

one-third probability then the individual should also be indifferent between living for 10 years with back pain or undergoing a treatment which may lead to full health for 10 years with a two-thirds probability or to death with a one-third probability. The second condition is '*constant proportional trade-off*', meaning that the life-years one would prefer to trade to accrue an increase in quality of life do not depend on the life years one has left. The last condition is '*risk neutrality*' with respect to life duration, which means that a certain life duration is equally preferred to a non-certain life duration, when the quality of life is fixed. If the quality of life varies over time, i.e. if the health state is not chronic, an additional condition should be fulfilled in the calculation of QALYs for them to represent individual utility. The condition of '*additive utility independence*' will allow the QALYs of a health profile that is composed of different health states to be calculated as a sum of the QALYs of each of these states, see Han Bleichrodt, "QALYs and HYEs: Under what Conditions are they Equivalent?," *Journal of Health Economics* 14 (1995), pp. 17–37. However, the condition of risk neutrality does not always hold as people are usually risk averse with respect to life years. Therefore, another formulation of QALY is required that is more descriptively valid, namely in line with individual preferences. John M. Miyamoto et al., "The Zero-Condition: A Simplifying Assumption in QALY Measurement and Multiattribute Utility," *Management Science* 44, no. 6 (1998), pp. 839–849 have identified two conditions under which QALYs can be calculated to be consistent with individual preferences when people are not risk neutral. The first is quite intuitive, referred to as the '*zero condition*' according to which all health conditions are equally preferred when the life duration is 0. The second is the '*standard gamble invariance*' meaning that if an individual is indifferent between living with a health condition for a certain duration or undergoing a treatment which may lead with probability p to a shorter life expectancy and with a probability of 1 – p to a longer life expectancy with the same condition, then this indifference holds with any other health condition as long as it is positive.

292   Graham Loomes and Lynda McKenzie, "The use of QALYs in Health Care Decision Making," *Social Science & Medicine* 28, no. 4 (1989), pp. 299–304.

293   See for instance Graham Loomes, "Evidence of a New Violation of the Independence Axiom," *Journal of Risk and Uncertainty* 4, no. 1 (1991), pp. 91–108 and R. Duncan Luce, "Where does Subjective Expected Utility Fail Descriptively?," *Journal of Risk and Uncertainty* 5, no. 1 (1992), pp. 5–27.

294   Daniel Kahneman and Amos Tversky, "Prospect Theory: An Analysis of Decision Under Risk," *Econometrica* 47, no. 2 (1979), pp. 263–292; Amos Tversky and Daniel Kahneman, "The Framing of Decisions and the Psychology of Choice," *Science* 211 (1981), pp. 453–458; Amos Tversky and Daniel Kahneman, "Advances in Prospect Theory: Cumulative Representation of Uncertainty," *Journal of Risk and Uncertainty* 5, no. 4 (1992), pp. 297–323.

295   See e.g. Han Bleichrodt, Jose Luis Pinto and Peter P. Wakker, "Making Descriptive use of Prospect Theory to Improve the Prescriptive use of Expected Utility," *Management Science* 47, no. 11 (2001), pp. 1498–1514; Jose Maria Abellan-Perpiñan, Han Bleichrodt and Jose Luis

criticism and the alternative theories that have been proposed to replace it, von Neumann-Morgenstern utility theory is still used in the economic appraisal of health care providing guidance regarding the behavior of individuals under uncertainty.[296]

Evidently, the choice of the welfarist approach as the theoretical foundation of CEA has methodological implications for the calculation of the QALY, since certain conditions must be fulfilled for QALY to reflect health related utility. Besides these implications however, the welfarist approach to CEA has some additional implications for the representation of individual preferences with respect to health and wealth in the cost/monetary value per QALY, which are addressed in section 4.6 below.

According to the extra-welfarist approach, CEA does not aim to improve social welfare merely as a function of individual utilities. Extra-welfarism allows for the maximization of additional outcomes apart from utility.[297] Culyer, who first submitted this view noted that 'extra-welfarism [...] transcends traditional welfare: it does not exclude individual welfares from the judgment about the social state, but it does supplement them with other aspects of individuals'.[298] In the context of evaluating health care programs and interventions, focusing on health is thus legitimate and more pragmatic than maximizing individual utility exclusively.[299] The focus on health may be explained by the view that health is a 'merit good', namely a good that is so valuable to consume that even if individuals do not perceive its value the state should finance its provision.[300] According to another explanation, health should be pursued because it is an important prerequisite that is fundamental for individuals to flourish. Under this view, drawing heavily upon Sen's capability approach,[301] health is viewed as a capability enabling individuals to develop and therefore it is valuable as such and not just because of the utility it yields.[302]

If the extra-welfarist approach is adopted as the foundation of QALY-based CEA, a broader conception of the QALY is possible, according to which the

---

Pinto-Prades, "The Predictive Validity of Prospect Theory Versus Expected Utility in Health Utility Measurement," *Journal of Health Economics* 28, no. 6 (2009), pp. 1039–1047.

[296] Drummond et al., *Methods for the Economic Evaluation of Health Care Programmes*, pp. 141–143.

[297] Werner B. F. Brouwer et al., "Welfarism Vs. Extra-Welfarism," *Journal of Health Economics* 27, no. 2 (2008), p. 330.

[298] Culyer, *The Normative Economics of Health Care Finance and Provision*, p. 36.

[299] Brouwer and Koopmanschap, *On the Economic Foundations of CEA. Ladies and Gentlemen, Take Your Positions!*, pp. 445–447.

[300] Culyer, *The Normative Economics of Health Care Finance and Provision*, p. 36. See also Sugden and Williams, *The Principles of Practical Cost-Benefit Analysis*, p. 179, explaining what merit goods are.

[301] Amartya Sen, "Equality of what?", *The Tanner Lecture on Human Rights* (Stanford University, 22 May 1979); Amartya Sen, *Commodities and Capabilities* (New Delhi: Oxford University Press, 1999).

[302] Brouwer et al., *Welfarism Vs. Extra-Welfarism*, p. 332.

QALY can measure health outcomes and potentially account for other considerations, rather than just express utilities. This implies that the calculation of QALYs under the extra-welfarist approach need not submit to the restrictive conditions stipulated by the welfarist approach.[303] Other implications of the choice of extra-welfarism as the basis of QALY-based CEA pertain to the cost side of CEA and will be elaborated below.[304]

Many scholars have defended the view that QALY-based CEA should be consistent with the welfarist approach.[305] They regard any approach that does not provide clear theoretical underpinnings for CEA as unsatisfactory and of little relevance for policy making.[306] Other important scholars in the field of health care and medical technology economic appraisal support the extra-welfarist approach as being more pragmatic.[307] Nevertheless, the differences between the two approaches are not so apparent and concrete, causing some scholars to question where the 'extra' is in extra-welfarism.[308] Others submit that CEA should not strictly adhere to one of the two approaches but rather leave policy makers to decide how CEA should be implemented and what it should aim to maximize depending on the context of the policy evaluated.[309]

4.2. WHAT IS THE QUALITY ADJUSTED LIFE YEAR?

Regardless of the theoretical underpinning chosen for CEA, the innovation of the QALY addressed the demand for a way of measuring in a common metric the benefit arising from interventions to both quality of life and life expectancy. It thus made possible in the context of CEA the comparison of interventions yielding different types of outcomes, and, most importantly, it combined in a single measure of effect, morbidity and mortality. Offering these significant advantages, compared to other methods of economic evaluation, the innovation of QALYs actually expanded the application of CEA as a method for the economic appraisal of health care.

---

[303] Brouwer and Koopmanschap, *On the Economic Foundations of CEA. Ladies and Gentlemen, Take Your Positions!*, p. 445.
[304] See *infra* section 4.6 and accompanying notes.
[305] Garber et al., *Theoretical Foundations of Cost-Effectiveness Analysis*, pp. 26 ff.; Adler, *QALY's and Policy Evaluation: A New Perspective*, pp. 6 ff., however he suggests adopting a welfarist approach that uses another criterion instead of the Kaldor-Hicks efficiency criterion.
[306] Johannesson, *Theory and Methods of Economic Evaluation of Health Care*, p. 174.
[307] Culyer, *The Normative Economics of Health Care Finance and Provision*, pp. 34–58; Brouwer and Koopmanschap, *On the Economic Foundations of CEA. Ladies and Gentlemen, Take Your Positions!*, pp. 439–459.
[308] Stephen Birch and Cam Donaldson, "Valuing the Benefits and Costs of Health Care Programmes: Where's the 'extra' in Extra-Welfarism?," *Social Science & Medicine* 56 (2003), pp. 1121–1133.
[309] Tsuchiya and Williams, *Welfare Economics and Economic Evaluation*, p. 43.

The QALY is a measure of health outcome, and more specifically it expresses the value of living one year with a certain health condition. Health outcome may encompass a variety of health-related effects generated by the intervention that do not pertain strictly to symptoms of disease but may for instance include improvement in self-care and social activities. Hence, the health condition evaluated, under the broad description used for health, is an indicator of the life quality the individual experiences during the particular year.[310] In other words, the QALY measures the value of life expectancy adjusted for quality.

To calculate QALYs, the different health conditions an individual experiences throughout her lifespan have to be first assessed. By health conditions, anything between perfect health and death can be implied; from a migraine and a fracture, to cancer or AIDS. The assessment results to an assignment of a different quality-weight to every health condition for the time it was experienced, varying from 0.00 to 1.00 with 0.00 representing death and 1.00 representing perfect health.[311] Conditions that are regarded as being worse than death can be assigned negative quality-weights. Quality-weights are alternatively also referred to in the literature as preference-weights, QALY-weights and health-related quality of life (HRQL), terms that will also be used hereafter interchangeably. After quality-weights for each condition have been established, QALYs are calculated by multiplying the value of the preference-weight with the time duration spent in that state.[312] Therefore, for an individual suffering under a chronic health condition that persists until the end of her life, QALYs would be calculated as:

$$QALYs = q(h) * T^{313}$$

The QALY-weight (q(h)) of the condition in combination with the remaining life expectancy (T) will yield the total QALYs experienced. If, for instance, living with an amputated leg above the knee were assigned a QALY-weight of 0.7, then having a remaining life expectancy of 30 years would yield 21 QALYs. Therefore, experiencing leg amputation for 30 years would be equivalent to 21 years of perfect health, as each QALY expresses one year in

[310] Brazier et al., *A Review of the Use of Health Status Measures in Economic Evaluation*, pp. 3–4; Folland, Goodman and Stano, *The Economics of Health and Health Care*, p. 81.
[311] Nord, *Methods for Quality Adjustment of Life Years*, p. 559; Garber et al., *Theoretical Foundations of Cost-Effectiveness Analysis*, p. 29; M. V. Bala et al., "Valuing Outcomes in Health Care: A Comparison of Willingness to Pay and Quality-Adjusted Life-Years," *Journal of Clinical Epidemiology* 51, no. 8 (1998), p. 667; Dolan, *The Measurement of Health-Related Quality of Life for use in Resource Allocation Decisions in Health Care*, p. 1726; Drummond et al., *Methods for the Economic Evaluation of Health Care Programmes*, pp. 174–177.
[312] Brazier et al., *A Review of the Use of Health Status Measures in Economic Evaluation*, pp. 3–4;.
[313] James K. Hammitt, "QALYs Versus WTP," *Risk Analysis* 22, no. 5 (2002), pp. 986–987.

full health. The calculation is also possible for more complicated cases, where the individual experiences many different health states throughout her lifetime. In these cases QALYs are calculated as the sum of the individual's quality-weighted health conditions (q(h)) for the duration (t) these conditions were experienced.[314] The lifetime of the individual is divided into time periods during which only one health condition is present. These time periods are indexed by i and the health condition related to that period is denoted as h_i hence:

$$QALYs = \Sigma_i\, q(h_i) * t_i^{[315]}$$

By applying QALYs, one can form an opinion on the relative value of different treatment possibilities. As an example, suppose that for a person with a certain ailment two equally expensive treatments exist. Treatment A increases the quality of life by 0.1 for five years, treatment B by 0.2 for three years. Calculating QALYs gained for both conditions results to treatment B being preferred, because it yields 0.6 QALY (0.2*3) while treatment A 'only' yields 0.5 QALY for the same amount of money.[316] Evidently, the most important advantage of QALY is that it can measure and compare the gains of various interventions both when they improve health-related quality of life as well as when they extent life duration. The graph below illustrates how a medical intervention that improves quality of life (A) and a medical intervention that extends life expectancy (B) can be compared on the basis of the benefit generated, expressed in QALYs, over the lifetime of a person adjusted for quality without medical intervention.[317]

To enable these comparisons, however, QALY-weights should be first established to allow the calculation of QALYs. The following section discusses the various existing methods to generate QALY-weights.

---

[314] Adler, *QALY's and Policy Evaluation: A New Perspective*, p. 2.

[315] Ibid., p. 2.

[316] This comparison does not yet show whether treatment A and/or B are worth their costs. For this, one has to evaluate how much a QALY is worth in money terms. See *infra* section 4.6. and accompanying notes.

[317] The first time that QALYs were depicted in this fashion was in Williams, *Economics of Coronary Artery Bypass Grafting*, pp. 326–329 who used a graphical illustration to show the quality and length of life gained for patients who are operated for coronary artery bypass grafting. See also the graphical illustrations in Marthe R. Gold et al., "Identifying and Valuing Outcomes," in *Cost-Effectiveness in Health and Medicine*, eds. Marthe R. Gold et al. (New York, Oxford: Oxford University Press, 1996), p. 92; Drummond et al., *Methods for the Economic Evaluation of Health Care Programmes*, p. 15.

Figure 1. Comparison of medical interventions A and B on the basis of the QALYs generated

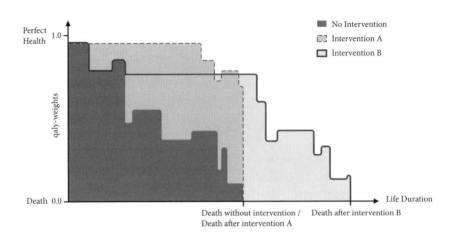

4.3. CALCULATION OF QALY-WEIGHTS

The initial calculation of QALYs for a particular health condition is conditional on the availability of quality-weights. The derivation of quality-weights is a demanding and complicated task, as numerous different techniques exist to elicit individuals' preferences regarding the quality of life associated with different health conditions. A useful distinction of the techniques separates them in single question format valuation techniques and the so-called 'generic measures' or 'multi-attribute health status classification systems' in which respondents have to answer a series of questions to indicate their valuation for a particular health condition.

4.3.1. SINGLE QUESTION FORMAT VALUATION TECHNIQUES

In single question format valuation techniques the respondents are asked to indicate their valuation for a particular health condition by answering a specific question. The question may involve indicating their preference for a particular health state or making a choice between different health state alternatives.

The *'standard gamble'* method[318] asks respondents to choose between living with an ailment on the one hand, and on the other hand undergoing a treatment

---

[318] Torrance, *Measurement of Health State Utilities for Economic Appraisal: A Review*, pp. 20–22; R. A. Carr-Hill, "Background Material for the Workshop on QALYs. Assumptions on the QALY Procedure," *Social Science and Medicine* 29, no. 3 (1989), p. 472; Nord, *Methods for*

which, with varying probabilities, leads either to perfect health or to death. The probabilities of experiencing perfect health or death after the treatment are complementary, with p the probability of perfect health and $1 - p$ the probability of death.[319] These probabilities are altered until the respondents are indifferent between living with the ailment and undergoing the treatment with the gamble of surviving in perfect health or dying immediately. The lowest probability of living in perfect health that the respondents still assess as high enough to undergo the treatment, determines the QALY-weight of the ailment. If for instance, one is indifferent between continuing to live with the ailment in question or undergoing a treatment which has 70% probability to restore her in perfect health and 30% probability of leading to death, then the QALY-weight of the ailment is 0.7. With a somewhat different formulation of the trade-off, the values for temporary health states, as well as for health states that are considered as being worse than death, can also be elicited.[320]

It has been argued by many scholars that the standard gamble (SG) is the 'gold standard' for the economic evaluation of health care because it has strong theoretical foundations in expected utility theory.[321] The process of eliciting QALY-weights with the SG method is based on the way people make decisions under conditions of uncertainty so as to maximize their expected utility generated by different outcomes, exactly as the theory predicts.[322] Remember that, according to the theory, if an intervention has both a positive and a negative outcome, the probability of each outcome is multiplied by its utility and the sum of these probability-weighted utilities yields the expected utility of the intervention. This calculation is performed for all the interventions being compared, so that in the end, individuals are able to rank interventions on the basis of the expected utility they generate. The SG can thus reflect the decisions

Quality Adjustment of Life Years, p. 569; Gold et al., *Identifying and Valuing Outcomes*, p. 113; Brazier et al., *A Review of the Use of Health Status Measures in Economic Evaluation*, pp. 25–26; Hammitt, *QALYs Versus WTP*, p. 994; Drummond et al., *Methods for the Economic Evaluation of Health Care Programmes*, pp. 149–151; Adler, *QALY's and Policy Evaluation: A New Perspective*, p. 2; Brazier et al., *Measuring and Valuing Health Benefits for Economic Evaluation*, pp. 87–90.

[319] At the point of indifference between living with the ailment and undergoing the treatment with the gamble, the QALY-weight of the ailment h_i is equal to $p*q(H)+(1-p)*q(D)$. Since the QALY-weight of perfect health is 1.0 and the QALY-weight of death is 0.0, the QALY-weight of the ailment will be equal to p. See Torrance, *Measurement of Health State Utilities for Economic Appraisal: A Review*, pp. 20–22.

[320] See ibid., pp. 21–22. However, the formulation of Torrance for the health states that are perceived as being worse than death may yield values ranging from $-\infty$ to $+1$ and therefore it has been proposed that negative values should be constrained to the negative of the best possible value, which is –1. See Brazier et al., *Measuring and Valuing Health Benefits for Economic Evaluation*, p. 88.

[321] Johannesson, *Theory and Methods of Economic Evaluation of Health Care*, pp. 176–179; Brazier et al., *Measuring and Valuing Health Benefits for Economic Evaluation*, p. 89.

[322] Drummond et al., *Methods for the Economic Evaluation of Health Care Programmes*, pp. 139–143; Adler, *QALY's and Policy Evaluation: A New Perspective*, p. 21.

of people regarding uncertain health outcomes, which is another advantage of the method as most health care decisions are also made under uncertainty and risk. However, the strong theoretical foundations of the SG in expected utility theory have caused some scholars to challenge its prevalence as the 'gold standard' on the grounds that expected utility theory is based on axioms that are violated in real life, since people do not follow the suggested model to make decisions.[323]

A shortcoming of the SG is that risk-averse individuals are likely to opt for the certainty of the ailment rather than the gamble of the treatment.[324] Therefore, they may be reluctant to accept any gamble but one that involves a high probability of perfect health resulting in turn to high QALY-weights for many health conditions. An additional concern for SG is that individuals may be unable to grasp the differences in the probabilities or in general misunderstand the task due to cognitive limitations.[325]

In the 'time trade-off' method,[326] respondents are asked to trade off x years in perfect health with t years in a certain health condition h_i which is less desirable. In other words, the respondent is required to indicate how much length of life she would sacrifice in order to gain life quality. The ratio x/t determines the QALY-weight of the health condition.[327] Hence, the more life years the respondent is willing to forego in order to achieve perfect health, the lower the QALY-weight for the health condition involved. So, if one assesses 30 years of life expectancy with the ailment as equal to 15 years in perfect health, then the QALY-weight of the health condition is 0.5. A somewhat different formulation of

---

[323]   Brazier et al., *Measuring and Valuing Health Benefits for Economic Evaluation*, pp. 100–101.

[324]   Nord, *Methods for Quality Adjustment of Life Years*, p. 561; Dolan, *The Measurement of Health-Related Quality of Life for use in Resource Allocation Decisions in Health Care*, p. 1736.

[325]   Johannesson, *Theory and Methods of Economic Evaluation of Health Care*, p. 179; Brazier et al., *A Review of the Use of Health Status Measures in Economic Evaluation*, p. 33. See also Mark Brisson and John Edmunds, *Valuing the Benefit of Varicella Vaccination: Comparison of Willingness to Pay and Quality-Adjusted Life Years* (City University Department of Economics, 2002), p. 20, suggesting that the level of education influences the responses in SG.

[326]   Torrance, *Measurement of Health State Utilities for Economic Appraisal: A Review*, pp. 22–24; Carr-Hill, *Background Material for the Workshop on QALYs. Assumptions on the QALY Procedure*, p. 472; Nord, *Methods for Quality Adjustment of Life Years*, p. 569; Karen Blumenschein and Magnus Johannesson, "Incorporating Quality of Life Changes into Economic Evaluations of Health Care: An Overview," *Health Policy* 36 (1996), p. 159; Gold et al., *Identifying and Valuing Outcomes*, p. 113; Brazier et al., *A Review of the Use of Health Status Measures in Economic Evaluation*, p. 26; Hammitt, *QALYs Versus WTP*, p. 994; Drummond et al., *Methods for the Economic Evaluation of Health Care Programmes*, pp. 151–153; Adler, *QALY's and Policy Evaluation: A New Perspective*, p. 2; Brazier et al., *Measuring and Valuing Health Benefits for Economic Evaluation*, pp. 91–93.

[327]   At the point of indifference between living with health condition h_i for t years and perfect health for x years we have $q(h_i)^*t=q(H)^*x$. Since the QALY-weight of perfect health is 1.0, the QALY-weight of h_i becomes x/t. See Torrance, *Measurement of Health State Utilities for Economic Appraisal: A Review*, pp. 22–24.

---

the trade-off can elicit values for temporary health states as well as for chronic health states that are perceived as being worse than death.[328]

The time trade-off method (TTO) is considered as being capable of eliciting the choices of respondents by asking them to decide between two alternatives, albeit without having clear theoretical foundations like the SG.[329] However, it is criticized on the grounds that the alternatives offered regard certain health outcomes, namely living with perfect health or living with an ailment, while actual health care choices involve risk and uncertainty.[330] The TTO is founded on the basic assumption of *'constant proportional trade-off'*, according to which the life years one would prefer to trade in order to accrue an increase in quality of life do not depend on the life years one has left.[331] This however may not hold, as individuals may be willing to trade-off life expectancy for increased life quality only when they have many years of life left, and be reluctant to do so if they have a short life expectancy.[332] Moreover, it may be the case that individuals have a certain goal of life expectancy that they want to reach, for instance because they want to become grandparents, before which they would not trade off any years for increased life-quality.[333] It has been demonstrated that for some severe health conditions there exists indeed a 'maximum endurable time' after which the utility of the health condition declines and individuals are expected to be willing to trade off many life years in order to gain quality of life.[334] A similar concept, which however focuses on quality of life instead of quantity, is referred to as 'threshold of tolerability' suggesting that only below a certain threshold of life quality would individuals consider trading off just a few days of life.[335] The time preference of individuals may also influence their responses in the TTO. Therefore, individuals

---

[328] See ibid., pp. 23–24. However, like in SG, the formulation of Torrance for the health states that are perceived as worse than death may lead to qaly-weights ranging from $-\infty$ to +1 and therefore it has been proposed that negative values should be constrained to the negative of the best possible value, which is –1. See Brazier et al., *Measuring and Valuing Health Benefits for Economic Evaluation*, pp. 91–92.

[329] Brazier et al., *A Review of the Use of Health Status Measures in Economic Evaluation*, p. 36.

[330] Brazier et al., *Measuring and Valuing Health Benefits for Economic Evaluation*, p. 101.

[331] See Pliskin, Shepard and Weinstein, *Utility Functions for Life Years and Health Status*, pp. 206–224 who have identified *'constant proportional trade-off'* as one of the three assumptions about preferences that must hold to derive QALYs for chronic health states.

[332] Stephen G. Pauker, "Coronary Artery Surgery: The use of Decision Analysis," *Annals of Internal Medicine* 85, no. 1 (1976), pp. 8–18; John M. Miyamoto and Stephen A. Eraker, "A Multiplicative Model of the Utility of Survival Duration and Health Quality," *Journal of Experimental Psychology.* 117, no. 1 (1988), p. 9.

[333] Miyamoto et al., *The Zero-Condition: A Simplifying Assumption in QALY Measurement and Multiattribute Utility*, p. 845.

[334] Heather J. Sutherland, Hilary Llewellyn-Thomas and James E. Till, "Attitudes Toward Quality of Survival – the Concept of "Maximal Endurable Time"," *Medical Decision Making* 2 (1982), pp. 299–309.

[335] Angela Robinson, Paul Dolan and Alan Williams, "Valuing Health Status using VAS and TTO: What Lies Behind the Numbers?," *Social Science & Medicine* 45, no. 8 (1997), pp. 1293, 1295–1296.

who have a positive time preference, meaning that they prefer to benefit from present gains and tend to value less any gains of the same magnitude realized in the future, will indicate low QALY-weights, as these individuals will be willing to trade life years at the end of their lives in return for a better life-quality in the present.[336] On the other hand people may prefer to experience a bad health state as soon as possible, in order to leave it behind them.[337]

The *'person trade-off'* method,[338] asks respondents to choose between two alternatives. The one involves helping by expanding the life or improving the life quality of x number of people in health condition A and the other helping y number of people in the worse health condition B. The number of people in both conditions is varied until respondents are indifferent between the two alternatives. At that point the ratio x/y yields the QALY-weight of health condition B. To give a numerical example, if respondents replied they are indifferent between improving quality of life for 20 people in health condition A and improving quality of life for 25 people in a more impaired health condition B, then the QALY-weight of health condition B is 0.8. Other alternatives in person trade-off (PTO) may include extending life duration in both health conditions or extending life in one health condition and improving quality of life in another.

The PTO is different from other valuation techniques because the choices made by the respondents do not involve their own health but rather concern the health treatment of others. It does not have a clear connection to theory, like SG has, but due to the ability to elicit the preferences of respondents regarding the health of other people it has been supported as being more appropriate to elicit QALY-weights for health care decisions in a societal context than other valuation techniques.[339] Nevertheless, the choices in the PTO are likely to be influenced by the opinion of respondents regarding whose health is more important to improve, whose life is more important to save/extend, and how the health benefits should be distributed to the people in need. Additionally, respondents may answer the question in accordance with what they believe the majority of people would opt for. In other words, PTO may reflect equity and distributional

---

[336] Nord, *Methods for Quality Adjustment of Life Years*, p. 561.

[337] Brazier et al., *A Review of the Use of Health Status Measures in Economic Evaluation*, p. 37.

[338] In early literature it was referred to as 'equivalence of numbers'. See Torrance, *Measurement of Health State Utilities for Economic Appraisal: A Review*, p. 25; Carr-Hill, *Background Material for the Workshop on QALYs. Assumptions on the QALY Procedure*, p. 472. However, the term 'person trade-off' was considered more appropriate as it differentiates this method from SG and TTO, which are also in essence equivalence methods. See Nord, *Methods for Quality Adjustment of Life Years*, pp. 568–569 where the term person trade-off is introduced. Also Brazier et al., *A Review of the Use of Health Status Measures in Economic Evaluation*, pp. 26–27; Hofstetter and Hammitt, *Human Health Metrics for Environmental Decision Support Tools: Lessons from Health Economics and Decision Analysis*, p. 17; Hammitt, *QALYs Versus WTP*, p. 995; Drummond et al., *Methods for the Economic Evaluation of Health Care Programmes*, pp. 153–154; Brazier et al., *Measuring and Valuing Health Benefits for Economic Evaluation*, pp. 93–94.

[339] Brazier et al., *Measuring and Valuing Health Benefits for Economic Evaluation*, pp. 103–104.

concerns of the respondents, influencing in an indeterminate way the QALY-weights for different health states.[340] Such concerns, it is suggested, will tend to yield QALY-weights that do not fluctuate noticeably between severe and less severe health conditions, as the respondents will try to disperse benefits to health in such a way that people enjoy comparable quality of life.[341] The formulation of PTO, asking respondents to decide for the health of other people, can also have the implication that respondents may refuse to answer the question.[342] The PTO has to date been used less frequently than other valuation techniques perhaps due to the fact that it is considered demanding for respondents to understand.[343]

The last technique in this category is referred to as the *'visual analogue scale'*, *'rating scale'* or *'category scale'*.[344] The terms are used interchangeably in the literature, although different terminology does indicate some real differences in practice.[345] In the visual analogue scale (VAS), respondents are asked to rank the ailment on a line with concrete endpoints. Between the endpoints the line is divided into equivalent intervals so that a distance between 20 and 25 on a 100-point scale equals the distance between 80 and 85.[346] The respondents have to rank different health conditions on the scale so that the spacing between the chosen points represents the difference in their preferences for the health conditions at hand.[347] There are many possible variations as the scale may range from 0 to 10 or from 0 to 100, be vertical or horizontal, etc. The endpoints of the scale will usually represent full health and death but it is also possible that to account for ailments that are perceived as being worse than death, the endpoints of the scale may be modified so that 0 represents the worst imaginable health condition and 100 represents the best imaginable health condition.[348] The ranking of the ailment on the scale yields its QALY-weight.

---

[340] Nord, *Methods for Quality Adjustment of Life Years*, p. 562; James K. Hammitt and Jin-Tan Liu, "Effects of Disease Type and Latency on the Value of Mortality Risk," *Journal of Risk and Uncertainty* 28, no. 1 (2004), p. 995.

[341] Nord, *Methods for Quality Adjustment of Life Years*, p. 562.

[342] Erik Nord, "The Person-Trade-Off Approach to Valuing Health Care Programs," *Medical Decision Making* 15, no. 3 (1995), pp. 201–208.

[343] Brazier et al., *A Review of the Use of Health Status Measures in Economic Evaluation*, p. 39; Brazier et al., *Measuring and Valuing Health Benefits for Economic Evaluation*, p. 103.

[344] Torrance, *Measurement of Health State Utilities for Economic Appraisal: A Review*, pp. 18–20; Nord, *Methods for Quality Adjustment of Life Years*, p. 568; Blumenschein and Johannesson, *Incorporating Quality of Life Changes into Economic Evaluations of Health Care: An Overview*, p. 159; Gold et al., *Identifying and Valuing Outcomes*, pp. 115–117; Brazier et al., *A Review of the Use of Health Status Measures in Economic Evaluation*, pp. 23–24; Hammitt, *QALYs Versus WTP*, pp. 994–995; Drummond et al., *Methods for the Economic Evaluation of Health Care Programmes*, pp. 147–149; Brazier et al., *Measuring and Valuing Health Benefits for Economic Evaluation*, pp. 84–87.

[345] David Parkin and Nancy Devlin, "Is there a Case for using Visual Analogue Scale Valuations in Cost-Utility Analysis?," *Health Economics* 15, no. 7 (2006), p. 655.

[346] Brazier et al., *A Review of the Use of Health Status Measures in Economic Evaluation*, p. 23.

[347] Drummond et al., *Methods for the Economic Evaluation of Health Care Programmes*, p. 147; Brazier et al., *Measuring and Valuing Health Benefits for Economic Evaluation*, pp. 83–86.

[348] The latter form of VAS is the one used by the EQ-5D questionnaire. See *infra* section 4.3.2.

For example, an ailment rated with 73 points on the scale has a QALY-weight of 0.73. The VAS can, with a certain formula, also elicit QALY-weights for temporary health states as well as for chronic states that are perceived as being worse than death.[349]

Respondents consider the technique of VAS as being easier to use and understand than other valuation techniques.[350] Nevertheless, VAS is criticized on the grounds that it lacks a theoretical foundation.[351] The fact that respondents just rank a health condition on a scale, without engaging in a trade-off between alternatives, creates the concern that the method is not based on choice and therefore cannot reflect individual preferences.[352] On the other hand, some commentators submit that the VAS does in fact involve trade-offs, which are more relevant to the valuation of health states with respect to each other than the trade-offs involved in the SG and the TTO, because by asking respondents to rank health states on a scale on the basis of their characteristics it actually compares health states to each other and not to perfect health like the TTO does or perfect health and death like the SG does.[353] Another opinion defends the VAS against the SG and the TTO on the grounds that unlike these techniques it does not suffer from problems relating to time preference and risk aversion.[354] Nevertheless, some scholars have suggested that to 'correct' the lack of theoretical underpinning, values generated from the VAS can be transformed into SG values or TTO values using specific power functions.[355] A possible shortcoming of the VAS is that it has been found to suffer from 'context effects', meaning that people are influenced by the seriousness of other health states presented and tend to rank a particular health state at hand lower on the scale when the rest of the health states are severe, and higher on the scale when the

[349] Torrance, *Measurement of Health State Utilities for Economic Appraisal: A Review*, p. 19; Brazier et al., *Measuring and Valuing Health Benefits for Economic Evaluation*, pp. 84–86.

[350] Blumenschein and Johannesson, *Incorporating Quality of Life Changes into Economic Evaluations of Health Care: An Overview*, p. 159; George W. Torrance, David Feeny and William Furlong, "Visual Analog Scales: Do they have a Role in the Measurement of Preferences for Health States?," *Medical Decision Making* 21, no. 4 (2001), p. 335.

[351] Magnus M. Johannesson, Bengt Jönsson and Göran Karlsson, "Outcome Measurement in Economic Evaluation," *Health Economics* 5, no. 4 (1996), p. 175. See also Han Bleichrodt and Magnus Johannesson, "An Experimental Test of a Theoretical Foundation for Rating-Scale Valuations," *Medical Decision Making* 17, no. 2 (1997), pp. 208–216 who conducted an experimental test but did not find theoretical justification for the use of rating scale.

[352] Johannesson, Jönsson and Karlsson, *Outcome Measurement in Economic Evaluation*, p. 175; Brazier et al., *A Review of the Use of Health Status Measures in Economic Evaluation*, pp. 34–35.

[353] Parkin and Devlin, *Is there a Case for using Visual Analogue Scale Valuations in Cost-Utility Analysis?*, p. 659.

[354] John Broome, "Qalys," *Journal of Public Economics* 50 (1993), pp. 149–167.

[355] Brazier et al., *Measuring and Valuing Health Benefits for Economic Evaluation*, pp. 97–99. However, Angela Robinson, Graham Loomes and Michael Jones-Lee, "Visual Analog Scales, Standard Gambles, and Relative Risk Aversion," *Medical Decision Making* 21, no. 1 (2001), pp. 17–27 find that there are no grounds for transforming VAS into SG utilities.

rest of the health states are mild.[356] Another problem that may occur is 'end scale aversion', namely a bias that makes people reluctant to rank health states close to the endpoints of the scale.[357] In addition to these potential problems the VAS may be vulnerable to 'response spreading', which implies that when respondents rank health conditions they may be inclined to use all the space on the scale and avoid placing health states close to each other, even if they perceive them as being alike.[358] A further concern for the VAS is that respondents may not be familiar with ranking health conditions on a scale, which could result in assigning QALY-weights to different health states that are inconsistent with their perceptions.

It follows from the foregoing description of the single question format valuation techniques that they are different in many aspects. What is worth emphasizing is that each method presents the respondents with a different cognitive task and a different question format. While the cognitive task pertaining to every technique has been explained above, the framing of the questions should also be highlighted here as it may potentially play an important role with respect to individuals' responses. Respondents may perceive the situation projected first in the question (full health, death or another ailment) as a reference point, which may influence their answers accordingly. This 'anchoring effect' could result for instance in the attachment of a high QALY-weight to a health condition if it is compared to death.[359]

A comparison of the valuation techniques shows that the SG, the TTO and the PTO are difficult and expensive to implement, as they are preferably applied through personal interviews rather than through self-administered questionnaires.[360] The VAS, on the contrary, is obviously easier to administer and more user friendly compared to the other methods that involve trade-offs in probabilities and risks.[361] It is furthermore cheaper and faster to implement as it can also be conducted via postal surveys.[362] The TTO and SG methods have been further criticized as only being appropriate to elicit QALY-weights for severe health states.[363] According to this view it is intuitive that one would be reluctant

356 Robinson, Loomes and Jones-Lee, *Visual Analog Scales, Standard Gambles, and Relative Risk Aversion*, p. 23; Torrance, Feeny and Furlong, *Visual Analog Scales: Do they have a Role in the Measurement of Preferences for Health States?*, p. 330.
357 Torrance, Feeny and Furlong, *Visual Analog Scales: Do they have a Role in the Measurement of Preferences for Health States?*, pp. 330–333.
358 Drummond et al., *Methods for the Economic Evaluation of Health Care Programmes*, p. 149; Parkin and Devlin, *Is there a Case for using Visual Analogue Scale Valuations in Cost-Utility Analysis?*, pp. 659–661.
359 Nord, *Methods for Quality Adjustment of Life Years*, pp. 562–563.
360 Brazier et al., *A Review of the Use of Health Status Measures in Economic Evaluation*, pp. 30, 36, 39 for SG, TTO and PTO respectively.
361 Brazier et al., *Measuring and Valuing Health Benefits for Economic Evaluation*, p. 95.
362 Parkin and Devlin, *Is there a Case for using Visual Analogue Scale Valuations in Cost-Utility Analysis?*, p. 662.
363 Carr-Hill, *Background Material for the Workshop on QALYs. Assumptions on the QALY Procedure*, p. 472.

to make a trade-off involving death or be willing to exchange future life years for a mild health condition such as an ankle strain or a broken finger. Moreover, some scholars submit that the choice scenarios the individuals are presented with in the SG and the TTO may be regarded as unlikely to materialize, thus influencing the elicitation of QALY-weights.[364]

Despite their relative merits and shortcomings that have been identified, even today there is no consensus as to which technique should be used to elicit QALY-weights. Given the differences in the valuation methods the critical issue emerges as to whether they reach the same QALY-weights for one health condition. According to empirical research, QALY-weights elicited with the SG actually tend to be higher than QALY-weights elicited with the TTO, which in turn are usually higher than those elicited with VAS.[365] The discrepancy observed is important to take into consideration and deal with, as different QALY-weights may lead to different health care decisions.[366] The last paragraph of section 4.3.2 below presents some of the ways that have been proposed to deal with the problem of discrepancy.

4.3.2. GENERIC MEASURES

The second category of techniques utilized to establish QALY-weights are frequently referred to as 'generic measures' because they value health states across their general attributes without emphasizing on a particular ailment.[367] Other terms used interchangeably are 'multi-attribute health status classification systems', 'multi-attribute utility scales' or 'quality of life measures', also indicating that these instruments focus on different dimensions of health rather than on a particular health state.[368] In generic measures respondents are asked to indicate how a particular health condition affects different dimensions of their health. These dimensions have been previously assigned QALY-weights with the

---

[364] Johannesson, *Theory and Methods of Economic Evaluation of Health Care*, pp. 178, 181; Blumenschein and Johannesson, *Incorporating Quality of Life Changes into Economic Evaluations of Health Care: An Overview*, p. 159.

[365] Bleichrodt and Johannesson, *An Experimental Test of a Theoretical Foundation for Rating-Scale Valuations*, p. 208. See Dolan, *The Measurement of Health-Related Quality of Life for use in Resource Allocation Decisions in Health Care*, p. 1736 who explains why risk aversion and time preference will cause SG values to be larger than TTO values.

[366] Han Bleichrodt and Magnus M. Johannesson, "Standard Gamble, Time Trade-Off and Rating Scale: Experimental Results on the Ranking Properties of QALYs," *Journal of Health Economics* 16 (1997), p. 156.

[367] Blumenschein and Johannesson, *Incorporating Quality of Life Changes into Economic Evaluations of Health Care: An Overview*, p. 158; Hammitt, *QALYs Versus WTP*, p. 995–996; Dolan, *The Measurement of Health-Related Quality of Life for use in Resource Allocation Decisions in Health Care*, pp. 1731–1732.

[368] Brazier et al., *A Review of the Use of Health Status Measures in Economic Evaluation*, p. 57; Drummond et al., *Methods for the Economic Evaluation of Health Care Programmes*, pp. 154–155.

use of the SG, the TTO or the VAS. The descriptions of respondents regarding the different dimensions are combined with their predetermined QALY-weights to yield the QALY-weight for the health condition at hand. Generic measures thus differ from the other valuation techniques in that the measurement of different health conditions actually took place at a time prior to their application. Generic measures consist of two parts.[369] The first part is the descriptive component of the measure, where respondents report their health condition on the basis of multilevel dimensions with the help of a questionnaire. The second part involves a table of values or an algorithm that combines the responses and yields a QALY-weight for the health condition reported.

Numerous generic measures exist but some of the most widely employed include the *EQ-5D*,[370] the *Health Utilities Index* (HUI) *mark one, two and three* (HUI1, HUI2, HUI3),[371] the *SF-6D*,[372] the *Quality of Well Being Scale* (QWB),[373] the *15D*[374] and the *Rosser disability/distress scale*.[375]

The *EQ-5D* instrument was developed by the *EuroQoL Group*, which came together in 1987 to devise a method for valuing health-related quality of life.[376] EQ-5D differentiates health states using five dimensions: mobility, self-care, usual activities, pain/discomfort and anxiety/depression. In the first part of the questionnaire, respondents are asked to mark their health condition on the basis of these five dimensions by indicating whether they have no problems, some problems or extreme problems in each dimension.[377] Each of these levels is assigned a weight previously elicited by the VAS or the TTO method. The most

---

[369]   Brazier et al., *Measuring and Valuing Health Benefits for Economic Evaluation*, p. 176.

[370]   EuroQol Group, "EuroQol: A New Facility for the Measurement of Health-Related Quality of Life," *Health Policy* 16, no. 3 (1990); James W. Shaw, Jeffrey A. Johnson and Stephen Joel Coons, "US Valuation of the EQ-5D Health States: Development and Testing of the D1 Valuation Model," *Medical Care* 43, no. 3 (2005), pp. 203–220.

[371]   John Horsman et al., "The Health Utilities Index (HUI*): Concepts, Measurement Properties and Application," *Health and Quality of Life Outcomes* 1 (2003).

[372]   John Brazier et al., "Deriving a Preference-Based Single Index from the UK SF-36 Health Survey," *Journal of Clinical Epidemiology* 51, no. 11 (1998), pp. 1115–1128; John Brazier, Jennifer Roberts and Mark Deverill, "The Estimation of a Preference-Based Measure of Health from the SF-36," *Journal of Health Economics* 21, no. 2 (2002), pp. 271–292.

[373]   Robert M. Kaplan and John P. Anderson, "A General Health Policy Model: Update and Applications," *Health Services Research* 23, no. 2 (1988), pp. 203–235.

[374]   Harri Sintonen, "An Approach to Measuring and Valuing Health States," *Social Science & Medicine* 15, no. 2 (1981), pp. 55–65; Harri Sintonen and Markku Pekurinen, "A Fifteen Dimensional Measure of Health-Related Quality of Life (15D) and its Applications," in *Quality of Life Assessment: Key Issues in the 1990s*, eds. Stuart R. Walker and Rachel M. Rosser (Dordrecht, the Netherlands: Kluwer Academic Publishers, 1993), pp. 185–195.

[375]   Rachel M. Rosser and Vincent C. Watts, "The Measurement of Hospital Output," *International Journal of Epidemiology* 1, no. 4 (1972), pp. 361–368; Rachel R. Rosser and Paul Kind, "A Scale of Valuations of States of Illness: Is there a Social Consensus?," *International Journal of Epidemiology* 7, no. 4 (1978), pp. 347–358.

[376]   See the official site of the EuroQoL Group and of the EQ-5D instrument www.euroqol.org/ (accessed 31.03.2014).

[377]   Mandy Oemar and Mark Oppe, *EQ-5D-3L User Guide: Basic Information on how to use the EQ-5D-3L Instrument*, EuroQol Group (2013), pp. 3–8.

---

widely used set of QALY-weights has been elicited in a UK general population survey.[378] However, there are also sets of QALY-weights elicited from other countries' population such as Belgium, Denmark, Germany, the Netherlands, Spain, USA, etc.[379] In the second part, respondents are asked to rank their health condition on a visual analogue scale thus communicating their overall perception of the ailment. All possible combinations of dimensions and their levels yield 243 different health states to which death and unconsciousness are added. The total QALY-weight for the health state described by the respondent is calculated from the overall evaluation of the respondent of all health dimensions by adding up the relevant QALY-weights and subtracting them from 1.00, i.e. perfect health.[380]

EQ-5D was renamed as EQ-5D-3L to differentiate from a newer version of the instrument that was launched in 2009, which comprises five rather than three levels in each health dimension. In the new version, referred to as EQ-5D-5L,[381] the respondents are asked to mark their health condition by indicating whether they have no problems, slight problems, moderate problems, severe problems or extreme problems. The additional two levels (slight problems and severe problems) increase the number of health states that can be realized to a total of 3,125. So far, there are no sets of QALY-weights corresponding to these levels but studies are being conducted in several countries to generate them in the near future.[382] However, the EQ-5D-5L can still be used by translating the QALY-weights from the EQ-5D-3L into QALY-weights appropriate for use in the EQ-5D-5L with the technique of 'cross-walking' that estimates conversion rates between instruments.[383]

The EQ-5D is a practical instrument, easy to use and open to self-completion. It has been widely used in the economic appraisal of health care and its three-level version has been translated into more than 170 languages to make its utilization possible in local populations.[384] In 2008, the National Institute for Health and Clinical Excellence (NICE), which provides guidance for health care decision-making in UK,[385] indicated that the EQ-5D was the preferred instrument to generate QALY-weights from adults.[386] Nevertheless, the concern that has

---

[378] Brazier et al., *Measuring and Valuing Health Benefits for Economic Evaluation*, p. 200.

[379] Oemar and Oppe, *EQ-5D-3L User Guide: Basic Information on how to use the EQ-5D-3L Instrument*, p. 10.

[380] Hammitt, *QALYs Versus WTP*, p. 996.

[381] Mandy Oemar and Bas Janssen, *EQ-5D-5L User Guide: Basic Information on how to use the EQ-5D-5L Instrument*, EuroQol Group (2013).

[382] Ibid., p. 12.

[383] Ibid.

[384] Oemar and Oppe, *EQ-5D-3L User Guide: Basic Information on how to use the EQ-5D-3L Instrument*, p. 16.

[385] Recently NICE established NICE International to offer health care guiding advice to other countries.

[386] National Institute for Health and Clinical Excellence, *Guide to the Methods of Technology Appraisal* (London, UK: National Institute for Health and Clinical Excellence, [2013]), p. 38.

been expressed with regard to the EQ-5D-3L is that the three levels in each dimension may not be sensitive enough to capture certain aspects of a health condition. More specifically, it is suggested that the instrument suffers from 'ceiling effects', namely it is insensitive to the valuation of mild health states.[387] Indeed some insensitivity of EQ-5D to some health conditions has been detected; however, it is not clear whether it is due to the small number of levels.[388] The five level version of the instrument was partly devised to address this problem and it remains to be seen whether it succeeds to do so.[389]

The *Health Utilities Index* is an instrument that was developed in McMaster University to assist in the measurement of health related quality of life.[390] Its first version was the HUI1, which is rarely used today, as it has been replaced by two more recent versions of the instrument, the HUI2 and HUI3. The HUI3[391] uses eight dimensions to classify health states: vision, hearing, speech, ambulation, dexterity, emotion, cognition and pain. Each dimension comprises five or six different levels (speech, emotion and pain have five levels) indicative of a gradual deterioration in that dimension. The dimension of pain for instance includes the following levels: free of pain and discomfort, mild to moderate pain that prevents no activities, moderate pain that prevents a few activities, moderate to severe pain that prevents some activities and severe pain that prevents most activities. The levels of each dimension are assigned a weight previously elicited by the SG and the VAS methods. The set of QALY-weights corresponding to these levels have been elicited from a general population sample in Ontario, Canada.[392] In the first part of the instrument, respondents indicate with the help of a questionnaire how much a certain condition affects the various health dimensions by choosing the corresponding level. The second part consists of a multiplicative function that combines the QALY-weights corresponding to the reported levels and yields the overall QALY-weight for the health condition at hand. Combining all dimensions and levels, 972,000 health states can be realized in total.

The HUI2, in comparison to the HUI3, is a descriptively inferior version of the instrument, consisting of seven dimensions with three to five levels each and can measure 24,000 health states in total.[393] It was developed prior to HUI3 to

---

[387]   Brazier et al., *Measuring and Valuing Health Benefits for Economic Evaluation*, p. 221.

[388]   Ibid., p. 221.

[389]   Rabin et al., *EQ-5D-5L User Guide: Basic Information on how to use the EQ-5D-5L Instrument*, p. 5.

[390]   Horsman et al., "The Health Utilities Index (HUI®): Concepts, Measurement Properties and Application," *Health and Quality of Life Outcomes* 1 (2003). See also the official site of the Health Utilities Index instruments www.healthutilities.com/.

[391]   David Feeny et al., "Multiattribute and Single-Attribute Utility Functions for the Health Utilities Index Mark 3 System," *Medical Care* 40, no. 2 (2002), pp. 113–128.

[392]   Ibid., p. 121.

[393]   George W. Torrance et al., "Multiattribute Utility Function for a Comprehensive Health Status Classification System: Health Utilities Index Mark 2," *Medical Care* 34, no. 7 (1996), p. 711.

measure children's health suffering from cancer. Therefore, although it is not recommended as a standalone measure of health, it is considered complementary to HUI3, especially when children's health evaluation is involved.[394]

The HUI is an easy instrument, susceptible both to self- and interview completion.[395] It has been translated into many languages including Chinese, Dutch, French, German, Greek, Italian and Spanish, with more translations being prepared.[396] However, a concern that is frequently expressed with respect to the instrument involves the origin of the QALY-weights assigned to the different levels of each dimension. Since the QALY-weights used in the HUI have been elicited from the Canadian population, it is doubted whether the instrument can also be applied in other countries.[397] The concern has been alleviated by a study that has reproduced the QALY-weight measurement in local populations and found they are consistent with the original QALY-weights from the Canadian population;[398] however, more research may be required in that direction.

The *SF-6D* is an instrument that has been developed in the University of Sheffield for the evaluation of health related quality of life.[399] It is derived from a preexisting measure, the SF-36, which has been extensively used to describe health status. Developing the SF-6D from the SF-36 aimed at devising a shorter instrument that can take advantage of the existing studies' results and can moreover represent individual preferences.[400] The SF-6D comprises two parts. The first part consists of a table with six dimensions: physical functioning, role limitations, social functioning, pain, mental health and vitality.[401] The dimensions of role limitations and vitality comprise four levels, the dimensions of mental health and social functioning comprise five levels, while the dimensions of physical functioning and pain comprise six levels. Respondents indicate the level they (would) experience in each dimension. For instance in the dimension of vitality they indicate whether they have a lot of energy all of the

---

[394]   Horsman et al., *The Health Utilities Index (HUI*): Concepts, Measurement Properties and Application*, p. 2; Brazier et al., *Measuring and Valuing Health Benefits for Economic Evaluation*, p. 227.

[395]   Horsman et al., *The Health Utilities Index (HUI*): Concepts, Measurement Properties and Application*, p. 3.

[396]   Ibid., p. 9.

[397]   Drummond et al., *Methods for the Economic Evaluation of Health Care Programmes*, p. 172.

[398]   Catherine Le Galès et al., "Development of a Preference-Weighted Health Status Classification System in France: The Health Utilities Index 3," *Health Care Management Science* 5, no. 1 (2002), p. 49 replicated the HUI3 QALY-weights in a general population survey in France.

[399]   Brazier et al., *Deriving a Preference-Based Single Index from the UK SF-36 Health Survey*, pp. 1115–1128; Brazier, Roberts and Deverill, *The Estimation of a Preference-Based Measure of Health from the SF-36*, pp. 271–292.

[400]   The SF-36 can describe millions of health states and has been very widely used. However, its scoring system does not represent individual preferences. Brazier et al., *Deriving a Preference-Based Single Index from the UK SF-36 Health Survey*, p. 1116; Brazier, Roberts and Deverill, *The Estimation of a Preference-Based Measure of Health from the SF-36*, p. 272.

[401]   Drummond et al., *Methods for the Economic Evaluation of Health Care Programmes*, p. 164; Brazier et al., *Measuring and Valuing Health Benefits for Economic Evaluation*, pp. 203–204.

time, most of the time, some of the time or none of the time in the perceived health condition. In total, 18,000 health states can be realized and evaluated. The second part of the instrument involves a scoring table, which indicates a QALY-weight for each level of every dimension. The set of QALY-weights corresponding to each level has been elicited from a UK population sample using the method of SG.[402] Adding up the QALY-weights for all levels and subtracting them from 1.00 (perfect health), yields the QALY-weight for the health condition at hand.[403]

The SF-6D is an easy instrument to administer as it can be self-completed by respondents.[404] It furthermore has the advantage of being able to identify and evaluate a significant number of health states (18,000). A shortcoming that has been observed, however, with respect to certain dimensions of the instrument is the so-called 'floor effect'.[405] Responses in the dimensions of physical functioning, social functioning and role limitations tend to concentrate in the lower levels indicating that perhaps more low levels should be added to these dimensions to capture the severity of certain health states.[406]

It is not possible to compare the instruments and reach definite conclusions regarding which is best to use. One reason is that the instruments do not perfectly coincide in the health dimensions they include, so that, depending on the health condition at hand, one or the other may be more appropriate to use. The HUI3 for instance is considered more appropriate to evaluate vision-related health conditions, as it specifically includes the dimension of sight, whereas the EQ-5D and the SF-6D do not include it.[407] Another reason is that each of these instruments uses QALY-weights elicited with different basic valuation techniques, namely the EQ-5D uses sets of QALY-weights elicited by the TTO and the VAS, the HUI uses QALY-weights elicited by the SG and the VAS, whereas the SF-6D uses QALY-weights elicited by the SG. Therefore, the use of the HUI, the EQ-5D or the SF-6D can be advocated depending on which basic valuation technique one considers superior. Apart from the concerns raised in the analysis above, the rest of the criticism with respect to the generic measures

---

[402] Brazier, Roberts and Deverill, *The Estimation of a Preference-Based Measure of Health from the SF-36*, p. 276. More specifically a selection of 249 health states have been valued and the QALY-weights for the rest have been extrapolated from these values. See also Benjamin M. Craig et al., "US Valuation of the SF-6D," *Medical Decision Making* 33, no. 6 (2013), pp. 793–803 for the first SF-6D valuation study in the United States.

[403] Drummond et al., *Methods for the Economic Evaluation of Health Care Programmes*, p. 165.

[404] Although the completion rates for the SF-6D were found to be worse that those of the EQ-5D. See Brazier et al., *Measuring and Valuing Health Benefits for Economic Evaluation*, p. 228.

[405] Ibid., p. 221.

[406] John J. Brazier et al., "A Comparison of the EQ-5D and SF-6D Across Seven Patient Groups," *Health Economics* 13, no. 9 (2004), pp. 873–884.

[407] Alan Wailoo, Sarah Davis and Jonathan Tosh, *The Incorporation of Health Benefits in Cost-Utility Analysis using the EQ-5D*, Report Decision Support Unit (National Institute for Health and Clinical Excellence, 2010), p. 90, available at: www.nicedsu.org.uk/EQ5D(2474845).htm (accessed 31.03.2014) reporting that in a review of cases studies, HUI3 was found to be more sensitive to changes in vision than the EQ-5D.

pertains to a large extent to shortcomings of their composite valuation techniques (the SG, the TTO and the VAS), which have also been addressed in the previous paragraphs. On the other hand, a major common advantage of the instruments is that all three can be easily administered. The questionnaires are simple and susceptible to self-completion, thus reducing the costs of their utilization. Notwithstanding the difficulties mentioned above to evaluate the instruments in comparison to each other, one review of five of the instruments, namely of the QWB, the 15D, the Rosser disability/distress scale, the HUI and the EQ-5D has concluded that the EQ-5D and the HUI present particular advantages so as to be considered the best instruments for QALY-weight elicitation.[408] Given these results, the effort is made to use mostly QALY-weights generated with the EQ-5D and the HUI in the following chapters to illustrate how the QALY can be utilized for the assessment of pain and suffering damages.

An important concern that reemerges in the context of generic measures is whether different instruments can elicit the same QALY-weights for a health condition. A potential divergence in the QALY-weights would imply that QALY calculations are affected accordingly, thus influencing health care decision-making. In light of this concern a series of studies compared the QALY-weights generated by different instruments for the same health condition and found that there is some variation, yet the results are ambiguous with respect to the significance of that variation. Some studies indicate that the QALY-weights differ to a large extent, whereas others have moderate or even insignificant variations.[409]

The discrepancy of QALY-weights is a problem arising not only for generic measures but also for the SG, TTO and VAS valuation techniques. While variation is to a certain extent justified by the fact that valuation techniques involve different cognitive tasks, large discrepancies are problematic; they do not provide clear guidance to health care decision-making and they create doubt as to whether they are actually capable of eliciting individual preferences regarding health conditions. Nevertheless, despite potential occurrence of discrepancy between the QALY-weights elicited with different valuation techniques, it should be emphasized that when the same method is used to elicit QALY-weights regarding a health condition from different people, then results are consistent.[410] In addition, each of the methods analyzed above yields the same or similar QALY-weights, when measurement is repeated over time to evaluate the same

---

[408]   Brazier et al., *A Review of the Use of Health Status Measures in Economic Evaluation*, p. 76.

[409]   Brazier et al., *A Comparison of the EQ-5D and SF-6D Across Seven Patient Groups*, p. 879 find that the mean QALY-weights generated with the SF-6D exceeds the QALY-weights generated with the EQ-5D by 0.045. Hind T. Hatoum, John E. Brazier and Kasem S. Akhras, "Comparison of the HUI3 with the SF-36 Preference Based SF-6D in a Clinical Trial Setting," *Value in Health* 7, no. 5 (2004), pp. 602–609 find that the difference in the mean QALY-weights generated by the SF-6D and the HUI3 was 0.04. For more studies see Brazier et al., *Measuring and Valuing Health Benefits for Economic Evaluation*, p. 219.

[410]   See Brazier et al., *A Review of the Use of Health Status Measures in Economic Evaluation*, pp. 31, 34, 36, 67, 72 for SG, VAS, TTO, HUI and EQ-5D respectively.

health condition.[411] In other words, the use of one method only produces consistent results with respect to eliciting QALY-weights. It has been proposed that to alleviate the problem of potential variation in QALY-weights, only one method should be used for all economic evaluations.[412] A different solution involves using the technique of 'cross-walking' to translate QALY-weights from one method to another.[413]

A great deal of attention has been devoted to the potential and the limitations of all methods. The interest can be justified by the belief that more refined methods will yield more consistent QALY-weights to individuals' perceptions and consequently provide better guidance to health care decision-making. Additional research is still needed and refinement of methods is necessary to acquire more uniform QALY-weights for different health conditions.

4.4. WHO SHOULD VALUE HEALTH?

Another important issue that sparks the debate surrounding QALYs is which group of people is best suited to answer the relevant questions for the elicitation of quality-weights.

The general public is viewed by many scholars as the most appropriate target group for the elicitation of QALY-weights. The US Panel on cost-effectiveness in health and medicine recommends the use of QALY-weights elicited from members of the general public for societal health care decision-making.[414] To justify this recommendation the panel uses the notion of a 'veil of ignorance', according to which members of the general public who may not experience adverse health conditions and do not know what their own future health condition will be can objectively evaluate different health states and contribute to the choice and prioritization of health care programs without self-interest.[415] An additional reason for favoring the use of QALY-weights elicited from the general population is the fact that many health care programs are likely to be financed by the public budget. Therefore, the general population's QALY-weights, and more specifically those of the taxpayer, should be used to decide which health care program will be implemented.[416] Using general population values is

---

[411] Ibid.

[412] Brazier et al., *Measuring and Valuing Health Benefits for Economic Evaluation*, p. 237.

[413] Erik Nord, Norman Daniels and Mark Kamlet, "QALYs: Some Challenges," *Value in Health* 12, no. s1 (2009), p. S10.

[414] Gold et al., *Identifying and Valuing Outcomes*, p. 106.

[415] Louise B. Russell et al., "Cost-Effectiveness Analysis as a Guide to Resource Allocation in Health: Roles and Limitations," in *Cost-Effectiveness in Health and Medicine*, eds. Marthe R. Gold et al. (Oxford, New York: Oxford University Press, 1996), pp. 6–7; Garber et al., *Theoretical Foundations of Cost-Effectiveness Analysis*, p. 35; Gold et al., *Identifying and Valuing Outcomes*, p. 100.

[416] Brazier et al., *Measuring and Valuing Health Benefits for Economic Evaluation*, p. 115.

unsurprisingly also the position of scholars who support a welfarist approach for QALY-based CEA.[417] However, opponents of general population values argue that the elicitation of QALY-weights from the general public inevitably requires the respondents to imagine living with health conditions they have never experienced, a demanding task that respondents may not be able to cope with.

People currently experiencing a health condition may indeed be more able to evaluate it and describe its consequences. Moreover, it is also reasonable that people targeted by a proposed health care program, namely those suffering from the health condition at hand, should perform its valuation.[418] The idea of eliciting QALY-weights from patients received a lot of support after a recent publication by Dolan and Kahneman, suggesting that health care decisions should rather be based on experiences of actual patients and not on general population values.[419] The main argument underlying their proposal is that patients' valuations are better able to represent the effects of health conditions because members of the general public tend to focus on becoming impaired and cannot anticipate potential adaptation.[420] Therefore, they tend to overestimate the severity of adverse health conditions. However, it may be unethical to ask patients to evaluate their health condition especially if the valuation technique used to elicit QALY-weights involves thinking about one's own death.[421] This type of evaluation may be very upsetting for the elderly and for respondents who are seriously ill. Another disadvantage of patient-elicited QALY-weights is that the seriously ill may not be able to answer the questions due to cognitive deficiencies caused by their health condition.[422] Moreover, it is conceivable that patients may answer the relevant questions in a strategic fashion so as to ensure that the health care program related to their health condition will be implemented.[423] However, there is no empirical evidence indicating that patients provide such strategic answers.[424] Furthermore, given that to determine

---

[417]   Remember that under a welfare economics approach the aim of CEA is to improve social welfare, which is considered to be a function of individual preferences. Therefore, individual preferences need to be elicited regarding health states. Moreover, the monetary value of a QALY depends either on the available budget (financed by taxpayers) or on the WTP for a QALY increase (see *infra* section 4.6 and accompanying notes).

[418]   Johannesson, Jönsson and Karlsson, *Outcome Measurement in Economic Evaluation*, p. 283.

[419]   Paul Dolan and Daniel Kahneman, "Interpretations of Utility and their Implications for the Valuation of Health," *The Economic Journal* 118, no. 525 (2008), pp. 215–234. See also Paul Dolan, "Developing Methods that really do Value the 'Q' in the QALY," *Health Economics, Policy and Law* 3, no. 1 (2008), pp. 69–77.

[420]   Dolan and Kahneman, *Interpretations of Utility and their Implications for the Valuation of Health*, pp. 223–226. See also Matthew Adler and Eric A. Posner, "Happiness Research and Cost-Benefit Analysis," *The Journal of Legal Studies* 37, no. 2 (2008), p. S253; Cass R. Sunstein, "Illusory Losses," *The Journal of Legal Studies* 37 (2008), pp. S157–S194. See *infra* chapter 6 for a more thorough discussion on patient values and potential adaptation.

[421]   Brazier et al., *Measuring and Valuing Health Benefits for Economic Evaluation*, p. 234.

[422]   Ibid., p. 234.

[423]   Brazier et al., *Measuring and Valuing Health Benefits for Economic Evaluation*, p. 115.

[424]   Johannesson, Jönsson and Karlsson, *Outcome Measurement in Economic Evaluation*, p. 283.

the effect of a medical intervention the QALY-weights are elicited from patients in different phases of a health condition, it would in any case be unclear in which direction potential strategic behavior could influence the results.

Doctors, health care professionals and other people working in the field of health care are also proposed as reliable sources for QALY-weights as they can assess health conditions from a scientific perspective, namely they can provide a total evaluation for a health condition, being aware of its long-term effects.[425] Nevertheless, the constant occupation of health professionals with adverse health conditions may make them insensitive to the negative consequences of various health states. Furthermore, health professionals may be more prone to providing strategic answers regarding health states if they have self-interest in the promotion of a particular health care program.[426]

Evidently, the choice of a target group for the elicitation of QALY-weights is not straightforward. In view of the arguments presented above, some scholars submit that patient values are the most appropriate to use in clinical decision contexts whereas general population values should be preferred for planning health care on a societal level.[427] So far, however, no agreement has been reached on the issue.

4.5. QALYs AND FAIRNESS CONSIDERATIONS

Besides the ability to evaluate health outcomes both in terms of quality and quantity, the use of QALYs has also been praised because of its allegedly egalitarian nature, as one QALY is considered to be worth the same for everyone, regardless of whose quality of life it improves.[428] Nevertheless, this assertion has been heavily contested.

One important counterargument holds that health care decisions based on QALYs will tend to discriminate against the old.[429] As the calculation of QALYs depends partly on life expectancy, it is indeed plausible that younger people will benefit more from a given treatment than older people will, because they have more life years left. According to this line of reasoning, it is likely that between two different treatments, priority is given to the one benefiting younger people,

---

[425] Gold et al., *Identifying and Valuing Outcomes*, p. 104.

[426] Johannesson, Jönsson and Karlsson, *Outcome Measurement in Economic Evaluation*, p. 283.

[427] Carr-Hill, *Background Material for the Workshop on QALYs. Assumptions on the QALY Procedure*, p. 473.

[428] Torrance, *Measurement of Health State Utilities for Economic Appraisal: A Review*, p. 17; Alan Williams, Roger W. Evans and Michael F. Drummont, "Quality-Adjusted Life-Years," *The Lancet* 329, no. 8546 (1987), p. 1372; Ichiro Kawachi, "QALYs and Justice," *Health Policy* 13 (1989), p. 118; Adam Wagstaff, "QALYs and the Equity-Efficiency Trade-Off," *Journal of Health Economics* 10 (1991), p. 27.

[429] John Harris, "Qalyfying the Value of Life," *Journal of Medical Ethics* 13, no. 3 (1987), p. 118; Alwyn Smith, "Qualms about QALYs," *The Lancet* 329, no. 8542 (1987), p. 1135.

as it consequently produces more QALYs. Scholars adhering to the view consider this 'ageist' effect of QALYs unacceptable and instead argue that every life should be valued equally irrespective of how much it is left and/or of what quality,[430] and that there is a moral obligation on society to care for the elderly.[431] Challenging this opinion, it is submitted that although life of young individuals can be considerably extended, life of older individuals can also be substantially improved in terms of quality meaning that resulting gains in QALYs may balance.[432] A much stronger argument against ageism, the so-called 'fair innings' argument, further supports the fairness of QALYs, maintaining that there is a certain threshold of lifetime in good quality that every person is entitled to.[433] Taking this fact into consideration, promoting fairness would actually entail that priority is given to young people who have not reached that threshold level yet (egalitarian ageism). Exactly this can be achieved by using QALYs in health care decision-making. According to a different view, prioritizing younger people in health care is more efficient as they are expected to be more productive than older people (utilitarian ageism).[434] Other scholars submit that the QALY is in fact not ageist enough, and it should actually discriminate more in favor of young people to address equality concerns.[435]

Another major criticism against the QALY concerns the second component it is dependent upon, namely the expected future health state. Using QALYs for health care allocation decisions would imply that between two potential candidates for a medical intervention, priority is to be given to the one whose health condition can be restored to a better state.[436] In a plausible scenario, QALYs would opt for a treatment that improves the health of moderately impaired individuals instead of a treatment which would grant its beneficiaries the opportunity to stay alive in poor health.[437] QALY-based decisions could therefore generate a sort of 'double jeopardy' for seriously ill people who have already been

---

[430] Harris, *Qalyfying the Value of Life*, p. 119; John Harris, "Unprincipled Qalys – a Response to Cubbon," *Journal of Medical Ethics* 17, no. 4 (1991), pp. 185 ff.

[431] Alan Williams and Richard Cookson, "Equity in Health," *Handbook of Health Economics* 1 (2000), p. 1876.

[432] Kawachi, *QALYs and Justice*, p. 117.

[433] Alan Williams, "Intergenerational Equity: An Exploration of the 'Fair Innings' Argument," *Health Economics* 6, no. 2 (1997), pp. 117–132. The term 'fair innings' however was originally coined by Harris. See John Harris, *The Value of Life. an Introduction to Medical Ethics*, 5th ed. (London, New York: Routledge, 1985), pp. 91–94.

[434] David L. B. Schwappach, "Resource Allocation, Social Values and the QALY: A Review of the Debate and Empirical Evidence," *Health Expectations* 5, no. 3 (2002), p. 212; Paul Dolan et al., "QALY Maximisation and People's Preferences: A Methodological Review of the Literature," *Health Economics* 14, no. 2 (2005), p. 205; Brazier et al., *Measuring and Valuing Health Benefits for Economic Evaluation*, p. 292.

[435] Klemens Kappel and Peter Sandøe, "Qalys, Age and Fairness," *Bioethics* 6, no. 4 (1992), pp. 313–316.

[436] Hammitt, *QALYs Versus WTP*, p. 991.

[437] Sunstein, *Lives, Life-Years and Willingness to Pay*, pp. 245–246.

unfortunate in life, as they would preclude them from receiving treatment and improving their health condition.[438]

Both critical views originate from the fact that one QALY counts the same for a young and an old person, and for a seriously and a mildly ill person. Therefore, what is considered an acclaimed advantage of QALYs with allegedly positive implications for fairness is in fact opposed as being inequitable. The essence of the counterarguments is that an additional QALY may actually be of greater value to an individual with few QALYs, such as a person who is old and/or in a very impaired state of health, than to an individual with more QALYs.[439] To decide which theoretical assertion is more consistent with the views of people, it is necessary to refer to empirical evidence. Indeed, empirical evidence seems to confirm that under certain conditions individuals do not assign the same value to all QALYs. More specifically two eloquent reviews of existing studies submit that, overall, people tend to give priority to the young.[440] Moreover, they frequently favor those who suffer severe health problems and those who face an imminent threat to life.[441] Another reoccurring result in the studies is that people with children should be given priority in health care in comparison to those with no dependents.[442] Less frequent and somewhat controversial is the tendency to discriminate against people with self-inflicted illnesses. This view would for instance entail that people whose daily routine does not involve cigarettes or alcohol would preferably be treated over smokers and frequent drinkers of alcohol in the case of lung cancer or cirrhosis of the liver. However, this preference is not very strongly supported by empirical findings.[443]

---

[438]   Harris, *Qalyfying the Value of Life*, pp. 119–120.

[439]   M. Johannesson, "On Aggregating QALYs: A Comment on Dolan," *Journal of Health Economics* 18 (1999), pp. 381–382. See also Broome, *Qalys*, pp. 149–167.

[440]   Schwappach, *Resource Allocation, Social Values and the QALY: A Review of the Debate and Empirical Evidence*, p. 212; Dolan et al., *QALY Maximisation and People's Preferences: A Methodological Review of the Literature*, pp. 201–202. See for instance Magnus Johannesson and Per-Olov Johansson, "Is the Valuation of a QALY Gained Independent of Age? some Empirical Evidence," *Journal of Health Economics* 16, no. 5 (1997), p. 595 who find that respondents consider saving one 30-year-old as equivalent to saving forty-one 70-year-olds.

[441]   Schwappach, *Resource Allocation, Social Values and the QALY: A Review of the Debate and Empirical Evidence*, p. 214; Dolan et al., *QALY Maximisation and People's Preferences: A Methodological Review of the Literature*, p. 199. See for instance Richard Cookson and Paul Dolan, "Public Views on Health Care Rationing: A Group Discussion Study," *Health Policy* 49, nos. 1–2 (9, 1999), p. 68 who find that respondents in a survey chose to allocate health using 'immediate need' as one of the guiding principles.

[442]   Schwappach, *Resource Allocation, Social Values and the QALY: A Review of the Debate and Empirical Evidence*, p. 213; Dolan et al., *QALY Maximisation and People's Preferences: A Methodological Review of the Literature*, pp. 202–203.

[443]   Williams and Cookson, *Equity in Health*, p. 1905; Schwappach, *Resource Allocation, Social Values and the QALY: A Review of the Debate and Empirical Evidence*, p. 213; Dolan et al., *QALY Maximisation and People's Preferences: A Methodological Review of the Literature*, p. 203.

Yet another argument challenges the egalitarian nature of the QALY on somewhat different grounds. The argument maintains that QALYs are actually dependent upon wealth and income; therefore using QALYs in health care decision-making will discriminate against the poor. Affluent individuals may indeed be better able to preserve a high level of QALYs, for instance because they eat healthy foods and exercise, and they can also lessen the negative consequences accompanying a health condition through income-related means, such as affording better nursing, consulting specialist doctors, etc.[444] Thus, the argument continues, it is cheaper to improve the health of rich people, as they already have a higher level of QALYs, than the health of the poor. Another opinion submits that health valuation may be affected by changes in income and vice versa, in other words income may also be affected by changes in health.[445] This may be the case for people whose income capacity significantly depends on their health, such as factory workers, professional athletes, etc. It is unclear how valuation techniques deal with the complicated relationship between health and income.[446] Empirical evidence on how QALYs are affected by income is limited. A study conducted with data from Sweden suggests that along different age groups people with higher income have more remaining QALYs than people with lower income.[447] Nevertheless, the authors remark that this relationship should not be interpreted in terms of cause and effect, as other factors may be influencing the results.[448] Again, it is important to look at whether people assign a greater value to the QALYs of the rich or the poor because that would justify their prioritization in health care. However, existing studies present mixed evidence on the matter.[449]

The discussion regarding how equitable QALY utilization is in the context of health care, and most importantly the criticism that has been expressed against using QALYs, gave rise to a series of proposals for calculating them, which claim to be able to alleviate the aforementioned concerns and incorporate peoples' preferences. One of these proposals is to attach equity weights to QALYs.[450]

---

[444] Hammitt, *QALYs Versus WTP*, p. 991; Brazier et al., *Measuring and Valuing Health Benefits for Economic Evaluation*, pp. 288–289.

[445] Hammitt, *QALYs Versus WTP*, p. 992.

[446] See Mark J. Sculpher and Bernie J. O'Brien, "Income Effects of Reduced Health and Health Effects of Reduced Income: Implications for Health State Valuation," *Medical Decision Making* 20, no. 2 (2000), pp. 207–215 who discuss this problem with respect to multi-attribute health status classification techniques.

[447] Ulf-G. Gerdtham and Magnus Johannesson, "Income-Related Inequality in Life-Years and Quality-Adjusted Life-Years," *Journal of Health Economics* 19, no. 6 (2000), pp. 1007–1026.

[448] Income may for instance be correlated with education, unemployment etc. See ibid., pp. 1024–1025.

[449] See Dolan et al., *QALY Maximisation and People's Preferences: A Methodological Review of the Literature*, p. 203 for a review of the studies on the relationship of socioeconomic status and health valuation.

[450] Brazier et al., *Measuring and Valuing Health Benefits for Economic Evaluation*, pp. 291–297; Nord, Daniels and Kamlet, *QALYs: Some Challenges*, pp. S13–S14.

Doing so will allow certain cases and groups of people to be given more gravity in health care decision-making and therefore enhance utilization of QALYs in health care according to peoples' preferences. Another way that has been advocated to address equity concerns in QALY utilization is to use the method of PTO to elicit QALY-weights.[451] Remember that in the PTO method respondents choose to improve health and/or extend life between groups of people who are in different conditions. Therefore it is argued that the PTO method can already incorporate into the values elicited the relative weight people attach to different cases and thus also include their preferences for equity.[452] A proposal that concentrates on the income-related equity problem is to use population average values to calculate QALYs. General population values would allegedly incorporate preferences of people with different socioeconomic status, hence reducing the effect of wealth in the calculation of QALYs. The foregoing exposition of existing proposals is far from being exhaustive. Other, more technical, methods have also been proposed to alleviate equity-related concerns and incorporate peoples' preferences with respect to QALY utilization in health care decision-making.[453] Efforts are constantly made to improve them and therefore refine the use of QALYs on the basis of peoples' preferences.

4.6. MONETIZATION: COST OR WTP PER QALY?

So far, the exposition of the QALY should have made clear in what context the QALY has been conceived and used as a measure of health outcome, how is it calculated and what are its most important characteristics, merits and disadvantages. A very short description of the QALY summarizing the most important points could state that *the QALY is a non-monetized measure of health outcome, competent to reflect the impact on health and longevity generated by different health care interventions.* However, to complete the discussion, it is necessary to further explain how a monetary value is derived for a QALY in the context of CEA to facilitate the evaluation of different health programs, treatments, and interventions. A choice between different treatments based only on their relative QALYs is not possible; the amount of money required to implement a treatment is relevant, to the extent that decisions regarding alternative treatments are subject to budget constraints. Therefore, the intervention that yields the most QALYs will not be unquestionably adopted unless it is the best choice among other alternatives regarding both QALYs

---

451 Williams and Cookson, *Equity in Health*, p. 1903; Michael Drummond et al., "Toward a Consensus on the QALY," *Value in Health* 12, no. s1 (2009), p. S32.
452 Williams and Cookson, *Equity in Health*, p. 1903. See also Erik Nord, *Cost-Value Analysis in Health Care* (New York: Cambridge University Press, 1999), pp. 123–129 who proposes the use of PTO elicited health state values in a type of analysis he terms 'cost-value analysis' to resolve, among others, fairness issues across patients.
453 See Nord, Daniels and Kamlet, *QALYs: Some Challenges*, pp. S13–S14 for an overview.

generated and costs incurred. In view of the limited resources available, the monetary value of a QALY is important for the health care decision-maker, who consequently allocates resources on the basis of the information on costs and health outcomes.

The information regarding the QALYs generated from an intervention and the costs incurred for its implementation is combined in a ratio of costs over QALYs, which is used as the measure of cost-effectiveness of the intervention.[454] The ratios of all competing interventions are then ordered from low to high. Evidently, low costs and high benefits are preferred to high costs and low benefits, implying that the lower the ratio, the more cost-effective the intervention. In cases where a budget has been stipulated to finance health care, interventions with low ratios will be implemented first as being more cost-effective, moving up to interventions with higher ratios. The intervention that will lead to the exhaustion of the financial resources, as the final one to be implemented under the budget constraint, will yield *a shadow price per QALY*.[455] Alternatively, if no specified budget for health care exists, a cutoff price can be assigned to the gain of one QALY so that only interventions with equal or lower ratio than the cutoff price will be implemented.[456]

In cases where a decision needs to be made regarding alternative interventions for the same type of health problem, such as for instance between different types of surgery (e.g. laser surgery, canaloplasty, implants) to treat glaucoma, a somewhat different procedure is followed. After the ordering of interventions on the basis of their effectiveness, namely on the QALYs gained, the incremental cost-effectiveness ratio is calculated for every successive intervention. If an incremental cost-effectiveness ratio shows that the intervention at hand is less effective (and/or more expensive) than consecutive interventions, then it is excluded from implementation.[457] Again, with a pre-specified budget, the most cost-effective interventions are implemented first and the cost per QALY gain of the last intervention to be funded yields a potential monetary value for a QALY. Otherwise, if no budget has been stipulated, a chosen price per QALY will provide the cutoff value so that interventions with an incremental cost-effectiveness ratio above that price will not be implemented.[458]

---

[454] Weinstein and Stason, *Foundations of Cost-Effectiveness Analysis for Health and Medical Practices*, p. 717.

[455] Magnus Johannesson and Milton C. Weinstein, "On the Decision Rules of Cost-Effectiveness Analysis," *Journal of Health Economics* 12, no. 4 (1993), p. 460.

[456] Ibid., p. 460.

[457] Alan M. Garber, "Advances in Cost-Effectiveness Analysis of Health Interventions," in *Handbook of Health Economics*, eds. Anthony J. Culyer and J. P. Newhouse, 1st ed., Vol. 1 (Elsevier, 2000), pp. 193–196. See also Brazier et al., *Measuring and Valuing Health Benefits for Economic Evaluation*, pp. 276–277.

[458] Johannesson and Weinstein, *On the Decision Rules of Cost-Effectiveness Analysis*, pp. 460–461; Magnus M. Johannesson, "The Relationship between Cost-Effectiveness Analysis and Cost-Benefit Analysis," *Social Science and Medicine* 41, no. 4 (1995), pp. 483–484.

Apparently, two basic approaches exist to attach a monetary value to the QALY and consequently perform a CEA of the competing programs. The first involves adopting as the monetary value of a QALY the cost per QALY gained of the last intervention that is implemented within a fixed budget. The second involves explicitly stipulating a price based on willingness to pay (WTP) for a QALY gain. It has been argued that deriving a monetary value for a unit of effect, namely per QALY gained, makes CEA similar to CBA because then CEA implicitly assigns a monetary value to health gains and arrives at a decision by essentially comparing costs and benefits.[459] At this point, the debate regarding the choice between a welfare economics and a decision-maker approach for CEA becomes relevant again.

Scholars adhering to the welfarist position maintain that the stipulated budget approach to derive a cost per QALY and consequently perform CEA is on the one hand unrealistic and on the other hand theoretically unsustainable.[460] Unrealistic because it is usually not the case that a single fixed budget is identified for health care.[461] Theoretically unsustainable because if the goal is to put society's resources to their most efficient use, all societal costs should be included in the analysis and not just the health care-related ones, as is implied by the use of a fixed budget for health care.[462] Therefore, the argument continues, assigning an acceptable price per QALY that incorporates all costs, and not only health-related ones, is the most appropriate way to perform a CEA. Evidently, an assignment of WTP per QALY involves not only an effort to monetize the QALY but also an attempt to provide a link between CEA and CBA, which would solve the problem of the weak theoretical foundation of CEA in welfare economics. Scholars who support the welfare economics basis for CEA have contributed numerous papers in this direction, stipulating the necessary conditions under which cost-effectiveness ratios would reach the same results as the Kaldor-Hicks

---

[459]   Charles E. Phelps and Alvin I. Mushlin, "On the (Near) Equivalence of Cost-Effectiveness and Cost-Benefit Analyses," *International Journal of Technology Assessment in Health Care* 7, no. 1 (1991), pp. 12, 18–19 submit that CEA and CBA actually require the same type of assumptions. However, CBA explicitly states a monetary value for a life while CEA implicitly attaches a monetary value for life with perfect health; CBA makes decisions on the basis of net benefits while CEA does this on the basis of the acceptability of the prices and CBA comes up with a certain recommendation while CEA leaves the decision unstated. See also Johannesson and Weinstein, *On the Decision Rules of Cost-Effectiveness Analysis*, p. 462.

[460]   Johannesson and Weinstein, *On the Decision Rules of Cost-Effectiveness Analysis*, p. 466; Johannesson, *The Relationship between Cost-Effectiveness Analysis and Cost-Benefit Analysis*, pp. 483–485. See also Magnus M. Johannesson and David Meltzer, "Some Reflections on Cost-Effectiveness Analysis," *Health Economics* 7, no. 1 (1998), pp. 1–7.

[461]   Johannesson and Weinstein, *On the Decision Rules of Cost-Effectiveness Analysis*, p. 466; Johannesson, *The Relationship between Cost-Effectiveness Analysis and Cost-Benefit Analysis*, p. 484; M. Johannesson and R. M. O'Conor, "Cost-Utility Analysis from a Societal Perspective," *Health Policy* 39 (1997), pp. 243–244.

[462]   Johannesson, *The Relationship between Cost-Effectiveness Analysis and Cost-Benefit Analysis*, pp. 483–485; Johannesson and O'Conor, *Cost-Utility Analysis from a Societal Perspective*, p. 243; Johannesson and Meltzer, *Some Reflections on Cost-Effectiveness Analysis*, pp. 1–7.

criterion.[463] A basic point is that WTP per QALY should be constant and of the same amount for everyone.[464] Pratt and Zeckhauser provide an important argument supporting this position by showing that if individuals have the same level of wealth, and health care programs are publicly financed, the use of a single WTP is justified.[465] However, it is difficult to strike a compromise between using a uniform WTP per QALY and the welfare economics tradition, as the WTP depends on peoples' preferences and can be expected to differ depending on personal characteristics. One of these characteristics, as indicated above, is the individual wealth level which affects marginal utility of wealth. It has thus been argued that if all necessary assumptions hold for QALYs to represent utility,[466] then differences in WTP per QALY are due to the different marginal utility of wealth of the individuals.[467] This submission, however, provides yet another argument for using a single WTP per QALY because, allowing the use of diverging WTP values would discriminate against the poor, who have high marginal utility of wealth and are therefore reluctant to spend.[468] On the other hand, other scholars stipulating the conditions under which CEA would reach the optimal cutoff value that is consistent with consumers' preferences for the implementation of health programs, emphasize that a uniform cutoff value would not be appropriate to assist health care decisions regarding people of different age, gender, income level and risk aversion.[469] It is apparent that eliciting a WTP per QALY that is consistent with the welfare economics tradition

---

[463]   Garber et al., *Theoretical Foundations of Cost-Effectiveness Analysis*, p. 34; Brazier et al., *Measuring and Valuing Health Benefits for Economic Evaluation*, p. 44; Johannesson and O'Conor, *Cost-Utility Analysis from a Societal Perspective*, pp. 247, 251 for instance stipulate that if summed QALYs are a measure of societal utility and the financing sources are the same for all health care programs, a fixed price per QALY can allow CEA to maximize societal utility; Han Bleichrodt and John Quiggin, "Life-Cycle Preferences Over Consumption and Health: When is Cost-Effectiveness Analysis Equivalent to Cost-Benefit Analysis?," *Journal of Health Economics* 18 (1999), pp. 681–708 show that it is feasible to derive a WTP for a QALY that depends on wealth, life-expectancy, health condition and consumption, when some rather restrictive conditions hold to make 'QALY maximization consistent with life-cycle preferences'; Thomas Klose, "A Utility-Theoretic Model for QALYs and Willingness to Pay," *Health Economics* 12 (2003), pp. 17–31 suggests that WTP per QALY is influenced by the severity of the health condition and the amount of the QALYs gained when health affects the marginal utility of wealth; finally B. O. Hansen et al., "On the Possibility of a Bridge between CBA and CEA: Comments on a Paper by Dolan and Edlin," *Journal of Health Economics* 23, no. 5 (2004), pp. 887–898 submit that a relationship between CBA and CEA exists if the problem of aggregating health effects is solved.

[464]   See Johannesson, *The Relationship between Cost-Effectiveness Analysis and Cost-Benefit Analysis*, p. 485.

[465]   John W. Pratt and Richard J. Zeckhauser, "Willingness to Pay and the Distribution of Risk and Wealth," *The Journal of Political Economy* 104, no. 4 (1996), pp. 758–759.

[466]   See *supra* text at section 4.1.1 and accompanying notes.

[467]   Johannesson and O'Conor, *Cost-Utility Analysis from a Societal Perspective*, pp. 245–248.

[468]   Ibid., pp. 245–248.

[469]   Alan M. Garber and Charles E. Phelps, "Economic Foundations of Cost-Effectiveness Analysis," *Journal of Health Economics* 16, no. 1 (1997), pp. 1–31.

and establishes a link between CBA and CEA requires a set of restrictive conditions to hold which are rather unrealistic and difficult to satisfy.[470] If these conditions do not hold then CEA aims at maximizing other outcomes such as health, apart from utility, and is distinct from CBA.[471]

On the other hand, the scholars who regard CEA just as a tool to assist decision-making, namely they adhere to the decision-maker approach for CEA, face no restrictions in terms of conditions that should be satisfied to monetize the QALY. For them, both eliciting a monetary value from cost-effectiveness ratios and accepting at the outset a cutoff value (WTP) per QALY are admissible ways to assign a price per QALY provided that they can both lead to health optimization under certain financial constraints.

4.6.1. COST PER QALY

Cost-effectiveness analyses conducted over the last 30 years have ended up with different acceptable cost-effectiveness ratios as shown by a recent overview of the relevant literature.[472] Interventions have been considered cost-effective at approximately €37,300 per QALY, while the amount of about €186,600 per QALY has been regarded as the upper limit below which an additional QALY is worth its costs.[473] The cost of kidney dialysis is frequently cited as an admissible

---

[470] Hammitt, *QALYs Versus WTP*, p. 998; Dorte Gyrd-Hansen, "Willingness to Pay for a QALY. Theoretical and Methodological Issues," *PharmacoEconomics* 23, no. 5 (2005), p. 427. See also Paul Dolan and Richard Edlin, "Is it really Possible to Built a Bridge between Cost-Benefit Analysis and Cost-Effectiveness Analysis?," *Journal of Health Economics* 21, no. 5 (2002), pp. 827–843 who establish an 'impossibility theorem' to show that it is not possible to connect CBA with CEA.

[471] Alistair McGuire, "Theoretical Concepts in the Economic Evaluation of Health Care," in *Economic Evaluation in Health Care: Merging Theory with Practice*, eds. Michael Drummond and Alistair McGuire (Oxford, New York: Oxford University Press, 2001), pp. 1–14.

[472] Don Kenkel, "WTP- and QALY-Based Approaches to Valuing Health for Policy: Common Ground and Disputed Territory," *Environmental & Resource Economics* 34 (2006), p. 421.

[473] Robert M. Kaplan and James W. Bush, "Health-Related Quality of Life Measurement for Evaluation Research and Policy Analysis," *Health Psychology* 1, no. 1 (1982), p. 74. The authors actually use the term 'Well-Year' instead of QALY to emphasize the health related aspect of the outcome generated by health care interventions. In essence however, the QALY and the Well-Year have the same meaning since the later is also described as one life-year adjusted for quality. See ibid., pp. 63–64. See also Andreas Laupacis et al., "How Attractive does a New Technology have to be to Warrant Adoption and Utilization? Tentative Guidelines for using Clinical and Economic Evaluations," *Canadian Medical Association Journal* 146, no. 4 (1992), pp. 473–481 for Canadian estimates of cost per QALY. The amounts in this and the next section have been calculated first by expressing the amounts from the original American publications in dollars from 2013 (see www.bls.gov/data/inflation_calculator.htm) and subsequently in euro on the basis of the 2013 Purchasing Power Parity (PPP) of the Euro-area as published by the OECD: 0.773 (see http://stats.oecd.org/Index. aspx?DataSetCode=PPPGDP). Acknowledging the differences between the PPP of the Member States, the PPP for the euro-area is applied henceforth to avoid having to list separate amounts for all Member States.

cost per QALY based on the consideration that kidney dialysis is a treatment which is (more than) worth its costs, posing a limit of about €83,000 to €106,600 for one QALY.[474] The National Institute for Clinical Excellence in the UK uses a lower limit of £20,000 to £30,000 (about €23,500 to €35,300), which many commentators regard as too low, while opponents of this view support that the threshold is too high and advocate a reduction.[475] This is the cost effectiveness ratio of the treatments whose implementation is considered acceptable, which consequently yields a price per QALY. According to the latest NICE guidelines, interventions that exceed the cost-effectiveness ratio of £20,000 to £30,000 per QALY require particular justification to be accepted for implementation.[476] An extensive database of cost-effectiveness ratios providing information on the acceptable cost per QALY for various health care programs can be found in the CEA registry, which periodically publishes recently conducted CEAs.[477]

---

[474]   Richard A. Hirth et al., "Willingness to Pay for a Quality-Adjusted Life Year: In Search of a Standard," *Medical Decision Making* 20, no. 3 (2000), p. 333. The kidney dialysis value that has been extensively cited is actually $50,000 per QALY. See e.g. Christopher Evans, Manouche Tavakoli and Bruce Crawford, "Use of Quality Adjusted Life Years and Life Years Gained as Benchmarks in Economic Evaluations: A Critical Appraisal," *Health Care Management Science* 7, no. 1 (2004), p. 44; Ashenfelter, *Measuring the Value of a Statistical Life: Problems and Prospects*, p. C14. However since this figure has remained static for years, Hirth et al. provide an upper and lower estimate of the dialysis value that is more up to date.

[475]   NICE, *Guide to the Methods of Technology Appraisal,* pp. 66–67. NICE has been using the same range of £20,000–30,000 as the acceptable cost per QALY for many years. See Evans, Tavakoli and Crawford, *Use of Quality Adjusted Life Years and Life Years Gained as Benchmarks in Economic Evaluations: A Critical Appraisal,* p. 46; Nancy Devlin and David Parkin, "Does NICE have a Cost Effectiveness Threshold and what Other Factors Influence its Decisions? A Discrete Choice Analysis," *Health Economics* 13, no. 5 (2004), pp. 437, 449 show that in practice the upper threshold limit is higher, at approximately £40,000; Marc Pomp, Werner Brouwer and Frans Rutten, *QALY-Tijd Nieuwe Medische Technologie, Kosteneffectiviteit En Richtlijnen (QALY-Ty. New Medical Technology, Cost-Effectiveness and Guidelines)* (Den Haag: Centraal Planbureau, [2007]). On the other hand Karl Claxton et al., "Methods for the Estimation of the NICE Cost Effectiveness Threshold. Revised Report Following Referees Comments," Centre for Health Economics, University of York (2013), pp. 98–99, support that the current threshold range is too high and should be lowered. See also Andrian Towse and James Raftery, "Should NICE's threshold range for cost per QALY be raised? Yes. No," *British Medical Journal* 338 (2009): 268–269 arguing in favor and against an increase in the threshold values per QALY. The amounts of £20,000–30,000 are converted to euro by using the annual average exchange rate of 2013 published by European Central Bank. See European Central Bank, "Annual Average Exchange Rate UK Pound Sterling to Euro," European Central Bank, http://sdw.ecb.europa.eu/quickview.do;jsessionid=3B7684CC6E9FC6A5CC6643B99E2E596C?node=2018794&SERIES_KEY=120.EXR.A.GBP.EUR.SP00.A (accessed 10.03.2014). UK pound sterling/euro= 0.84926.

[476]   National Institute for Health and Clinical Excellence, *Guide to the Methods of Technology Appraisal,* p. 67.

[477]   Center for the Evaluation of Value and Risk in Health, "Cost-Effectiveness Analysis Registry," Institute for Clinical Research and Health Policy Studies, Tufts Medical Center, www.cearegistry.org (accessed 31.03.2014).

4.6.2. WTP PER QALY

Two approaches have been followed so far to derive a WTP for a QALY. The first involves obtaining peoples' WTP for a QALY gain. Some of the first attempts to do so arrived at a monetary value for a QALY by eliciting the WTP for the overall QALY gain generated by a treatment.[478] However, WTP may be affected by the size of the health gain as it is possible that people will be willing to pay more money for the first QALYs gained and less money as their health improves.[479] In addition, spending money to improve one's health condition will increase one's marginal utility of wealth, as money will become more valuable. Therefore, to avoid the size of the health gain influencing the elicitation of the monetary value of a QALY, it has been proposed that it would be better for the WTP to be based on marginal changes in QALYs.[480] From the WTP elicited for marginal changes in QALYs it is possible to arrive at the WTP for a QALY gain; for instance, an individual who would be willing to pay €5,000 for a treatment that improves her health by 0.05 QALYs would have a WTP per QALY of €100,000. This method, among others, has been applied in a European project under the name 'European Value of a Quality Adjusted Life Year' which aimed at determining a monetary value for a QALY for ten countries over the period 2007–2010.[481] According to the results of the project, the overall mean WTP per QALY over all ten countries is at most approximately €68,000.[482] Another study from 2010 elicited the WTP per QALY for the Netherlands arriving at a maximum of about €26,000.[483]

---

[478]   Niklas Zethraeus, "Willingness to Pay for Hormone Replacement Therapy," *Health Economics* 7, no. 1 (1998), pp. 34–35 estimated the WTP per QALY gained for hormone replacement therapy in Sweden; Karen Blumenschein and Magnus Johannesson, "Relationship between Quality of Life Instruments, Health State Utilities, and Willingness to Pay in Patients with Asthma," *Annals of Allergy, Asthma & Immunology* 80, no. 2 (1998), pp. 189–194 estimated the WTP per QALY for asthma cure in Kentucky, USA.

[479]   Johannesson, *The Relationship between Cost-Effectiveness Analysis and Cost-Benefit Analysis*, pp. 486–487.

[480]   Johannesson and Meltzer, *Some Reflections on Cost-Effectiveness Analysis*, pp. 4–5.

[481]   See Angela Robinson et al., "Estimating a WTP-based value of a QALY: The 'chained' approach," *Social Science & Medicine* 92 (2013), pp. 92–104. *European Value of a Quality Adjusted Life Year Final Publishable Report* (2010), pp. 35 ff. explains how two alternative approaches were used (the 'chained approach' and the 'direct approach') to elicit a WTP per QALY for marginal QALY gains.

[482]   This amount resulted by using the 'direct approach' and an expected gain of 0.05 QALYs. Additionally, the top 1% of the data was trimmed to avoid including very high responses in the calculations (the initial overall mean amount before trimming was about €145,000). The 'chained approach' resulted in overall trimmed means ranging between about €15,100 and €63,900. See ibid, pp. 72, 91–92.

[483]   Ana Bobinac et al., "Willingness to Pay for a Quality-Adjusted Life-Year: The Individual Perspective," *Value in Health* 13, no. 8 (2010), p. 1052. The amount arrived at in the study is €24,500. This amount is expressed in euro from 2013 on the basis of the annual average inflation rates published by Eurostat. See Eurostat, "Annual Average Inflation Rates 2000–2012," Eurostat, http://epp.eurostat.ec.europa.eu/statistics_explained/index.php/Consumer_prices_-_inflation_and_comparative_price_levels (accessed 31.03.2014).

However, the authors submit that using more marginal gains in QALYs would have probably resulted in higher WTP values and therefore they note that the value elicited should be regarded as a lower limit for WTP per QALY.[484] In a more recent study from 2012 involving Dutch respondents, the WTP per QALY estimated, ranged from about €82,000 to €113,000.[485]

The second way that has been used to estimate a WTP per QALY involves taking advantage of the existing literature on the VSL.[486] The existing WTP values readily found in the VSL literature can be used to derive a value per QALY if certain assumptions are made.[487] In an overview from 2000 where QALY values are elicited on the basis of VSL research, an amount of about €298,000 per QALY is mentioned as the median value of different estimates.[488] The same overview reports that 28 out of the 35 estimates exceed about €112,000 per QALY while 30 out of 35 estimates exceed €56,000 per QALY.[489] Another study assesses the monetary value of a QALY on the basis of a regression-based meta-analysis of 68 VSL studies, arriving at a value of about €182,000.[490] This value is derived by dividing the VSL by the current number of life years left, excluding the costs of lost productivity and applying a discount factor to express it in current values.[491] Another study estimated the WTP per QALY on the basis of VSL values at approximately between €210,000 and €497,000.[492] In the USA, various amounts per QALY have been used by different agencies in the context of health decisions.

---

[484] Ibid., p. 1053.

[485] Ana Bobinac, *Economic Evaluations of Health Technologies: Insights into the measurement and valuation of benefits*, Dissertation Erasmus University Rotterdam (The Netherlands, 2012), pp. 104–129. The original amounts arrived at in the study (before adjusting for 2013 inflation) range between €80,000–110,000.

[486] Kenkel, *WTP- and QALY-Based Approaches to Valuing Health for Policy: Common Ground and Disputed Territory*, pp. 419–437 proposed an 'intellectual trade' between the two approaches in another direction, namely that of QALY-fying the VSL.

[487] Johannesson, Jönsson and Karlsson, *Outcome Measurement in Economic Evaluation*, p. 289; Hirth et al., *Willingness to Pay for a Quality-Adjusted Life Year: In Search of a Standard*, p. 335; Kenkel, *WTP- and QALY-Based Approaches to Valuing Health for Policy: Common Ground and Disputed Territory*, p. 427; *European Value of a Quality Adjusted Life Year Final Publishable Report*, p. 5.

[488] Hirth et al., *Willingness to Pay for a Quality-Adjusted Life Year: In Search of a Standard*, pp. 338–339.

[489] Ibid., p. 340.

[490] Ted R. Miller, "Valuing Nonfatal Quality of Life Losses with Quality-Adjusted Life Years: The Health Economist's Meow," *Journal of Forensic Economics* 13, no. 2 (2000), p. 161.

[491] Remember that VSL incorporates both monetary and nonmonetary aspects of life (e.g. productivity costs and loss in quality of life). For a discussion of the discount factor see *infra* section 4.7 and accompanying notes. Instead of using VSL values to elicit the WTP per QALY it has been suggested that the Value of Statistical Life Year (VSLY) should be used instead, which is arrived at by dividing the VSL by remaining life expectancy. A VSLY approach would conceptually be expected to reflect the monetary value for one QALY if productivity costs were excluded from the VSLY and the year was lived under a condition of perfect health. See Johannesson, *The Relationship between Cost-Effectiveness Analysis and Cost-Benefit Analysis*, p. 488.

[492] Johannesson and Meltzer, *Some Reflections on Cost-Effectiveness Analysis*, p. 5.

The USA Food and Drug Administration (FDA) for instance, used a value derived from the VSL of about €98,000 per QALY, while it has also utilized values of approximately €294,000 and €489,000 per QALY.[493] The EuroVaQ project has also attempted to estimate the value of one QALY on the basis of the VSL.[494] Two approaches were used. In the first the country-specific VSL was divided by the average life expectancy. In the second, an attempt was made to additionally isolate the effect of age and income on the resulting values. The value per QALY resulting from the first approach was approximately €81,500 in the Netherlands, €85,500 in UK and €75,000 in Sweden while the amounts resulting from the second approach were somewhat lower, namely €74,000, €73,000 and €74,500 respectively.[495]

To date, no consensus has been reached regarding the method that should be used to assign a monetary value to one QALY and, consequently, no single value or range of values for a QALY has met with wide acceptance. Thus, the values suggested so far for a QALY are highly divergent. Basing the monetary value of a QALY on the cost-effectiveness ratio approach may result in arbitrary cutoff values. On the other hand, there is limited research on eliciting a WTP for a QALY. For this reason, recent projects have tried to develop more robust methods to determine the WTP for a QALY. More research is necessary in this regard.

4.7. DISCOUNTING

Another matter that deserves attention in the context of the QALY approach is how to deal with present and future costs incurred to implement an intervention as well as with present and future health gains generated. To be able to compare them on equal footing and reach correct health care decisions, costs and health gains occurring in the future should be first reflected in present values through discounting.[496] However, although the reason for discounting costs is evident, the justification for doing so with respect to health gains is not that obvious.

Costs incurred in the future are given less weight in the present because a certain amount of money in the future would buy fewer goods than it would today, due to inflation.[497] In addition, an amount of money today can be invested

---

[493] Adler, *QALY's and Policy Evaluation: A New Perspective*, pp. 59–61.

[494] It is referred to as Value Per Fatality in the report, but essentially it is the same measure as VSL. See *European Value of a Quality Adjusted Life Year Final Publishable Report*, pp. 20–30.

[495] The original amounts in the publication (before adjusting for 2013 inflation) are €76,640, €80,591 and €70,323 for the first approach and €69,399, €68,359 and €70,119 for the second approach.

[496] Joseph Lipscomb, Milton C. Weinstein and George W. Torrance, "Time Preference," in *Cost-Effectiveness in Health and Medicine*, eds. Marthe R. Gold et al. (Oxford, New York: Oxford University Press, 1996), p. 214.

[497] Weinstein and Stason, *Foundations of Cost-Effectiveness Analysis for Health and Medical Practices*, p. 719; Shane Frederick, George Loewenstein and Ted O'Donoghue, "Time

---

and generate a return, so that the same amount in the future will be less valuable.[498] Therefore, in order to express future costs in present terms, discounting is necessary. There has been discussion, however, as to whether the health benefits realized in the future should also be discounted, because they do not concern money that can be invested, but rather increases in the quality of life. In order to account for the positive time preference, namely peoples' inclination to experience health gains in the present rather than have their health improved in the future, it has been accepted that future health benefits should also be discounted to express them in present terms. However, it is not necessary that discounting should occur at the same rate for benefits as for costs.[499]

NICE in UK and the US Panel on Cost-effectiveness in Health and Medicine have recommended that both costs and health gains, expressed in QALYs, should be discounted at the same rate.[500] However, the prevailing opinion in the Netherlands and Belgium submits that a higher rate should be employed to discount future costs than future benefits.[501] Discounting costs and health benefits at the same rate is based on the argument that health is valued in relation to money and thus it should also be discounted like money is, for consistency reasons.[502] An additional argument is that if health gains are not discounted or are discounted at a lower rate than costs, the paradoxical result will be that the more an intervention is postponed, the more cost-effective, and thus desirable it will be.[503] On the other hand, proponents of differential discounting of costs and benefits note that the monetary value of a QALY gain is expected to grow over

---

[498]   Discounting and Time Preference: A Critical Review," *Journal of Economic Literature* 40, no. 2 (2002), pp. 382–383.

  Weinstein and Stason, *Foundations of Cost-Effectiveness Analysis for Health and Medical Practices*, p. 719; Frederick, Loewenstein and O'Donoghue, *Time Discounting and Time Preference: A Critical Review*, pp. 382–383.

[499]   David J. Torgerson and James Raftery, "Discounting," *British Medical Journal* 319 (1999), pp. 914–915.

[500]   See Lipscomb, Weinstein and Torrance, *Time Preference*, pp. 216, 233 with respect to the US panel and National Institute for Health and Clinical Excellence, *Guide to the Methods of Technology Appraisal*, p. 44 for NICE. See also Milton C. Weinstein, George Torrance and Alistair McGuire, "QALYs: The Basics," *Value in Health* 12, no. s1 (2009), p. S9.

[501]   Werner Brouwer et al., "Need for Differential Discounting of Costs and Health Effects in Cost Effectiveness Analyses," *British Medical Journal* 331 (2005), pp. 446–448; Weinstein, Torrance and McGuire, *QALYs: The Basics*, p. S9; Mehraj B.Y. Parouty, Daan Krooshof and Maarten J. Postma, "Differential Time Preferences for Money and Quality of Life," *PharmacoEconomics* (2014). See College voor Zorgverzekeringen (CVZ), *Richtlijnen voor Farmacoeconomisch Onderzoek; geactualiseerde versie* (Dieman: CVZ 2006) and Federaal Kenniscentrum voor de Gezondheidszorg (KCE), *Richtlijnen voor Farmacoeconomische Evaluaties in Belgie* (Brussels: KCE 2008) for the Netherlands and Belgium respectively.

[502]   Weinstein and Stason, *Foundations of Cost-Effectiveness Analysis for Health and Medical Practices*, p. 720.

[503]   Emmett B. Keeler and Shan Cretin, "Discounting of Life-Saving and Other Nonmonetary Effects," *Management Science* 29, no. 3 (1983), pp. 300–306. Remember that health effects are the denominator of the cost-effectiveness ratio.

time so that consistency between health and wealth does not really hold.[504] The argument continues that in order to reflect the growing value of health gains, QALYs should be discounted at a lower rate.[505] Moreover, the observation that no recommendation has been expressed to postpone health care programs, when in the past NICE guidelines stipulated a lower discount rate for health gains, is an indication that the 'postponing paradox' may not hold.[506] In a recent study it has been sustained that the decision regarding the appropriate discounting of benefits is ultimately connected with judgments on values and facts such as whether the maximization of welfare or of health is the objective that should be pursued in CEA or whether a fixed budget for health care exists, etc.[507] The authors show that, depending on the judgments of values and facts one adheres to, it may be more appropriate to apply the same or a different discount factor to costs and health gains.

Besides the proposal that the discount factor should differ for benefits, it has further been argued that the discounting applied to QALYs should differ depending on which method has been used to elicit the quality-weights for their calculation. More precisely, discounting should be exercised with caution in the case where the TTO method has been employed.[508] Responses generated using the TTO question format already incorporate evaluations of the individuals for the relative value of health quality through time.[509] Thus, additional discounting in this case would result to an underestimation of QALYs.[510]

To date, the opinion that both costs and health gains should be discounted at the same rate prevails.[511] In practice, a discount factor of about 3–5% is often applied.[512] In the most recent version of its guidelines, NICE indicated that

---

[504]   Brouwer et al., *Need for Differential Discounting of Costs and Health Effects in Cost Effectiveness Analyses*, pp. 446–447.

[505]   Hugh Gravelle and Dave Smith, "Discounting for Health Effects in Cost-Benefit and Cost-Effectiveness Analysis," *Health Economics* 10 (2001), pp. 587–599.

[506]   Brouwer et al., *Need for Differential Discounting of Costs and Health Effects in Cost Effectiveness Analyses*, p. 447.

[507]   Karl Claxton et.al., "Discounting and decision making in the economic evaluation of health-care technologies," *Health Economics* 20, no. 1 (2011), pp. 2–15.

[508]   Linda D. MacKeigan, Amiram Gafni and Bernie J. O'Brien, "Double Discounting of QALYs," *Health Economics* 12 (2003), pp. 165–166.

[509]   Johannesson, Jönsson and Karlsson, *Outcome Measurement in Economic Evaluation*, p. 287; MacKeigan, Gafni and O'Brien, *Double Discounting of QALYs*, pp. 165–166. Remember that the TTO method elicits quality-weights by requesting from the respondent to make a trade-off between life years in the future, and perfect present health.

[510]   MacKeigan, Gafni and O'Brien, *Double Discounting of QALYs*, pp. 166, 169 expressed similar concerns also for SG based QALYs. See also Bleichrodt and Johannesson, *Standard Gamble, Time Trade-Off and Rating Scale: Experimental Results on the Ranking Properties of QALYs*, p. 155 where undiscounted TTO-QALYs were found to be more consistent with individual preferences elicited by direct ranking, than discounted TTO-QALYs.

[511]   Drummond et al., *Methods for the Economic Evaluation of Health Care Programmes*, p. 111.

[512]   Brouwer et al., *Need for Differential Discounting of Costs and Health Effects in Cost Effectiveness Analyses*, p. 446; Drummond et al., *Methods for the Economic Evaluation of Health Care Programmes*, p. 111.

discount rates of both costs and benefits should be set at 3.5%.[513] Nevertheless, studies often contain a sensitivity analysis using different discount factors to evaluate their influence on the results.[514] In the absence of a commonly accepted discounting approach, this practice is recommended in order to establish if and how different discount factors may affect the economic appraisal of health care programs.[515]

4.8. DISABILITY ADJUSTED LIFE YEARS: AN ALTERNATIVE TO QALYs?

This chapter has aimed to present the origin and characteristics of the QALY as well as the way it has been used so far in the context of health economics to assess the cost-effectiveness of medical interventions and allocate health budgets, concentrating especially on the QALY's ability to measure changes in both health quality and life duration. Before concluding the analysis, however, it is worthwhile to briefly refer to another measure, the Disability Adjusted Life Year (DALY), which has also been used as an alternative to measure health. The brief discussion of the DALY aims to show that, contrary to the QALY, the DALY does not have the characteristics that could render it an appropriate measure to be used in the alternative context of assessing pain and suffering damages in a tort law setting. By excluding the DALY, the choice of the QALY as the measure of health from the domain of health economics that could alternatively be used for assessing pain and suffering damages is thus justified.

The DALY measures the lost life years due to mortality, as well as the lost life years due to ill health, physical disability, etc., on a population level.[516] It has been developed on behalf of the World Bank and the World Health Organization as the measurement unit for the Global Burden of Disease Study and has subsequently been employed to quantify the burden of disease and disability in different regions of the world.[517] The DALY expresses the difference between the actual health and longevity of a population and the ideal longevity and health of a population; it therefore does not involve individual experiences of health. In

---

[513]   National Institute for Health and Clinical Excellence, *Guide to the Methods of Technology Appraisal*, p. 44.

[514]   NICE suggests to perform a sensitivity analysis using a discount factor of 1.5% for both costs and health benefits. See ibid., pp. 44, 65. Torgerson and Raftery, *Discounting*, p. 915.

[515]   Torgerson and Raftery, *Discounting*, p. 915; Drummond et al., *Methods for the Economic Evaluation of Health Care Programmes*, p. 111.

[516]   World Health Organization, *The Global Burden of Disease. 2004 Update* (Geneva, Switzerland: World Health Organization, [2008]).

[517]   Ibid.; Marthe R. Gold, David Stevenson and Dennis G. Fryback, "HALYS and QALYS and DALYS, Oh My: Similarities and Differences in Summary Measures of Population Health," *Annual Review of Public Health* 23 (2002), p. 117.

other words the DALY measures a population's lost healthy years given a life of ideal health and longevity. To perform this measurement, the life expectancy at birth of Japanese women, which is considered to be the highest in the world at 86 years, is considered to be the ideal life expectancy.[518] The degree of disability experienced by a group of people is evaluated on the basis of values provided by health experts.[519] Furthermore, the degree of disability is measured only with respect to a specific disease.

These few characteristics of the DALY already render it inappropriate for use in the assessment of pain and suffering damages. For instance, the fact that DALYs involve measurements of population health rather than of individual health is not compatible with assessing pain and suffering damages, which by definition involves individual losses. Moreover, the fact that DALYs refer only to specific diseases is also a feature that is inappropriate for the assessment of immaterial losses resulting from accidents in a tort law context, as these may involve a multitude of health conditions and/or injuries. Although this section does not provide a thorough account of the DALY, these few characteristics already sufficiently show that the DALY is not appropriate for assessing pain and suffering damages resulting from personal injury.

---

[518] Institute for Health Metrics and Evaluation, *The Global Burden of Disease: Generating Evidence, Guiding Policy*, (Seattle, WA: IHME, 2013), p. 12. The Global Burden of Disease Study of 1990 used as reference cases the life expectancy of Japanese men and women, which was at the time 80 and 82.5 years respectively. See Christopher J. L. Murray and Arnab K. Acharya, "Understanding DALYs," *Journal of Health Economics* 16, no. 6 (1997), p. 711.

[519] Drummond et al., *Methods for the Economic Evaluation of Health Care Programmes*, pp. 187–188.

CHAPTER 5

USING QALYs IN A TORT LAW CONTEXT

Assessing Pain and Suffering Damages

The preceding detailed description of the QALY, although far from being complete, aimed to show that the QALY is a reliable measure of the quality and duration of life that has resulted from and is supported by thorough scientific research. The previous analysis emphasized the QALY's strengths and weaknesses in the context of the economic appraisal of health care programs and interventions, where it has been used so far. The ability of QALYs to represent the consequences of different health treatments and interventions in terms of morbidity and mortality in a relatively simple manner has led many researchers to recognize the QALY as the best method currently available to assist the allocation of health care resources, although this assertion has not been uncontested.[520] Taking advantage of these characteristics, the current chapter revisits the problem underlying the assessment of pain and suffering damages for personal injuries, offering a solution that is based on an alternative use of the QALY.

As explained previously in chapter 2, the problem with the assessment of pain and suffering damages, as it is currently performed in most of the countries examined, is that it lacks a framework which can take into account the relative consequences of different types of injuries on the remaining life expectancy and the health and quality of life of the victim and translate them into monetary awards. The result is that damages awarded may be unpredictable and not reflect the gravity of the immaterial loss incurred. Under these circumstances it is doubtful whether the amounts granted can provide fair compensation to the victim, and offer appeasement for her loss. Analogous negative repercussions are generated from current assessment practices for deterrence and loss spreading. To deter potential tortfeasors, the magnitude of pain and suffering damages should depend on the gravity of the losses and be easily expected to induce

---

[520]   See the report of Smith, Drummond and Brixner, *Moving the QALY Forward: Rationale for Change* written on the occasion of the International Society for Pharmacoeconomics and Outcomes Research workshop on the future of the QALY, at pp. S2–S3.

individuals to take precautions. Similarly, to ensure that liability insurance is sustainable and encourage its provision and purchase, the size of pain and suffering damages should be verifiable ex ante to allow incorporation of the losses into the premiums and product/service prices offered. The lack of a framework with these traits for the assessment of pain and suffering damages seriously impedes the attainment of these goals. Furthermore, the additional complication arising with respect to the realization of deterrence and loss spreading of immaterial losses is that to attain both goals, people should only receive as pain and suffering damages the amount they would have been willing to spend themselves to reduce the probability of an accident. Accommodating this additional requirement on top of all the others in a single method of assessment seems to be a very challenging task.

The current chapter combines information from the preceding analysis to suggest that QALYs are able to provide a framework with these characteristics for the ex ante assessment of pain and suffering damages for non-fatal injuries, which is based on the impact of the health impairment on the victim and allows a more systematic valuation of pain and suffering damages than the current legal approach. The proposed framework is described and an example is provided to illustrate how it would work in practice. Possible implications of its implementation for compensation, deterrence, insurance and the administrative costs of justice are discussed.

5.1. EXPLOITING EXISTING QALY RESEARCH

The analysis of the QALY and of its components in the previous chapter serves as the basis for the proposed method to assess pain and suffering damages. The specialized research of QALYs from the domain of health economics enables assessing the impact of different health conditions on the quality of life. By using the QALY-weight derived for each condition, an educated assessment of the QALY loss due to the health impairment can be made. The QALY loss represents the decrease in quality of life due to the injury and is subsequently translated in a monetary award by using the existing literature on the monetary value of the QALY. The resulting amount is the average damage amount for the pain and suffering experienced in one year due to the injury. Finally, by taking into consideration the duration of the injury (and/or the remaining life expectancy of the victim), one can arrive at the total pain and suffering damages that correspond to the immaterial losses inflicted. By applying a discount factor, future damages can be expressed in their net present value, to enable the award of a lump sum. The following sections make the suggested method more concrete by explaining precisely which QALY-weights, monetary values and discount factors will be used below and address important questions regarding the proposed method that might arise.

5.1.1. UTILIZING AVAILABLE QALY-WEIGHTS

There exists a vast amount of research investigating the impact of different treatments on the health condition and quality of life of individuals and expressing it in terms of QALYs. The Center for the Evaluation of Value and Risk in health (CEVR), which is part of the Institute for Clinical Research and Health Policy Studies at Tufts Medical Center, has collected the relevant articles in English published from 1976 onwards and has compiled a large archive, the Cost-Effectiveness Analysis (CEA) registry, which comprises more than 14,000 QALY-weights.[521] The registry is searchable per reference and publication date of the article, health state, type of method used to elicit QALY-weights, population sample, QALY-weights corresponding to the medical condition at hand, etc. Of course, non-English articles also exist which provide additional QALY-weights. However they are fewer in number and have not yet been systematized in a database similar to the CEA registry.

The proposed method for assessing pain and suffering damages for personal injuries suggests taking advantage of the information on QALY-weights already generated. Therefore, the registry will be used as a source of QALY-weights, as it is the most extensive compilation of relevant information. More specifically QALY-weights from the registry pertaining to particular illnesses and medical conditions will be utilized to estimate the loss in health and quality of life incurred after an injury. The collected QALY-weights available in the registry will enable the relative ranking of different types of immaterial losses and provide a non-arbitrary basis to estimate pain and suffering damages. However, since QALYs have been predominantly used to assess the effectiveness of different medical interventions and treatments for medical conditions, namely mainly illnesses, it may be the case that a QALY-weight is not readily available for an injury as such. Therefore, at this stage some calculations will inevitably have to be based on QALY-weights of medical conditions that have comparable consequences to the injuries at hand. For instance, if a QALY-weight for loss of sight is not available, the QALY-weight for a severe cataract may be used, as a cataract is a disease that causes vision loss in its last stages. Nevertheless, the lack of QALY-weights for particular injuries is a shortcoming that can be dealt with in the future if additional research is undertaken to assess the impact of injuries as such on health and the quality of life. This book does not undertake QALY research but instead relies on the CEA registry and the existing QALY-weights for illnesses (and injuries) which can be used to evaluate the quality of life loss after an injury. However, a concern may arise as to whether it is appropriate to use a QALY-weight for an illness to express the immaterial loss due to an injury.

---

[521]   Center for the Evaluation of Value and Risk in Health, "Cost-Effectiveness Analysis Registry," Institute for Clinical Research and Health Policy Studies, Tufts Medical Center, www. cearegistry.org (accessed 31.03.2014).

A pragmatic response to this reasonable concern would be that the lack of a method, reflecting the gravity of the injury and translating it to a monetary award, has already led courts to use yardsticks which are much more remote from the essence of the losses they seek to compensate than QALY-based damage assessment could ever be. An example is the reliance of courts on previously awarded amounts for similar impairments, which establishes a link with previous case law but not necessarily a meaningful connection between the award and the immaterial loss incurred. Therefore, even if QALY-weights of illnesses are used to approximate injury losses, assessing pain and suffering damages by applying a QALY framework would be considered an improvement compared to judicial practices which award damages with less reference to the health and quality of life reduction actually inflicted. Besides, the use of QALY-weights for illnesses will actually be warranted for cases in which pain and suffering damages are claimed after a product-inflicted illness. Some examples of illnesses for which pain and suffering damages have been awarded in the past include mesothelioma and lung cancer manifesting as a result of contact with asbestos, HIV being contracted by blood transfusion and, in a fairly recent case, neurological problems caused by using certain pesticides.[522] In these cases the use of the QALY-weight for the relevant illness will make it possible to fully capture the consequences of the illness to the health and quality of life of the victim and estimate the corresponding pain and suffering damages.

It may also be the case that the registry provides several QALY-weights for one type of medical condition which do not necessarily coincide. Searching the registry for 'blindness', for instance, yields QALY-weights between 0.36 and 0.95. Nevertheless, this significant difference in the QALY-weights can be explained if one takes into consideration that blindness is a broad term which may describe lack of vision in one eye, blindness for both eyes or even blindness in combination with other medical conditions such as diabetes, sclerosis or other illnesses leading to loss of vision, etc. In this particular case the QALY-weight of 0.36 indeed corresponds to a combination of blindness and diabetes. Therefore the difference in the QALY-weights reflects the difference in the gravity of the medical condition and may even be indicative of comorbid conditions. Less severe types of blindness, e.g. vision loss in one eye, will accordingly have a high QALY-weight, whereas more severe types of blindness, for instance complete loss of sight, will yield lower QALY-weights. It is thus important to use the QALY-weights from the registry that most accurately describe the immaterial loss one wants to assess. In the subsequent estimations of pain and suffering damages (for loss of hearing in this chapter and for other types of injuries in chapter 7), it was

---

[522] See for instance one of the class actions against cigarette manufacturer Philip Morris for exposing smokers in increased risk of lung cancer: Xavier v. Philip Morris USA Inc., 787 F. Supp. 2d, 1075 (N.D. Cal. 2011). See also the recent case of a farmer filling a lawsuit against an insecticide company for incurring chemical poisoning that led to neurological problems: François v. Monsanto, T.G.I. Lyon, 13 fév. 2012, n° 2012/144.

therefore necessary to read the underlying publications in order to decide which of the elicited QALY-weights are best fitting to assess the immaterial loss of a given injury type.

It is however possible that other reasons account for a difference in the QALY-weights. A notable concern pertains to the possibility that QALY-weights for the same health condition may differ because of the use of different methods of elicitation. The issue was extensively discussed in the previous chapter where it was shown that some variation does exist between the QALY-weights elicited for the same health condition if different methods are used, although is it not clear whether this variation is significant. Additional attention and efforts are devoted to refine the methods and acquire more uniform QALY-weights. It should however be stressed that, when only one method is used to elicit QALY-weights from different people regarding the same health condition, then results are consistent. Likewise, QALY-weights are stable if one method is used to evaluate the same health condition over time. In other words, most methods score well in terms of *inter-rater* and *test-retest* reliability.[523] This fact has led to the proposal that only one method should be used for all economic evaluations in the context of health economics.[524] If the proposal is implemented, the generation of more uniform QALY-weights will also be beneficial for the use of QALYs in a legal context to assess pain and suffering damages. Nevertheless, it should be emphasized that while variation in QALY-weights is an important reason for concern for the cost-effectiveness analyses of different treatments, where a small difference may be decisive for the choice of the intervention, the situation is not the same for the proposed use of QALYs as a method to assess pain and suffering damages. In this alternative context, variation of QALY-weights due to differences in the severity of the medical condition or even due to the use of a different method of elicitation is desirable to some extent. The variation of QALY-weights will generate a range of QALY losses for the same health condition which, multiplied by the monetary value of a QALY, will yield a range of pain and suffering damages, rather than a fixed amount, allowing judges the margin to choose which amount to award for the case at hand. The decision on the size of pain and suffering damages will therefore depend on the impact of the objective injury based on specialized research and the consequences of that injury for the specific victim. The latter issue will give the judge the opportunity to exercise a critical discretion regarding the magnitude of the award by choosing the appropriate amount from the range of values. This is considered a very important characteristic of the proposed approach and will be further analyzed in section 5.3.1.

---

[523] See Brazier et al., *A Review of the Use of Health Status Measures in Economic Evaluation*, pp. 12, 31, 34, 36, 67, 72 for SG, VAS, TTO, HUI and EQ-5D respectively.

[524] Brazier et al., *Measuring and Valuing Health Benefits for Economic Evaluation*, p. 237.

The subsequent analysis uses QALY-weights derived from publications included in the CEA registry, which have received a quality score of at least 4.0 on a scale from 1.0 to 7.0 indicating lowest and highest quality respectively. Therefore, they are considered publications of high quality according to the registry's evaluation. Moreover, publications including QALY-weights that have been elicited with the EQ-5D and the HUI are taken into consideration in large part, because these instruments are considered to be better for QALY-weight elicitation than other instruments.[525] The publications used in the subsequent analysis have been chosen among others after thoroughly reading all of them to determine which of them provide QALY-weights that are best fitting to assess the immaterial loss of a given injury type.

5.1.2. DECIDING THE MONETARY VALUE OF A QALY

The QALY loss inflicted provides a measure of gravity for the injury sustained but it is its combination with a monetary value that expresses the loss incurred in monetary terms and allows pain and suffering damages to be estimated. Determining a monetary value for a QALY has been an issue in the domain of health economics for quite some time, as was explained in the previous chapter. To recapitulate, the two basic approaches followed are to regard as the monetary value of a QALY the cost of the last treatment that is implemented given a budget constraint or to elicit the value of a QALY using WTP. From the two approaches, only the latter involving WTP is relevant for the purpose of providing a monetary value for a QALY to be used in the assessment of pain and suffering damages. The first approach should be ruled out because it seems inappropriate that the size of the award for pain and suffering depends on a QALY value arrived at on the basis of stipulated budgets. The constraints imposed by the available resources on the implementation of different QALY-generating medical interventions have no relevance for the assessment of pain and suffering damages.

One way followed to obtain WTP values for a QALY is to extrapolate them from the WTP-based values of the VSL.[526] However, since the QALY is better suited than the VSL to assess pain and suffering damages for non-fatal injuries, the other way, namely a direct elicitation of the WTP for a QALY as such, is more appropriate for the purpose of monetizing the QALY. Asking people what value they would place on avoiding the (probability of) occurrence of a QALY loss provides a WTP per QALY that can be utilized in the context of assessing damage awards. The large-scale project of EuroVaQ that was recently undertaken in Europe has estimated the WTP per QALY in nine European countries by

---

[525]   Brazier et al., *A Review of the Use of Health Status Measures in Economic Evaluation*, p. 76.
[526]   See *supra* chapter 4 in section 4.6.2.

asking similar questions. Different variants of questions were used, including questions eliciting WTP for one QALY and for smaller fractions of a QALY to avoid the size of the health gain influencing the willingness to pay, questions involving a certainty or a risk of losing QALYs, etc. The overall mean WTP per QALY was estimated at an upper limit of approximately €68,000.[527] Another study estimating the WTP per QALY with respect to temporary health states associated with herpes zoster arrived at values between €24,000 and €41,500 approximately,[528] whereas a different study arrived at an amount of about €26,000 as a WTP per QALY for the Netherlands, acknowledging however that the amount would have been higher if smaller fractions of QALYs had been used.[529] In a more recent study involving Dutch respondents, the WTP per QALY estimated ranged from about €82,000 to €113,000.[530]

Emphasis should be placed on the fact that in the context of economic evaluation of health care programs it may not be possible to regard a single value as the all-applicable WTP per QALY.[531] Although a single value would make the decision process regarding the implementation of different medical interventions and techniques fairly easy, in reality the value of a QALY may fluctuate under the influence of contextual factors. For instance, a WTP may be higher for a QALY generated through chemotherapy than for a QALY generated through cosmetic plastic surgery or, even if a WTP has been assigned for a QALY, it is possible that a QALY may be regarded as being of greater value if it is accrued to young individuals or to people who have fewer QALYs overall. This may explain why so

---

[527] This amount resulted by using the 'direct approach' and an expected gain of 0.05 QALYs. Additionally, the top 1% of the data was trimmed to avoid including very high responses in the calculations (the initial overall mean amount before trimming was about €145,000). The 'chained approach' resulted in overall trimmed means ranging between about €15,100 and €63,900. See *European Value of a Quality Adjusted Life Year Final Publishable Report*, pp. 89–94.

[528] Tracy A. Lieu et al., "Willingness to Pay for a QALY Based on Community Member and Patient Preferences for Temporary Health States Associated with Herpes Zoster," *PharmacoEconomics* 27, no. 12 (2009), p. 1006. The amounts from the original American publication have been first expressed in dollars from 2013 (see www.bls.gov/data/inflation_calculator.htm) and subsequently in euro on the basis of the 2013 Purchasing Power Parity (PPP) of the euro-area as published by the OECD: 0.773 (see http://stats.oecd.org/Index.aspx?DataSetCode=PPPGDP).

[529] Bobinac et al., *Willingness to Pay for a Quality-Adjusted Life-Year: The Individual Perspective*, pp. 1052–1053. The original amount in the publication is €24,500. It has been adjusted for inflation on the basis of the annual average inflation rates published by Eurostat. See Eurostat, "Annual Average Inflation Rates 2000–2012," Eurostat, http://epp.eurostat.ec.europa.eu/statistics_explained/index.php/Consumer_prices_-_inflation_and_comparative_price_levels (accessed 31.03.2014).

[530] Ana Bobinac, *Economic Evaluations of Health Technologies: Insights into the measurement and valuation of benefits*, Dissertation Erasmus University Rotterdam (The Netherlands, 2012), pp. 104–129. The original amounts in the publication (before adjusting for inflation) range between €80,000 and €110,000.

[531] See Werner Brouwer et al., "The New Myth: The Social Value of the QALY," *PharmacoEconomics* 26, no. 1 (2008), pp. 1–4.

far in the domain of health economics there has been no clear consensus on a 'correct', unique monetized value of a QALY. However, it should be stressed again that what may be considered a limitation of QALYs in the domain of health care allocation is not necessarily such in the domain of tort law. QALYs in the domain of health care allocation have a particular aim, namely to provide a decision tool with which the resources will be allocated so as to generate better health for more people. To make sure that such an allocation takes place according to the preference of the people, the QALY has to be subject to certain assumptions to make sure that it indeed reflects what people would have wanted for themselves and for others. However, in the context of awarding pain and suffering damages, there is no common resource that needs to be allocated to the most health generating treatment, nor are there considerations on distributional effects or equity. The QALY can be utilized in the domain of tort law by taking into consideration only those elements that are important for its utilization, namely the ability to express quality and quantity of life and reflect the relative severity of different injuries, while at the same time not being restricted by the limitations pertaining to its implementation in the context of health care. Therefore, although an all-applicable WTP for a QALY might not be accepted in the domain of health care allocation, a unique amount per QALY that has some basis in the amount individuals would be willing to pay to avoid a QALY loss would be appropriate to use in the assessment of pain and suffering damages.

Given that a single WTP per QALY may not be available in the domain of health economics, the amount to be used as the value of a QALY in the legal context for the purpose of assessing pain and suffering damages is something to be decided upon primarily on the basis of ongoing scientific research in health economics but also taking into consideration other factors. These factors may include the economic situation in a country, the GDP, the input from consultation with insurance companies and other potentially involved parties like for instance consumer organizations etc. Thus, although the monetary value assigned to the QALY will be largely affected by research results, it will ultimately be a product of multilevel consultation and of political decision. Each country would choose to implement a value per QALY that best corresponds to the existing economic and other circumstances in that country, implying that different monetary values per QALY may be used by different countries. Even though research results do not stipulate a single 'correct' monetized value of a QALY, the amounts arrived at by the EuroVaQ and by other research provide at least the range within which the value of a QALY should lie. In the ensuing analysis, the value of €50,000 per QALY is applied to estimate pain and suffering damages for different injuries. It is not argued that this is the best possible amount, but until more research is undertaken to determine whether a different amount may be better suited to assess pain and suffering damages, it makes sense to apply an amount that lies within the range of values stipulated by the most recent EuroVaQ project.

5.1.3. APPLYING A DISCOUNT FACTOR TO REFLECT PRESENT VALUE

Apart from the monetary value of the QALY, which is a crucial element to make it possible to express the damage incurred in monetary terms, another important issue that affects the size of the awards is discounting. A differentiation should be made between the discounting applied on QALYs in the context of health economics and the discounting that takes place when courts award damages for future losses. The latter involves calculating the net present value of future losses by taking into consideration the duration of the injury, in order to enable the award of pain and suffering damages in a lump sum.

When courts award (pain and suffering) damages in a lump sum, as is the case in most of the examined jurisdictions,[532] the amounts corresponding to present losses are taken at their nominal value while the amounts corresponding to (expected) future losses should be first expressed in present terms before being taken into consideration. The rationale behind this practice is that inflation and the possibility of returns on investment make an amount awarded today more valuable than the same amount awarded in the future.[533] Therefore, a discount rate is applied to reduce pain and suffering damages for future immaterial loss on the grounds that by receiving today an amount of money that would normally be due in the future, the victim has the opportunity to invest it and make profit. If, for instance, the decrease in quality of life caused by a certain permanent injury is estimated at €10,000 per year and the remaining life expectancy of the injured is ten years, then for a period of ten years the damages should not simply be assessed at €100,000 but at the net present value of ten annual future payments of €10,000. The exact size of pain and suffering damages would then depend on the discount factor being applied. As an example, a discount factor of 4% would result in a lump sum payment of €84,353 while a discount factor of 6% would lead to €78,017.

Following the court practice, the proposed method applies a discount rate to account for the duration of the injury. Hence, if the immaterial loss due to an injury persists in the future, the amount derived on the basis of QALYs as the monetary expression of pain and suffering for one year is discounted to express the loss in present values.

In the previous chapter it was explained that, in the context of health economics, discounting is implemented in two instances with respect to QALYs, namely it is applied for future costs arising from the implementation of QALY-

---

[532]   See *supra* chapter 2 in section 2.2.1.
[533]   See *supra* chapter 4 in section 4.7. See also Christopher Bruce, "Selecting the Discount Rate," *Expert Witness* 1, no. 3 (1996), at: www.economica.ca/ew01_3p3.htm (accessed 31.03.2014); Laura Weir et al., "The Discount Rate Revisited," *Expert Witness*, no. 1 (2008), at: www. economica.ca/ew13_1p1.htm (accessed 31.03.2014).

generating treatments and for QALY gains that occur in the future. Evidently, the relevance of this two-stage discounting is obfuscated in the proposed framework. Here, the QALY is used to express losses that have already been inflicted and therefore no discounting of the QALY itself is necessary. Hence, the discussion with respect to applying the same or differential discounting to costs and benefits in the context of health economics loses its relevance for the proposed application of the QALY in the context of tort law. However, one could argue that a different way of discounting QALYs, which is not performed in health economics, is required in the suggested framework for the assessment of pain and suffering damages to account for the fact that quality of life deteriorates over time as people grow older. If for instance an individual incurs an injury that restricts her mobility, should she receive an amount of damages corresponding to that deterioration when she is likely to experience mobility restrictions due to old age even if she had been injured? The implication of applying a discount rate to QALYs to reflect the health deterioration due to aging would be that, to some extent, the loss in quality of life inflicted by the injury would be cancelled out. Such discounting inadvertently assumes that growing old has the same percentage of health deterioration for all individuals, which is clearly not the case. To accurately reflect the decrease in quality of life occurring when growing old would require the application of different discount rates whose estimation would involve thorough research. In addition, discounting QALYs to account for aging would offset the immaterial loss arising from the injury with the deterioration of health relating to senescence even when the consequences of the injury are not part of the declining health dimensions. A significant facial scar or an acute finger injury, for instance, reduces the quality of life of the victim in a way that does not normally happen in old age. Therefore, it should not be taken for granted that deterioration of health due to aging occurs in the same proportion for all individuals or that the impact of an injury is necessarily lessened with seniority. Discounting QALYs to reflect that quality of life deteriorates with old age would unjustifiably underplay the detrimental effects of an injury. After all, aging is a natural cause of health deterioration, which is expected to take place regardless of the involuntary worsening of the quality of life inflicted by an injury. For these reasons a discount rate should not be applied to QALYs when assessing pain and suffering damages.[534]

What should be done however in the process of evaluating the QALY loss incurred in a given injury case is that the judges should take into consideration

---

[534] Nevertheless, there may be other arguments in favor of discounting QALYs. People incurring a significant immaterial loss due to injury in an early period of their life may be able to overcome it and adapt to the new situation. Whether adaptation actually occurs or not is an empirical matter, nonetheless its manifestation may provide a justification for discounting QALYs. See *infra* chapter 6 and accompanying notes.

the health condition of the victim at the time of the accident. At this point, it is appropriate for the potential effect of age on quality of life to figure in the assessment of pain and suffering damages if it can be demonstrated that the effect of a certain injury is different for people belonging in different age clusters. So, for instance, if there is QALY research showing that a given injury reduces the quality of life of 20- to 30-year-olds by 0.2 QALYs whereas it causes a 0.15 decrease to 60- to 70-year-olds, then these quality-weights should be taken into consideration when assessing damages for people of the relevant age. This implies that the calculation of pain and suffering damages may be significantly refined if QALY research is conducted not only on the basis of particular health conditions but also taking into consideration different age clusters. Nevertheless, preexisting unfavorable health conditions should generally be accounted for irrespective of the age of people they are attributed to. For example, in the case of losing sight in one eye, a person who has severe myopia and astigmatism and cannot see without glasses should not be regarded as incurring the same loss as a person having perfect vision. Although this is not considered to be discounting, it has a similar effect as it reduces the estimated QALY loss on reasonable grounds by accounting for health problems that may already persist at the time of the accident.[535]

It follows that the only applicable discounting for the proposed method of assessing pain and suffering damages is the one already applied by courts to express future monetary amounts in present values. The size of the discount rate may vary per country. In UK, a statutory order stipulates that a discount rate of 2.5% should be applied.[536] In other countries, legally binding rules regarding the discount rate that should be implemented by courts are missing entirely. In the ensuing analysis, a discount rate of 4% will be applied to express

---

[535] This line of reasoning reminds of the so-called 'thin skull rule' implemented in some legal systems which suggests that if the victim suffers an unusually high level of damage *the tortfeasor has to take the victim as he finds him* and be held liable for all damages. The proposed QALY approach can indeed enable judges to account for all the losses inflicted to the quality of life of a victim, even if these losses have been aggravated due to a special characteristic of the victim, such as e.g. a proneness to bone fractures. Here however, a different thing is suggested; that QALYs can differentiate between the loss incurred due the injury and a pre-existing detrimental health condition, thus making the injurer liable for the magnitude of loss she inflicted.

[536] Note that this rate applies for future pecuniary loss. The amounts awarded for (future) immaterial loss in cases of personal injury are not discounted. See the Damages (Personal Injury) Order 2001, SI 2001/2301 for England and Damages (Personal Injury) (Scotland) Order 2002 (SSI 2002/46) for Scotland. The Scottish Government is currently under consultation with relevant parties to review the discount rate in Scotland. See Ministry of Justice Scottish Government and Department of Justice Northern Ireland, "Damages Act 1996: The Discount Rate. Review of the Legal Framework," Consultation Paper 3/2013 (2013). In Canada, rule 59.03(1) and (2) of the Ontario Rules of Civil Procedure, stipulate that a fixed rate of 2.5% should be used to discount pecuniary losses occuring after the first 15 years since the start of the trial; during the first 15 years a different discount rate is applicable.

the damages corresponding to future pain and suffering in present terms. The chosen rate is somewhat higher than the rate currently applied in many jurisdictions to avoid the risk of overestimating the monetary value of immaterial losses due to inadequate discounting. Nevertheless, it should be kept in mind that a revision and an adjustment of the discount rate on the basis of the most recent inflation rate and interest rate on investment might yield a somewhat different percentage.

5.2. SYNTHESIS

The previous section identified which pieces of information from QALY research are relevant for the assessment of pain and suffering damages. The essence of the proposal is to take advantage of an already existing research field, which provides readily available evaluations of the gravity of immaterial losses related to quality of life, as well as a way to evaluate the loss in monetary terms, hence offering all that is necessary and sufficient to calculate pain and suffering damages. It should be mentioned here that the QALY's potential for the assessment of pain and suffering damages has not gone completely unnoticed. An earlier proposal by Miller stipulated that forensic experts could apply QALY methodology to help guide jury valuations in tort cases involving non-fatal injury and illness.[537] According to his proposal, qualified medical and economic experts assisting the court would have to choose among several existing QALY scales, the scale that is more appropriate to reflect the immaterial loss incurred by the plaintiff at hand. Then, by using the selected scale they would evaluate the plaintiff's losses themselves and poll the plaintiff and/or his caregivers to elicit their valuations. Additionally for some cases they would examine existing surveys or survey people similar to the victim.[538] The resulting QALY loss could be then used to guide the jury or be further monetized. Evidently, this proposal involves eliciting the QALY loss of each and every individual plaintiff claiming for damages. Besides being very costly to implement, Miller's approach is thus distinctly different from the framework suggested below, which takes advantage of the readily available QALY research in a more extensive way. Disregarding this highly relevant and freely accessible information would be difficult to justify. In addition, the proposed framework presents further advantages that are extensively discussed in the following sections.

---

[537] Miller, *Valuing Nonfatal Quality of Life Losses with Quality-Adjusted Life Years: The Health Economist's Meow*, pp. 145–167.
[538] Ibid., pp. 155–156.

5.2.1. A GRAPHICAL REPRESENTATION OF THE PROPOSED FRAMEWORK

The idea can be further illustrated by the use of the following graphs. The horizontal axis shows that time is limited by the normal life expectancy ($t^\dagger$) of the victim who has suffered immaterial loss. At time t^* the accident takes place. The vertical axis represents the QALY-level of the victim. The upper (bold) horizontal line indicates the QALY-level of the victim before the accident, while the lower (fine) horizontal line indicates the QALY-level after the accident in which she suffered the immaterial loss. The vertical distance between both lines represents the severity of the injury. Finally, the shaded area reflects the total loss of quality of life, which pain and suffering damages seek to prevent and compensate.

Figure 2. A lasting injury that does not affect life expectancy

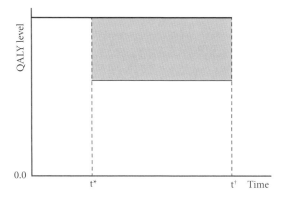

Figure 3. An injury that heals

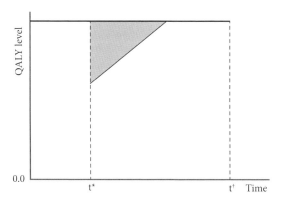

Figure 2 shows a lasting injury that does not affect the life expectancy of the victim, such as for instance scar tissue, remaining pain or paralysis of lower limbs. A different situation, this time of an injury that does not last but heals in a finite amount of time, is illustrated in figure 3. If during the healing time quality of life gradually increases, then the shaded triangular area reflects the immaterial loss incurred. It is also possible that some injuries not only affect quality of life but also the remaining life expectancy, as depicted in figure 4. This may occur for example when an injury causes the victim to be more susceptible to infections or abstain from physical exercise. Of course, many more situations are conceivable such as injuries which do not heal completely, so that the victim no longer reaches her pre-accident QALY-level.[539] The best depiction of a given situation depends, of course, on the type of injury, but also on the information that is available in health economics literature regarding the impact of such injuries on the quality of life.

Figure 4. An injury affecting both quality of life and life expectancy

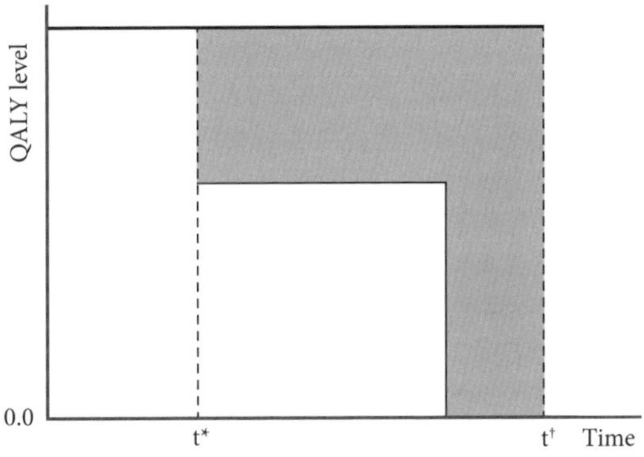

The next section combines the relevant insights from QALY research and provides a concrete example of the proposed QALY framework for the assessment of pain and suffering damages.

5.2.2. THE CASE OF DEAFNESS

Loss of hearing may occur as a consequence of being exposed to extreme levels of noise, improper use of drugs, extensive head injury, etc. It is therefore possible that it results from work-related or product-related accidents, traffic accidents or

---

[539] Another possibility is that the victim may hedonically adapt to the injury so that the decrease in the QALY-level will be large in the period directly after the accident and lower in the subsequent periods.

medical malpractice. Deafness has a negative impact on quality of life extending beyond the inability to hear, as it also generates problems in speech and causes difficulties in daily and social life.

There is extensive research on the cost-effectiveness of cochlear implants, which are hearing devices implanted in the inner ear allowing people with profound and milder deafness to regain the sense of sound to a greater or a lesser extent.[540] In this research, it is investigated whether cochlear implants increase the quality of life of deaf individuals to a considerable degree so that their additional costs are worth incurring. To allow a comparison of the quality of life experienced before and after the implantation, QALY-weights are elicited in both health states, namely in the state of profound or milder deafness and in the state of increased hearing after the cochlear implants are placed in the inner ear. The QALY-weights indicating the reduction in quality of life due to profoundly impaired hearing can be used to assess the immaterial loss resulting from incurring deafness.

In a relatively recent study, Summerfield et al. investigated the cost-effectiveness of bilateral cochlear implants as opposed to unilateral cochlear implants.[541] They examined how the quality of life of adult individuals with profound deafness may improve after undergoing a bilateral cochlear surgery. To compare the resulting quality of life after surgery with the quality of life that would have been experienced without any hearing problems they elicited the QALY-weights for profound deafness, for a state with no hearing problems and for the state after the implantation.[542] They also took into consideration the fact that some people can already benefit from traditional acoustic devices before the implantation, whereas other people are unable to benefit from traditional hearing aids. Using the Health Utilities Index Mark II (HUI2) to elicit QALY-

---

[540]   J. Robert Wyatt et al., "Cost Utility of the Multichannel Cochlear Implant in 258 Profoundly Deaf Individuals," *Laryngoscope* 106, no. 7 (1996), pp. 816–821; Cynthia S. Palmer et al., "A Prospective Study of the Cost-Utility of the Multichannel Cochlear Implant," *Archives of Otolaryngology – Head & Neck Surgery* 125, no. 11 (1999), pp. 1221–1228; A. Quentin Summerfield et al., "A Cost-Utility Scenario Analysis of Bilateral Cochlear Implantation," *Archives of Otolaryngology – Head & Neck Surgery* 128, no. 11 (2002), pp. 1255–1262; UK Cochlear Implant Study Group, "Criteria of Candidacy for Unilateral Cochlear Implantation in Postlingually Deafened Adults II: Cost-Effectiveness Analysis," *Ear & Hearing* 25, no. 4 (2004), pp. 336–360. See also a meta-analysis reviewing the then up to date research results André K. Cheng and John K. Niparko, "Cost-Utility of the Cochlear Implant in Adults. A Meta-Analysis," *Archives of Otolaryngology – Head & Neck Surgery* 125 (1999), pp. 1214–1218.

[541]   Summerfield et al., *A Cost-Utility Scenario Analysis of Bilateral Cochlear Implantation*, pp. 1255–1262. The quality of this research is a 5.0 on a scale from 1.0 to 7.0; see https://research.tufts-nemc.org/cear4/SearchingtheCEARegistry/SearchtheCEARegistry.aspx.

[542]   To estimate the QALY loss due to profound deafness, Summerfield et al. first asked from patients with profound deafness to provide their QALY weights with HUI2. Then, they estimated the loss in quality of life due to profound deafness by redoing the same HUI2 questionnaires with the difference that in the functions of hearing and speech they indicated that the patients had the highest level. This way they managed to rule out only the effect of the impaired hearing on the quality of life.

weights, they found that the QALY loss as a result of profoundly impaired hearing (and relatedly, speech) is 0.235 for people who cannot benefit at all from hearing devices and 0.164 for those who can use traditional acoustic devices to improve their situation.[543]

These research results convey the information that a person who suffers from profound deafness incurs an immaterial loss of 0.235 QALYs per year unless she is able to mitigate the loss by using hearing aids, in which case the immaterial loss is 0.164 QALYs. Expressing this loss in monetary terms by using the value of €50,000 per QALY yields a damage amount of €11,750 per year for those who cannot benefit from acoustic devices, and €8,200 for those who can. These amounts can be used to assess pain and suffering damages when the victim of an accident suffers a total loss of hearing. For example, assuming an average life expectancy of 80 years and applying a discount rate of 4%, a 48-year-old would be entitled to approximately €222,000 for pain and suffering.[544] However, if she were able to use traditional hearing devices to alleviate the gravity of her condition, then she should receive about €155,000.[545]

The preceding example serves as a brief illustration of how pain and suffering damages can be assessed using the proposed QALY framework. Any potential special circumstances of the individual are not taken into consideration in this elementary hypothetical example. One such circumstance could for instance be that the victim is an amateur singer and after the accident cannot do her hobby anymore. Or, in a worse scenario, the victim is already blind, so that an additional loss of hearing would in essence deprive her of a means of perceiving her surroundings. Another possibility is that the victim may already have had reduced hearing before the accident. Such aggravating or mitigating circumstances can be easily factored into the resulting amounts, especially if a range of values has already been generated by the existing QALY research for the injury at hand. The judge then will be able to choose from the range the value that best fits the case at hand and retain the discretion to further adjust the award recommended by the specialized research, upwards or downwards. The research of Summerfield et al. was used in this particular example because it calculates the QALY loss incurred due to profound deafness in a very clear way by comparing the quality of life with no hearing problems and the quality of life with complete loss of hearing. The rest of the existing literature uses a slightly

---

[543] Ibid., p. 1259. These are the values elicited by community members-volunteers participating in the research. The research also provides the extent of QALY loss due to deafness as indicated by the actual patients who experienced profound deafness. Their evaluation of the QALY loss due to deafness was 0.281 for deafness that cannot be mitigated with traditional acoustic aids and 0.145 for deafness, which can be alleviated by using traditional hearing devices.

[544] The net present value of 33 annual payments of €11,750 (0.235 * €50,000), applying a discount factor of 4% equals €221,764.

[545] The net present value of 33 annual payments of €8,200 (0.164 * €50,000), applying a discount factor of 4% equals €154,763.

more indirect way to arrive at the QALY loss due to profound deafness, by comparing the quality of life experienced with total hearing loss with the quality of life resulting after the bilateral cochlear implantation, when allegedly the hearing capacity has significantly improved, assuming it approximates the quality of life with no hearing problems. Although this may not be quite accurate, it should be mentioned that this research has estimated the QALY loss due to profound deafness at 0.2 QALYs[546] and 0.26 QALYs.[547] In these studies, and in the study of Summerfield et al., the QALY loss due to deafness was estimated for an adult population and therefore was the one appropriate to use in the hypothetical example of the 48-year-old victim. However, if the victim in a given case is a child or an elderly person, the QALY loss due to deafness should be derived from the research available that focuses on the effects of profound deafness and cochlear implantation on children or the elderly.[548] If the impact of deafness on quality of life is different depending on the age of the victim, then using more age-specific research results for the assessment of the immaterial loss will also yield more refined pain and suffering damages.

5.3. CAN THE GOALS OF TORT LAW WITH RESPECT TO PAIN AND SUFFERING DAMAGES BE REACHED?

The previous section demonstrated how existing results from a research field that specializes in monitoring changes in quality of life could be used for the purpose of awarding pain and suffering damages for personal injury. If these

---

[546] Wyatt et al., *Cost Utility of the Multichannel Cochlear Implant in 258 Profoundly Deaf Individuals*, p. 817 find a QALY loss of 0.204 QALYs; Palmer et al., *A Prospective Study of the Cost-Utility of the Multichannel Cochlear Implant*, p. 1225 find a QALY loss of 0.2 QALYs, whereas in a more recent study UK Cochlear Implant Study Group, *Criteria of Candidacy for Unilateral Cochlear Implantation in Postlingually Deafened Adults II: Cost-Effectiveness Analysis*, pp. 336–360 finds an overall QALY loss of 0.2 QALYs which spans between 0.18 and 0.22 depending on the age group of the respondents. See also Mark H. Rozenbaum et al., "Vaccination of risk groups in England using the 13 valent pneumococcal conjugate vaccine: economic analysis," *British Medical Journal* 345 (2012), p. 9, who stipulate that the QALY-weight of deafness is 0.81. Assuming a perfect health of 1, then the QALY loss related to deafness would be 0.19 QALYs. However the paper does not clarify which way was used to elicit this QALY-weight.

[547] This QALY loss is the result of a meta analysis by Cheng and Niparko, *Cost-Utility of the Cochlear Implant in Adults. A Meta-Analysis*, p. 1217.

[548] Research that focuses on older patients found a mean difference before and after the cochlear implantation of 0.24 QALYs. See Howard W. Francis et al., "Impact of Cochlear Implants on the Functional Health Status of Older Adults," *The Laryngoscope* 112, no. 8 (2002), p. 1484. On the other hand, research focusing on children, found a difference in QALYs ranging from 0.22 to 0.39, depending on the method used (time trade-off, visual analogue scale or HUI3). See André K. Cheng et al., "Cost-Utility Analysis of Cochlear Implant in Children," *JAMA-Journal of the American Medical Association* 284, no. 7 (2000), p. 855.

research results are translated as per injury in the way that was demonstrated above, then the large number of available QALY-weights for different types of health conditions will enable the evaluation of the immaterial loss resulting from personal physical injuries and will make the assessment of pain and suffering damages seem like merely a computation exercise. However, apart from being potentially relatively easy to implement, the proposed QALY framework should exhibit other significant virtues to be able to adequately justify a prospective generalized use in courts. The following sections discuss how basing the assessment of pain and suffering damages on QALY research can provide the long-needed framework that serves as a catalyst to attain the goals stipulated by tort law and the economic analysis of tort law with respect to pain and suffering damages.

5.3.1. IMPLICATIONS FOR COMPENSATION AND SATISFACTION

According to the preceding analysis, pain and suffering damages should meet certain criteria to fulfill the goal of fair compensation. They should reflect as much as possible the immaterial loss incurred and be characterized by consistency in that they are of similar size for comparable injuries and of proportionally dissimilar size to express the relative severity of different types of injuries.[549] Moreover, to attain the secondary goal of satisfaction, pain and suffering damages should additionally take into consideration the personal circumstances of the victim so that the resulting amount is sufficient to acknowledge her harm and appease her for her loss. These criteria are not met by many of the existing legal approaches, which award pain and suffering damages on the basis of previously awarded amounts. They are however met by the proposed QALY framework.

In health economics research the negative consequences of different types of injuries are expressed in QALY losses. Combining information on the QALY loss experienced due to an injury with its expected duration and the monetary value of the QALY will yield a pain and suffering amount that comes as close as possible to reflecting the immaterial loss incurred. The QALY loss suffered under different health conditions is an indicator of their severity, allowing comparison of the conditions and their relative ranking. Therefore, the resulting amounts generated on the basis of QALY losses will be consistent with the relative severity of the injuries, hence achieving the desired horizontal and vertical fairness. The proposed QALY framework thus promotes fair compensation by making the amount awarded for pain and suffering dependent on the gravity and duration of the immaterial loss incurred. Besides accounting for the relative severity of

---

[549] See *supra* chapter 2.

different types of injuries, the proposed approach is also able to differentiate pain and suffering damages when the difference in severity does not result from the injury as such but from a preexisting health condition of the victim. For instance under the QALY framework, a person who was already paralyzed from the waist down and was unable to use her leg will receive less for pain and suffering if she experiences leg amputation than a person who is in full use and command of her leg.

Apart from achieving fair compensation, the proposed approach generates pain and suffering damages that can facilitate satisfaction. As mentioned previously, in QALY research people themselves indicate how a certain health condition may impact their overall well-being as well as how they monetarily evaluate this impact. These evaluations are made in a completely different context, in which, unlike the context of a trial, people do not have an interest in magnifying their loss.[550] Therefore, the resulting amounts of pain and suffering damages based on these evaluations can be safely assumed to reflect more sincerely the amount a victim would consider appropriate to acknowledge the harm she has suffered than the amounts awarded under the current legal approaches.

Besides these positive features, however, what is also important in the proposed approach is that it allows the judge the necessary margin to individuate pain and suffering damages based on particular personal characteristics of the plaintiff.[551] As was briefly explained in section 5.1.1, given that health economics research often results in an average QALY loss accompanied by an upper and a lower limit, compiling the readily available information on QALY losses will result in ranges of QALY losses, each pertinent to a different type of injury. By assigning a monetary value to the QALY, a range of pain and suffering damages, rather than a fixed amount, will be estimated for a particular type of injury. The task of judges will then be to position the case they have before them within the range and, depending on the particular circumstances of the case, award an amount close to the high, medium or low points of the range. If for instance a person whose hobby is to play the piano were to have their hand amputated, it is plausible to assume that she would suffer a grave loss from this particular reduction in physical ability. The judge would thus award her an amount of damages corresponding to one of the highest QALY losses in the range of values for hand amputation. It becomes obvious that individuation of the awards is hence not compromised by the fact that the size of pain and suffering damages is delineated by QALY research. The judge retains the discretion to decide the

---

550   See *infra* at section 5.4.1 for more details regarding how the proposed approach deals with strategic behavior.

551   See Leebron, *Final Moments: Damages for Pain and Suffering Prior to Death*, p. 265 stating very eloquently that "the valuation of the loss depends on the extent of the objective injury, and the degree to which the effect of that injury is amplified or muted by the circumstances of a particular plaintiff's life".

amount from the given range depending on the circumstances of the particular plaintiff. If certain personal circumstances aggravate or extenuate the experience of the injury, they can be taken into account by awarding higher or lower amounts within the range. Pain and suffering damages will normally not exceed the higher amounts stipulated in the range unless there is a particular reason that warrants special treatment, such as for instance extreme or multiple injuries. In that case, the judge will be required to provide a justification for deciding to award higher amounts. The assessment of pain and suffering damages for multiple injuries is a topic that will be dealt with more thoroughly in section 5.5.2 below.

One could argue that the proposed framework turns an issue that is more susceptible to subjective evaluation into a logistic matter by depriving the judge of the ability to 'judge from the heart' which amount of money is appropriate to be awarded to the victim at hand. However, as was explained above, although the proposed framework uses the objective impact of the injury on the quality of life as the baseline for estimating the magnitude of pain and suffering damages, the judge still has the final word regarding the size of the award. The judge therefore still 'judges from the heart' under the suggested approach. What is instead restricted is the liberty to deliver boundless and standardless judgments regarding the size of the awards, which has so far been a source of arbitrariness, complicating the attainment of tort law goals with respect to pain and suffering damages. Allowing the judge the margin to award the amount she thinks best corresponds to the case at hand is an aspect of the proposed framework that provides an additional point of differentiation from the approach suggested by Miller. Under Miller's approach, qualified experts elicit the QALY loss of the injured plaintiff on the spot. The product of this evaluation is a single number representing the immaterial loss incurred, which can then be used as such or be further monetized by the experts, yielding one specific amount for pain and suffering.[552] In contrast with the proposed QALY framework, Miller's approach thus results in only one amount that is defensible from a scientific point of view, putting the pressure on the jury to refrain from significantly deviating from it.

In general, utilizing QALY research for the assessment of pain and suffering damages is expected to have positive implications with respect to compensation and satisfaction, significantly facilitating their attainment. Insights from QALY research can actually provide the non-arbitrary basis that was lacking and yield predictable and consistent pain and suffering damages that consequently promote legal certainty. Moreover, the proposed framework gives the opportunity to the judge to exercise her discretion by individuating the award on the basis of special characteristics of the plaintiff.

---

[552] Miller, *Valuing Nonfatal Quality of Life Losses with Quality-Adjusted Life Years: The Health Economist's Meow*, p. 161.

5.3.2. IMPLICATIONS FOR DETERRENCE AND LOSS SPREADING: STRIKING A BALANCE BETWEEN THE GOALS

It is clear that to achieve deterrence, immaterial losses should be fully reflected and compensated with pain and suffering damages to make the injurer internalize the harm she inflicted. On the other hand, however, to attain loss spreading it may not be necessary to award pain and suffering damages for immaterial losses. The prevailing view so far suggests that tort damages are a form of compulsory insurance and therefore only if individuals are inclined to insure themselves against immaterial losses should they also receive pain and suffering damages. A discrepancy therefore exists between the two goals with respect to the treatment of immaterial losses. However, as was explained in chapter 3, several authors submit that even if a rational person were to not self-insure against non-pecuniary losses, she would still be willing to spend resources to avoid such losses, or at least to reduce the probability of suffering such losses.[553] These resources form the basis of *ex ante determined damages*, which are correct both from a deterrence as well as from an insurance point of view. They satisfy the requirements set by both goals, because the injurer correctly internalizes the costs the victim would be willing to spend on accident avoidance, while the victim is not 'over-insured' against her will. The injurer should thus pay the amount that the victim was willing to spend on accident avoidance divided by the expected number of accidents since the accident has now materialized. In line with this idea of ex ante determined damages, Posner and Sunstein have proposed that a measure which exactly reflects how many resources people are willing to spend on reducing the probability and/or magnitude of fatal accidents, namely the VSL(Y), should be employed to assess damages for fatal injuries in a tort context.[554] However, a comparable methodology is still lacking for non-fatal injuries.[555]

The proposed framework fills this gap. Remember that in QALY research the QALY loss for any given health condition is arrived at on the basis of peoples' responses. Likewise, the WTP per QALY is also derived from people who indicate what value they would place in avoiding the (probability of) occurrence of a QALY loss. The damage awards generated on the basis of this information

---

[553] Danzon, *Tort Reform and the Role of Government in Private Insurance Markets*, p. 526; Miller, *Willingness to Pay Comes of Age: Will the System Survive*; Ott and Schäfer, *Schmerzensgeld Bei Körperverletzungen. Eine Ökonomische Analyse*, p. 568; Geistfeld, *Placing a Price on Pain and Suffering: A Method for Helping Juries Determine Tort Damages for Nonmonetary Injuries*, p. 779; Arlen, *Tort Damages*, pp. 708–710; Schäfer and Ott (2005), p. 371.
[554] Posner and Sunstein, *Dollars and Death*, pp. 537–598. It should be reminded that it is not in the scope of this thesis to discuss and conclude whether VSL should be used to assess pain and suffering damages in cases of personal injuries. For more information regarding the VSL see *supra* at chapter 3.
[555] Schäfer and Ott, *Lehrbuch Der Ökonomischen Analyse Des Zivilrechts*, p. 371.

will therefore reflect how many resources people are willing to spend on reducing the probability and/or magnitude of non-fatal injuries inflicting QALY losses. In other words, using QALY research in the assessment of pain and suffering damages provides the framework that was lacking to estimate the ex ante determined damages that can overcome the discrepancy between the goals of deterrence and loss spreading with respect to compensating immaterial losses.[556] In that sense, the proposed framework can be viewed as analogous to the utilization of the VSL(Y) for fatal injury cases.

One could argue that the QALY should not be utilized in the proposed context because it was not initially developed to determine the size of damages. Although this is a legitimate objection to the proposed approach, this chapter so far should have made clear that the QALY is characterized by certain elements which are more than suitable for use in the context of assessing pain and suffering damages. A measure that is competent to express the loss in both life quality and duration due to health impairment and also evaluate it in monetary terms is in fact missing from the current legal approach. The preceding discussion should have also clarified that the suggestion to use the QALY for the assessment of pain and suffering damages does not imply that results from QALY research will be automatically accepted. It has been explained that QALY research results should be scrutinized to decide whether they are appropriate for use in the proposed alternative setting. For instance, only if the monetary value per QALY has been arrived at by eliciting the WTP per QALY and not differently, will it be accepted to guide the assessment of pain and suffering damages. In addition, quality-weights will be used for the assessment only if they pertain to the injury at hand or a health condition with comparable impact. Other issues under scrutiny will be which method was used to elicit QALY-weights, what part of the population responded to the questions and whether research that generates QALY-weights reaches a certain threshold of scientific quality. The possibility of using the QALY in the alternative context of damage assessment should therefore not be excluded simply because of the fact that the QALY was initially intended for use in health care allocation. Despite its origins in a different field, the QALY is characterized by certain elements which make its use compatible with the proposed context. After all, even the VSL(Y) which has also been suggested as a way to determine damages for pain and suffering was initially a measure the intended use of which was to assist cost-benefit analyses of programs that affected human lives. As long as the QALY's different origin is acknowledged, attention is paid to the issues mentioned above and effort is put into making it even more fitting in the legal context, the QALY could be utilized to assist the damage assessment. Deciding to use the QALY in the context of assessing pain and suffering damages will likely stimulate research and further refine it for the targeted purpose.

---

[556] See *supra* chapter 3 in section 3.2.2 and chapter 4 in section 4.6.2.

The proposed QALY framework for the assessment of pain and suffering damages will generate awards that reflect to a great extent the immaterial loss incurred, as they are based precisely on the total quality of life decrease experienced due to the injury. In addition, the awards will be foreseeable and non-arbitrary as they will be based on the readily available QALY losses related with various injuries and the predetermined monetary value for a QALY. These elements are important from a law and economics point of view because to achieve deterrence all immaterial losses must be reflected in damage awards in a predictable and consistent way so that potential injurers can anticipate the size of liability costs and incorporate them into their decision on care and activity. On the other hand, including all losses in damage awards is also crucial for loss spreading, as those losses will be subject to spreading between the parties. The utilization of the QALY in the assessment of damages may result in higher damage awards. However, this will not be detrimental to loss spreading. On the contrary, higher damage awards may actually lead to a better spreading of the losses, because by receiving higher amounts, victims will now have a lower residual loss.

The envisaged QALY tables will offer injury-specific ranges of amounts for pain and suffering damages allowing potential plaintiffs and defendants to know in advance the upper and lower limits of a prospective award for pain and suffering pertaining to an injury. The resulting predictability and consistency of the awards will facilitate deterrence, as potential injurers will be able to anticipate the expected accident losses and incorporate them in their care and activity decisions.[557] If the upper and lower limits of the prospective awards are known ex ante, insurance supply will also be facilitated, as insurance companies will be able to use this information and set their premiums accordingly. Of course, the size of the award is not the only factor that determines the supply of insurance. Another factor is the unpredictability of the accident risk. To the extent, however, that uncertainty regarding the size of pain and suffering damages is a reason for shortage of insurance supply, the proposed approach could facilitate loss spreading. By making the premium fixing more transparent, ex ante foreseeable pain and suffering damages could also increase the demand for insurance.

Obviously, predictability and consistency of the resulting awards is another distinctive difference of the proposed approach from the proposition put

---

[557] Remember that a criticism against the deterrent goal is that the amounts awarded are so arbitrary and unpredictable that they cannot possibly provide any guidance towards the end of reducing accidents. See King, *Pain and Suffering, Noneconomic Damages, and the Goals of Tort Law*, pp. 185–191, 209: "Deterrence and incentive goals of tort law are corrupted when the assessment of damages is arbitrary and lacks any objective referent". For a milder assertion of the same argument see Geistfeld, *Placing a Price on Pain and Suffering: A Method for Helping Juries Determine Tort Damages for Nonmonetary Injuries*, p. 786: "the element of arbitrariness and resultant unpredictability of pain-and-suffering awards undermine the deterrence function of the tort system"; and Schäfer and Ott, *The Economic Analysis of Civil Law*, p. 131.

forward by Miller. His suggestion to evaluate every injury on a case per case basis would impede potential injurers (and insurers) from taking into consideration the magnitude of pain and suffering damages and consequently would hinder the attainment of deterrence and the facilitation of loss spreading.[558]

5.3.3. ECONOMIZING ON ADMINISTRATIVE COSTS OF THE LEGAL SYSTEM

Besides the aforementioned benefits accruing especially to compensation and deterrence, the proposed QALY framework is also expected to result in significant litigation cost savings. A first fact supporting this expectation is that the suggested framework is relatively inexpensive to implement as it involves incurring one-time only costs. QALY research provides a reservoir of evaluations of QALY losses relating to different injuries, which, in combination with a predetermined monetary value for a QALY, can yield pain and suffering damages for a large number of injuries. In some cases, the existing research may even function as focal points that can be used to fill in the blanks. If, for example, the QALY loss for an amputation of the foot and for an amputation of the entire leg have been measured in QALY research, but the QALY loss for an amputation of the lower leg is not yet known, one could safely assume that it lies in between the two known QALY losses for the foot and the whole leg. Only for a few types of injuries, for which the QALY loss has not yet been evaluated, may it be necessary to undertake additional research, and hence to incur additional costs. However, even if more research is required, the cost incurred to generate the relevant information will be a one-time only cost, while the resulting information will likely be utilized in a multitude of future cases. The same applies for the cost that will be incurred in order to make this research more fitting to be used in a legal context. The preparation preceding the implementation of the suggested framework involves reading the relevant publications and deciding which QALY-weights can be used to express the immaterial loss incurred with different injuries. The preceding analysis provided a range of QALY-weights for the immaterial loss arising from deafness, while four more cases are explored in chapter 7. Given that in this book the preparation for these five cases has been performed by a lawyer, it can be generally expected that lawyers are able to read the relevant publications and point to the QALY-weights that could be used for the case at hand. If this is not possible, however, the task of preparation could be assigned to a committee of experts, who will take the bulk of QALY research and translate it for all

---

[558]   Miller, *Valuing Nonfatal Quality of Life Losses with Quality-Adjusted Life Years: The Health Economist's Meow*, pp. 145–167.

conceivable personal injuries in the way indicated previously in section 5.2.2. Although this implies that an additional cost will have to be incurred in order to implement the proposed framework, nevertheless this cost will be incurred only once, while the information generated will be used repeatedly and without cost by courts for future damage assessments.

If the proposed framework is implemented for the assessment of pain and suffering damages, litigation costs will also reduce because a smaller number of qualified experts (if any) will be required in court in order to assist it. Since the type of injury or impairment of a person due to an accident will be established before the trial, for instance during the usual hospitalization after the occurrence of an accident, no additional medical expert will be necessary during the trial to re-diagnose the condition, unless of course a significant change has occurred in the meantime. The judge will only need to be aware of the genre of the injury, e.g. hand amputation, spine fracture, paralysis, deafness, scarring, loss of sight, etc. to be able to take advantage of the relevant range of values based on QALYs. Moreover, given that under the proposed framework the monetary value of the QALY will be used to translate the QALY losses into pain and suffering awards, forensic experts, who are used in some jurisdictions to determine which monetary amount corresponds to the immaterial loss, will also be redundant. It is evident that in this respect the proposed approach can be further differentiated by the proposition made by Miller. His suggestion to elicit QALY-weights on the spot for every injury would obviously require qualified experts to be present in the courtroom. Hence, it would have the exact opposite implications for the administrative costs of the legal system than the QALY framework, namely it would increase them. The availability and accessibility of the QALY research, in combination with the fact that less specialized testimony will be required under the proposed approach, will accelerate adjudication, benefiting the parties and further reducing the costs of litigation. Speedier adjudication of each case will consequently result in more cases being decided in less time and improve the overall reliability of the judicial system.

It is evident that the QALY approach does not suggest assessing the immaterial losses in a very precise way for each and every individual accident case. The QALY research in essence gives the judge access to information regarding the average losses incurred due to a personal injury as these have been evaluated by a number of respondents in different studies. This practice may somewhat compromise accuracy but on the other hand will yield pain and suffering amounts that are correct on average and will not result in major under- or overestimations. After all it is legitimate to try to improve and accelerate the decision-making process for a large number of people rather than trying to improve it as much as possible for one person only. The proposed method therefore places at the center of the assessment the type of injury incurred and subsequently takes into account the victim's age and the injury duration or, in the case of a permanent injury, the life expectancy of the victim. By doing so, it follows exactly the recommendation by Kaplow and Shavell who argued in a seminal paper that basing damages on the average harm is superior to calculating them with accuracy as it saves in litigation costs and does not distort incentives.[559] The authors continued by suggesting that it is not actually necessary for courts to know the average loss because 'at the outset of a case, courts will possess, essentially free of cost, a simple physical description of the plaintiff's injury for instance, that a 35-year-old person suffered a broken leg'.[560] The QALY research provides a framework that ranks injuries according to their relative severity on the basis of easily verifiable immaterial effects and additionally allows the objective characteristic of the victim's age to figure in the assessment. It therefore completely adheres to the law and economics recommendations with respect to the appropriate level of accuracy in the assessment of damages. An accurate assessment of immaterial losses would yield pain and suffering damages that are not predictable ex ante. Predictability of the awards however is a necessary element to allow the tortfeasor to incorporate the expected accident cost in her care and activity decisions.[561] Therefore, it is preferable that damages are based on average losses, and hence that they are foreseeable, rather than be accurate ex post. This practice also enables insurers to set their premiums on the basis of average expected losses, consequently offering insurance in a more transparent manner, which may eventually facilitate loss spreading. Although the benefits of the QALY approach for deterrence and loss spreading have been explained in previous sections, it should be emphasized here that by generating damages on the basis of the average losses incurred due to an injury, the proposed framework significantly lowers the costs of deterrence and loss spreading, hence further reducing overall administrative costs.

A generalized implementation of the proposed framework implies that the magnitude of pain and suffering damages would be predictable ex ante. This can potentially further reduce the administrative costs of the legal system by incentivizing opposing parties to enter settlements.[562] If victims know in advance approximately how much they will receive for incurring an injury and tortfeasors are aware of how much they will have to pay if they inflict an injury, both may be induced to settle to avoid engaging in litigation.[563] Increased settlement rates will further alleviate the administrative cost burden of the courts.

---

[559] Kaplow and Shavell, *Accuracy in the Assessment of Damages*, pp. 202–204.
[560] Ibid., p. 202.
[561] Kaplow, *The Value of Accuracy in Adjudication: An Economic Analysis*, pp. 309 ff.
[562] Bovbjerg, Sloan and Blumstein, *Valuing Life and Limb in Tort: Scheduling "Pain and Suffering"*, p. 925.
[563] Frederick S. Levin, "Pain and Suffering Guidelines: A Cure for Damages Measurement Anomie Note," *University of Michigan Journal of Law Reform* 22 (1989), p. 320.

5.4. BENEFITS EXTENDING BEYOND THE GOALS OF TORT LAW

The preceding section illustrated that the proposed approach has positive implications for the attainment of the goals stipulated by tort law and the economic analysis of tort law with respect to pain and suffering damages. The fact that the proposed QALY framework significantly facilitates the attainment of these goals in comparison to the approaches currently followed is already sufficient to support its generalized implementation for the assessment of pain and suffering damages. However, besides these principal advantages, the proposed method brings about some additional benefits that deserve mention.

5.4.1. DEALING WITH STRATEGIC BEHAVIOR

One of the benefits accompanying the proposed approach is its ability to deal more effectively with strategic behavior than the current legal approaches. In the context of a trial it is typically expected that any plaintiff will behave strategically to receive a higher amount of money for pain and suffering damages by exaggerating the loss incurred, and that any defendant will strategically contest claims for higher damages. In some cases the judge and medical experts may actually be convinced by the plaintiff and consequently agree to award a higher amount. The proposed QALY approach can ameliorate potential problems of strategic behavior, since the information on QALY values comes from (other) community members and/or patients who evaluate the health condition prior to the trial and in a different context. Of course, it may still be the case that respondents may have other goals to pursue in a QALY measurement setting. For instance, a patient may behave strategically and exaggerate the improvement that a medicine or a treatment has had on her health to make sure that the medicine or treatment is found to be cost-effective and continues to be provided to the patients with that condition.[564] However, as explained in the previous chapter, there is no empirical evidence for strategic responses with respect to QALY-weights.[565] Nevertheless, even if people were to exaggerate their answers, the effect would be much more indirect than in the case of asking a victim to describe her condition in the courtroom and to state how much money she would require for her loss.

---

[564] Brazier et al., *Measuring and Valuing Health Benefits for Economic Evaluation*, p. 115.
[565] See *supra* section 4.4.

5.4.2. INDUCING VICTIM MITIGATION OF LOSSES

Another important advantage of the proposed QALY framework is that it can assist courts to arrive at pain and suffering damages that take into consideration the victims' prospects to mitigate the losses, as well as the extent of the potential mitigation. In the law and economics literature it is already accepted as common knowledge that mitigation is desirable if mitigation costs are lower than the decrease achieved through mitigation in the actual losses.[566] In cases of injuries, there is a possibility that there may be medical treatments or interventions that can alleviate the immaterial loss at hand, while at the same time posing no risk and being anodyne for the victims. In that case, if the cost of these treatments is lower than the reduction of the immaterial loss, plaintiffs should be encouraged to undergo them. The health economics literature can provide information regarding the costs of implementation and the effectiveness in terms of generating QALYs, of different medical treatments, interventions, techniques or devices that could potentially be used for mitigating immaterial losses. By incorporating this information, the proposed QALY framework will assist courts in awarding pain and suffering damages that are restricted to the optimally mitigated immaterial losses and, in granting an amount that corresponds to the costs of mitigation. In this way, the proposed framework will provide incentives to victims to optimally mitigate their losses.[567]

The example of deafness in section 5.2 can be used by means of illustration to explain practically how the proposed QALY approach can induce mitigation. Even major hearing losses can in some cases be alleviated by using simple hearing aids, which can be worn on or in the ear and are absolutely safe. As described in the example, they may significantly reduce the immaterial loss incurred. More specifically, the QALY loss experienced due to profound hearing loss is 0.235 QALYs per year if the person cannot benefit from traditional hearing aids and 0.164 QALYs if simple acoustic devices can be used to improve hearing. In the hypothetical example with the 48-year-old who incurs deafness, these QALY losses would result to pain and suffering damages in the magnitude of approximately €222,000 if traditional hearing devices are not used, and of about €155,000 if they are.[568] This is obviously a significant difference in the awards, which most likely exceeds the costs of purchasing simple hearing aids. Therefore, victims who can benefit from hearing devices should be induced to mitigate their losses by receiving as pain and suffering damages an amount equivalent to their mitigated hearing loss. In addition, the amount corresponding to the costs of the hearing aids should be added to the damages awarded for pecuniary losses resulting from the injury. The proposed approach

---

[566] Shavell, *Foundations of Economic Analysis of Law*, p. 248.
[567] Shavell, *Foundations of Economic Analysis of Law*, pp. 248–249.
[568] Assuming that the value per QALY is €50,000 and applying a discount factor of 4%.

based on QALY research can provide the necessary information to enable the generation of pain and suffering awards that can induce mitigation, hence lowering the overall accident costs.

5.5. CHALLENGES

The advantages of the proposed framework for the assessment of pain and suffering damages are evident. The analysis in the previous sections should have made clear that the QALY approach is to be preferred on a multitude of grounds to the approaches that are currently implemented to assess pain and suffering damages. Above all, it is to be preferred because it is able to achieve the goals of tort law and of the economic analysis of tort law with respect to pain and suffering damages. Additionally, it can potentially be implemented in a number of countries, provided that each of them uses a monetary value per QALY that best corresponds with its existing economic and other circumstances. Finally, it is to be preferred because it has adjacent positive consequences which further facilitate the adjudication procedure and reduce its costs. Nevertheless, as was mentioned previously in section 5.3.2, cautiousness should be exercised in the process of implementing the proposed approach.

5.5.1. USING THE APPROPRIATE RESEARCH RESULTS

Particular attention should be paid with respect to which research results are appropriate to use for the assessment of pain and suffering damages. QALY research results should be carefully scrutinized to decide whether they reach a certain quality threshold. Using the CEA registry as a source of QALY research can significantly facilitate this screening, since publications included in its database have already been classified in terms of quality. Moreover, it is important that the QALY-weights used to arrive at pain and suffering damages for the injury incurred are derived from research pertaining to that injury or a related health condition. Based on this information and after taking into account the personal circumstances of the victim, the judge will decide on an amount of pain and suffering damages that best reflects the immaterial loss incurred due to the injury. It is possible however, that the judge is confronted with the case of a victim that has experienced multiple injuries. Deciding on the magnitude of pain and suffering damages in cases of multiple injuries is a more challenging task in comparison to typical, single injury cases and is therefore discussed below.

5.5.2. HOW TO DEAL WITH MULTIPLE INJURIES?

Multiple injuries occur frequently as a result of traffic-related accidents. The assessment of pain and suffering damages for multiple injuries is generally a challenging task for judges, who are required to take into consideration the consequences of the inflicted injuries altogether. Under the proposed QALY framework, an amount of pain and suffering damages for multiple injuries can ideally be arrived at if there is already QALY research dealing with the particular combination of injuries. Judges will then be able to utilize the QALY loss from the relevant research and combine it with the monetary value of the QALY to arrive at pain and suffering damages for the multiple injuries in that case. For instance, the QALY loss resulting from multiple bone fractures may already be available in the QALY research on osteoporosis. This QALY loss could therefore be cautiously used to assess pain and suffering damages in cases of accidents that result in multiple bone fractures.

Nevertheless, if there is no QALY research for the combination of the injuries at hand, the judge will have to take into consideration QALY research regarding the loss resulting from each of the injuries. This however does not mean that the total immaterial loss will be estimated by adding up the QALY loss of each injury. Take for instance the case of a person who incurs waist-down paralysis, but at the same time has one of her legs amputated. The pain and suffering damages in this case should not be assessed by merely adding up the QALY loss resulting from waist-down paralysis and leg amputation. Being paralyzed means that one cannot use one's legs anymore. Therefore, in this case the judge would take into consideration only the QALY loss of incurring waist-down paralysis and award an amount corresponding to the highest loss in the range of values in order to reflect the aesthetic loss suffered with leg amputation. Many more similar cases are conceivable. Multiple injuries will usually lead to an increase in the size of pain and suffering damages, which is not in proportion to the sum of their QALY losses. In general, the judge will decide how the information contributed by QALY research is to be used for the assessment of pain and suffering damages, depending on the case at hand.

The challenge of estimating damages for multiple injuries would be addressed in the long run through the generalized implementation of the QALY framework for the assessment of pain and suffering damages. The decision to use QALYs would stimulate research and generate research results for injuries for which QALY information is currently missing. Therefore, if a certain combination of injuries were to frequently reoccur, research could be undertaken to evaluate the relevant QALY loss.[569] Generic instruments such as the HUI and EQ-5D, which evaluate health states on the basis of general attributes and can thus reflect the severity of multiple injuries, could be used to evaluate the QALY loss inflicted.

---

[569]   See *supra* section 5.3.3.

CHAPTER 6

PAIN AND SUFFERING DAMAGES BASED ON QALYs

Circumventing Victims' (and Judges') Hedonic Misperceptions

Calculating pain and suffering damages due to personal injury is a difficult task. To achieve the goals of tort law, as those are stipulated both in legal theory and in law and economics scholarship, the method that should be used to perform this calculation should be able to account for the decrease in health and bodily integrity, as well as the duration of the injury suffered, in a predictable and consistent manner, and at the same time allow the judge to incorporate into her decision particular circumstances pertaining to the case at hand which may influence the amount awarded.

The previous chapter illustrated how a measure that is 'state of the art' in the domain of health economics, commonly used to inform the allocation of health care budgets and evaluate the cost-effectiveness of medical interventions, meets the requirements above and is thus well suited to provide a systematic basis for assessing pain and suffering damages. The use of QALYs in the calculation of pain and suffering damages allows the overall reduction in quality of life as a result of the diminution in health and bodily integrity as well as the age of the victim and the duration of injury to figure in the amounts awarded. The range of QALY values in turn allows judges to retain their discretion in choosing the correct value within the range that corresponds to the personal conditions and the specific circumstances of the case.

Besides these qualities, the current chapter suggests that using QALYs in the calculation of pain and suffering damages may have an additional advantage. Under the influence of insights from cognitive psychology, behavioral law and economics have proposed that victims (i.e. plaintiffs) as well as judges may make false predictions about the victims' future subjective well-being. These false predictions are attributed to the psychological phenomena of hedonic adaptation neglect and the focusing illusion which can influence the calculation of pain and suffering damages and lead to awards that do not correctly reflect the loss of enjoyment of life of the victim due to the injury. As a result, several frameworks have so far been proposed to take into account these psychological phenomena in the assessment of pain and suffering awards.

The following sections sketch the theoretical underpinnings and review the existing empirical studies on the occurrence of hedonic adaptation neglect and focusing illusion. The framework proposals that have been submitted so far to take these psychological insights into account in the assessment of pain and suffering damages are presented, as is the criticism against them. It is argued that a framework based on QALYs can accommodate these insights and lead to a better calculation of pain and suffering damages than other currently proposed approaches, by circumventing the problem of victims' and judges' hedonic misperceptions. However, attention is drawn to the fact that present research results are insufficient to draw definite conclusions with respect to incorporating insights from psychology into tort law and the assessment of pain and suffering damages, while it also remains to be discussed whether such an inclusion would be desirable from a normative standpoint. Therefore, the chapter concludes that current thinking favors the non-incorporation of these insights into the assessment of pain and suffering damages and that more discussion on the topic is warranted.

6.1. RELEVANCE OF PSYCHOLOGICAL INSIGHTS FOR PAIN AND SUFFERING DAMAGES

Under the influence of insights from cognitive psychology, a series of scholarly papers have suggested that the loss of enjoyment of life resulting from an injury is not as grave as previously thought, mainly because people adapt to adverse conditions, but also because after a while they do not focus that much on their injury.[570] More specifically, this strand of literature explains that the psychological phenomenon of *hedonic adaptation* causes a rebound in the subjective well-being of the victim, while another psychological phenomenon referred to as the *focusing illusion* or *focalism* prevents victims and external observers from realizing that the injury only affects particular areas of their life.[571] The two psychological phenomena have especially been claimed to have a significant influence in the context of a trial involving adjudication for pain and

---

[570] Samuel R. Bagenstos and Margo Schlanger, "Hedonic Damages, Hedonic Adaptation, and Disability," *Vanderbilt Law Review* 60, no. 3 (2007), pp. 745–797; Sunstein, *Illusory Losses*, pp. S157–S194; Peter A Ubel and George Loewenstein, "Pain and Suffering Awards: They Shouldn't be (just) about Pain and Suffering," *The Journal of Legal Studies* 37 (2008), pp. S195–S216.

[571] David A. Schkade and Daniel Kahneman, "Does Living in California make People Happy? A Focusing Illusion in Judgments of Life Satisfaction," *Psychological Science* 9, no. 5 (1998), pp. 340–346; Timothy D. Wilson et al., "Focalism: A Source of Durability Bias in Affective Forecasting," *Journal Personality & Social Psychology* 78, no. 5 (2000), pp. 821–836.

suffering damages. The allegedly resulting implication for the assessment of pain and suffering damages is that victims (and judges) disregard the gradual improvement in life satisfaction after an adverse event and thus claim for (decide for) a higher damage award than what would correspond to the actual losses incurred. Likewise, a focusing illusion concentrates the attention of the victim and the judge on the consequences of the personal injury and exaggerates its impact, possibly also leading to excessive damages for pain and suffering that do not correctly reflect the true loss of enjoyment of life of the victim. In light of these insights several proposals have been put forward to decrease or even abolish damages awarded for loss of enjoyment of life thus reducing the overall amount of pain and suffering damages.

It becomes obvious that these psychological phenomena are relevant for tort law, especially in the context of awarding damages for nonpecuniary losses arising from personal injuries. If the idea is taken seriously that pain and suffering damages should reflect the actual immaterial loss of the victim,[572] then there is no need to provide compensation for a lasting loss in subjective well-being if, due to adaptation, that loss is only temporary. To be sure, this does not mean that the victim should receive almost no damages at all for immaterial losses. An injured individual not only suffers a loss in subjective well-being but also suffers pain and experiences diminution in physical abilities. Damages for the objective fact of suffering a diminution in health such as hand amputation, loss of hearing, etc. should always be granted. Hence, hedonic adaptation (and focusing illusion) calls for a decrease only in the damages awarded for loss of enjoyment of life. After all, adaptation, as will be explained below, refers only to the emotional response of the victim to the adverse health event influencing subjective well-being and life satisfaction. Likewise, the occurrence of focusing illusion may hinder the realization of the actual loss due to the injury only with regard to subjective well-being and life satisfaction.

The discussion on whether hedonic adaptation and focusing illusion should be accounted for and reflected in immaterial damage awards initiated in the USA, where loss of enjoyment of life, which is allegedly influenced by these psychological phenomena, is either recognized as part of an all-encompassing notion of pain and suffering damages or is considered a separate element of damages.[573] Nevertheless, the discussion is also important for Europe. The fact

---

[572]   Herman Cousy and Dimitri Droshout, "Belgium," in *Compensation for Personal Injury in a Comparative Perspective*, eds. Bernhard A. Koch and Helmut Koziol (Springer: Wien, New York, 2003), p. 68; Cooter and Ulen, *Law and Economics*, pp. 327–328; Shavell, *Foundations of Economic Analysis of Law*, p. 236.

[573]   Stan V. Smith, "Hedonic Damages in Personal Injury and Wrongful Death Litigation," in *Litigation Economics*, eds. Patrick A. Gaughan and Robert J. Thornton (Greenwich, CT and London: JAI Press Inc., 1993), pp. 40–41; Susan Poser, Brian H. Bornstein and E. Kiernan McGorty, "Measuring Damages for Lost Enjoyment of Life: The View from the Bench and the Jury Box," *Law and Human Behavior* 27, no. 1 (2003), pp. 53–68; Bagenstos and Schlanger, *Hedonic Damages, Hedonic Adaptation, and Disability*, p. 748.

that in many European countries pain and suffering damages are not divided into separate categories, as may be the case in the USA, obfuscates its relevance. However, to the extent that pain and suffering damages in Europe also seek to compensate for the loss of enjoyment of life,[574] the discussion remains as important and requires thorough investigation.

Thus, it becomes crucial for tort law scholars to delve into the psychological phenomena of hedonic adaptation and focusing illusion and investigate whether they actually occur after experiencing an injury and, if yes, to what extent. The answers to these questions will show how big an influence, if any, these psychological phenomena exert on the enjoyment of life and subsequently advise on whether hedonic adaptation and focusing illusion should be taken into consideration in the assessment of pain and suffering damages.

6.1.1. HEDONIC ADAPTATION NEGLECT

Hedonic adaptation, as defined by Frederick and Loewenstein, refers to the gradual decrease of emotional responses to both positive and negative circumstances.[575] In other words, hedonic adaptation is the adjustment that follows after an initial peak of affective response to an adverse or a favorable condition. This adjustment is not instant; it takes place overtime and is facilitated by cognitive and physiological processes and can even be assisted by factors unrelated to the individual experiencing the positive or negative circumstances.[576] For instance, an individual incurring an adverse health condition may undergo a cognitive change that alters her aspirations, values and priorities in life, and will eventually allow her not to view her condition as a source of discomfort and unhappiness.[577]

On the physiological level, an individual may find that her unimpaired senses sharpen or that her body mass increases to respond to an adverse health event. Waist-down paralyzed individuals are thus found to develop upper body strength and the popular belief that blind people develop acute hearing has long been scientifically proven.[578] As for external factors, infrastructure that

---

[574] Giovanni Comandé, "Doing Away with Inequality in Loss of Enjoyment of Life," in *Personal Injury and Wrongful Death Damages Calculations: Transatlantic Dialogue*, eds. John O. Ward and Robert J. Thornton, Vol. 91 (Emerald Group Publishing, 2009), pp. 255–263; Magnus and Fedtke, *Germany*, p. 112.

[575] Shane Frederick and George Loewenstein, "Hedonic Adaptation," in *Well-being: The Foundations of Hedonic Psychology*, eds. Daniel Kahneman, Ed Diener and Norbert Schwarz (New York: Russell Sage Foundation, 1999), pp. 302–303.

[576] Ibid., 302; Ubel and Loewenstein, *Pain and Suffering Awards: They Shouldn't be (just) about Pain and Suffering*, S198.

[577] Frederick and Loewenstein, *Hedonic Adaptation*, 302; Paul Menzel et al., "The Role of Adaptation to Disability and Disease in Health State Valuation: A Preliminary Normative Analysis," *Social Science & Medicine* 55, no. 12 (2002), p. 2151.

[578] Thomas Elbert et al., "Expansion of the Tonotopic Area in the Auditory Cortex of the Blind," *The Journal of Neuroscience* 22 (2002), pp. 9941–9944; Kenneth Hugdahl et al., "Blind

accommodates the needs of disabled persons and other things that promote their independence are the most important to facilitate hedonic adaptation.[579] Examples of such arrangements include ramps in buildings, voice or touch signaling traffic lights, wheelchair-accessible vehicles, and disabled-friendly streets, bus stops and working environments. With the help of these factors individuals may regain their life satisfaction and subjective well-being to a certain extent.

There is a vast amount of empirical research exploring hedonic adaptation to disability.[580] In a very frequently cited study, Brickman, Coates and Janoff-Bulman investigate how winning the lottery or suffering a serious accident affects life enjoyment and everyday pleasure.[581] They interview lottery winners, paralyzed accident victims and a group of control individuals to obtain information regarding their evaluation of past, present and future happiness. According to the results of the cross-sectional study, lottery winners almost return to their previous levels of life satisfaction some time after winning the lottery, while paraplegic and quadriplegic victims report lower levels of life enjoyment than healthy individuals, but the difference is not as significant as might be expected.[582] Findings of hedonic adaptation are also confirmed in more recent studies. In a cross-sectional study on the effect of a colostomy on quality of life, colostomy patients report higher quality of life than do healthy individuals and former patients who are asked to imagine living with a colostomy.[583] Another study finds that both hemodialysis patients and healthy individuals report a positive mood for the majority of time during a week, thus concluding that patients have adapted to their condition.[584] In a review of research conducted on

---

Individuals show Enhanced Perceptual and Attentional Sensitivity for Identification of Speech Sounds," *Cognitive Brain Research* 19, no. 1 (2004), pp. 28–32; Frédéric Gougoux et al., "Voice Perception in Blind Persons: A Functional Magnetic Resonance Imaging Study," *Neuropsychologia* 47, no. 13 (2009), pp. 2967–2974.

[579]   Bagenstos and Schlanger, *Hedonic Damages, Hedonic Adaptation, and Disability*, p. 767; Ubel and Loewenstein, *Pain and Suffering Awards: They Shouldn't be (just) about Pain and Suffering*, p. S198.

[580]   For eloquent overviews see Bagenstos and Schlanger, *Hedonic Damages, Hedonic Adaptation, and Disability*, pp. 745–797; John Bronsteen, Christopher Buccafusco and Jonathan C. Masur, "Hedonic Adaptation and the Settlement of Civil Lawsuits," *Columbia Law Review* 108 (2008), pp. 1516–1550; Rick Swedloff and Peter H. Huang, "Tort Damages and the New Science of Happiness," *Indiana Law Journal* 85 (2010), p. 553.

[581]   Philip Brickman, Dan Coates and Ronnie Janoff-Bulman, "Lottery Winners and Accident Victims: Is Happiness Relative?," *Journal of Personality and Social Psychology* 36, no. 8 (1978), pp. 917–927.

[582]   Ibid., pp. 920–921. The lottery winners and accident victims had experienced winning or injury not less than one month and not more than one and a half year before participating in the study (with the sole exception of a participant who had found out that he won the lottery less than a month before the study was conducted).

[583]   Dylan M. Smith et al., "Misremembering Colostomies? Former Patients Give Lower Utility Ratings than do Current Patients," *Health Psychology* 25, no. 6 (2006b), pp. 688–695.

[584]   Jason Riis et al., "Ignorance of Hedonic Adaptation to Hemodialysis: A Study using Ecological Momentary Assessment," *Journal of Experimental Psychology* 134, no. 1 (2005).

quality of life and life satisfaction of people with disabilities, it is shown that life satisfaction of disabled people does not decrease with disability.[585] Furthermore, according to the results of yet another study, the emotional status of patients with spinal cord injury is shown not to differ from the status of the control population sample.[586] Finally, in a review of studies on psychosocial adaptation of children with limb deficiencies, it is reported that young amputees adapt well to their disability.[587]

Other research, however, suggests that individuals do not adapt to adverse health conditions. Lucas criticizes many of the earlier studies on hedonic adaptation to adverse events on the grounds that they are cross-sectional and thus do not measure the change in subjective well-being before and after the adverse event.[588] He conducts a longitudinal study using nationally representative panel data of German and British households which report the subjective well-being of participants before becoming disabled and for an average of 7.39 and 5.31 years respectively after the onset of disability.[589] According to the results, life satisfaction is found to decrease considerably after a disability and not to rebound in the long run, signifying that there is essentially no hedonic adaptation.[590] However, a later study using the same data set arrives at somewhat different results. Oswald and Powdthavee use the British household panel data and conduct a longitudinal study showing that life satisfaction rebounds to about 30% for severely disabled and to about 50% for moderately disabled three years after the onset of the disability.[591] Thus, hedonic adaptation is found to occur but it is not as powerful as to return the disabled individuals to their pre-disability levels of life satisfaction. Another study using longitudinal data reports that hedonic adaptation is almost complete for mild disability two years after the onset of disability.[592] On the other hand, in the same study evidence for hedonic

---

[585]   Carol J. Gill, "Health Professionals, Disability, and Assisted Suicide: An Examination of Relevant Empirical Evidence and Reply to Batavia," *Psychology, Public Policy, and Law* 6, no. 2 (2000), pp. 528–529.

[586]   Christofer Lundqvist et al., "Spinal Cord Injuries: Clinical, Functional, and Emotional Status," *Spine* 16, no. 1 (1991), pp. 78–83.

[587]   Vida L. Tyc, "Psychosocial Adaptation of Children and Adolescents with Limb Deficiencies: A Review," *Clinical Psychology Review* 12, no. 3 (1992), pp. 275–291.

[588]   Richard E. Lucas, "Long Term Disability is Associated with Lasting Changes in Subjective Well-being: Evidence from Two Nationally Representative Longitudinal Studies," *Journal of Personality and Social Psychology* 92 (2007), pp. 719, 721–722.

[589]   Ibid., pp. 719–725.

[590]   Ibid., pp. 726–728.

[591]   Andrew J. Oswald and Nattavudh Powdthavee, "Does Happiness Adapt? A Longitudinal Study of Disability with Implications for Economists and Judges," *Journal of Public Economics* 92, no. 5–6 (2008), pp. 1070, 1072.

[592]   Nattavudh Powdthavee, "What Happens to People before and After Disability? Focusing Effects, Lead Effects, and Adaptation in Different Areas of Life," *Social Science & Medicine* 69, no. 12 (2009), pp. 1839–1843.

adaptation appears to be very weak for serious disability even after four years or more of becoming disabled.[593]

Apart from these studies presenting mixed empirical evidence on hedonic adaptation, another set of studies suggests that adaptation does not occur at all for certain health conditions. Adverse health conditions generating chronic pain, distress, and progressive and degenerative disorders seem to resist hedonic adaptation.[594] In a longitudinal study on adaptation to rheumatoid arthritis there are no findings of hedonic adaptation.[595] Likewise, in a review of research regarding psychosocial adaptation to multiple sclerosis, little evidence of adaptation is reported.[596] What multiple sclerosis and rheumatoid arthritis have in common is that they are both illnesses with periodic exacerbations and remissions that gradually lead to health deterioration.[597] The characteristics of instability and progressive deterioration, which do not leave patients the margin to get used to the current health state and consequently cope with the illness, are considered to be the reason why people do not adapt to these health conditions.[598] Other health conditions involving persistent pain, ringing in the ears (i.e. tinnitus), anxiety and depression are also believed to defy adaptation.[599] However, the explanation of why these symptoms may cause significant loss in subjective well-being and impede adaptation rests on somewhat different reasons than those of progressive and degenerative illnesses. As will be explained in the next section, focusing illusion may be responsible in these cases for the significant loss in subjective well-being.

If one excludes adverse health conditions involving chronic pain or progressive and degenerative health disorders where hedonic adaptation is either limited or nonexistent, signs of adaptation manifest for most of the rest of the health conditions investigated. People are found to hedonically adapt to adverse health conditions such as colostomy, paralysis, blindness and kidney dialysis;[600] however results do not clarify with certainty how long after the manifestation of

---

593   Ibid., pp. 1839–1844.

594   Frederick and Loewenstein, *Hedonic Adaptation*, p. 312; Swedloff and Huang, *Tort Damages and the New Science of Happiness*, p. 567.

595   Craig A. Smith and Kenneth A. Wallston, "Adaptation in Patients with Chronic Rheumatoid Arthritis: Application of a General Model," *Health Psychology* 11, no. 3 (1992), p. 159.

596   Richard F. Antonak and Hanoch Livneh, "Psychosocial Adaptation to Disability and its Investigation among Persons with Multiple Sclerosis," *Social Science & Medicine* 40, no. 8 (4, 1995), pp. 1099–1108.

597   "Rheumatoid arthritis," in *Concise Medical Dictionary* (Oxford University Press: 2010), Oxford Reference Online (accessed 14.03.2014); "Multiple sclerosis," in *Concise Medical Dictionary* (Oxford University Press: 2010), Oxford Reference Online (accessed 14.03.2014).

598   Frederick and Loewenstein, *Hedonic Adaptation*, p. 312. See also Antonak and Livneh, *Psychosocial Adaptation to Disability and its Investigation among Persons with Multiple Sclerosis*, pp. 1100 ff.

599   Sunstein, *Illusory Losses*, pp. S166–S168, S174–S175.

600   Ubel and Loewenstein, *Pain and Suffering Awards: They Shouldn't be (just) about Pain and Suffering*, p. S196.

the adverse health event hedonic adaptation occurs and how powerful it is. Another shortcoming is that not all studies investigating subjective well-being and potential hedonic adaptation use the same methodology. This may create problems not only when comparing their results but more importantly it can cast doubt on the validity of their results, as it is possible that studies using the same data may reach different conclusions due to application of different methodologies.[601]

Nevertheless, in spite of the mixed evidence on the existence and extent of adaptation, many of the studies on hedonic adaptation arrive at a reoccurring result: If healthy people are asked to assess the impact of certain adverse health conditions on their level of subjective well-being, they generally assess it as being much larger than actual patients or victims report it to be.[602] Similar results are replicated when healthy respondents are asked to evaluate the quality of life of a certain health condition in general, rather than just their subjective well-being.[603] This finding, which is partly attributed to adaptation neglect,[604] implies that victims themselves may also report a much larger loss in enjoyment of life at the onset of their disability than after they have experienced the relevant medical condition for a longer time. These results are reached even in cases where hedonic adaptation is not complete; patients or victims are found to assess their subjective well-being as being much higher than healthy individuals imagine it to be, even in cases where hedonic adaptation is imperfect.[605]

---

[601]   See for instance Lucas, *Long Term Disability is Associated with Lasting Changes in Subjective Well-being: Evidence from Two Nationally Representative Longitudinal Studies*, pp. 717–730 and Oswald and Powdthavee, *Does Happiness Adapt? A Longitudinal Study of Disability with Implications for Economists and Judges*, pp. 1061–1077 who used the same panel data but reached different results with respect to adaptation. Lucas concluded that there is no adaptation while Oswald & Powdthavee concluded that adaptation exists but is not so powerful as to return disabled individuals to their pre-disability life satisfaction levels.

[602]   Riis et al., *Ignorance of Hedonic Adaptation to Hemodialysis: A Study using Ecological Momentary Assessment*, p. 3; Peter A. Ubel et al., "Misimagining the Unimaginable: The Disability Paradox and Health Care Decision Making," *Health Psychology* 24, no. 4 (2005a), p. S57; Bagenstos and Schlanger, *Hedonic Damages, Hedonic Adaptation, and Disability*, pp. 769 ff.

[603]   Gill, *Health Professionals, Disability, and Assisted Suicide: An Examination of Relevant Empirical Evidence and Reply to Batavia*, p. 530; George Loewenstein, Ted O'Donoghue and Matthew Rabin, "Projection Bias in Prediction Future Utility," *The Quarterly Journal of Economics* 113, no. 4 (2003), pp. 1212–1213; Peter A. Ubel, George Loewenstein and Christopher Jepson, "Whose Quality of Life? A Commentary Exploring Discrepancies between Health State Evaluations of Patients and the General Public," *Quality of Life Research* 12, no. 6 (2003), p. 599; Ubel et al., *Misimagining the Unimaginable: The Disability Paradox and Health Care Decision Making*, pp. S57 ff.; Bagenstos and Schlanger, *Hedonic Damages, Hedonic Adaptation, and Disability*, pp. 769 ff.

[604]   Ubel et al., *Misimagining the Unimaginable: The Disability Paradox and Health Care Decision Making*, p. S61; Sunstein, *Illusory Losses*, p. S164. The other explanation for its occurrence is considered to be focusing illusion, see *infra* section 6.1.2.

[605]   Ubel et al., *Misimagining the Unimaginable: The Disability Paradox and Health Care Decision Making*, p. S60.

Several researchers express the concern that apart from hedonic adaptation neglect, scale recalibration may also be responsible for these findings.[606] People evaluate their subjective well-being by using a certain reference point or reference group, which may change after an event, consequently affecting respective evaluations. Therefore, victims and patients of an adverse health condition may be giving a higher evaluation of their life satisfaction because when they are asked to report their levels of subjective well-being they now do so by unconsciously comparing themselves with other people suffering from the same condition. This may pose a problem as it implies that hedonic adaptation (and focusing illusion) is not the only cause of the difference observed between the responses regarding subjective well-being of patients and non-patients. The difference can be entirely or partly due to the fact that patients may use the adverse health condition as a reference point and report higher levels of subjective well-being considering how much worse their condition could be. If this is the case, it could be difficult to distinguish what is the effect of scale recalibration and what of hedonic adaptation on subjective well-being. To test the possibility that scale recalibration may explain differences in quality of life as reported between patients and non-patients, Ubel, Loewenstein and colleagues conducted a series of studies.[607] According to the results reported, some of the studies show that scale recalibration does not play a role in the discrepancy of subjective well-being between patients and non-patients,[608] whereas other studies corroborate the influence of scale recalibration[609] or provide mixed evidence.[610] The authors conclude that the discrepancies between the responses of patients and the general public cannot be attributed solely to scale recalibration and that evidence of hedonic adaptation is considerable.[611] A different group of researchers on the other hand maintains that scale recalibration is just another

---

[606]   Wim Groot, "Adaptation and Scale of Reference Bias in Self-Assessments of Quality of Life," *Journal of Health Economics* 19, no. 3 (2000), pp. 404–408; Ubel et al., *Misimagining the Unimaginable: The Disability Paradox and Health Care Decision Making*, pp. S58–S59; Oswald and Powdthavee, *Does Happiness Adapt? A Longitudinal Study of Disability with Implications for Economists and Judges*, p. 1071; Sunstein, *Illusory Losses*, p. S165; Ubel and Loewenstein, *Pain and Suffering Awards: They Shouldn't be (just) about Pain and Suffering*, p. S200.

[607]   Ubel and Loewenstein, *Pain and Suffering Awards: They Shouldn't be (just) about Pain and Suffering*.

[608]   Jonathan Baron et al., "Effect of Assessment Method on the Discrepancy between Judgments of Health Disorders People have and do Not have: A Web Study," *Medical Decision Making* 23 (2003), pp. 422–434; Heather Lacey et al., "Are they really that Happy? Exploring Scale Recalibration in Estimates of Well-being," *Health Psychol* 27, no. 6 (2008), pp. 669–675.

[609]   Peter A. Ubel et al., "What Is Perfect Health to an 85-Year-Old? Evidence for Scale Recalibration in Subjective Health Ratings," *Medical Care* 43 (2005), pp. 1054–1057.

[610]   Dylan M. Smith et al., "Why are You Calling Me? How Study Introductions Change Response Patterns," *Quality of Life Research* 15, no. 4 (2006a), pp. 621–630.

[611]   Ubel et al., *Misimagining the Unimaginable: The Disability Paradox and Health Care Decision Making*, p. S58; Ubel and Loewenstein, *Pain and Suffering Awards: They Shouldn't be (just) about Pain and Suffering*, p. S202.

effect of the adaptive process, a change of reference in order to adapt to the new condition[612] and should therefore not be considered as a measurement problem influencing the extent to which hedonic adaptation is responsible for differences in subjective well-being between patients or victims and healthy individuals. By arguing that scale recalibration is part of adaptation and not an alternative explanation for the difference in responses, this view thus enforces the argument that neglecting the possibility of hedonic adaptation to adverse health conditions is responsible for the divergence in subjective well-being that is observed between patients or victims and healthy individuals.

Hedonic adaptation and its neglect pose a challenge for tort law as they imply that neither victims making a claim for pain and suffering damages, nor the judge who has to decide on the size of the award will be able to take the potential occurrence of hedonic adaptation into consideration.[613] Victims will not be able to realize that there is a chance of hedonic adaptation to the adverse health condition, which will reduce their loss of subjective well-being in the long run. Therefore, they will indicate a higher loss of life satisfaction than what will actually be incurred, and claim an award for immaterial losses that overstates the part of the damages related to loss of enjoyment of life. This exaggeration of course may be due not only to adaptation neglect, but also to strategic behavior of the victims and their lawyers.[614] On the other hand, the judge will have to reflect on the evidence, and award an amount of damages for immaterial losses taking into consideration, among other things, how much the victim's subjective well-being is influenced by the loss. If victims themselves are not able to predict the potential occurrence of hedonic adaptation, then there is a high chance that the judge will also not be able to anticipate potential adaptation to the adverse health condition unless of course they have themselves experienced the adverse health event in the past and therefore are aware of the possibility of adaptation.[615] Hedonic adaptation neglect will thus lead courts to award higher amounts of pain and suffering damages than would be required to reflect the actual impact of the injury on enjoyment of life. Of course, in situations where people do not adapt (e.g. because they are suffering from chronic pain, progressive or degenerative disorders, depression, etc.), the problem of excessive damages for loss of enjoyment of life, and consequently excessive pain and suffering damages, will not exist.

---

[612] Mirjam A. G. Sprangers and Carolyn E. Schwartz, "Do not throw out the baby with the bath water: build on current approaches to realize conceptual clarity. Response to Ubel, Peeters, and Smith," *Quality of Life Research* 19 (2010), pp. 477–479; Yvette Edelaar-Peeters and Anne M. Stiggelbout, "Anticipated adaptation or scale recalibration?," *Health and Quality of Life Outcomes* 11 (2013), p. 172.

[613] Sunstein, *Illusory Losses*, p. S172.

[614] Bagenstos and Schlanger, *Hedonic Damages, Hedonic Adaptation, and Disability*, pp. 752–755.

[615] Sunstein, *Illusory Losses*, pp. S169, S173–S175.

6.1.2. FOCALISM/FOCUSING ILLUSION

'Focusing illusion' is a term used for the first time in 1998 by Schkade and Kahneman to describe the phenomenon that people tend to disproportionately focus their attention on certain consequences of life events and exaggerate their impact.[616] Two years later, Wilson and colleagues independently use the term 'focalism' to signify the same phenomenon, namely that people attend too much on a '*focal event*' and disregard other important areas of their life that remain unaffected.[617] The terms are used interchangeably in the remainder of this chapter.

A focusing illusion implies that when people are asked to evaluate the impact of a certain event on their subjective well-being, they might concentrate on specific consequences of the event and subsequently exaggerate the gain or loss in subjective well-being depending on whether these consequences had positive or negative implications. For an individual who suffers an adverse health condition due to a tortious act, this may mean that during the initial period following the act, the victim will focus on the loss incurred because she will concentrate on the activities affected, disregarding areas of her life that remain unchanged.[618] If for instance, an individual becomes deaf due to an accident, she will concentrate on the fact that she is no longer able to listen to music, make a conversation without lip-reading, enjoy a play at the theatre, etc. Therefore, she may indicate that she has suffered a large loss in enjoyment of life. However, in time she will realize that a considerable number of activities such as shopping for groceries, going on vacation, doing gymnastics, etc., remain more or less unaffected by her disability.

The phenomenon of focalism may provide an alternative explanation for the findings of the famous article by Brickman and colleagues according to which lottery winners almost return to their previous levels of life satisfaction some time after winning the lottery, and paraplegic victims report relatively high levels of life enjoyment which would not have been expected for people experiencing such an adverse health condition.[619] While hedonic adaptation was previously suggested as an explanation for this result, focalism implies that the life satisfaction of lottery winners and paraplegics rebounds because after a while they do not concentrate so much on the focal event of winning the lottery or

---

616   Schkade and Kahneman, *Does Living in California make People Happy? A Focusing Illusion in Judgments of Life Satisfaction*, pp. 340–346.

617   Wilson et al., *Focalism: A Source of Durability Bias in Affective Forecasting*, pp. 821–836.

618   Ubel, Loewenstein and Jepson, *Whose Quality of Life? A Commentary Exploring Discrepancies between Health State Evaluations of Patients and the General Public*, p. 601; Riis et al., *Ignorance of Hedonic Adaptation to Hemodialysis: A Study using Ecological Momentary Assessment*, p. 3.

619   Brickman, Coates and Janoff-Bulman, *Lottery Winners and Accident Victims: Is Happiness Relative?*, pp. 917–927.

becoming paraplegic.[620] This example illustrates that hedonic adaptation and focusing illusion can be interrelated. A focusing illusion can impede adaptation to the extent that victims of adverse health events constantly concentrate on their loss, thus blocking cognitive and physiological processes that facilitate adjustment to the new situation.[621] Therefore, the maladaptation to health conditions involving persistent pain, tinnitus, anxiety and depression can be attributed to focalism because by default people focus on these symptoms.[622] Focalism is also likely to be the explanation of why people cannot get used to being facially disfigured. The inevitable constant concentration of attention on facial disfigurement impedes hedonic adaptation.[623]

Focalism is more likely to occur at the onset of disability when the victim or patient directs excessive attention to the losses incurred and underestimates areas of life that remain intact. However, focalism may also occur at a later stage, long after the onset of the disability, whenever the individual is reminded of certain consequences of her adverse health condition. Thus it has been reported that disabled people continue to indicate their poor health as a very negative aspect of their life every time they are primed to think about it, even four or more years after the onset of disability.[624]

Yet focalism may affect not only people experiencing disability, but also any person who is prompted to reflect on how she would feel in the same circumstances. In a study by Schkade and Kahneman, healthy individuals were asked to evaluate the life satisfaction of paraplegics.[625] According to the results, individuals who knew a paraplegic ranked the subjective well-being of paraplegia higher than individuals who had no acquaintance with people suffering from the condition.[626] This outcome confirmed the hypothesis of the researchers, namely that when people are unfamiliar with an adverse health condition they tend to concentrate on its negative consequences and disregard the fact that disabled people do not focus all the time on these consequences.[627]

Focusing illusion has been suggested, in addition to hedonic adaptation, as an additional reason why patients or victims assess their subjective well-being, and generally their quality of life, much higher than healthy individuals imagine

---

[620]   Schkade and Kahneman, *Does Living in California make People Happy? A Focusing Illusion in Judgments of Life Satisfaction*, p. 340.
[621]   Powdthavee, *What Happens to People before and After Disability? Focusing Effects, Lead Effects, and Adaptation in Different Areas of Life*, p. 1835.
[622]   Sunstein, *Illusory Losses*, pp. S166–S168, S174–S175.
[623]   Ibid., p. S168.
[624]   Powdthavee, *What Happens to People before and After Disability? Focusing Effects, Lead Effects, and Adaptation in Different Areas of Life*, p. 1842.
[625]   Schkade and Kahneman, *Does Living in California make People Happy? A Focusing Illusion in Judgments of Life Satisfaction*, pp. 340–346.
[626]   Ibid., p. 340.
[627]   Ibid., p. 340.

it would be.[628] To test this idea, a series of studies was conducted employing 'defocusing exercises' in which the subjects indicated their quality of life for an adverse health condition (paraplegia, below-knee amputation and partial blindness) before and after they were prompted to think about areas of life that remain unaffected.[629] If focalism accounts for the disparity in quality of life between disabled and healthy people, then healthy respondents would increase the reported quality of life estimates after considering life domains not influenced by disability. Nevertheless, the results did not support the idea, as most respondents indicated an even lower quality of life after considering unaffected areas of life.[630] Therefore, even though the results of the experiment did not negate the existence of focusing illusion in general, they certainly refuted the proposition that focusing illusion is responsible for the disparity between the estimation of healthy and of disabled respondents regarding the subjective well-being of the same adverse health condition.[631]

The phenomenon of focusing illusion poses a challenge for tort law, in the same way that hedonic adaptation neglect does, namely if it really occurs, it may lead to excessive amounts of pain and suffering damages in cases of personal injury. The victim of a tortious act will be forced to reflect a lot on her resulting injury in the context of a court trial. By focusing on her adverse health condition and the negative consequences it may have for certain aspects of her life, the victim may overestimate the impact of the injury[632] and indicate a higher loss of subjective well-being than she actually incurs, thus exaggerating those damages related to loss of enjoyment of life. However, even if the victim realizes that the injury will not deprive her of all life activities, so that her loss of enjoyment of life will not be dramatically reduced after injury, it will most likely still be in her interest to exaggerate the loss, thus behaving strategically in order to receive a higher amount of pain and suffering damages. On the other hand, during the trial the judge will necessarily focus on the losses of the victim in the process of

---

[628]   Ubel et al., *Misimagining the Unimaginable: The Disability Paradox and Health Care Decision Making*, p. S61.

[629]   Peter A. Ubel et al., "Do Nonpatients Underestimate the Quality of Life Associated with Chronic Health Conditions because of a Focusing Illusion?," *Medical Decision Making* 21 (2001), pp. 190–199; Peter A. Ubel, George Loewenstein and Christopher Jepson, "Disability and Sunshine: Can Hedonic Predictions be Improved by Drawing Attention to Focusing Illusions Or Emotional Adaptation?," *Journal of Experimental Psychology: Applied* 11, no. 2 (2005b), pp. 111–123.

[630]   Ubel et al., *Do Nonpatients Underestimate the Quality of Life Associated with Chronic Health Conditions because of a Focusing Illusion?*, p. 199; Ubel, Loewenstein and Jepson, *Disability and Sunshine: Can Hedonic Predictions be Improved by Drawing Attention to Focusing Illusions Or Emotional Adaptation?*, p. 116.

[631]   Ubel et al., *Do Nonpatients Underestimate the Quality of Life Associated with Chronic Health Conditions because of a Focusing Illusion?*, p. 199; Ubel, Loewenstein and Jepson, *Disability and Sunshine: Can Hedonic Predictions be Improved by Drawing Attention to Focusing Illusions Or Emotional Adaptation?*, p. 116.

[632]   Timothy D. Wilson and Daniel T. Gilbert, "Affective Forecasting," *Advances in Experimental Social Psychology* 35 (2003), pp. 366 ff.

assessing the damages and awarding an amount for pain and suffering.[633] If the judge is not aware of the possibility that her judgment may be subject to a focusing illusion, she may end up awarding higher amounts of pain and suffering damages than would be required to reflect the actual impact of the injury on the enjoyment of life of the victim.

6.1.3. A COUNTERINTUITIVE EMPIRICAL RESULT OR JUST A PREFERENCE FOR BEING HEALTHY?

According to the preceding analysis, hedonic adaptation and focalism suggest that life satisfaction of victims will, sometime after sustaining the injury, return to (almost) its pre-injury levels, provided that victims do not constantly focus on their injuries and that they adjust to their new life circumstances. Empirical evidence demonstrates that this is not always the case. However, if people indicate that they enjoy the same levels of subjective well-being before and after the injury, one would expect that after the injury has occurred, they would be indifferent between living with the injury and being healthy. In other words, if people perfectly adapt to the adverse health condition and continue to enjoy life in the same way that they did before the injury occurred, they should in theory not be concerned about returning to perfect health. Yet empirical results refute this presumption.

People who report lower levels of life satisfaction after the adverse health condition are expected to, and indeed do, indicate their willingness to pay to return to their pre-disability state because they believe that subjective well-being is higher in that state.[634] The more striking reaction, however, comes from people who report themselves as having the same level of life satisfaction before and after the injury: they are still willing to sacrifice wealth and also life years to return to a healthy condition.[635] In a study investigating the subjective well-being of people with colostomies, even though patients indicated that their subjective well-being was not much different than that of people who did not have colostomies, they were still willing to sacrifice approximately 15 percent of their remaining life expectancy to return to a life without a colostomy.[636]

Apart from the actual victims and patients, however, healthy people also indicate that they would be willing to trade off life years to avoid being disabled.

---

[633] Schkade and Kahneman, *Does Living in California make People Happy? A Focusing Illusion in Judgments of Life Satisfaction*, p. 340; Bagenstos and Schlanger, *Hedonic Damages, Hedonic Adaptation, and Disability*, p. 773; Sunstein, *Illusory Losses*, p. S173.

[634] Sunstein, *Illusory Losses*, p. S172; Ubel and Loewenstein, *Pain and Suffering Awards: They Shouldn't be (just) about Pain and Suffering*, p. S203.

[635] George Loewenstein and Peter A. Ubel, "Hedonic Adaptation and the Role of Decision and Experience Utility in Public Policy," *Journal of Public Economics* 92, nos. 8–9 (2008), p. 1799.

[636] Smith et al., *Misremembering Colostomies? Former Patients Give Lower Utility Ratings than do Current Patients*, pp. 691–692.

This response is attributed to hedonic adaptation neglect and focalism, which, as the preceding analysis clearly illustrated, cause healthy people to assess the consequences of an injury as being much worse than victims do. Nevertheless, if the response persists even after explaining to non-patients the implications of adaptation neglect and of a focusing illusion, it may be the case that other considerations influence their answers. In a relevant study, people were asked to consider that hedonic adaptation might occur after incurring amputation below the knee, severe pain, colostomy or paraplegia.[637] Although it was hypothesized that drawing their attention to the possibility of adaptation would positively affect their ratings regarding living with these conditions, respondents instead indicated that they would be willing to trade off life years to avoid being disabled.[638]

These results appear to be counterintuitive if one takes the premises of hedonic adaptation (and of focusing illusion) seriously. However, they also indicate that both healthy and disabled people are concerned with more than just emotional well-being and life satisfaction.[639] People care about good health and bodily integrity and appreciate the opportunity to be able to choose between the options that exist in various domains of life, provided one is healthy. In other words, health diminution is not only important as such, but also because it curtails the capability of an individual to function.[640] The fact that people are willing to exchange their money and life expectancy for health indicates that health diminution is regarded as an important loss even in cases where subjective well-being is not affected. If tort law is interested in compensating for the actual losses incurred, then this is something to be taken seriously under consideration in the assessment of pain and suffering damages as it implies that even when victims perfectly adapt to their injury, pain and suffering damages should be awarded to reflect the loss in health and bodily integrity.

6.2. PAIN AND SUFFERING DAMAGES INCORPORATING INSIGHTS FROM COGNITIVE PSYCHOLOGY: PROPOSALS SO FAR

In spite of the inconclusive empirical support, the idea of hedonic adaptation has influenced legal scholarship in the USA. The main argument in the newly

---

[637] Laura J. Damschroder, Brian J. Zikmund-Fisher and Peter A. Ubel, "Considering Adaptation in Preference Elicitations," *Health Psychology* 27, no. 3 (2008), pp. 395–396.

[638] Ibid., pp. 397–398.

[639] Sunstein, *Illusory Losses*, pp. S176 ff.; Ubel and Loewenstein, *Pain and Suffering Awards: They Shouldn't be (just) about Pain and Suffering*, pp. S205 ff.

[640] Loewenstein and Ubel, *Hedonic Adaptation and the Role of Decision and Experience Utility in Public Policy*, p. 1803. See also Amartya Sen, *Resources, Values and Development* (Oxford: Basil Blackwell, 1984), pp. 315–317 and Sen, *Commodities and Capabilities*.

emerging strain of literature is that hedonic adaptation reduces the loss of enjoyment of life and therefore pain and suffering damages awarded for personal injury should be lowered accordingly. The most far-reaching proposition following from this argument with respect to pain and suffering damages is expressed in Bagenstos and Schlanger who suggest the abolishment of damages for loss of enjoyment of life.[641] They conjecture that awarding damages for loss of enjoyment of life is redundant not only because people return to the same life satisfaction after injury, but also, and more importantly, because granting damages for loss of enjoyment of life communicates the idea that life with disability is miserable and pitiful.[642] Moreover, in order to become more persuasive, victims are often required to 'perform' their disability in court, which may in itself generate a loss of enjoyment of life.[643] Therefore, they suggest that damages should be awarded only for pain and for loss of opportunities created by social exclusion, leaving open the possibility to compensate a person for the objective loss of a permanent impairment.[644]

A somewhat different proposition is put forward by Sunstein. The unpredictability of pain and suffering damages awards is pointed out, with the suggestion that it emanates from the fact that when any immaterial loss due to an injury has to be assessed in dollars, 'jurors are being asked to judge without a modulus – that is, [...] without a standard'.[645] This realization, in combination with the acknowledgement of hedonic adaptation neglect on the part of judges and juries leads Sunstein to propose the development of a set of civil damages guidelines. The set of guidelines will incorporate existing information about the effect of an injury on subjective well-being as well as on physical and cognitive abilities and will assist courts in assessing pain and suffering damages consisting of loss of enjoyment of life and loss of capabilities.[646]

A third proposal incorporating adaptation in pain and suffering damages assessment is moving along the same lines.[647] It involves a three-stage procedure to arrive at the assessment of pain and suffering damages. In the first stage a 'panel of citizens' ranks injuries depending on their severity, taking into consideration the effect of the injury on life satisfaction and the physical ability to function.[648] In the second stage, legislators set a maximum amount for pain and suffering damages and the panel of citizens determines a range of awards for each group of injury.[649] In the third stage the juries match the actual injury of

---

[641] Bagenstos and Schlanger, *Hedonic Damages, Hedonic Adaptation, and Disability*, pp. 745–797.

[642] Ibid., pp. 774, 784.

[643] Ibid., pp. 785–787.

[644] Ibid., pp. 751, 775, 787, 791.

[645] Sunstein, *Illusory Losses*, p. S183.

[646] Ibid., pp. S184–S186.

[647] Ubel and Loewenstein, *Pain and Suffering Awards: They Shouldn't be (just) about Pain and Suffering*, pp. S207 ff.

[648] Ibid., pp. S208–S210.

[649] Ibid., pp. S210–S211.

the victim at hand with the existing category and decide whether the victim should be awarded damages at the upper or lower end of the range depending on personal circumstances.[650]

All three proposals are influenced by the insights of research into hedonic adaptation, although the extent to which they endorse the idea and propose its incorporation into the assessment of pain and suffering damages differs. At the same time, they all acknowledge the need to compensate for the loss of physical and cognitive ability, namely the health diminution following from an injury. Other scholars voice the concern that courts lack a way to evaluate the initial decrease and subsequent improvement in life satisfaction due to hedonic adaptation when deciding on pain and suffering damages.[651] Hedonic adaptation has also been argued to increase the propensity of victims to enter into settlements.[652] Since life satisfaction gradually improves as a result of adaptation, victims do not perceive their condition to be as bad as they did at the onset of their injury and thus less money seems to suffice to compensate them. Hedonic adaptation is therefore suggested to cause a stronger inclination for victims to settle.[653]

It should be noted that proposals involving guidelines, tables and damage caps are not novel for the assessment of pain and suffering damages in the USA. The topic has long triggered significant discussion, which arose from the recognition that pain and suffering damages in the USA are highly unpredictable, arbitrary[654] and of considerable magnitude. This realization, in combination with the fact that pain and suffering damages awards represent a significant fraction of the total amounts for both economic and noneconomic losses granted in tort law cases in the USA[655] has led academics to propose ideas for the rationalization of their assessment ranging from schedules,[656]

---

650   Ibid., pp. S211–S213.

651   Oswald and Powdthavee, *Does Happiness Adapt? A Longitudinal Study of Disability with Implications for Economists and Judges*, pp. 1065, 1071.

652   Bronsteen, Buccafusco and Masur, *Hedonic Adaptation and the Settlement of Civil Lawsuits*, pp. 1536–1540.

653   Ibid., pp. 1536–1540.

654   Leebron, *Final Moments: Damages for Pain and Suffering Prior to Death*, pp. 256–363; Levin, *Pain and Suffering Guidelines: A Cure for Damages Measurement Anomie Note*, p. 309; Gregory B. Rodgers, "Estimating Jury Compensation for Pain and Suffering in Product Liability Cases Involving Nonfatal Personal Injury," *Journal of Forensic Economics* 6, no. 3 (1993), p. 251; Geistfeld, *Placing a Price on Pain and Suffering: A Method for Helping Juries Determine Tort Damages for Nonmonetary Injuries*, pp. 783–785; Paul V. Niemeyer, "Awards for Pain and Suffering: The Irrational Centerpiece of our Tort System Essay," *Virginia Law Review* 90 (2004), pp. 1401–1422.

655   Viscusi, *Pain and Suffering in Product Liability Cases: Systematic Compensation Or Capricious Awards?*, p. 208; Viscusi, *The Value of Life: Has Voodoo Economics Come to the Courts?*, p. 13.

656   Bovbjerg, Sloan and Blumstein, *Valuing Life and Limb in Tort: Scheduling "Pain and Suffering"*, pp. 908–976.

guidelines[657] and caps,[658] to their abolishment.[659] Under these circumstances, insights into hedonic adaptation that support the decrease of damages for loss of enjoyment of life seem to be in line with the ideas of rationalizing pain and suffering damages awards by implementing, among other measures, a general decrease in the awards. Moreover, reducing pain and suffering damages awards, as implied by hedonic adaptation, accommodates the appeals by the insurance industry for lower amounts.[660]

In European legal systems, the situation is quite different. Pain and suffering damages awards may also be unpredictable and considerably different between and even within countries, yet the amounts awarded are certainly significantly lower than the amounts awarded in the USA.[661] As explained previously in chapter 2, tables that consist of previously adjudicated amounts exist for standardization purposes but judges may depart from the amounts stipulated therein, provided they justify their decision.[662] It is common belief in most European countries that pain and suffering damages awards in cases of personal injury are rather low and thus an upward adjustment is frequently advocated.[663] In fact, a 10% uplift in pain and suffering damages has been recently endorsed by the Court of Appeal in England, while a discussion on the topic is currently ongoing in the Netherlands.[664] Therefore, a proposal to decrease pain and suffering damages awards due to hedonic adaptation would be most likely treated with reluctance. So far, no discussion on hedonic adaptation and its potential effect for pain and suffering damages has taken place in Europe. However, it is reasonable to assume that insofar as pain and

---

[657] Levin, *Pain and Suffering Guidelines: A Cure for Damages Measurement Anomie Note*, pp. 303–332.
[658] Marcus L. Plant, "Damages for Pain and Suffering," *Ohio State Law Journal* 19 (1958), pp. 210–211.
[659] King, *Pain and Suffering, Noneconomic Damages, and the Goals of Tort Law*, pp. 163–209.
[660] See Ronen Avraham, "Putting a Price on Pain-and-Suffering Damages: A Critique of the Current Approaches and a Preliminary Proposal for Change," *Northwestern University Law Review* 100, no. 1 (2006), p. 92 suggesting that insurance companies advocate the minimization of damage awards. Reducing the amounts awarded for pain and suffering seems to be an everlasting request of the insurance industry. Already in 1959 Prof. Morris remarked that "it would not be surprising if insurance companies soon decide to sponsor legislation drastically limiting awards for pain and suffering", Clarence Morris, "Liability for Pain and Suffering," *Columbia Law Review* 59 (1959), p. 485.
[661] Anthony J. Sebok, "Translating the Immeasurable: Thinking about Pain and Suffering Comparatively," *DePaul Law Review* 55 (2005–2006), pp. 389–393.
[662] See e.g. Markesinis et al., *Compensation for Personal Injury in English, German and Italian Law*, pp. 67–68 and Wissink and van Boom, *The Netherlands*, p. 148 for Germany and the Netherlands respectively. For a detailed description of the assessment of immaterial losses in several European countries see *infra* text in chapter 2.
[663] See for instance Karner and Koziol, *Austria*, pp. 1, 14; Rogers, *England. Damages Under English Law* (2001b), pp. 70–71; Magnus and Fedtke, *Germany*, p. 119 for Austria, England and Germany respectively.
[664] See *infra* chapter 2, section 2.3.1.

suffering damages in Europe also aim at providing compensation for the loss of enjoyment of life,[665] the effect exerted on enjoyment of life by hedonic adaptation is a matter of importance. Nevertheless, any change proposed to the size of the amounts awarded for pain and suffering due to hedonic adaptation should be accompanied by compelling arguments and evidence.

The idea of incorporating hedonic adaptation into the assessment of pain and suffering damages has found some strong supporters in legal scholarship in the USA but has also generated significant criticism. Opponents of the idea argue that empirical evidence is so far not totally assertive of hedonic adaptation and therefore its potential utilization in a legal context would be premature and unjustified.[666] An additional point is that by proposing a general decrease in the damages awarded for loss of enjoyment of life, proponents of the idea disregard the fact that between the injurious event and the occurrence of hedonic adaptation, the victim may have incurred a significant loss in subjective well-being.[667] By generally lowering the amount of damages awarded to account for hedonic adaptation, this loss will not be reflected. Moreover, it is asserted that if the jury is provided with additional information, it will be able to correctly account for the possibility of hedonic adaptation[668] and therefore an *a priori* general decrease of damages for loss of enjoyment of life will not be necessary.

It becomes obvious that the overall amount of pain and suffering damages cannot be lowered to reflect potential adaptation, without further investigation and discussion on the phenomenon of adaptation. On the other hand, it may be useful to contemplate whether and how hedonic adaptation should be taken into account in the assessment of pain and suffering damages, especially in the event that future research eventually corroborates the effect of hedonic adaptation on enjoyment of life. The problem with the proposals presented so far is that they do not supply concrete and practical instructions on how the framework could be implemented, namely how pain and suffering damages incorporating potential adaptation will be measured and monetized, hence remaining at a theoretical level. Moreover most of the proposals take the occurrence of hedonic adaptation for granted and consequently presume that enjoyment of life rebounds due to adaptation. However, as reported in empirical studies, this is not always the case. For this reason, proposals should be revised to take into account the different extent of adaptation as well as the possibility that adaptation may not occur at all for a certain injury.

---

[665] Magnus and Fedtke, *Germany*, p. 112; Busnelli and Comandé, *Italy* (2001), p. 142.
[666] Swedloff and Huang, *Tort Damages and the New Science of Happiness*, pp. 567–575.
[667] Ibid., p. 557.
[668] Ibid., p. 589.

6.3. QALYs AND HEDONIC ADAPTATION: PAIN AND SUFFERING DAMAGES BASED ON THE QALY FRAMEWORK

Evaluating losses resulting from personal injury primarily requires a method that takes into account the reduction in health and bodily integrity. A monetized version of QALYs can help judges perform this task and moreover can provide information regarding the decrease in quality of life and subjective well-being. Being capable of capturing the changes in subjective well-being, QALYs can also provide information regarding the occurrence of potential hedonic adaptation. The following paragraphs illustrate how QALYs may be utilized to provide judges with the *modulus* lacking according to Sunstein, namely the framework to connect the size of pain and suffering damages to the actual injuries and loss of enjoyment of life of the victim and thus accommodate the potential occurrence of hedonic adaptation.

According to the preceding analysis, people may adapt to their life circumstances so that an evaluation of the health condition shortly after it is incurred may differ from a later evaluation.[669] If QALY-weights are elicited right after the onset of an adverse health condition, patients are likely not to have adapted, while QALY-weights elicited a significant amount of time after the onset of the condition may be signficantly affected by adaptation.[670]

The phenomenon of adaptation and its potential influence on the evaluation of health conditions is one of the arguments presented in health economics literature *against* using patient values.[671] The reason is that assigning high QALY-weights to living with an ailment due to adaptation may affect the conclusions of cost-effectiveness analysis regarding medical treatments and interventions. If patients assign high QALY-weights to poor health, then the added value of a health-improving treatment in terms of QALYs gained is reduced.[672] Therefore, it becomes evident that the question of whether or not to include adaptation is also relevant in the area of health economics, because it affects the outcome of cost-effectiveness analyses regarding the value of medical interventions. In recognition of the influence of adaptation on cost-effectiveness analysis, a study has tried to devise a method to allow the isolation of the adaptation effect from patients' responses.[673] According to the results, utilizing

---

[669] Dolan, *The Measurement of Health-Related Quality of Life for use in Resource Allocation Decisions in Health Care*, pp. 1738–1739; Bagenstos and Schlanger, *Hedonic Damages, Hedonic Adaptation, and Disability*, pp. 763–765.

[670] Dolan, *The Measurement of Health-Related Quality of Life for use in Resource Allocation Decisions in Health Care*, pp. 1738–1739.

[671] Brazier et al., *Measuring and Valuing Health Benefits for Economic Evaluation*, p. 115.

[672] Ibid., p. 115; Dolan and Kahneman, *Interpretations of Utility and their Implications for the Valuation of Health*, p. 220.

[673] Groot, *Adaptation and Scale of Reference Bias in Self-Assessments of Quality of Life*, pp. 403–420.

the proposed method to isolate the adaptation effect indeed yielded lower QALY-weights for the health conditions involved.[674] Another study suggests that the adjustment costs associated with adaptation after a health change can significantly influence the preference for different health states and create implications for cost-effectiveness analysis.[675] Adjustment costs may for instance involve the costs related to acquiring new skills, ensuring functional independence, performing usual tasks in new ways, changing family, friend and work relationships, etc. The model constructed shows that adjustment costs incurred due to health deterioration render maintenance of good health more attractive to an individual in good health, while adjustment costs incurred due to improvement render good health less attractive to an individual in poor health.[676] This explains, according to the authors, why individuals in poor health assign a higher QALY-weight to their condition than would healthy individuals assessing the same state. The resulting implication is that preventive treatments, which keep people in their current state of health, yield more QALYs than curative treatments that help people recover better health.[677]

If patients' values incorporating adaptation are taken into consideration for the allocation of resources to different medical treatments and health programs, the paradoxical result is that patients who make the praiseworthy effort to adapt to an adverse health condition are 'rewarded' with fewer resources allocated to treatments that improve their condition.[678] Eight key features of adaptation illustrate the moral controversy created by the inclusion or exclusion of adaptation in health state valuation.[679] According to Menzel et al. adaptation may consist of cognitive denial of a functional health state, failure to realize what full health is like, a decrease in life expectations, heightened stoicism, skill enhancement in the capacities that are left, activity adjustment, a change in goals, and the alteration in conception of what 'healthy' actually means. The first three elements have a negative connotation, the fourth can be regarded as either positive or negative and the last four elements are considered to be laudable accomplishments. Depending on whether adaptation manifests as a product of positive or negative elements, it should be included or excluded from evaluation of state of health and cost-effectiveness analyses.[680] The same reasoning may also be applied when deciding whether adaptation should be included in the

---

[674] Ibid., pp. 416–417.
[675] Rajiv Sharma, Miron Stano and Mitchell Haas, "Adjusting to Changes in Health: Implications for Cost-Effectiveness Analysis," *Journal of Health Economics* 23, no. 2 (2004), pp. 335–351.
[676] Ibid., pp. 339, 348–349.
[677] Ibid., pp. 348–349.
[678] Menzel et al., *The Role of Adaptation to Disability and Disease in Health State Valuation: A Preliminary Normative Analysis*, p. 2155; Dolan and Kahneman, *Interpretations of Utility and their Implications for the Valuation of Health*, p. 220.
[679] Menzel et al., *The Role of Adaptation to Disability and Disease in Health State Valuation: A Preliminary Normative Analysis*, p. 2151.
[680] Ibid., p. 2153.

assessment of pain and suffering damages: if a victim for instance lowers her expectation in life and over time forgets how it was to be fully healthy, should the injurer benefit from this adaptation through lower damages?

The controversy arising from the utilization of QALY-weights that incorporate adaptation into cost-effectiveness analysis is not relevant in the context of tort law. The important point for the assessment of pain and suffering damages emerging from the discussion above is that QALYs elicited by patients are competent to incorporate potential adaptation to the health condition evaluated. QALYs are able to encompass the reduction in quality of life attributed to both the deterioration of health and the loss of enjoyment of life resulting from an injury. Quality of life can be positively affected if the individual adapts to her impairment and negatively affected if the impairment imposes a diminution in health. Therefore, QALY values of patients, elicited long enough after the occurrence of the relevant medical condition, will incorporate the consequences of potential adaptation on loss of enjoyment of life as well as the loss due to health deterioration. After all, if a victim has adapted to the new situation, this is reflected in her own assessment of her current situation. At the same time, if the deterioration in health affects the quality of life of the victim, this also shows from her answers. On the other hand, if adaptation does not occur, QALY values will reflect that as well.

Adaptation can be incorporated into QALY-weights, especially if these are elicited with 'generic measures', also referred to as 'quality of life' measures.[681] Generic measures allow the assessment of different health conditions on the basis of how they rank in various dimensions. Among the dimensions, those referring to emotion and mood provide respondents with the possibility to express how the health state in question affects their subjective well-being. If the individual has adapted to the health condition at hand, she may rank other dimensions as being low, but indicate that her subjective well-being is high. If for instance HUI3 is used to elicit QALY-weights, the respondent will have to indicate in the dimension of 'emotion' whether she is 'happy and interested in life', 'somewhat happy', 'somewhat unhappy', 'very unhappy' or 'so unhappy that life is not worthwhile'. At the same time, she will have to rank her health condition on the basis of the dimensions of vision, hearing, speech, ambulation, dexterity and cognition. A paralyzed victim who has adapted may therefore indicate that she is 'happy' or 'somewhat happy' while at the same time in the dimension of ambulation she may answer that she 'cannot walk at all'. Another victim who has incurred partial blindness may likewise be 'happy' or 'somewhat happy', but in the dimension of vision she may indicate herself as 'able to recognize a friend on the other side of the street with or without glasses but unable to read ordinary newsprint even with glasses or contact lenses'.[682] The

---

[681]   Brazier et al., *Measuring and Valuing Health Benefits for Economic Evaluation*, p. 114.
[682]   Ibid., pp. 190–192.

combination of answers for *all* dimensions in the HUI3 determines the QALY-weight for the specific injury. The same happens with other generic measures such as EQ-5D, HUI2, SF-36, etc., namely different health conditions are assessed on the basis of various dimensions, including a dimension that reflects subjective well-being.

The experience of pain, which is frequently thought to impede adaptation, as mentioned previously, can also be accounted for in the elicitation of QALY-weights, again especially when using generic measures. Pain is likely to affect the level of subjective well-being that is reported by the patient in the dimension relating to emotion. Moreover, in many generic measures such as the EQ-5D, the HUI2, the HUI3 and the SF-6D, 'pain' is a separate dimension. Thus, if for instance EQ-5D is used to elicit QALY-weights, the respondent will be asked to indicate whether she experiences 'no pain or discomfort', 'moderate pain or discomfort' or 'extreme pain or discomfort'. Likewise, the overall quality of life of a victim who, in the pain dimension of HUI2, reports to be 'free of pain and discomfort', will be higher than that of a victim who reports 'severe pain that is not relieved by drugs and constantly disrupts normal activities'.[683]

It follows that QALY-weights elicited from patients long enough after the health impairment occurred can tackle the problem of measuring potential adaptation to an adverse health condition. A QALY-based evaluation of the health state at hand can reflect both the loss of enjoyment of life after hedonic adaptation, as well as the reduction in physical abilities. If judges utilize QALY-weights elicited from patients to assess and award pain and suffering damages, then the problem of adaptation neglect will be avoided, as QALY-weights will reflect hedonic adaptation, and the resulting amount of pain and suffering damages will correspond to the reduction in quality of life caused by the personal injury. However, it is not certain whether utilization of QALYs in the assessment of pain and suffering damages can also avoid the influence of the focusing illusion. If the focusing illusion occurs, loss of enjoyment of life may be overestimated, thus yielding amounts for pain and suffering damages that are too high. The use of QALYs may not be able to alleviate this problem, if during the elicitation of QALY-weights the attention of the respondent is focused on the losses incurred, disregarding areas of life that remain unaffected after the injury. However, using generic measures for the elicitation of QALY-weights may be able to limit the problem of the focusing illusion, because a respondent will be required to consider many different dimensions of life, some of which may not be affected by the injury at all. For example, for a victim who incurred amputation of her arm, the dimensions of vision, hearing, speech, ambulation and cognition included in the HUI3 generic measure are not relevant at all, while those of dexterity, emotion and pain may be. Yet the respondent will have to indicate how the injury affects *all* dimensions. Drawing the attention of the

---

[683]   Ibid., p. 186.

respondent to different dimensions of life may achieve the desired *defocused* evaluation of the injury. Similar defocusing exercises using comparable methods to achieve less concentration of the respondents on negative circumstances have sometimes been successful[684] while other attempts have failed.[685] Therefore, it is an empirical matter whether elicitation of QALY-weights with generic measures can avoid the inclusion of the focusing illusion in the assessment of the injury. In any case, even if the focusing illusion is not fully avoided, it will most likely be less severe than when judges assess the impact of the injury and consequently estimate what an appropriate amount of pain and suffering damages would be. Because judges are not themselves the ones suffering the injuries, they tend to focus on their negative effects and have no good way of evaluating the impact of the injuries in everyday life. The patients/victims who fill out the HUI3, EQ-5D or other generic measures are better able to do so.

In conclusion, QALYs are able to incorporate potential adaptation, if the QALY-weights are elicited from actual patients/victims a significant amount of time after they have suffered a loss. Their responses will be affected by whether or not adaptation has taken place and, if it has, to what extent. Of course the essence of what pain and suffering damages seek to express, namely the reduction in the quality of life caused by personal injuries will also be reflected in QALYs. Generic measures are the most appropriate to derive QALY values as they explicitly distinguish between factors relating to subjective well-being and to physical abilities. However, if a more simple method such as the standard gamble or the visual analogue scale is used, the responses will provide an evaluation of the injury as a whole, on the basis of both subjective well-being and physical ability. The focusing illusion may also be overcome by the use of QALYs but even if it is not, it will probably be less problematic than if the judge has to assess what an appropriate amount of pain and suffering damages would be.

The suggested framework based on QALYs is better equipped to deal with victims' and judges' hedonic misperceptions than the frameworks proposed so far because it can take into account the extent of hedonic adaptation and the fact that hedonic adaptation may not occur at all for certain types of injuries. Therefore, it presents a more refined solution for incorporating adaptation into the assessment of pain and suffering damages compared with the other proposals so far, which advocate a decrease in the awards or the abolishment of damages for loss of enjoyment of life. The QALY framework circumvents victims' and judges' hedonic misperceptions by allowing the size of pain and suffering damages to be corrected for hedonic adaptation neglect and focusing illusion without putting the pressure on victims and judges to realize and acknowledge

---

[684]   Wilson et al., *Focalism: A Source of Durability Bias in Affective Forecasting*, pp. 821–836.

[685]   Ubel et al., *Do Nonpatients Underestimate the Quality of Life Associated with Chronic Health Conditions because of a Focusing Illusion?*, pp. 190–199; Ubel, Loewenstein and Jepson, *Disability and Sunshine: Can Hedonic Predictions be Improved by Drawing Attention to Focusing Illusions Or Emotional Adaptation?*, pp. 111–123.

the effects of these phenomena. What is more, it does so without compromising other crucial features that a method for assessing pain and suffering damages should have, namely the ability to primarily allow the severity and duration of the injury to figure in the awards.

6.4. SHOULD PSYCHOLOGICAL INSIGHTS INFLUENCE THE ASSESSMENT OF PAIN AND SUFFERING DAMAGES?

The preceding analysis suggests that using a variant of the proposed QALY framework, namely only using for the damage assessment QALY-weights that have been elicited by patients or victims a significant amount of time after incurring an adverse health condition, enables the incorporation of potential hedonic adaptation into pain and suffering damages. Contrary to the approaches currently proposed to take hedonic adaptation into account in damage assessment, this framework provides concrete instructions and could be practically implemented provided that the relevant QALY-weights are available. However, despite the fact that the proposed framework could incorporate the phenomenon of adaptation if it occurs, it still remains an open question whether insights from psychology such as hedonic adaptation and focusing illusion should actually influence the assessment of pain and suffering damages.

The review of empirical literature shows that hedonic adaptation may occur for many adverse health conditions that exert a positive influence on subjective well-being, while at the same time the prospect of adaptation may be neglected by both injured and third parties, influencing the injured to claim higher pain and suffering damages and the judge to award them. Taking into consideration the fact that pain and suffering damages should reflect the true loss of enjoyment of life, it would perhaps make sense to lower pain and suffering damages accordingly, to account for hedonic adaptation and correct for focusing illusion to the extent (and if) these phenomena occur.[686] However, empirical results are inconclusive as to whether, how long after the adverse health condition and to what extent hedonic adaptation occurs. For instance, research results have shown that people who incur severe injuries may not adapt to them or may do so only partly. Furthermore, there are some health conditions, such as conditions involving chronic pain, anxiety, depression and/or progressive deterioration, which have been found not to be receptive to hedonic adaptation. With regard to focusing illusion, empirical literature shows that the extent of its influence on

---

[686] However, see also de Pianto, David, "Tort Damages and the (Misunderstood) Money-Happiness Connection," *Arizona State Law Journal* 44, no. 4 (2012), pp. 1385–1430 claiming that if adaptation is placed in the context of the larger empirical literature of well-being then a downward threat to damage awards is not necessarily posed.

subjective well-being is difficult to measure, if it is possible at all, and it is not possible to specify the point in time at which focusing illusion may occur. In fact, even from its theoretical description, it becomes obvious that it is a phenomenon that may reappear every time someone is induced to focus on the negative aspects of an injury. These ambiguous research results on the existence and effect of hedonic adaptation and focusing illusion do not provide a solid scientific justification for their inclusion in the assessment of pain and suffering damages. Under the current circumstances it would therefore be reasonable to abstain from incorporating psychological insights into damage assessment, until more injury-specific research is conducted to supply more information on the extent of their occurrence.

Apart from the lack of persuasive empirical evidence on the effect of these phenomena, a further argument against their inclusion in damage assessment is that the assessment methods that have so far been proposed to incorporate these phenomena into pain and suffering damages are not competent to reflect them to the extent they occur. Proposals that take the manifestation of hedonic adaptation and focusing illusion for granted and implement a uniform reduction in pain and suffering damages for any type of injury, should in any case be rejected as being too crude and inconsistent with empirical findings. Until a better framework to reflect them is available, psychological phenomena should therefore not be included in the assessment of pain and suffering damages.

However, even in the existence of sufficiently eloquent empirical evidence on the occurrence of hedonic adaptation (and focusing illusion) and of a framework, such as the proposed QALY framework, that can correctly incorporate its effect into pain and suffering damages, it may still not be appropriate to take hedonic adaptation into account in damages assessment based on normative considerations. Reducing pain and suffering damages to reflect adaptation would, for instance, retrospectively influence the incentives of potential injurers to take precautions. In that case, lower pain and suffering damages would induce the injurer to take fewer precautions, resulting inadvertently in more accidents. It follows from this simple line of thinking that incorporating insights from cognitive psychology into tort law is a prospect that should be contemplated very carefully as it may have adverse effects on the fulfillment of tort law goals with respect to pain and suffering damages. This chapter has provided an account of the empirical research and the ongoing discussion so far on the topic of psychological insights and their potential implications for pain and suffering damages, without addressing such normative concerns. However, a thorough discussion on the normative desirability of including psychological insights in the assessment of pain and suffering damages is necessary, before any such decision is made.

CHAPTER 7

THE QALY FRAMEWORK APPLIED

Practical Examples and Implementation Recommendations

The assessment of pain and suffering damages as it is currently performed in many countries does not seem to take into account all the crucial elements that would allow the objectives of tort law and of the economic analysis of tort law to be attained. The preceding analysis clearly demonstrated that there is a large scope for improvement, which could be achieved by utilizing a measure that has been used so far to evaluate health treatments and medical interventions.

The proposed QALY approach can take into consideration elements that are important for the attainment of compensation and satisfaction, such as the intensity of the pain, the type, severity and duration of the injury, the loss of life expectancy, and the personal characteristics of the victim, and express them in the resulting awards in a predictable and consistent manner. Moreover, the QALY can offer the missing framework to estimate the ex ante determined damages; it can set the damages so as to ensure that the injurer correctly internalizes the costs the victim would be willing to pay and that the victim is not over-insured against her will. By treating immaterial losses arising from personal injuries in a way that is consistent with both deterrence and insurance considerations, the suggested framework can therefore strike a balance between the two goals with respect to the treatment of immaterial losses. Besides the abovementioned advantages of the QALY, chapter 5 also explained that the proposed approach is expected to result in a decrease in litigation costs and to facilitate speedier adjudication, consequently enhancing the overall reliability of the judicial system. Finally, chapter 6 examined whether, under certain conditions, the QALY framework could be able to address the possibility that victims (and judges) disregard the gradual improvement in life satisfaction after an adverse event due to hedonic adaptation and focusing illusion and thus claim for (or decide in favor of) a higher damage award than what would correspond to the actual losses incurred. If additional empirical evidence were indeed to corroborate that these misperceptions occur regularly, and at the same time legal scholarship were to reach the conclusion that they should be accounted for in the assessment of pain and suffering damages, then the proposed QALY framework could perform this task.

The overview of the advantages that would in theory be generated by a potential utilization of the QALY for the assessment of pain and suffering damages could convince even skeptical commentators as to the desirability of its implementation. However, referring to practical examples of how the QALY can be applied is necessary to reinforce the theoretical arguments and prove the readiness and the relative ease with which the proposed approach can enable the assessment of pain and suffering damages for numerous injuries. In chapter 5, the example of deafness illustrated how QALY research can be used practically for the assessment of pain and suffering damages. This chapter will provide additional examples of the proposed approach for some frequently occurring immaterial losses arising from injuries such as paralysis, amputation of lower extremities and loss of vision. It will also illustrate how the QALY framework could enable the assessment of pain and suffering damages for the nowadays rare cases of HIV contraction in hospitals and other medical practices. The amounts resulting from the QALY approach will be juxtaposed with the amounts that have actually been awarded by courts for the same type of injuries in England, Germany, Greece, Italy and the Netherlands. It should be noted that this juxtaposition is not intended to serve as a comparison of the amounts resulting from the proposed framework and of the amounts that have been awarded in the countries studied. A proper comparison would have required a much larger number of observations and a thorough report of all the factors playing a role in the decision of the award, which is not possible in the context of this book. The juxtaposition merely intends to give an idea of the amounts resulting from the approaches followed in these countries, which were extensively discussed in chapter 2, and the amounts that would instead result from the suggested QALY framework. The chapter concludes with some recommendations on how the envisaged QALY approach could presently be introduced into the judicial system.

7.1. PERSONAL INJURY CASES

The subsequent sections provide additional illustrations of the proposed approach for the cases of paralysis, amputation of lower extremities, loss of sight and contraction of HIV through medical practice. The first three health conditions have in common that they all inflict large immaterial losses and may plausibly occur as a result of traffic accidents, medical malpractice, work-related accidents or the use of a defective product. The contraction of HIV through blood transfusion or infected medical devices (syringes, etc.) is a somewhat different case as it involves the infliction of a disease, rather than an injury. It imposes very high immaterial loss, which is difficult to assess and reflect in pain and suffering damages. It is therefore interesting to show how the proposed approach would deal with this type of immaterial loss. The availability of past judicial adjudications awarding pain and suffering damages for these particular immaterial losses was an additional reason for their selection.

The methodology to be followed below is the one that was extensively described in chapter 5. The CEA registry will be used to obtain the relevant information regarding the QALY loss pertaining to the injury suffered. The monetary value of €50,000 per QALY will be utilized to express this loss in monetary terms. Taking into consideration the average life expectancy and/or duration of the injury and applying a discount factor of 4% will finally yield the amount of pain and suffering damages for the case at hand. The average life expectancy of both men and women that will be used to perform the calculations will be the age of 80 years.[687] This is currently about the total average life expectancy in the countries studied (England, Germany, Greece, Italy and the Netherlands).[688]

7.1.1. THE CASE OF PARALYSIS/SEVERE SPINAL CORD INJURY

Paralysis is a generic term referring to the loss of mobility and sensation in body parts. It usually results after severe spinal cord injuries, which affect the nerve roots and the spinal cord. Such injuries are likely to occur in traffic- or work-related accidents. The most serious cases of paralysis may involve the inability to move and feel both legs (paraplegia) or entail inability to control and sense all four limbs (quadriplegia). In both cases the impact on quality of life is extremely detrimental, as it pertains not just to the obvious deprivation of autonomous movement but it also affects social life, usual activities, sexual function and emotional well-being.

In England, the reported cases on paralysis and the pain and suffering damages that were awarded have been collected, along with information regarding other types of injuries, in a biennial publication providing guidelines to the judges.[689] In the latest edition, a bracket of £262,350 to £326,700, so approximately between €308,915 and €384,687, comprises the amounts that were awarded for pain and suffering damages in cases of severe paralysis (quadriplegia).[690] The guidelines clarify that factors such as the presence of

---

[687] More accurately the average life expectancy in the countries examined is approximately 78 years and 82 years for men and women respectively. See OECD, "Life expectancy", in *OECD Factbook 2013: Economic, Environmental and Social Statistics* (OECD Publishing: 2013), pp. 232–233.

[688] Ibid.

[689] See *supra* chapter 2 at section 2.3.1.

[690] Judicial College, *Guidelines for the Assessment of General Damages in Personal Injury Cases*, p. 3. These amounts have resulted after the 10% uplift endorsed by the Court of Appeal in Simmons v. Castle [2012] EWCA Civ 1288. The English amounts throughout this chapter are

physical pain, awareness of disability, the extent of any residual movement, the age and life expectancy, the degree of independence (if any), the presence of respiratory issues, and depression should determine where within the bracket pain and suffering damages should lie for a given case of quadriplegia.[691] The guidelines also give directions for the assessment of pain and suffering damages for paraplegia for which the awarded amounts range between £177,100 and £229,900, i.e. from approximately €208,534 to €270,706.[692] Again the clarification is made that crucial factors playing a role in the resulting magnitude of pain and suffering damages are 'i) the presence and extent of pain, ii) the degree of independence, iii) depression, and iv) age and life expectancy'. Nevertheless, as mentioned in chapter 2, these brackets are not binding on judges, who can still exercise their judgment regarding the size of pain and suffering damages but should provide adequate justifications if they decide to deviate.

In the Netherlands, decisive factors for the magnitude of the awards in cases of spinal cord injuries are the position of the lesion, remaining pain, possible influence on fertility, incontinence, etc.[693] The court granted €119,152 to a 22-year-old passenger of a bus who became paralyzed after the bus was involved in a traffic accident.[694] He has been wheelchair-bound ever since. €92,925 was awarded to a 35-year-old who suffered paralysis after hitting his back against a tree during a skating contest.[695] In another case, the court granted approximately €113,856 to a 37-year-old who suffered spinal cord injury, is bound to a wheelchair and can only move one arm.[696]

In Germany, the amounts awarded for pain and suffering also depend on the extent and duration of the injury, possible occurrence of depression as well as the

---

derived from the publication of the Judicial College and are converted to euro by using the annual average exchange rate of 2013 published by European Central Bank. See European Central Bank, *Annual Average Exchange Rate UK Pound Sterling to Euro*. UK pound sterling/euro= 0.84926.

[691] More specifically the guidelines stipulate among others that "the mid-range of this bracket is appropriate for cases in which the injured person is not in physical pain, has full awareness of their disability, has an expectation of life of 25 years or more, has retained powers of speech, sight and hearing but needs help with bodily functions. At the top of the bracket will be cases where physical pain is present or where there is a significant effect on senses or ability to communicate." Judicial College, *Guidelines for the Assessment of General Damages in Personal Injury Cases*, p. 3.

[692] Ibid., p. 4.

[693] ANWB Smartengeld, pp. 114 ff.

[694] Rb. Utrecht, 31–03–2004, rolnr. 03–155. The amounts in this chapter are expressed in euro from 2013 on the basis of the annual average inflation rates published by Eurostat. See Eurostat, "Annual Average Inflation Rates 2000–2012," Eurostat, http://epp.eurostat.ec.europa.eu/statistics_explained/index.php/Consumer_prices_-_inflation_and_comparative_price_levels (accessed 31.03.2014). The original amount awarded (before adjusting for 2013 inflation) was €102,101.

[695] Rb. Zwolle, 02–10–2002, rolnr. 01–1113. The original amount awarded (before adjusting for 2013 inflation) was €75,000.

[696] Hof Arnhem, 30–11–2004, VK 2005/73, 381. The original amount awarded (before adjusting for 2013 inflation) was €97,563.

effects the injury has on social life.[697] The amount of €371,350 was granted for pain and suffering to a 22-year-old man who incurred serious paralysis after a medical treatment error due to incorrect diagnosis of a CT scan.[698] A 50-year-old, who was injured in an accident and became paralyzed waist down, received €262,416.[699] €56,800 was awarded for pain and suffering to a 61-year-old man who incurred a spinal cord injury which resulted in paraplegia.[700] In another case, a 61-year-old woman received a higher amount, namely €218,115, as she also suffered from strong pain and post-traumatic stress.[701]

In Greece, a 35-year-old man who became paralyzed from the waist down after an accident at his workplace, received €171,700.[702] In another case the court awarded €170,240 to a 25-year-old man who was found comparatively negligent by 40% for the accident that resulted in his paraplegia due to a spinal cord lesion.[703] In yet another case, a 17-year-old who was involved in a car crash and was paralyzed received the amount of €474,981.[704] The court awarded €163,703 to a 14-year-old boy who was considered comparatively negligent by 70% for incurring paraplegia after falling from the seventh floor of a construction site.[705]

In Italy, the amounts awarded for damages to health are derived from invalidity tables and their magnitude depends on the percentage of invalidity experienced after injury. An additional amount is also awarded for moral

---

[697] Hacks, Ring and Böhm, *Schmerzensgeldbeträge 2009*, p. 11.

[698] OLG Schleswig 09.10.2009 4 U 149/08. The original amount awarded (before adjusting for 2013 inflation) was €350,000.

[699] OLG Hamm 09.03.2006 6 U 62/05, NJW-RR 2006, 1251. The original amount awarded (before adjusting for 2013 inflation) was €231,000.

[700] LG Baden-Baden 24.10.2006 1 O 374/04. The original amount awarded (before adjusting for 2013 inflation) was €50,000.

[701] LG München I 23.08.2004 17 O 1089/03 SP 2005, 52. The original amount awarded (before adjusting for 2013 inflation) was €185,000.

[702] EfPirea 24/2012. The man received €100,000 for pain and suffering based on art. 932 CC and €70,000 based on art. 931 CC. The court ruled that the amount awarded on the basis of 931 CC relates to the negative effect of the injury on the victim's future social and economic development. The issue whether art. 931 CC is closer connected to pecuniary loss, immaterial loss or forms a third independent head of damages is a matter of divergence. Latest decisions of the Supreme Court maintain that amounts awarded on the basis of art. 931 CC do not aim to compensate for pecuniary losses. See *supra* chapter 2 at section 2.2.1. The original amount awarded (before adjusting for 2013 inflation) was €170,000.

[703] MonProtLeukadas 472/2004. The man received €80,000 for pain and suffering based on art. 932 CC and €48,000 based on art. 931 CC. The original amount awarded (before adjusting for 2013 inflation) was €128,000.

[704] EfThes 1328/2006, Armenopoulos, 8/2008, p. 1178. The teenager received €234,776 based on art. 932 CC and €146,735 based on art. 931 CC. The court ruled that the amount awarded on the basis of art. 931 CC relates to the negative effect of the injury on future social development. The original amount awarded (before adjusting for 2013 inflation) was €381,511.

[705] EfAth 6009/2005. The boy was awarded €100,000 as pain and suffering damages based on art. 932 CC. The rest of the amount was granted on the basis of art. 931 CC. See *supra* note as well as chapter 2 at section 2.2.1. The original amount awarded (before adjusting for 2013 inflation) was €127,000.

damages.[706] An 18-year-old victim who was paralyzed as a result of spinal cord injury in a car accident received the amount of €1,228,953 for the total immaterial loss incurred.[707] The victim's youth and the severity of the injury (85% invalidity) increased the damage award. In another case, a 63-year-old man who suffered paraplegia (90% invalidity) after medical malpractice received a total amount of €727,056.[708]

The cases mentioned above give an indication of the amounts that have been awarded for pain and suffering damages in cases of paralysis in the countries studied. The analysis now turns to the proposed QALY approach. In health economics literature there are cost-effectiveness analyses that investigate the extent to which certain medical interventions and techniques may avert paralysis resulting from spinal cord injuries at the lowest cost. One such technique is the computed tomography (CT) scan which can detect serious cervical spine fractures that are frequently the cause of spinal cord injuries and consequently paralysis. Another technique is the radiographic scan which is the standard procedure followed for trauma patients in medical centers to establish whether they have unstable cervical spine injuries. However, the radiographic scan does not always show the injury while the more expensive CT scan provides better information. In a publication from 1999 it was analyzed whether the CT scan or the radiographic scan is more cost-effective with respect to detecting cervical spine fractures which can result in paralysis.[709] The QALY-weight of paralysis was elicited with the Health Utilities Index Mark II by physiatrists who were expert in treating patients with spinal cord injury. It was assessed at 0.516 (ranging from 0.465 to 0.611).[710] Assuming people are enjoying a perfect health before the injury, the QALY loss due to paralysis is 0.484 (ranging from 0.389 to 0.535). However, it is possible that the victim is not in a state of perfect health before incurring paralysis. In that case the minuend will be less than 1.0 and therefore the QALY loss sustained will be lower as well. By applying €50,000 as the monetary value of a QALY, pain and suffering damages corresponding to one year of paralysis would equal €24,200 (0.484 * €50,000).[711]

---

[706]   See *supra* chapter 2 at section 2.3.1.

[707]   Tribunale Savona, 29/07/2005, online at De Jure: http://dejure.giuffre.it/psixsite/ PaginePubbliche/default.aspx. The original amount awarded (before adjusting for 2013 inflation) was €1,024,128.

[708]   Tribunale Roma sez. XIII, 24/11/2005. The original amount awarded (before adjusting for 2013 inflation) was €605,880.

[709]   C. Craig Blackmore et al., "Cervical Spine Screening with CT in Trauma Patients: A Cost-Effectiveness Analysis," *Radiology* 212, no. 1 (1999), pp. 117–125. The quality of this research is a 5.5/7.0, with 7 indicating research of the best quality. See *supra* chapter 5 at section 5.1.1.

[710]   Ibid., p. 121–122.

[711]   In fact, the monetary equivalent of the immaterial loss experienced due to paralysis within a year will lie between €19,450 and €26,750 corresponding to the range of QALY losses (0.389–0.535).

Assuming an average life expectancy of 80 years, a 22-year-old victim has 59 years of life expectancy remaining.[712] The pain and suffering damages are hence calculated as the net present value of 59 payments of €24,200, which amounts to about €567,000.[713] This is the amount that a 22-year-old who suffers paralysis, like the victim from the Dutch case, would receive as pain and suffering damages. The same type of calculation would yield an amount of approximately €175,100 for a 14-year-old victim who is comparatively negligent by 70% like the victim involved in the Greek case above.[714] The table below gives an overview of the amounts that have been actually awarded in actual court cases as well as of the amounts that would result for each of the cases discussed, if the proposed QALY framework was used to assess pain and suffering damages.

Table 2. Pain and suffering damages for severe spinal cord injuries

Health conditions	Actual amounts awarded			Pain and suffering based on QALYs
Quadriplegia	England	any age	€308,915–384,687	
Paraplegia	England	any age	€208,534–270,706	
	Germany	22 years old	€371,350	€566,995
	– " –	50 years old	€262,416	€442,667
	– " –	61 years old	€218,115	€342,041
	– " –	61 years old	€56,800	€342,041
	Greece	14 years old	€163,703 (comp. neg. 70%)	€175,124
	– " –	17 years old	€474,981	€578,072
	– " –	25 years old	€170,240	€335,537
	– " –	35 years old	€171,700	€525,625
	Italy	18 years old	€1,228,953	€573,900
	– " –	63 years old	€727,056	€318,609
	The Netherlands	22 years old	€119,152	€566,995
	– " –	35 years old	€92,925	€525,625
	– " –	37 years old	€113,856	€517,173

---

[712] However, the average life expectancy may be lower in cases of very severe paralysis, such as for instance those requiring the injured to use a ventilator. See National Spinal Cord Injury Statistical Center, "The Annual Statistical Report for the Spinal Cord Injury Model Systems," (Birmingham, Alabama: 2011) at https://www.nscisc.uab.edu/PublicDocuments/reports/pdf/2011%20NSCISC%20Annual%20Statistical%20Report%20-%20Complete%20Public%20Version.pdf (accessed 31.03.2014), p. 33.

[713] If one also wants to incorporate a normal expected worsening of health over time, the QALY decrease in later years will be lower, resulting in a lower final amount.

[714] Pain and suffering damages for a 14-year-old with an average life expectancy of 80 years would result in €583,747. However, if the victim was comparatively negligent by 70% the amount of pain and suffering damages would be reduced to approximately €175,100.

It is evident that the amounts resulting with the proposed approach are somewhat higher than the amounts that have actually been awarded. Only the amounts that were granted for pain and suffering damages in Italy exceed the amounts generated with the QALY framework. Amounts for England were not estimated given the lack of information on particular cases. However, given that the same monetary value per QALY is used in this chapter to illustrate how the proposed approach could be practically applied, the amounts resulting with the QALY approach for the victims in other countries are also valid for England, assuming a victim of the same age as the victim for which the amount was estimated.[715] Hence, based on the proposed approach, a 37-year-old victim in England would receive pain and suffering damages of €517,173. This amount is already much higher than the maximum amount that has been awarded in England for paraplegia according to the range stipulated in the publication of the Judicial College and it even exceeds the maximum amount that has been awarded for quadriplegia.

It should be noted that to arrive at these amounts the age and average life expectancy of the victim as well as the loss in quality of life were taken into consideration. Personal circumstances however were not taken into account, although in actual court decisions they are incorporated in the assessment. The examples provided here are therefore basic estimations of what pain and suffering damages would look like if the QALY approach were applied. Nevertheless, the QALY approach offers the possibility of incorporating personal and other circumstances. In the preceding example of paralysis, one could choose to apply a higher or lower QALY loss from the given range of values, if that would better reflect the aggravation or alleviation of the immaterial losses experienced from the injury due to personal circumstances. Using a higher or lower QALY loss would influence the size of pain and suffering damages. Different estimates of the QALY loss resulting from paralysis can be also found in other publications. The publication used for this example of the QALY approach was preferred over others because the state of health evaluated came closer to the injury inflicted in the given cases (paraplegia). However, information on QALY losses related to paralysis can also be found in other sources.[716]

---

[715] Remember that in order to assess pain and suffering damages it is advisable that the monetary value per QALY is not only based on scientific results but also on factors such as the economic situation in a country, GDP, input from consultation with insurance companies, consumer organizations etc. Therefore, it is possible that each country assigns a different monetary value per QALY. This chapter uses the same value of €50,000 per QALY as an indication for all countries in order to illustrate the proposed approach.

[716] In Rianne Oostenbrink et al., "Cost-Utility Analysis of Patient Care in Children with Meningeal Signs," *International Journal of Technology Assessment in Health Care* 18, no. 3 (2002), p. 485 the QALY loss resulting from severe paralysis (tetraplegia) and mental retardation is elicited with HUI3 and is estimated at 0.97. This QALY loss evidently involves a comorbid health state of higher severity than the cases utilized in this section and therefore it

7.1.2. THE CASE OF LOWER LEG AMPUTATION

Amputation of lower extremities is an injury that most frequently occurs as a result of a work- or traffic-related accident. The size of the amounts awarded for pain and suffering in the case of a lower leg amputation depends, as for other injuries, on factors such as the age of the victim and other personal circumstances, while the level of the amputation (above- or below-knee, foot amputation) may also influence the resulting awards. In many cases the immaterial loss generated by the amputation can be somewhat mitigated by using prosthetic limps.

In England, the amounts that have been awarded as pain and suffering damages for amputation of one leg above the knee, range between £84,700 and £111,100, so from approximately €99,734 to €130,820.[717] The highest amounts in the bracket were granted for severe cases, in which psychological problems, phantom pains or side effects such as backache were experienced after the amputation.[718] In the case of amputation below the knee, the amounts that have been awarded according to the guidelines range from £79,200 to £107,525.[719] The highest values were granted for painful amputations occurring during an accident or for amputations performed after a series of operations failed to restore the limb. Converted into euros, the amounts range between €93,257 and €126,610. Pain and suffering damages awarded for amputation of a foot lie in the bracket of £67,870 to £88,660, which is approximately €79,916 to €104,396.[720] However, the injury has also been awarded pain and suffering damages from the range of values for amputation below the knee, in cases where the ankle was also removed.

In the Netherlands, €48,498 was awarded for pain and suffering to a 54-year-old woman who was run over by a truck and had her left leg amputated just above the knee.[721] The court also granted €18,071 to a woman for the immaterial

---

was not used to calculate pain and suffering damages. In a more recent publication Frank J. Papatheofanis, Erin Williams and Steven D. Chang, "Cost-Utility Analysis of the Cyberknife System for Metastatic Spinal Tumors," *Neurosurgery* 64, no. 2 (2009), pp. A73–A83 the cost-effectiveness of surgical techniques against metastatic spinal tumors is investigated. The QALY loss due to paralysis is estimated at 0.3, however the method used to elicit it is different from the ones typically used, which explains why it was not utilized to calculate pain and suffering damages in this example.

[717] Judicial College, *Guidelines for the Assessment of General Damages in Personal Injury Cases*, p. 59.

[718] Ibid., p. 59.

[719] Ibid., pp. 59–60.

[720] Ibid., p. 67.

[721] Hof Den Haag, 19–03–1996, VR 1999/149. The amount awarded originally is equivalent to €34,034 in 1996 euro. This amount has been expressed in 2013 euro using the annual average inflation rates for the Netherlands for the years 1996–1999 from the Inflation EU database and the annual average inflation rates published by Eurostat for the years 2000–2012. See Inflation EU, Worldwide inflation data, "Historic Harmonized Inflation. The Netherlands," www.inflation.eu/inflation-rates/the-netherlands/historic-inflation/hicp-inflation-the-

losses incurred after the amputation of her lower leg. She was able to alleviate her condition by using a prosthetic limb.[722] In another case, a 43-year-old man who fell from his horse had to have his left leg amputated below the knee after a series of medical errors. He was awarded €29,541 for pain and suffering.[723] The court also granted €30,221 to an 86-year-old man who was hit by a car and had to have his leg amputated.[724]

In Germany, a 16-year-old man who incurred amputation of his lower leg, including the knee joint, received €158,850 for pain and suffering.[725] In another case, €59,500 was awarded to a 60-year-old man who had his leg amputated after an accident and was experiencing problems with his knee joint.[726] In a traffic accident case, the court awarded €45,440 for pain and suffering to a young woman who had her lower leg amputated.[727] €55,800 was granted to a 20-year-old man who had his right leg amputated below the knee as well as his left forefoot.[728]

In Greece, €335,140 was awarded to a 26-year-old man after an accident which resulted in the amputation of his leg just below the knee. He was able to alleviate his condition by using a prosthetic limb.[729] In a traffic accident case, a 19-year-old received €211,650 in pain and suffering damages for having her left leg amputated just below the knee.[730] At the time of the adjudication, she was already using a prosthetic limb. The amount of €180,750 was granted to a 23-year-old in a work-related accident. His right leg was amputated below the

---

netherlands.aspx (accessed 31.03.2014) and Eurostat, "Annual Average Inflation Rates 2000–2012," Eurostat, http://epp.eurostat.ec.europa.eu/statistics_explained/index.php/Consumer_prices_-_inflation_and_comparative_price_levels (accessed 31.03.2014).

[722] Rb. Rotterdam, 20–10–2010, VR 2011/135. The original amount awarded (before adjusting for 2013 inflation) was €17,000.

[723] Rb. Den Bosch, 23–11–2001, rolnr. 80–3786. The original amount awarded (before adjusting for 2013 inflation) was €22,689.

[724] Rb. Den Haag, 06–07–2000, VR 2000/198. The original amount awarded (before adjusting for 2013 inflation) was €22,689.

[725] OLG München 24.09.2010 10 U 2671/10, BeckRS 2010, 23467. The original amount awarded (before adjusting for 2013 inflation) was €150,000.

[726] OLG Frankfurt a. M. 01–12–2001 1 U 35/03. The original amount awarded (before adjusting for 2013 inflation) was €50,000.

[727] Lothar Jaeger and Jan Luckey, *Schmerzensgeld*, 4th ed. (Münster: ZAP Verlag, 2008), p. 776. The plaintiff claimed €50,000 but because of the poor financial situation and the lack of insurance of the injurer, who was the boyfriend of the victim, the court only granted €40,000, which adjusted in euro from 2013 equals €45,440.

[728] LG München I 11.01.2007 19 O 12070/04 RA Krumholz, München. The original amount awarded (before adjusting for 2013 inflation) was €50,000.

[729] EfAth 2570/2005. The original amount awarded (before adjusting for 2013 inflation) was €260,000. From this amount, €200,000 were awarded on the basis of 932 CC for immaterial loss and €60,000 on the basis of 931 CC for the negative effect of the injury on the victim's future social and economic development.

[730] EfThes 2601/2006, Armenopoulos 2007, p. 1921. The original amount awarded (before adjusting for 2013 inflation) was €170,000. From the total amount awarded, €90.000 was granted on the basis of art. 932 CC. The rest €80,000 was awarded based on art. 931 CC. See *supra* note as well as chapter 2 at section 2.2.1.

knee and he uses a prosthetic limb.[731] However, the court only granted about €81,606 to a 32-year-old man who was involved in a work-related accident and had his leg amputated below the knee.[732]

In Italy a man received €152,145 in pain and suffering damages for amputation of his foot after an accident.[733] In another case, a 59-year-old was involved in an accident for which he was comparatively negligent by 20% that resulted in the amputation of his leg. He received €534,215 for the resulting immaterial loss; nevertheless, although it is not clarified in the court decision text, the amount probably pertains to an amputation of the upper leg.[734]

In health economics literature, information can be found regarding the impact of amputation on the quality of life. Amputation of lower extremities is usually performed to patients of arteriosclerosis, whose lower limbs receive insufficient blood supply due to the blockage of their arteries.[735] Diabetes patients can likewise be potential candidates for lower leg amputation, as diabetes may also cause a hardening of the arteries.[736] There has been extensive research into the cost-effectiveness of medication and other types of treatment for these health conditions, in which the QALY loss related to amputation of a lower limb has been elicited.

A study by Ragnarson Tellvall et al. investigates whether increasing preventive efforts in diabetic patients can lower the probability of occurrence of foot ulcers and amputations, and whether these benefits are worth the costs.[737] Patients suffering from these conditions provide information on their quality of life based on the EQ-5D questionnaire. The difference in QALY value between diabetes patients after primary healing of a foot ulcer and diabetes patients who have healed with major amputation is 0.29.[738] This QALY loss indicates the net effect of amputation to the quality of life of the patients.

---

[731] EfKalamatas 16/2007. The original amount awarded (before adjusting for 2013 inflation) was €150,000. From the total amount, €120,000 was granted on the basis of art. 932 CC. The rest €30,000 was awarded based on art. 931 CC.
[732] EfThes 2717/2002. The original amount awarded (before adjusting for 2013 inflation) was €58,964.
[733] Corte di Cassazione, n. 25751, 24/10/2008. The original amount awarded (before adjusting for 2013 inflation) was €135,000.
[734] Corte di Appello di Bari sez. II, nr. 737, 23/05/2011.
[735] Judy Harker, "Wound Healing Complications Associated with Lower Limb Amputation," *World Wide Wounds* (2006).
[736] Ibid.
[737] Gunnel Ragnarson Tennvall and Jan Apelqvist, "Prevention of Diabetes-Related Foot Ulcers and Amputations: A Cost-Utility Analysis Based on Markov Model Simulations," *Diabetologia* 44, no. 11 (2001), p. 2077. The quality of this research is a 5.0 on a scale from 1.0 to 7.0.
[738] Ibid., p. 2079. See also Gunnel Ragnarson Tennvall and Jan Apelqvist, "Health-Related Quality of Life in Patients with Diabetes Mellitus and Foot Ulcers," *Journal of Diabetes and its Complications* 14, no. 5 (2000), p. 238. Note that as major amputation are considered those which are below or above the knee.

Another study investigates whether amputation of lower limbs or revascularization is more cost-effective to deal with vascular disease.[739] The QALY-weights relating to amputation of lower leg and revascularization are elicited by using the TTO from patients of vascular disease, who experience pain and difficulty in walking.[740] The QALY-weights of being cured after single or multiple revascularization are 0.95 and 0.9 respectively, indicating that there is a residual loss in quality of life even after the treatment, which relates to the experience of the vascular disease. On the other hand, the QALY-weight after incurring a successful amputation of the lower limb that restores the ambulation of the patient is 0.6. The difference between these QALY-weights therefore reflects the net loss incurred in quality of life due to amputation of lower limb, which ranges from 0.3 to 0.35. The amputation may regard more than just the foot, which may explain the higher QALY loss.

Other publications find the QALY loss related to amputation of lower extremity to be around 0.2[741] and 0.39 QALYs.[742] Apart from the studies cited, there are many others that are relevant to the amputation of lower extremities. Nevertheless, not all of them qualify to be used in this illustration of the QALY approach. One of the reasons is that some publications are, according to the CEA Registry, of a lower quality than the level that has been set as a prerequisite for consideration in this dissertation.[743] Other publications were excluded because they do not clearly differentiate between the QALY loss due to the amputation and the QALY loss suffered due to other health conditions.[744]

The existing research provides the necessary range of QALY losses that can be used for the assessment of the immaterial losses resulting from lower leg

---

[739] T. E. Brothers et al., "Justification of Intervention for Limb-Threatening Ischemia: A Surgical Decision Analysis," *Cardiovascular Surgery* 7, no. 1 (1999), pp. 62–69. The quality of this research is a 4.5 on a scale from 1.0 to 7.0.

[740] Ibid., p. 64.

[741] Sheela T. Patel et al., "Is Thrombolysis of Lower Extremity Acute Arterial Occlusion Cost-Effective?," *Journal of Surgical Research* 83, no. 2 (1999), pp. 106–112; CDA Cost-Effectiveness Group, "Cost-Effectiveness of Intensive Glycemic Control, Intensified Hypertension Control, and Serum Cholesterol Level Reduction for Type 2 Diabetes," *Journal of the American Medical Association* 287, no. 19 (2002), pp. 2542–2551.

[742] K. Visser et al., "Cost-Effectiveness of Diagnostic Imaging Work-Up and Treatment for Patients with Intermittent Claudication in the Netherlands," *European Journal of Vascular and Endovascular Surgery* 25, no. 3 (2003), pp. 213–223.

[743] See *supra* chapter 5 at section 5.1.1. For instance Richard Kahn et al., "Age at Initiation and Frequency of Screening to Detect Type 2 Diabetes: A Cost-Effectiveness Analysis," *The Lancet* 375, no. 9723 (2010), pp. 1365–1374 find a reduction in quality of life due to foot amputation of 0.105. The publication received from the CEA Registry a quality score of 3.5/7.

[744] In the study of Elbert S. Huang et al., "The Impact of Patient Preferences on the Cost-Effectiveness of Intensive Glucose Control in Older Patients with New-Onset Diabetes," *Diabetes Care* 29, no. 2 (2006), pp. 259–264 a QALY loss of 0.55 was reported for amputation of lower extremity. Another publication, Bruce Y. Lee et al., "The Economic Effect of Screening Orthopedic Surgery Patients Preoperatively for Methicillin-Resistant Staphylococcus Aureus," *Infection Control and Hospital Epidemiology* 31, no. 11 (2010), pp. 1130–1138 arrives at a QALY loss of 0.56.

amputation. By again applying the value of €50,000 per QALY and by assuming an average life expectancy of 80 years it is possible to estimate pain and suffering damages relating to amputation of a lower limb. However, the actual court cases reported above do not all refer to an amputation of the same severity. Therefore, in order to facilitate the juxtaposition of the amounts generated from the proposed method with the actual amounts granted in court, the QALY loss of 0.29 will be used to estimate pain and suffering damages resulting from amputation of lower leg while the QALY loss of 0.35 will enable the assessment of pain and suffering damages for amputation of the leg above the knee. The table below gives an overview of the pain and suffering amounts that have been awarded in actual court cases and of the amounts that would result by applying the QALY approach for cases of amputation above the knee and below the knee. Some of the cases reported above have been excluded from this table because they regard an amputation of the foot, because it is unclear whether the amputation is below or above the knee, because they refer to multiple injuries (e.g. the German case involving both amputation of leg below knee and forefoot) or because the age of the victim is not verifiable in the text of the court decision.

Table 3. Pain and suffering damages for amputation of the lower leg

Health conditions	Actual amounts awarded			Pain and suffering based on QALYs
Amputation above the knee	England	any age	€99,734–130,820	
	Germany	16 years old	€158,850	€419,449
	Italy	59 years old	€534,215	€263,010
	The Netherlands	54 years old	€48,498	€297,198
Amputation below the knee	England	any age	€93,257–126,610	
	Germany	young (19–32 years old)	€45,440	€343,865–321,829
	Greece	19 years old	€211,650	€343,865
	– " –	23 years old	€180,750	€338,237
	– " –	26 years old	€335,140	€333,397
	– " –	32 years old	€81,606	€321,829
	The Netherlands	43 years old	€29,541	€292,067

Utilization of QALYs for the assessment of pain and suffering damages resulting from amputation of the lower leg seems to result in higher amounts than the ones granted in most of the European countries investigated. The amount awarded in the Italian case was larger than the one arrived at by the QALY approach. Nevertheless, as was stated previously, it is not completely clear in the text of that court decision what the level of amputation was. If amputation in that case involves the upper leg then it is reasonable that the awarded amount would be higher than the amount calculated based on the QALY loss of amputation above the knee. The amount granted to the 26-year-old victim in Greece is also higher than the amount resulting with the proposed approach. However, this is not the case with the rest of the Greek cases, where a wide divergence in the amounts awarded can be observed. In the rest of the countries, implementation of the QALY approach would result at least in a threefold increase of the amounts currently awarded. Again it should be stressed that the amounts calculated here only take into consideration the injury inflicted and the remaining life expectancy and do not incorporate other personal circumstances of the victim. In a particular case, however, the judge will be able to refine the award resulting from the QALY approach by using the value within the range that best takes into account the personal circumstances of the case besides the age of the victim.

7.1.3. THE CASE OF VISION LOSS IN ONE EYE

Eye injuries leading to a complete loss of sight in one eye may occur under any circumstances and are not particularly related to a specific setting. The size of pain and suffering damages awarded for complete vision loss in one eye may differ depending on age, the remaining visual ability of the victim, and the potential residual aesthetic effect that the injury may inflict. It should be noted that loss of vision might occur after an injury which leaves the eye intact, destroys part of it or results in the removal of the eyeball. In the last two cases an increased amount for pain and suffering can be reasonably expected to reflect the gravity of the additional loss.

In England, a special section of the guidelines publication reports the amounts that have been awarded for injuries affecting sight. A bracket of £44,330 to £53,020, so between approximately €52,198 and €62,430, comprises the amounts that were awarded for pain and suffering damages in cases of total loss of one eye.[745] The guidelines also give directions for the assessment of pain and suffering damages regarding the complete loss of sight in one eye for which the awarded amounts range between £39,820 and £44,330, i.e. from approximately €46,887 to €52,198.[746] The highest amounts in the range are granted, according to the guidelines, for cases of eye injuries which also inflict aesthetic damage in addition to loss of sight.

---

[745]   Judicial College, *Guidelines for the Assessment of General Damages in Personal Injury Cases*, p. 16.
[746]   Ibid., p. 17.

In the Netherlands, €22,489 was awarded to an 8-year-old boy who lost his right eye during a soccer game.[747] In another case, a 16-year-old was hit in the right eye with an air gun and suffered total loss of sight. He received €21,940 for pain and suffering.[748] In a work-related accident, a 24-year-old received €17,010 for loss of an eye.[749] In another case, a woman who became blind in one eye after being hit by fireworks, was granted €26,325 for pain and suffering.[750]

In Germany a 7-year-old girl who was injured in the playground and lost her left eye as a result, was awarded €12,470.[751] A much higher amount of €119,000 was awarded to a 36-year-old man who suffered blindness in his left eye due to medical error.[752] In another case, a 12-year-old boy received €14,737 for pain and suffering. He lost the sight in his right eye during an accident for which he was found comparatively negligent by one third.[753]

In Greece, the court awarded €32,700 to a 37-year-old woman who became blind in her left eye as a result of misuse of a syringe by her dentist.[754] A 21-year-old man received €30,000 for loss of vision in his right eye resulting from a work-related accident.[755] The amount of €99,600 was awarded to a 36-year-old man who was injured in one eye by a flare and lost 80% of his vision.[756] However, a 46-year-old man whose left eye was destroyed after someone kicked him in the face only received about €37,828.[757]

Similarly to the injuries studied in the previous two sections, courts in Italy have granted the highest amounts also for pain and suffering for the complete loss of vision in one eye. The court of Pisa awarded €154,074 to a 43-year-old man who lost sight in his right eye in a hunting accident.[758] The amount of €159,481 was awarded to a young man who incurred a serious eye injury at work.

---

[747] Rb. Den Haag, 19–06–2002, rolnr. 99–791. The original amount awarded (before adjusting for 2013 inflation) is €18,151.

[748] Rb. Alkmaar, 24–12–2008, VR 2009/60. The original amount awarded (before adjusting for 2013 inflation) is €20,000.

[749] Hof Den Bosch, 17–10–2006, VR 2007/11. The original amount awarded (before adjusting for 2013 inflation) is €15,000.

[750] Hof Leeuwarden, 08–02–2011, JA 2011/87. The original amount awarded (before adjusting for 2013 inflation) is €25,000.

[751] OLG Schleswig 15.03.2000 11 U 5/2000. The original amount awarded (before adjusting for 2013 inflation) is €10,000.

[752] OLG Stuttgart 18.03.2003 1 U 81/02 NJOZ 2003, 3064. The original amount awarded (before adjusting for 2013 inflation) is €100,000.

[753] OLG Koblenz 18.03.2004 5 U 1134/03 NJW-RR 2004, 1025. The original amount awarded (before adjusting for 2013 inflation) is €12,500.

[754] EfAth 2591/2010, NV 61/2013, 2695. The original amount awarded (before adjusting for 2013 inflation) is €30,000. The amount was awarded on the basis of art. 931 CC.

[755] EfPirea 278/2013.

[756] DPrAth 3441/2006. The original amount awarded (before adjusting for 2013 inflation) is €80,000.

[757] EfDod 307/2005. The original amount awarded (before adjusting for 2013 inflation) is €29,347.

[758] Tribunale di Pisa, 01/07/2009, n.189/2002 R.G. The original amount awarded (before adjusting for 2013 inflation) is €141,482.

The pupil of his right eye was deformed and it became blind.[759] In another case, a man suffered a retinal rupture of his right eye while practicing kung fu. Eventually, vision in the injured eye was lost despite the effort and the eye surgeries he underwent in the meantime. The court granted him €86,111.[760]

Losing sight in one eye may be the unfortunate outcome of an eye injury, as illustrated in the cases above, or it may result from a disease that affects the eye such as cataract, diabetes, glaucoma, etc. There has been extensive health economics research into the cost-effectiveness of surgery and other types of treatment for these health conditions. In a publication from 2001, Brown et al. investigate whether people with good vision in both eyes have a higher quality of life than people who have good vision only in one eye.[761] If that is the case, then a treatment improving the vision in the second, least potent eye could be cost-effective depending on the cost incurred to achieve the improvement.[762] The quality of life of patients who have unilateral or bilateral good vision is elicited with the TTO. According to the results the difference in quality of life between good vision in both eyes and good vision in one eye is 0.08.[763] Although the difference involves having bad vision in one eye rather than being completely blind in one eye, it is still indicative of how quality of life is affected. The same estimate regarding the difference in quality of life between good vision of both eyes versus good vision of one eye only has been corroborated by other studies.[764]

In another publication, Busbee et al. investigate whether cataract surgery in the second eye after a successful treatment of the first eye is cost-effective.[765] The methodology of their study also applies for cases in which only one eye has restricted vision due to a cataract while the other has no problems.[766] Earlier research has already showed that surgery to the first eye is very cost-effective.[767]

---

[759] Tribunale di Modena, sez. Lav., 30/11/2011, n. 287. The original amount awarded (before adjusting for 2013 inflation) is €150,030.

[760] Cassazione Civile sez. III, 21/04/2011, n. 9147. The original amount awarded (before adjusting for 2011 inflation) is €68,234.

[761] Melissa M. Brown et al., "Quality of Life Associated with Unilateral and Bilateral Good Vision," *Ophthalmology* 108, no. 4 (2001), pp. 643–647. Although this research is not reported as such in the CEA Registry, it is cited by other research that is listed. See e.g. Michael B. Rothberg, Anunta Virapongse and Kenneth J. Smith, "Cost-Effectiveness of a Vaccine to Prevent Herpes Zoster and Postherpetic Neuralgia in Older Adults," *Clinical Infectious Diseases* 44, no. 10 (2007), pp. 1280–1288. This publication has a quality score of 4/7.

[762] Brown et al., *Quality of Life Associated with Unilateral and Bilateral Good Vision*, pp. 643, 646.

[763] Ibid., p. 644.

[764] See Philip Clarke, Alastair Gray and Rury Holman, "Estimating Utility Values for Health States of Type 2 Diabetic Patients using the EQ-5D (UKPDS 62)," *Medical Decision Making* 22, no. 4 (2002), pp. 340–349;.

[765] Brandon G. Busbee et al., "Cost-Utility Analysis of Cataract Surgery in the Second Eye," *Ophthalmology* 110, no. 12 (12, 2003), p. 2312.

[766] Ibid. The quality of this research is a 4.5 on a scale from 1.0 to 7.0.

[767] Brandon G. Busbee et al., "Incremental Cost-Effectiveness of Initial Cataract Surgery," *Ophthalmology* 109, no. 3 (2002), p. 609.

The quality of life values after cataract surgery in the first and in the second eye are elicited from patients using the TTO method. The resulting QALY-weight after a cataract surgery in the first eye is 0.858, while the QALY-weight after a cataract surgery in the second eye is 0.967.[768] Hence, the QALY gain of a cataract surgery to the second eye after a successful treatment of the first eye is 0.109 per year. This QALY difference of seeing with one eye and seeing with two eyes can be used as an estimate of the loss of the quality of life if one loses sight in one eye.

Other research investigating the quality of life experienced by people suffering from diabetes-related complications arrived at a QALY loss related to blindness in one eye of 0.074. This QALY loss was elicited from diabetes patients using the EQ-5D questionnaire.[769] Apart from the publications cited here, there are other publications that provide information on the quality of life experienced with blindness. Nevertheless, some of those publications are of low quality according to the CEA registry, while many of them only concern blindness in both eyes or do not differentiate the loss of quality of life that is experienced as a result of blindness in one eye from the loss of quality of life that is experienced from other comorbid health conditions. Therefore, their results are not used here for the illustration of the QALY approach.

It should be noted that the QALY values in the studies presented above have been elicited from patients who are actually experiencing the relevant health condition, e.g. have really had a surgery for a cataract. Nevertheless, in other studies it may be the case that the effects of a health-improving treatment are explained to people (patients and non-patients), who are then asked to imagine and indicate how their quality of life would be affected. These studies are therefore framed so as to elicit QALY-weights as a product of prospective QALY gains and not of QALY losses. However, risk-averse people are expected to weigh a loss of a certain size more heavily than a gain of the same size. This suggests that people evaluating a health condition after an improvement are likely to indicate that it has a higher QALY-weight than people evaluating the same health condition after a deterioration. The influence of loss aversion in the second group of people will cause them to attach a lower QALY-weight to the same health condition. Therefore, the utilization of QALY-weights that have been elicited as a product of health gains should be done cautiously, by taking into consideration that they may be an underestimation of the losses.

The research reviewed provides a range of QALY losses (from 0.074 to 0.109) that can be used for the assessment of the immaterial losses resulting from loss

---

[768] Busbee et al., *Cost-Utility Analysis of Cataract Surgery in the Second Eye*, p. 2312.

[769] Clarke, Gray and Holman, *Estimating Utility Values for Health States of Type 2 Diabetic Patients using the EQ-5D (UKPDS 62)*, p. 344. See also Bernhard Schwarz et al., "Cost-Effectiveness of Sitagliptin-Based Treatment Regimens in European Patients with Type 2 Diabetes and Haemoglobin A1c Above Target on Metformin Monotherapy," *Diabetes, Obesity & Metabolism* 10, no. s1 (2008), pp. 43–55, who use the results of Clarke et al. for their study. The publication has a quality score of 5/7.

of sight in one eye. Depending on the circumstances of the case at hand such as for instance the remaining vision ability of the victim, the residual aesthetic effect, etc., the judge may choose to apply one of the values included in the range in order to assess pain and suffering damages. The table below presents on the one hand the amounts that have been awarded in the court cases reviewed in the preceding paragraphs and on the other hand the amounts that would result from the implementation of the QALY approach. It lists separately the amounts corresponding to the cases in which people lost vision in one eye and the amounts corresponding to the cases in which people lost the eye itself. Acknowledging the fact that the immaterial loss is likely to be larger in the latter cases, the QALY loss of 0.109, which is at the higher end of the range, is used to estimate pain and suffering damages for the loss of an eye. The lower QALY loss of 0.08, which reflects the difference in quality of life between unilateral and bilateral good vision, is used to arrive at pain and suffering damages for loss of vision in one eye. By applying a monetary value of €50,000 per QALY as well as an average life expectancy of 80 years and a discount factor of 4%, pain and suffering damages for the given cases are estimated.

Table 4. Pain and suffering damages for loss of sight in one eye and loss of an eye

Health conditions	Actual amounts awarded			Pain and suffering based on QALYs
Loss of sight	England	any age	€46,887–52,198	
	Germany	12 years old	€14,737 (comp. neg. 1/3)	€64,702
	– " –	36 years old	€119,000	€86,195
	Greece	21 years old	€30,000	€94,113
	– " –	36 years old	€99,600	€86,195
	– " –	37 years old	€32,700	€85,483
	Italy	young (19–32 years old)	€159,481	€94,859–88780
	– " –	43 years old	€154,074	€80,570
	The Netherlands	16 years old	€21,940	€95,874
Loss of an eye	England	any age	€52,198–62,430	
	Germany	7 years old	€12,470	€133,921
	Greece	46 years old	€37,828	€105,791
	The Netherlands	8 years old	€22,489	€133,610
	– " –	24 years old	€17,010	€126,548

The proposed QALY framework for the assessment of pain and suffering damages for loss of sight in one eye does not seem to generally result in much higher amounts than the ones actually granted by courts, as was the case for the injuries investigated in the previous sections. However, as in the previous cases, Italy has granted the highest pain and suffering damages compared to the rest of the countries, also exceeding the amounts that would be generated using the proposed QALY approach. The results are mixed with respect to Germany and Greece, as they have each in one case awarded higher amounts than the ones estimated using QALYs. However, this may be due to the inclusion of personal circumstances other than the age of the victim, which were not taken into account in this basic illustration of the QALY approach. The Netherlands is again one of the countries awarding the lowest amounts. With respect to the case of loss of an eye, the pain and suffering damages generally awarded in all the countries that were investigated are somewhat lower than the amounts resulting from the proposed approach.

7.1.4. THE CASE OF HIV CONTRACTION

The Human Immunodeficiency Virus (HIV) can be contracted under different circumstances. However, the cases of HIV contraction for which pain and suffering damages can be claimed under civil procedure relate almost exclusively to hospital and other medical practice settings. In these environments, HIV can be contracted through blood transfusion and utilization of infected medical devices, e.g. syringes, etc. Contracting HIV through blood transfusion especially in western and central European countries is now highly unlikely, following the increase in safety measures that were implemented in the late eighties and the early nineties through national policies.[770] The risk is further reduced by the fact that European member states are required to conform to European Directives setting safety standards for the collection, storage and distribution of blood products and other related processes.[771] However, although the risk of HIV contraction through blood transfusion is quite remote,[772] the incidence of

---

[770] See Virginia Berridge, *AIDS in the UK, the Making of Policy, 1981–1994* (Oxford: Oxford University Press, 1996) and Bert de Vroom, "The Dutch Reaction to Contaminated Blood: An Example of Cooperative Governance," in *Success and Failure in Public Governance: A Comparative Analysis*, eds. Mark Bovens, Paul 't Hart and B. Guy Peters (Cheltenham, UK: Edward Elgar, 2001), pp. 508–532, for the relevant policies that were implemented in United Kingdom and the Netherlands respectively.

[771] See for instance the Directive 2002/98/EC, OJ L 33, 08.02.2003, pp. 30–40 on setting standards of quality and safety for the collection, testing, processing, storage and distribution of human blood and blood components and the Directive 2012/45/EU, OJ L 207, 06.08.2010, pp. 14–29 on standards of quality and safety of human organs intended for transplantation. See also Barbara Suligoi et al., "Epidemiology of Human Immunodeficiency Virus Infection in Blood Donations in Europe and Italy," *Blood Transfusion* 8, no. 3 (2010), p. 178.

[772] Yet still existent for western countries. See Eric L. Delwart et al., "First Report of Human Immunodeficiency Virus Transmission Via an RNA-Screened Blood Donation," *Vox Sang* 86,

accidents in hospitals and other medical practice settings potentially leading to an infection with HIV cannot be completely excluded. It is therefore still instructive to investigate how courts in the countries studied have dealt with the immaterial loss resulting from HIV contraction and juxtapose these findings with the approach suggested by the proposed QALY framework.

The guidelines published in England to assist judges in the assessment of pain and suffering damages in personal injury cases do not include HIV contraction in the list of injuries and harms for which pain and suffering damages have been awarded. An extensive search in WESTLAW database for relevant court cases confirms that civil claims for damages after contraction of HIV have not been made, with the exception of one case that was eventually dismissed.[773] The contraction of HIV after a hospital visit, for instance in order to receive treatment for hemophilia or other treatments involving blood products, is considered a special case in England for which special compensation recovery schemes apply. The absence of reported civil claims indicates that people have likely preferred to request compensation under these schemes. More specifically, people who have contracted HIV through a treatment in the National Health System (NHS) are entitled to compensation by the government. Payments are made through MFET Ltd, a company established for the purpose of making payments to people who have acquired HIV as a result of NHS treatment.[774] In 2009, the Minister of State for the Department of Health stipulated that tax-free payments to HIV-infected individuals will be made annually and will amount to £14,515, so approximately €17,091.[775]

In a landmark case in the Netherlands, a 57-year-old man received €216,044 for pain and suffering after he contracted HIV from an infected needle during his stay in the Academic Medical Center of Amsterdam.[776] The amount is

---

no. 3 (2004), pp. 171–177 and Ruby Phelps et al., "Window-Period Human Immunodeficiency Virus Transmission to Two Recipients by an Adolescent Blood Donor," *Transfusion* 44, no. 6 (2004), pp. 929–933.

[773] Search terms included: "pain and suffering", "general damages", HIV, AIDS, infection, contraction. The only civil claim found was one made by a 60-year-old man who claimed to have contracted HIV after he was injected with an infected syrinx. Nevertheless his claim was dismissed. See Alan Roger Plater v. Sonatrach [2004] EWHC 146 (Qb).

[774] The Social Security (Recovery of Benefits) (Lump Sum Payments) Regulations 2008, s.7 as amended by The Social Security (Miscellaneous Amendments) (No. 2) Regulations 2010, s. 13. See also Department for Work and Pensions, "Recovery of benefits and lump sum payments and NHS charges: technical guidance," (2013), s. 4.5 and HC Deb, 8 March 2010, written answer col. 51W. The establishment of the relevant funds was a response to what is considered to be the 'worst treatment disaster in the history of NHS', namely the infection of 4,670 people with HIV and hepatitis C after receiving contaminated blood transfusions in the late 1970s to the mid-1980s.

[775] The original amount stipulated by the Minister of State was £12,800. See HC Deb, 20 May 2009, written ministerial statements col. 82WS. This amount has been expressed in pounds sterling from 2013 and converted to euro by using the annual average exchange rate of 2013 published by European Central Bank.

[776] Hoge Raad, 08-07-1992, nr. 14852, NJ 1992, p. 714. The amount awarded originally is equivalent to €136,134 in 1992 euro. This amount has been expressed in 2013 euro using the

considered until today to be the highest amount for pain and suffering that can be awarded in the Netherlands. In a more recent case a 13-year-old boy received €90,665 for pain and suffering for contracting HIV through the use of infected blood products in a hospital.[777] He died about a decade later at the age of 26.

In Germany, a 60-year-old married man was awarded €32,950 as well as an amount of €500 per month after contracting HIV through infected blood.[778] In another case, a 9-year-old boy contracted HIV after the use of an infected blood-clotting device. He received €159,250 as well as €500 per month for pain and suffering.[779] His youth as well as the fact that 'the opportunity to lead a full and fulfilling life can be excluded from the outset with high probability' played an important role in the magnitude of the award. In a more recent case, a 40-year-old woman was granted an amount of €178,500 as well a monthly allowance of €500 for pain and suffering after she was infected by HIV and hepatitis C.[780]

No civil court decision awarding pain and suffering damages for HIV contraction existed in Greece until recently. The only case available today is the case of a 16-year-old girl who was infected with HIV after a blood transfusion in a hospital. The court awarded her €707,000 for pain and suffering.[781] Important factors playing a role for the court's decision were the health deterioration of the teenager, the reduction of her life expectancy and the depression following the realization of the infection.

In Italy, a woman received pain and suffering damages of €289,238 for contracting HIV in the process of a surgery.[782] In yet another case, a doctor contracted HIV while he was performing a hysterectomy. The hospital he worked for was ordered to pay him pain and suffering damages in the magnitude of €220,545.[783]

---

annual average inflation rates for the Netherlands for the years 1992–1999 from the Inflation EU database and the annual average inflation rates published by Eurostat for the years 2000–2012.

[777] Rb. Groningen 24–03–2000, rolnr. 98–1028. The original amount awarded (before adjusting for 2013 inflation) is €68,067.

[778] OLG Hamburg 20.04.1990 zfs 1990, 260; NJW 1990, 2322. The German amounts in this section awarded before 2000 have been expressed in 2013 euro using the factors included in Statistisches Bundesamt, "Statistisches Jahrbuch Deutschland und Internationales," (Wiesbaden, 2013), p. 315. The amount awarded originally in this case is equivalent to €25,000 in 1990 euro. The amount of €500 has not been adjusted for inflation.

[779] LG Bonn 02.05.1994 9 O 323/93. The original amount awarded (before adjusting for 2013 inflation) is €125,000. The amount of €500 has not been adjusted for inflation.

[780] OLG Frankfurt 23.12.2003 8 U 140/99. The original amount awarded (before adjusting for 2013 inflation) is €150,000. The amount of €500 has not been adjusted for inflation.

[781] DEfThes 1876/2012. The original amount awarded (before adjusting for 2013 inflation) is €700,000.

[782] Tribunale di Roma sez. II, 16/01/2009, n. 908. The original amount awarded (before adjusting for 2013 inflation) is €265,600.

[783] Corte d'Appello di Roma, 23/02/2009 online in LIDER LAB database www.lider-lab.sssup.it/lider/en.html. The original amount awarded (before adjusting for 2013 inflation) is €202,521.

The assessment of pain and suffering damages for the contraction of HIV is a more demanding task compared to the assessment of the injuries dealt with in the previous sections. HIV differs from the cases discussed above in that it is not an injury but a virus, which can nevertheless also be contracted as a result of an accident. HIV is a virus that infects the immune system, rendering it very weak and susceptible to infections. The last stage of the virus is referred to as the Acquired Immunodeficiency Syndrome (AIDS). Once the stage of AIDS is reached, death is unavoidable as the immune system submits to infections that it would have otherwise been able to cope with, meaning that the patient may eventually die from any regular flu. To date, there is no cure for HIV/AIDS. Existing medication can slow down the progression from HIV to AIDS, thus prolonging life. More specifically, in the years following the first occurrences of HIV, the incubation period of AIDS for adults was estimated at approximately eight years after contracting HIV.[784] Another study conducted a decade later found that the average time between infection and manifestation of AIDS is ten to eleven years for adults.[785] A more recent study concluded that the period of progression from HIV to AIDS spans up to twenty years.[786] The latest research results reveal a possibility of an even higher life expectancy for people infected with HIV. More specifically, in a study investigating the life expectancy of individuals from high income countries such as Germany, Italy, the Netherlands, England, USA, etc., who were receiving combined antiretroviral treatment, it was found that a 20-year-old patient of HIV can be expected to live about 43 years, implying that the life expectancy of a young HIV patient equals two thirds of the life expectancy of the general population.[787] Another study corroborated this result by concluding that in the UK the remaining life expectancy after contracting HIV may be up to 46 years for a 20-year-old who has been diagnosed promptly and received combined drug therapy.[788] Limited research results exist

---

[784] Graham F. Medley et al., "Incubation Period of AIDS in Patients Infected Via Blood Transfusion," *Nature* 328 (1987), p. 719 estimated the mean incubation period for adults at 8.23 years and Andrew R. Moss and Peter Bacchetti, "Natural History of HIV Infection," *AIDS* 3, no. 2 (1989), pp. 55–62 reported that in absence of medication the progression from HIV to AIDS takes place within 7 to 10 years from infection.

[785] John W. Mellors et al., "Prognosis in HIV-1 Infection Predicted by the Quantity of Virus in Plasma," *Science* 272, no. 5265 (1996), pp. 1167–1170.

[786] Alvaro Muñoz, Caroline A. Sabin and Andrew A. Phillips, "The Incubation Period of AIDS," *AIDS* 11 (1997), pp. S69–S76 conclude that up to 40% will not experience AIDS for 12 years after infection while up to 17% of infected will not experience AIDS for 20 years after infection. See also Debby den Uyl, van der Horst-Bruinsma, Irene E. and Michiel van Agtmael, "Progression of HIV to AIDS: A Protective Role for HLA-B27," *AIDS Reviews* 6 (2004), p. 89 who mention that progression to AIDS varies per individual and takes approximately 5–20 years.

[787] Antiretroviral Therapy Cohort Collaboration. "Life expectancy of individuals on combination antiretroviral therapy in high-income countries: a collaborative analysis of 14 cohort studies," *The Lancet* 372 (9635, 2008): 293–299.

[788] Losina, Elena and Kenneth A. Freedberg, "Life expectancy in HIV. Better but not good enough," *British Medical Journal* 343 (2011).

on the life expectancy of middle-aged HIV patients, although it is expected that older HIV patients above 50 years of age will not have a correspondingly higher life expectancy. After the virus has reached the stage of AIDS, the mean survival period ranges from 9.5 to 22 months without combined drug therapy,[789] which can be increased if combined drug therapy is used.

The information on the progression of the virus and the average survival times after its contraction is crucial for the assessment of pain and suffering damages with respect to HIV contraction. The preceding analysis should have made clear that the immaterial loss following HIV contraction is not restricted to the decrease in quality of life related to the virus, but principally regards the highly probable prospect of reduced life duration. Judges assessing pain and suffering damages for HIV contraction should therefore take into consideration this immaterial loss and incorporate it into the resulting amounts. The proposed QALY framework can significantly facilitate this assessment.

There has been extensive health economics research into how health-related quality of life changes after an HIV infection. In this research the QALY-weights relating to HIV infection and AIDS are elicited.[790] More specifically, in a study from 2006, patients were asked to evaluate the quality of life experienced with an HIV infection and with AIDS using the TTO method.[791] The patients indicated a QALY-weight of 0.99 for asymptomatic HIV infection and a QALY-weight of 0.85 for AIDS.[792] In another study, QALY-weights were elicited with the SG from both patients of HIV and community members, i.e. from people who are not infected from HIV. According to the results, patients indicated QALY-weights of 0.97 and 0.845 for asymptomatic HIV infection and AIDS respectively, while the

---

[789] Marcel Zwahlen and Matthias Egger, *UNAIDS Obligation no. HQ/05/422204. Progression and Mortality of Untreated HIV-Positive Individuals Living in Resource-Limited Settings: Update of Literature Review and Evidence Synthesis* (Bern: University of Bern, Division of International and Environmental Health, [2006]), refer to the results of six studies regarding countries in the industrialized world, i.e. USA, the Netherlands, Denmark, New Zealand. See also Patrizio Pezzotti et al., "Increasing Survival Time After AIDS in Italy: The Role of New Combination Antiretroviral Therapies," *AIDS* 13, no. 2 (1999), pp. 249–255, who find a reduced risk of death after the use of combination therapies.

[790] Most of the studies differentiate between asymptomatic HIV infection, namely infection in which symptoms of the virus have not manifested and symptomatic HIV infection in which they have. Asymptomatic HIV infection therefore entails a lower decrease in quality of life.

[791] Shyoko S. Honiden et al., "The Effect of Diagnosis with HIV Infection on Health-Related Quality of Life," *Quality of Life Research* 15, no. 1 (2006), pp. 69–82. The study is not included in the CEA Registry as such, however it is the source of QALY-weights for many studies that have been rated very highly in terms of quality. See for instance Gillian D. Sanders et al., "Cost-Effectiveness of Screening for HIV in the Era of Highly Active Antiretroviral Therapy," *The New England Journal of Medicine* 352, no. 6 (2005), pp. 570–585, which was rated with a quality score of 6 out of 7, as well as Gillian D. Sanders et al., "Cost-Effectiveness in HIV Screening in Patients Older than 55 Years of Age," *Annals of Internal Medicine* 148, no. 12 (2008), pp. 889–903, which received a quality score of 6.5 out of 7.

[792] Honiden et al., *The Effect of Diagnosis with HIV Infection on Health-Related Quality of Life*, pp. 74–76.

corresponding QALY-weights for community members were 0.937 and 0.778.[793] In a meta-analysis overviewing existing research, the QALY-weights elicited by patients with the TTO method were found to be 0.94 and 0.7 for an HIV infection without symptoms and for AIDS respectively.[794] However the QALY-weights were lower when community members evaluated the same health states, as they indicated QALY-weights of 0.68 and of 0.44 for the same health conditions.[795] The list of studies arriving at comparable results regarding the loss in quality of life experienced due to HIV infection and AIDS is very long.[796] In most of the studies QALY-weights for both stages of the disease range between 1.0 and 0.6. Assuming people enjoy perfect health before the infection implies that the QALY loss relating to HIV infection and AIDS is between 0.0 and 0.4. This range of QALY loss characterizes the whole period of suffering from HIV/AIDS. The fact that a QALY loss of 0.0 is included in the range might be surprising given the detrimental consequences of the specific disease. However it can be explained by the fact that the stipulated range includes all phases of the disease from asymptomatic HIV to AIDS. Therefore, it is reasonable to assume that the QALY loss of 0.0 corresponds to asymptomatic HIV, which is a phase of the virus with little or no negative symptoms, hence indicated by individuals as inflicting a QALY loss of 0.0.

As explained previously, however, the most detrimental outcome of HIV/AIDS is not the reduction in quality of life experienced during the disease but

---

[793] Bruce R. Schackman et al., "Comparison of Health State Utilities using Community and Patient Preference Weights Derived from a Survey of Patients with HIV/AIDS," *Medical Decision Making* 22, no. 1 (2002), p. 31. The results of this study are used in Andrew Coco, "The Cost-Effectiveness of Expanded Testing for Primary HIV Infection," *Annals of Family Medicine* 3, no. 5 (2005), pp. 391–399, that has been evaluated by the CEA Registry with a quality score of 4/7.

[794] Tammy O. Tengs and Ting H. Lin, "A Meta-Analysis of Utility Estimates for HIV/AIDS," *Medical Decision Making* 22 (2002), p. 478. The results of this study are used in Eugene J. Schweitzer et al., "Estimated Benefits of Transplantation of Kidneys from Donors at Increased Risk for HIV Or Hepatitis C Infection," *American Journal of Transplantation* 7, no. 6 (2007), pp. 1515–1525, that has been evaluated by the CEA Registry with a quality score of 4/7.

[795] This is consistent with the hedonic adaptation neglect explanation. See *supra* chapter 6.

[796] See for instance Jeff Etchason et al., "The Cost Effectiveness of Preoperative Autologous Blood Donations," *The New England Journal of Medicine* 332, no. 11 (1995), pp. 719–724; Joel Tsevat et al., "Health Values of Patients Infected with Human Immunodeficiency Virus: Relationship to Mental Health and Physical Functioning," *Medical Care* 34, no. 1 (1996), pp. 44–57; Ahmed M. Bayoumi and Donald A. Redelmeier, "Economic Methods for Measuring the Quality of Life Associated with HIV Infection," *Quality of Life Research* 8, no. 6 (1999), pp. 471–480; Robert MacLaren and Patrick W. Sullivan, "Cost-Effectiveness of Recombinant Human Erythropoietin for Reducing Red Blood Cells Transfusions in Critically Ill Patients," *Value in Health* 8, no. 2 (2005), pp. 105–116; Courtney C. Maclean and Jeffrey S. A. Stringer, "Potential Cost-Effectiveness of Maternal and Infant Antiretroviral Interventions to Prevent Mother-to-Child Transmission during Breast-Feeding," *Journal of Acquired Immune Deficiency Syndromes* 28, no. 5 (2005), pp. 570–577; Swati P. Tole et al., "Cost-Effectiveness of Voluntary HIV Screening in Russia," *International Journal of STD & AIDS* 20, no. 1 (2009), pp. 46–51. All find a QALY loss due to HIV infection or AIDS approximately between 0 and 0.4.

the anticipated reduction in lifespan. Apart from the loss of quality of life, the judge should therefore also take into consideration the reduction in lifespan of infected individuals and reflect this loss in the amount awarded for pain and suffering. Recall from chapter 4 that a QALY expresses the value of living one year under a certain health condition with the QALY-weight of 0.0 representing death and the QALY-weight of 1.0 representing perfect health.[797] Therefore, in case of death, a QALY loss of 1.0 is incurred for each year of life lost. A person who has contracted HIV will thus suffer a deterioration of her life quality with a QALY loss ranging between 0.0 and 0.4 for each year of survival as well as a QALY loss of 1.0 for each year of lost life expectancy.

The table below lists on the one hand the amounts that have been awarded as pain and suffering damages for HIV contraction, and on the other hand the amounts that would result by applying the QALY approach. For the Italian cases, where the age of the victim was not specified in the court decision text, it is assumed that the adult individuals are 45 years old. To calculate pain and suffering damages on the basis of the proposed framework the insights from health economics research are taken into consideration. In all cases, the infected individuals are assumed to survive for an average of 20 years during which they experience a QALY loss of 0.2. The survival period of 20 years lies within the range of life expectancy for HIV/AIDS patients, as was outlined above, and is realistic for middle-aged adults as the people in (most of) the cases below were. It furthermore takes into account the possibility that HIV-positive individuals may not receive a timely diagnosis, which will inevitably delay their treatment and result in a reduced life expectancy. The QALY loss of 0.2 is in the middle of the range of loss experienced due to HIV/AIDS. By applying €50,000 as the monetary value of a QALY, pain and suffering damages corresponding to one year of HIV/AIDS would equal €10,000 (0.2 * €50,000). The remaining years of life expectancy after this survival period will be considered as lost life expectancy. Assuming that the average life expectancy of an individual is 80 years, individuals who have been infected with HIV will incur a QALY loss of 1.0 for each year of lost life expectancy. Expressed in monetary terms, a year of lost life expectancy would correspond to €50,000 (1.0 * €50,000). As an example, a person who contracts HIV at 45 years of age, as is presumably the age of the victims in the Italian cases, would normally have 36 years of remaining life expectancy. The pain and suffering damages are hence calculated as the sum of the net present value of 20 payments of €10,000, corresponding to the survival period, and of 16 payments of €50,000, corresponding to the lost life expectancy. The resulting amount of €417,873 is the amount that a 45-year-old who contracts HIV would receive as pain and suffering damages under the proposed approach.

---

[797] See *supra* chapter 4 at section 4.2.

Table 5. Pain and suffering damages for HIV contraction

Health condition	Actual amounts awarded			Pain and suffering based on QALYs
HIV contraction	England	any age	€17,091 (annual payment)	
	Germany	60 years old	€32,950 (+ €500)	€164,158
	– " –	9 years old	€159,250 (+ €500)	€657,445
	Greece	16 years old	€707,000	€633,069
	Italy	adult – 45 years old	€289,238	€417,873
	– " –	adult – 45 years old	€220,545	€417,873
	The Netherlands	13 years old	€90,665	€644,344
	– " –	57 years old	€216,044	€227,484

The juxtaposition of the amounts that were actually awarded with the amounts that would result by applying the proposed QALY framework clearly reveals that pain and suffering damages based on the QALY approach are significantly higher in most cases. Only the amount awarded in Greece for the 16-year-old victim was higher than the amount arrived at on the basis of QALYs. Once again, the amounts awarded by Italian courts were on the high side. The Netherlands seems to have granted a quite low amount in the case of the 13-year-old victim, since applying the QALY approach would lead to more than a sixfold increase in the size of the award. However, the remaining life expectancy of 20 years may be too low, for young people such as the 13-year-old in the Dutch case, the 9-year-old from the German example and the 16-year-old in the Greek case. Applying a higher life expectancy in cases involving younger victims would yield lower amounts for pain and suffering damages. The QALY loss of 0.2 that was applied in this example lies in the middle of the range of QALY losses. However, judges deciding on a case at hand may choose to apply a different value from the range if they believe it better describes the condition of the infected individual.

The case of HIV contraction is particularly demanding to deal with when it comes to awarding pain and suffering damages as it inflicts a loss not only to the quality of life but it also affects life expectancy. The impact of HIV contraction is therefore difficult for courts to assess. However, relevant information on the influence of HIV/AIDS on the quality of life of infected individuals is extensive and can be easily found in existing health economics literature. Besides the information on the quality of life, additional information on the decrease in life expectancy is necessary to assess pain and suffering damages for HIV contraction. It is advised that the most recent evidence regarding the remaining life expectancy of HIV/AIDS patients should be taken into account before the relevant damage assessment is performed, because the constantly developing medical treatments and drug innovations tend to turn this fatal disease into a chronic one. Nevertheless, this demonstration of how the proposed QALY framework can be used to assess pain and suffering damages in the case of infection with HIV/AIDS can be used as a model for assessing other health conditions that reduce life expectancy and quality of life such as mesothelioma, lung cancer and asbestosis occurring as a result of exposure to asbestos. In any case, the QALY framework suggests that the specialized scientific information should be taken into consideration and be allowed to guide the process of determining pain and suffering damages amounts.

7.2. DISCUSSION OF THE RESULTING AMOUNTS

The previous section reviewed the amounts that have been awarded for pain and suffering in England, Germany, Greece, Italy and the Netherlands for particular injuries. As explained in the introduction of this chapter, the purpose was not to compare the amounts. After all, a full-fledged comparison would necessitate a sufficiently large number of observations regarding the pain and suffering damages that have been awarded, as well as a detailed description of the personal and other circumstances that played a role in the assessment of each case. The review merely intended to give an idea of the amounts that have resulted with the assessment approaches followed in these countries. Nevertheless, even from the mere juxtaposition of the amounts, it can be safely observed that the size of pain and suffering damages awarded differs significantly between the countries examined. In the Netherlands, for instance, judges appear to have granted the lowest pain and suffering damages for most of the injuries. Germany, England and Greece follow in ascending order of size of pain and suffering damages awarded, although this ordering does not strictly apply to all the injuries studied. In Italy, judges seem to have awarded the highest amounts for most of the injuries, which in many cases were even an order of magnitude higher than the amounts resulting from the QALY approach.

However, although the difference in magnitude raises some questions as it regards amounts that were awarded for the same type of injuries, it is not in itself problematic. After all, differences in for instance gross national income per capita and the level of social security may influence the assessment of pain and suffering damages relating to personal injury and, to a certain extent, explain the divergence of the resulting amounts.[798] Apart from the influence of these factors

---

[798] Still, the difference in the amounts is somewhat surprising for countries such as the Netherlands and Germany who have geographical proximity and allegedly share similar conditions. See for instance World Bank, "GNI Per Capita, Atlas Method," World Bank,

on the assessment of damages, which could be empirically investigated, there are also other reasons that may potentially explain the damages' divergence. However, these are subtler and their impact may be difficult to understand and isolate, let alone quantify. One such factor may be the existence, or lack of existence, of infrastructure accommodating the needs of disabled individuals. People who suffer permanent injuries, such as those who lose their sight or suffer leg amputation, can be significantly aided in their everyday life by the existence of e.g. ramps, automatic sliding doors, disabled-friendly public transportation, etc. Such arrangements promote the independence of the disabled individual and allow them to experience their injury in a less detrimental way, thus reducing the immaterial loss suffered. Total or partial absence of such infrastructure may account somewhat for the higher awards. A similar effect may be exerted on the pain and suffering amounts by the topography of a country. It is conceivable that it is less burdensome to suffer paralysis or leg amputation in a relatively flat country like the Netherlands, than in a country consisting mainly of mountainous regions. It is therefore reasonable to expect that damages in the second case may be pushed higher. Another factor that may also contribute to explaining the divergence of pain and suffering damages relates to how different cultural or religious groups perceive pain. It has been demonstrated for instance that north and south Europeans do not share the same culture of pain, as northern Europeans appear to be more tolerant and stoic than their southern counterparts.[799] This would imply that the amounts awarded in south European countries might also be an order of magnitude larger due to cultural differences. Similarly, it has been found that Protestants tend to be more tolerant to pain than Jews, who in turn have more tolerance to pain than Roman Catholics.[800] It should be stressed that it is by no means argued here that the factors briefly mentioned above are explicitly taken into consideration by the judge and reflected as such in the resulting awards. What is instead argued is that it is reasonable to expect that a judge who lives in a particular country, shares the mentality of its inhabitants and is aware of these conditions, may be subliminally influenced to award amounts corresponding, among others, to these circumstances.

---

http://data.worldbank.org/indicator/NY.GNP.PCAP.CD (accessed 31.03.2014), for the GNI per capita of the Netherlands $47,970 and Germany $44,260 in 2012.

[799] See B. Berthold Wolff, "Ethnocultural Factors Influencing Pain and Illness Behavior," *Clinical Journal of Pain* 1, no. 1 (1985), p. 23. He remarks, "the British [...] do not complain when in pain; Italians and other Mediterranean people are emotional and overreact to pain". See also Gary B. Rollman, "Culture and Pain," in *Cultural Clinical Psychology. Theory, Research and Practice*, eds. Shahé Kazarian and David R. Evans (New York, Oxford: Oxford University Press, 1998), p. 269. Summarizing the results of other studies on the issue they note that North Europeans were shown to be more tolerant to pain than people of Mediterranean ancestry e.g. Italians.

[800] B. Berthold Wolff and Sarah Langley, "Cultural Factors and the Response to Pain: A Review," *American Anthropologist* 70, no. 3 (1968), pp. 496–497.

It follows that a difference in the amounts *between* jurisdictions, although often stressed in the literature, is not in itself problematic. In the preceding paragraph it was explained that there are several factors that may account for the divergence. Differences *within* a jurisdiction on the other hand are more difficult to justify and may be caused by the lack of a coherent framework for assessment. It is unclear, for instance, why in Greece a 36-year-old who lost the sight in one eye received €99,600, while in another case a 37-year-old who also lost sight in one eye was granted only €32,700.[801] Personal circumstances probably played a role in influencing the decision of the judge. Nevertheless, one would expect that the amount awarded in the second case would be close to the amount granted in the first case, given that the victims were essentially of the same age.

However, even in countries in which the size of damages for comparable injuries rarely differs because a table or a tariff system is in place, as is the case in England, Germany and the Netherlands, is it correct to arrive at pain and suffering awards on the basis of amounts granted by courts in the past? The answer depends on the goals aimed at through pain and suffering damages. Chapter 2 showed that from a legal perspective, damages are awarded to attain fair compensation and satisfaction.[802] Chapter 3 in turn demonstrated that from a law and economics point of view one of the goals of awarding pain and suffering damages is to generate optimal deterrence incentives.[803] The foregoing analysis established that in order to accomplish these goals the total immaterial loss incurred should be systematically reflected in the awards. This implies that the impact of the injury on the quality of life of the victim, as well as the relative ranking of different types of injuries should be taken into account. Hence factors such as the nature and extent of the injury, the age of the victim, the loss of enjoyment of life, the reduction in life expectancy, inflicted pain and suffering, etc. should be considered in the assessment. The use of tables or tariffs, however, does not necessarily result in amounts that reflect the impact of the injury and its relative ranking in comparison to other injuries. Reliance on past rulings gives no information on the factors that influenced the decision. Moreover, reliance does not necessarily mean that the initial rulings were correct to start with. Juxtapose for instance, the amount of €21,940 awarded in the Netherlands to a 16-year-old for losing sight in one eye with the amount of €90,665 that was granted to a 13-year-old for contracting HIV.[804] Amounts awarded for similar types of harm in the past as well as personal circumstances may have influenced the decision of the judge regarding the size of the awards. However, given that the victims are of almost the same age, it can be held that the higher amount awarded for the case of HIV contraction indicates that the immaterial loss

---

[801] See *supra* section 7.1.3.
[802] See *supra* chapter 2 at section 2.1.
[803] See *supra* chapter 3 at section 3.1.1.
[804] See *supra* at sections 7.1.3 and 7.1.4.

incurred in that case is considered more severe. But does this amount really reflect how much more negative influence HIV contraction has on the life of the victim, in comparison to loss of sight in one eye?

The proposed QALY framework for the assessment of pain and suffering damages can precisely reflect the impact various injuries have on the quality and duration of life of the victim, as well as the relative severity of different types of injuries, which are both important factors for the attainment of fair compensation. Moreover, it can express the total immaterial loss incurred in a systematic and predictable way, thus facilitating the generation of deterrent incentives. These characteristics imply that the proposed framework would encourage the uniform treatment of pain and suffering damages throughout a country by arriving at similar amounts for comparable injuries, but at the same time also by differentiating the size of the awards on the basis of the relative ranking of the injuries. However, from the description in chapter 2 of the assessment approaches followed in different countries, it would seem that the assessment method implemented in Italy is also able to reflect these factors. One would then sincerely wonder, why not use the Italian system instead?

The approach followed in Italy is indeed able to take into account in a systematic way the reduction in the quality of life of the victim caused by an injury because it is based on medical information. In that respect, it certainly has an advantage compared to the rest of the approaches reviewed here. However, the fact that not all courts have agreed to use the tables of the court of Milan for the assessment of pain and suffering damages may cause systematic differences in amounts within the country's jurisdictions. Moreover, it is unclear whether and how personal circumstances of the victim amply figure in the assessment, given that damages to health are estimated by using predetermined amounts that correspond to points of invalidity, and moral damages are sometimes assessed as a proportion of damages to health. Finally, the fact that damages correspond to points of invalidity and not injuries as such implies that a medical expert is always necessary to translate the impact of a certain injury into invalidity points, which adds complexity and significantly raises the cost of the trial. It also does not facilitate settlements, as the parties may not be able to estimate in advance the invalidity points corresponding to their injury, leading to a further increase in the costs of the legal system.

On the contrary, the proposed QALY approach for the assessment of pain and suffering damages takes advantage of specialized research in which individuals themselves evaluate the impact of different types of injuries on the quality of life. The monetary value per QALY, which is used to translate the immaterial loss into monetary terms, is based on scientific results, which are also derived from individuals' evaluations, as well as on economic and other circumstances of the respective country. Moreover, the judge needs to be aware only of the genre of the injury, which is easy to establish, in order to be able to take advantage of the relevant values based on QALYs. In the previous section it was shown that pain and suffering damages generated with the application of the QALY approach were in most cases significantly higher than the amounts actually awarded by courts. Given that the amounts generated with the proposed framework reflect the immaterial loss relating to personal injury, as close as possible as individuals themselves perceive it, the implication of the QALY approach is that the amounts currently awarded in most of the countries examined are far too low and they should be significantly increased.

7.3. IMPLEMENTATION RECOMMENDATIONS

If the merits of the proposed framework for the assessment of pain and suffering damages are recognized and the decision is made to implement it in practice, it is recommended that the envisaged QALY approach be introduced into the judicial system in two stages.

The first stage of the implementation would involve making QALY research admissible to court. Lawyers could be encouraged to base the amount of damages which they claim for their clients on the relevant health economics literature and more specifically on the values generated by combining the range of QALY losses related to the injury with the monetary value of a QALY.[805] Courts would then have to decide whether to grant these (higher) claims. If they do, these amounts will find their way into the system currently applied for the rationalization of the awards in the respective country. In England, for instance, the amounts would be incorporated into the existing tariffs, in Germany they would be included in the tables with past court decisions, in the Netherlands they would be incorporated in the relevant publication, etc. The QALY approach would in this way gain ground from the bottom up. Alternatively, tables with amounts based on QALY research could be compiled by a committee of experts and be circulated to courts for consultation. These tables would replace the tables that are presently used in some jurisdictions, which include the amounts awarded in the past. Given that health economics research results in average QALY-weights accompanied by an upper and lower limit, the envisaged QALY tables would offer a range of amounts rather than a fixed amount for each injury. Judges would then consult the tables and award an amount from these tables that they would consider appropriate for the case at hand. The QALY approach would in this way be implemented top-down. This book provides information on five health conditions, namely deafness, paralysis due to spinal cord injury,

---

[805] It should be noted that in the process of writing the dissertation on which this book is based, the supervising professor was contacted by Dutch lawyers who wanted to use, among other evidence, information from QALY research in order to make a claim for pain and suffering damages. Unfortunately, the court found no negligence of the defendant and dismissed the claim for damages without ruling on its content.

amputation of lower limb (below and above knee), loss of sight in one eye (and loss of one eye), and contraction of HIV. Nevertheless, information on many more health conditions should be included in the tables before they could be used to assist the assessment of pain and suffering damages. For some injury cases, additional research may need to be undertaken. However, it may not be necessary to include in the table amounts for all conditions imaginable. For example, if the table includes amounts for amputation of an arm and amputation of a hand, even if there are no amounts with respect to amputation below the elbow, it can be assumed that these should lie in between the two others. Although at this stage mandatory legislation would not be in place regarding the implementation of the QALY framework, nevertheless the legislator could pass laws which provide financial or other incentives to undertake QALY research and generate QALY-weights for different health conditions. This would provide the information that is missing for some types of injuries and in the long run potentially facilitate the refinement of existing tables.

The second stage of the implementation would happen subsequently and would involve enforcing the applied QALY framework. Legislation or a less formal type of legal rule such as a circular issued by the ministry of justice or the head of the judiciary would incorporate the contents of the tables shaped during the first stage of implementation. In the meantime, judicial practice and QALY research would have further refined the approach and would have dealt with difficult issues relating to its application (e.g. the case of multiple injuries). At this point the upper and lower limits stipulated in the tables would become binding on the judge, who would be expected to award amounts complying with the set boundaries. Nevertheless, these boundaries would not become mandatory in an absolute sense. The occurrence of extreme cases and unforeseen contingencies cannot be safely excluded especially when, in this context, an extreme case would probably entail that the victim incurs a very high immaterial loss. The legal rule regarding the implementation of the QALY framework would therefore stipulate that only in exceptional cases would the judge be allowed to deviate from the predetermined range of values by awarding higher amounts. In that case, the judge would be required to provide a special justification. To incentivize the judges not to exceed the stipulated amounts but for highly extraordinary cases, an exception could additionally be introduced into the competence of the court of third instance, to admit appeals regarding the size of the awards only if they exceed the set limits.

CHAPTER 8
EPILOGUE

Discussing the proposed QALY approach for the assessment of pain and suffering damages and highlighting the advantages emanating from its potential utilization are important to realize the desirability of its implementation. However, the theoretical discussion is of little value if the suggested framework cannot be practically implemented. Concrete examples are therefore necessary to support the theoretical discussion and to prove that the proposed QALY framework can indeed be practically applied, bringing about an improvement in the assessment of pain and suffering damages for various personal injuries. In chapter 5, the example of deafness illustrated how QALY research can be used for the assessment of pain and suffering damages. Chapter 7 contributed four more examples to the analysis. More specifically, pain and suffering damages were assessed for four additional health conditions that inflict high immaterial losses, namely paralysis (paraplegia), lower leg amputation (above and below the knee), loss of sight in one eye (and loss of one eye) and contraction of HIV. Assessing pain and suffering damages for these five cases by implementing the proposed QALY approach clearly demonstrated that existing information from health economics could be practically utilized in the context of tort law after only minor processing and at relatively low cost.

Having demonstrated both in theory and in practice the competence of the proposed QALY framework to assess pain and suffering damages better than existing approaches in a number of ways, the analysis is concluded in the present chapter by revisiting the research questions posed in the introduction and summarizing the main results. Promising venues for future research relating to the results of this study are also suggested. Literature dealing with the impact of detrimental health states and personal injuries on health, physical integrity and the quality of life is highly relevant for the evaluation of the immaterial losses resulting from these injuries, even if it has been produced in the context of scientific fields other than law and the economic analysis of law. It is hence surprising that not many comprehensive proposals, and none suggesting the framework proposed in this book, have thus far been made that this literature should be taken into consideration in the assessment of pain and suffering damages. This chapter discusses this omission and closes with an overarching recommendation.

8.1. CAN THE PROPOSED QALY FRAMEWORK IMPROVE THE CURRENT ASSESSMENT OF PAIN AND SUFFERING DAMAGES?

Two main questions have been addressed in this study: How should pain and suffering damages in cases of personal physical injuries be assessed in order to fulfill the goals of tort law as these are stipulated by traditional legal theory and by law and economics? How can insights from health economics research involving the impact of different health conditions on the quality of life be used to this end?

By answering these questions, the present study has aimed to explore the possibility of an improvement in the pain and suffering damages currently awarded for non-fatal personal injuries. The analysis demonstrated that an improvement could indeed be made if the QALY, a measure used in health economics to express the impact of different health conditions on the quality of life, is used for the assessment of pain and suffering damages.

The analysis of the goals of tort law clarified that the assessment of pain and suffering damages and the resulting amounts should meet certain criteria in order to attain those goals. From a legal perspective, the goals of tort law aimed at through pain and suffering damages are fair compensation and satisfaction, with compensation being considered the paramount goal of tort law in most European countries.[806] Both goals imply that pain and suffering damages should reflect as much as possible the immaterial loss incurred. For compensation purposes the amounts awarded should be further characterized by consistency in that they are of similar magnitude for comparable injuries and of proportionally dissimilar magnitude to express the relative severity of different types of injuries. Moreover, to attain the goal of satisfaction, pain and suffering damages should additionally take into consideration the personal circumstances of the victim so that the resulting amount is sufficient to acknowledge her harm and appease her for her loss. The foregoing analysis held that both goals can be reached under the proposed QALY approach for the assessment of pain and suffering damages, as the amounts resulting from this approach incorporate the stipulated criteria.[807]

The preceding analysis explained that the proposed approach for the assessment of pain and suffering damages heavily relies on the QALY loss suffered as a result of different health conditions. The QALY loss expresses the negative consequences of a health condition; the existence and availability of information regarding the QALY losses of a multitude of different health conditions enables the relative ranking of the conditions according to their

---

[806] See *supra* chapter 2 at section 2.1.
[807] See *supra* chapter 5 at section 5.3.1.

severity. The QALY is also able to reflect the duration of a health condition. Basing the assessment of pain and suffering damages on this information therefore generates amounts that fulfill the goal of fair compensation, as the amounts reflect the immaterial loss incurred due to the injury and are proportionate to its relative severity. Besides reflecting the immaterial loss incurred, however, the amounts resulting from the proposed approach could also reflect personal circumstances, hence reaching the goal of satisfaction. The fact that health economics research results in a range of QALY losses for a given health condition implies that by assigning a monetary value to the QALY, a range of pain and suffering damages with upper and lower limits, rather than a fixed amount, will be estimated for a particular type of injury. This will enable the judge to consider the personal circumstances of the victim and choose an amount from within the range that better reflects those circumstances.

From a law and economics point of view, the goals of tort law aimed at through pain and suffering damages are deterrence, loss spreading and the reduction of the costs of the legal system.[808] The preceding analysis illustrated that pain and suffering damages should meet certain criteria in order to attain those goals. For deterrence purposes, pain and suffering damages should fully reflect the immaterial losses inflicted in a consistent and predictable way so that tortfeasors can anticipate the size of their liability costs and incorporate them into their decisions about care and activity. On the other hand, including all losses in damage awards is also crucial for loss spreading, as those losses will be subject to spreading between the parties. However, to induce loss spreading, there is no agreement as to how pain and suffering damages should be treated, although the prevailing opinion suggests that immaterial losses should not be compensated or should be compensated only in part because people do not (want to) insure against such losses. The preceding analysis showed that it is possible to strike a balance between deterrence and loss spreading with respect to the treatment of pain and suffering damages, if damages equal the amount a victim would be willing to forego to avoid or reduce the probability of suffering such losses. The proposed QALY approach for the assessment of pain and suffering damages can express these ex ante determined damages and strike a balance between the goals of deterrence and insurance by promoting both goals.[809]

The preceding analysis explained that under the proposed QALY approach the QALY loss suffered from different types of injuries is combined with a monetary value for a QALY to yield the pain and suffering damages due annually for the injury at hand. The QALY loss for any given health condition is arrived at on the basis of peoples' responses. Likewise, the monetary value for a QALY is also derived from people who indicate what value they would place on avoiding the occurrence or lowering the probability of a QALY loss. This monetary value

---

[808] See *supra* chapter 3.
[809] See *supra* chapter 5 at section 5.3.2.

can be adjusted so that it better corresponds to the economic and other circumstances of the country where the QALY framework is applied. The damage awards generated on the basis of this information will therefore reflect how many resources people are willing to spend on reducing the probability and/or magnitude of non-fatal injuries inflicting QALY losses. The proposed approach is hence capable of expressing the ex ante determined damages that can promote both deterrence and loss spreading, as the injurer correctly internalizes the amount the victim would be willing to spend to avoid incurring immaterial losses, and the victim is not over-insured against her will. Under the proposed approach, the existing evaluations of QALY losses related to different injuries will be combined with a predetermined monetary value for a QALY, generating ranges of amounts for pain and suffering damages with upper and lower limits for different types of injuries. The magnitude of the awards resulting from the proposed approach will thus be foreseeable and non-arbitrary. This will facilitate deterrence, as the injurer will be able to incorporate the expected accident losses in her care and activity decisions. It may additionally affect loss spreading, as it will enable producers and insurers to set their product prices and premiums accordingly to incorporate the expected accident losses. To the extent that uncertainty regarding the magnitude of pain and suffering damages is a reason for shortage of insurance supply, the proposed approach could hence facilitate loss spreading. Furthermore, by making the premium fixing more transparent, ex ante foreseeable pain and suffering damages could also increase the demand for insurance.

According to the foregoing analysis, the last, but not least important, goal aimed at through pain and suffering damages from a law and economics point of view is the reduction of the administrative costs of the tort system.[810] This implies that pain and suffering damages should be assessed by economizing on resources, and also that the resulting amounts should promote the attainment of the goals of deterrence and loss spreading, so as to further reduce the total administrative costs of the tort system. The preceding analysis demonstrated that the suggested framework for the assessment of pain and suffering damages can achieve this goal.[811] More specifically, it was explained that the proposed QALY approach is relatively inexpensive to implement. The preparation for the implementation involves reading the relevant publications and deciding which information on QALY losses is appropriate to use in the assessment of pain and suffering damages. Lawyers themselves or a specifically appointed committee of specialists could perform this task. In any case, the cost incurred for this preparation will be a one-time only cost, while the information generated will be used repeatedly and without cost by courts for future damage assessments. The existing information on QALY losses, combined with a predetermined monetary

---

[810]   See *supra* chapter 3 at section 3.1.3.
[811]   See *supra* chapter 5 at section 5.3.3.

value for a QALY, will inexpensively generate pain and suffering damages for a large number of injuries. It will also enable the assessment of pain and suffering damages for injuries, which lie in between other injuries for which information on the QALY loss already exists. Additional research will be undertaken only for injuries for which information on the inflicted QALY loss may not yet be available. In this case, however, the cost incurred to generate the relevant information will be a one-time only cost, while the resulting information will likely be utilized in a multitude of future cases. Besides the low costs required for its implementation, the proposed approach is also expected to result in significant litigation cost savings. Under the proposed framework, the judge will only need to be aware of the type of the injury to be able to take advantage of the relevant range of QALY losses and assess the corresponding pain and suffering damages. Given that a simple physical description of the injury will likely be available to the court, additional medical experts will therefore not be necessary to evaluate the condition. This will lower litigation costs and accelerate the adjudication. The fact that the proposed approach will generate predictable amounts may induce the opposing parties to enter settlements. Increased settlement rates will alleviate the administrative cost burden of the courts. Moreover, foreseeable awards will facilitate deterrence and loss spreading as explained in the previous paragraphs, hence further reducing the overall administrative costs of the tort system.

Employing insights from health economics regarding the impact of different types of injuries in the context of tort law to assess pain and suffering damages has been demonstrated in this study to positively affect the attainment of the goals of tort law both from a legal perspective and from a law and economics point of view. Given that current assessment approaches in European countries do not take into account such insights, the proposed QALY framework is undoubtedly a superior approach for generating pain and suffering damages. Besides being able to reflect the immaterial loss incurred after different types of injuries, the proposed approach can also assess damages for immaterial losses relatively inexpensively, can potentially achieve significant cost savings for the tort system and create incentives for people to reduce accidents and spread accident losses. It moreover takes into account peoples' evaluations of the immaterial loss incurred as a result of different personal injuries, which leads to amounts that perform better in compensating the victim and acknowledging her harm than the amounts resulting from current approaches based on previously awarded amounts. Besides the benefits generated by the proposed framework for the attainment of tort law goals, the analysis has demonstrated that the QALY approach has additional positive side effects. One of these positive side effects is the ability of the proposed framework to ameliorate the problem of victims' strategic behavior.[812] Assessing pain and suffering damages on the basis of

---

[812]   See *supra* chapter 5 at section 5.4.1.

evaluations of QALY losses, which have been generated prior to the trial and in a different context, allows the court to remain unaffected by potential exaggerated assertions of the victim regarding the magnitude of the loss experienced. Another positive side effect of the proposed approach is that it can induce victims to mitigate their losses, if and to the extent mitigation is possible, by awarding pain and suffering damages that are restricted to the optimally mitigated immaterial losses as well as an additional amount corresponding to the costs of mitigation.[813] Both adjacent benefits of the proposed approach, namely dealing with victims' strategic behavior and inducing victims to mitigate their losses, are expected to lead to a further reduction of the costs of the tort system.

An additional advantage of the proposed approach is the fact that it could be smoothly introduced into the judicial system in two stages. In the first stage, lawyers would be encouraged to incorporate into their claims existing QALY information regarding personal injuries. The resulting pain and suffering damages based on this information would then gradually find their way into the relevant damage tables, tariffs, etc., and the QALY approach would gain ground from the bottom up. Alternatively, tables with amounts based on QALY research could be compiled by a group of experts and be circulated to courts for consulting. This would lead to a more accelerated top-down implementation of the approach. In the second stage, the tables compiled over time in one way or another, would be incorporated into a legal rule and become binding for the judge, who would only be allowed to deviate from the stipulated range of amounts in extreme cases.

In conclusion, the present study has demonstrated that the proposed QALY framework based on insights from health economics research involving the impact of different health conditions on the quality of life can significantly improve the assessment of pain and suffering damages. This conclusion is not affected if insights from cognitive psychology are taken into account.[814] These insights suggest that the psychological phenomena of hedonic adaptation neglect and focusing illusion may influence victims (i.e. plaintiffs) to exaggerate their immaterial loss, and judges to award excessive pain and suffering damages that do not correctly reflect the true immaterial loss of the victim. The preceding analysis explained that if these phenomena truly manifest, the proposed QALY approach could potentially incorporate them in the assessment of pain and suffering damages. If people who have already suffered a certain health condition for a significant amount of time evaluate the QALY loss associated with that condition, then this evaluation would likely incorporate adaptation. Moreover, if generic measures are used to perform these evaluations, the problem of the focusing illusion may be limited, because the respondent will be required to

---

[813] See *supra* chapter 5 at section 5.4.2.
[814] See *supra* chapter 6.

consider many different dimensions of life, some of which may not be affected by the injury at all. Basing the calculation of pain and suffering damages on the QALY losses, which have been generated under these conditions, could potentially circumvent the problem of victims' and judges' hedonic misperceptions. However, the available empirical proof shows that the extent of the occurrence of hedonic adaptation and focusing illusion is still unknown for different types of injuries. Therefore, more injury-specific research is required before deciding to take them into consideration in the assessment of pain and suffering damages. However, even if sufficiently eloquent empirical evidence on the occurrence of hedonic adaptation becomes available, it may still not be appropriate to incorporate hedonic adaptation into damage assessment based on normative considerations. This study has aimed to demonstrate the ability of the proposed QALY approach to yield pain and suffering damages that can reflect these phenomena, without reaching definite conclusions on the normative desirability of such an inclusion. More research is therefore necessary to address these concerns.

8.2. USING A MEASURE FROM HEALTH ECONOMICS IN THE CONTEXT OF TORT LAW

The preceding analysis demonstrated that a QALY-based framework could significantly improve the current assessment of pain and suffering damages. However, although the benefits of utilizing the QALY in the context of tort law have been made obvious, the fact that the QALY is a measure that has its origin in a different discipline may generate some concerns as to whether it can actually be used in an alternative context. The detailed analysis in chapter 4 explained that the QALY is a measure used in the context of health economics that enjoys strong scientific support, as it has resulted from thorough research over the last 20 years. The QALY can evaluate health outcomes resulting from medical treatments and interventions that affect both quality of life and life expectancy. However, apart from having certain important qualities, such as the ability to evaluate the impact of different health conditions on health and longevity, which are also relevant for a potential use of the QALY in the context of tort law, the analysis pointed out that the QALY also suffers from certain shortcomings. These include for instance the fact that there may be different QALY values for one health condition, the fact that a single WTP per QALY may not exist or be accepted in the context of health economics, etc. The question then arises as to whether using QALYs in the alternative context of tort law should even be considered, given that the QALY is not just yet a perfect measure for the purpose for which it was created and employed. Although this is a reasonable concern, the analysis in chapter 5 demonstrated that many of the shortcomings of QALYs in the context of health economics lose their relevance if the QALY is used for the assessment of pain and suffering damages in the context of tort law. Using QALYs for the assessment of pain and suffering damages serves purposes other than the utilization of the QALY in the domain of health care allocation. Therefore, what is considered as a limitation of the QALY in that context does not necessarily pose a problem in the context of tort law. The fact, for instance, that a range of QALY values exists for a specific health condition is not problematic in the context of assessing pain and suffering damages. On the contrary, it is desirable, as it implies that a range of pain and suffering damages for a given injury will be generated which will leave the judge the discretion to award an amount of damages that corresponds to the personal circumstances of the victim.[815] Nevertheless, even if a few shortcomings persist, a potential general implementation of the QALY for the assessment of pain and suffering damages would likely stimulate research, hence refining the use of the QALY in the context of tort law and dealing with these shortcomings. In any case, even with the shortcomings that may persist, previous chapters have demonstrated that, compared to current methods, the proposed QALY framework would be an improvement for the assessment of pain and suffering damages.

The QALY can be utilized in the domain of tort law by taking into consideration those elements that are relevant, namely the ability to express quality and quantity of life. However, this does not imply that any results from QALY research will be automatically accepted. Chapter 5 explained that QALY research results should first be scrutinized to decide whether they are appropriate for use in the proposed alternative setting.[816] The relevant literature with information on evaluations of QALY losses should hence reach a threshold of certain scientific quality in order to be taken into consideration, should stipulate whether the evaluations pertain to the injury at hand or a health condition with comparable impact, and so on. The use of the QALY so far has been restricted in the context of health economics for health care allocation purposes and therefore any efforts to improve it have concentrated on its utilization in that context. Undertaking targeted research to make the QALY more compatible with assessing injuries in a tort law setting is hence reasonably expected to solve remaining issues relating to the implementation of the QALY in this alternative context.

Current legal and law and economics approaches for the assessment of pain and suffering damages lack a measure that is competent to express the loss in both life quality and duration due to health impairment and also to evaluate this loss in monetary terms. The present study addresses this lack by suggesting that an interdisciplinary information transfer should take place, i.e. existing research results from the domain of health economics that possess the aforementioned

---

[815] See *supra* chapter 5 at section 5.3.1.
[816] See *supra* chapter 5 at section 5.3.2.

desirable characteristics and are hence highly relevant for the assessment of pain and suffering damages, should be used in the context of tort law. Using this highly relevant and freely available information for the assessment of pain and suffering damages should not be excluded merely because of the fact that the QALY was initially intended for use in a different context.

8.3. QALYs IN LEGAL AND LAW AND ECONOMICS SCHOLARSHIP

The preceding analysis demonstrated that the QALY has some distinctive features which render it an appropriate measure to employ in alternative contexts involving assessments about health and life. Given that tort law primarily involves wrongful harms inflicted on health and life and necessitates a measure that can assess the resulting losses, it is surprising that only few pieces of legal and law and economics scholarship so far have realized and explored the potential of the QALY in this context.

Miller is one of the few authors who have advocated an alternative use of the QALY in the context of tort law.[817] In his paper from 2000, Miller proposes to use QALYs as a technique that forensic experts can apply to each and every individual injury case to help guide jury valuations on quality of life losses. The main aim of the paper is to '*define, categorize and demonstrate the usefulness of different QALY scales in a forensic economics context*'.[818] He suggests that forensic experts assisting the court could choose the most appropriate of these scales for the injury at hand and use it to evaluate the plaintiff's losses, first themselves and then by polling the plaintiff and/or his caregivers to find out their valuations. However, as explained in chapter 5, evaluating the QALY loss of an injury *ad hoc* as Miller suggests is in fact detrimental to the attainment of the goals of tort law. The *ad hoc* evaluation is expected to increase the administrative costs of the tort system because the presence of qualified experts would be required in the courtroom to perform the evaluations, which would also lead to slower adjudication and fewer cases being decided overall. Moreover, evaluating the QALY loss on the spot would result in highly individualized awards, hence hindering the achievement of deterrence and loss spreading as potential injurers (and insurers) would not be able to predict the size of the amounts and incorporate it into their care and activity (and premium setting) decisions. However the fact that Miller proposes to use QALYs for the assessment of pain and suffering damages, even if in a different way than it is proposed herein,

---

817   Miller, *Valuing Nonfatal Quality of Life Losses with Quality-Adjusted Life Years: The Health Economist's Meow*, pp. 145–167.
818   Ibid., p. 146.

shows that he acknowledges how desirable the characteristics of the QALY are for potential use in damages assessment in the context of tort law.

The idea to use QALYs in a tort context was revisited in 2010 by Karapanou and Visscher.[819] We observe a general consensus in legal scholarship, namely that in order to achieve the goals of compensation and satisfaction, pain and suffering damages for personal injuries should be based on the severity and duration of the impairment to health. However, the approaches used for the assessment of pain and suffering damages do not reflect these factors. After briefly reviewing these approaches, we argue that assessing damages on the basis of existing information from QALY research could indeed enable the impact of the health impairment on the victim to be reflected in the awards. We use QALY information to generate pain and suffering damages for a few types of injuries and compare the resulting amounts with amounts of pain and suffering damages that were awarded in concrete cases. The results indicate that the amounts currently awarded are too low when compared to the impact of the injuries on quality of life.

In a more recent paper of 2011, Studdert et al. review existing approaches for scheduling pain and suffering damages and suggest that the best alternative involves using insights from health economics.[820] Their analysis focuses particularly on awarding damages in cases of medical malpractice. By combining a dataset from a study of immaterial loss associated with work-related injuries that was conducted between 1988 and 1991 with original empirical work, they try to generate quality-weights for different types of injuries.[821] These quality-weights can then be used as a basis for ranking injuries to create a schedule for pain and suffering damages. The fact that the quality-weights generated may not capture all dimensions of injuries is not important given that the calculation is intended to serve as proof that building a schedule on the basis of such valuations is feasible. The paper puts the emphasis on demonstrating how a schedule based on insights from health economics could be constructed and hence does not deal with a number of other issues that would be relevant for actually implementing these schedules such as how the resulting quality-weights should be monetized so as to arrive at pain and suffering damages, how the amounts should be discounted, how these schedules would find their way into the tort system, etc. Nevertheless, the claim of the authors that using insights from health economics is a superior approach for the assessment of pain and suffering damages fully agrees with the conclusions arrived at in this study.

---

[819]   Vaia Karapanou and Louis Visscher, "Towards a Better Assessment of Pain and Suffering Damages," *Journal of European Tort Law* 1, no. 1 (2010), pp. 48–74. Parts of the paper have been elaborated on and extensively discussed in the present book.

[820]   David M. Studdert et al., "Rationalizing Noneconomic Damages: A Health-Utilities Approach," *Law and Contemporary Problems* 74 (2011), pp. 57–101.

[821]   The paper refers to quality-weights with the term health-utilities.

Another line of literature has linked QALYs with pain and suffering damages for personal injuries in a completely different manner. Some authors use the amounts that have been awarded for pain and suffering in combination with the QALY-weights relating to different types of injuries to derive the monetary value of a QALY that is implied by the awards.[822] The underlying idea is that these values could potentially be used for analyzing health and safety regulation.[823] Evidently, this line of literature is not relevant to the questions investigated in this study. Nevertheless it should be remarked that due to the problems attached to the current legal approaches, pain and suffering damages do not necessarily reflect with accuracy the severity of the injury and the immaterial loss incurred. Therefore, deriving the implied monetary value of a QALY from these amounts will likely result in an arbitrary value that should hence not be used for analyzing important issues like the ones involving safety and health. The potential of the QALY has also been acknowledged by some legal scholars who remark that using QALYs to facilitate assessments about the health and life of individuals could potentially bring about an improvement in the relevant tort law context.[824]

The review of literature that refers to QALYs in conjunction with pain and suffering damage assessment shows that the potential virtues of the QALY for the context of tort law have not yet been fully realized nor have they received due attention from legal and law and economics scholarship. A few reasons may account for this under-exploration of the QALY. The fact for instance that the QALY has been developed and utilized almost exclusively in the context of health economics, a discipline which has no communication with tort law and/ or the economic analysis of tort law, may have hindered the dissemination of QALY research in these fields. Moreover, the fact that the QALY is supported by voluminous research, from which it may be hard to distinguish what is relevant for the potential utilization of the QALY in the alternative context of tort law, may further account for the under-exploration of the QALY. The present study has recognized the competence of the QALY to be used in the context of tort law for the assessment of pain and suffering damages and has illustrated how a QALY-based framework could work in practice. By identifying and presenting the information from QALY research that is relevant in the context of tort law, this study has hopefully made this research more accessible to readers of a legal

---

[822] See for instance Deborah V. Aiken and William W. Zamula, "Valuation of Quality of Life Losses Associated with Nonfatal Injury: Insights from Jury Verdict Data," *Review of Law & Economics* 5, no. 1 (2009), pp. 287–310.

[823] Ibid., pp. 293, 306.

[824] See for instance Willem H. van Boom, "Structurele fouten in het aansprakelijkheidsrecht," inaugural address Tilburg University (The Hague: BJU, 2003), pp. 21–26, maintaining that it would be worthwhile to use the QALY in tort law to better determine the benefits of precaution with respect to the health and life of individuals. See also Lars Noah, "Comfortably numb: medicalizing (and mitigating pain and suffering damages)," *University of Michigan Journal of Law Reform* 42, no. 2 (2008).

and law and economics background, and has taken the first step for its further dissemination to lawyers and judges.

8.4. AVENUES FOR FUTURE RESEARCH

Multiple avenues will be opened for future research if the idea of using insights from the domain of health economics for the assessment of pain and suffering damages is considered. Additional research will have to be undertaken to generate QALY-weights with respect to personal injuries for which information may not yet be available. Moreover, although the monetary value of a QALY will ideally be a product of multilevel consultation between relevant parties (insurance companies, producers, victim and consumer associations, medical doctors, lawyers, judges, etc.) and of ongoing scientific results, more research may be required to arrive at the monetary value for a QALY that would be appropriate to use in each country.

The analysis herein has focused particularly on the European legal context. However, it would be interesting to investigate whether and how the proposed QALY framework for the assessment of pain and suffering damages should be modified for potential implementation in countries outside Europe. An issue that would emerge if the proposed approach were to be applied in USA, for example, relates to contingency fees. More specifically, given that in the USA contingency fees are in practice paid through the amounts awarded for pain and suffering, it would be interesting to explore how contingency fees would be dealt with if the QALY framework were to be implemented. Similar issues that would necessitate further research could arise in any country that considers the application of the proposed approach.

8.5. THE WAY FORWARD

> *'Where is the wisdom we have lost in knowledge?*
> *Where is the knowledge we have lost in information?'*
>
> Thomas S. Eliot (1934), *The Rock*

Scientific research has long been characterized by the acquirement of expertise in increasingly specialized scientific fields. The division is instructive, enabling in-depth exploration and analysis and resulting in the accumulation of an enormous amount of information. However, the exponentially growing volume of information combined with the highly specialized nature of this information makes the communication between research fields difficult and results in their compartmentalization. The lack of interdisciplinary communication hence undermines the product of specialization, since the information acquired cannot be used to facilitate the broader understanding and treatment of phenomena and problems that transcend disciplines.

This study has demonstrated that tort law alone is not competent to effectively answer the question of how the assessment of pain and suffering damages arising from personal physical injuries can be improved. The assessment of damages for personal injuries involves an evaluation of the impact of the immaterial loss incurred as a result of the injury, which also falls outside the competence of the economic analysis of tort law. Therefore, although law and economics can provide important insights that should be taken into account to answer the question, it still cannot provide the tools with which to evaluate the impact of injuries. These tools are to be found in a specialized research field dealing precisely with how personal injuries and other health conditions affect individuals. The present study has maintained that using insights from health economics regarding the impact of different health conditions on the quality of life could improve the assessment of pain and suffering damages. A framework was hence proposed to enable this interdisciplinary information transfer.

Besides responding to the research questions posed, this study has also presented a concrete example of how an interdisciplinary approach to a complex and practical problem may lead to better understanding and treatment of it. The overarching recommendation that follows is that for problems sharing these characteristics and requiring a multi-dimensional, holistic treatment, interdisciplinarity is to be encouraged. Despite the increased efforts required to delve into the specialized information from an unfamiliar discipline, this study suggests that the benefits of doing so outweigh the costs.

BIBLIOGRAPHY

Abellan-Perpiñan, Jose Maria, Han Bleichrodt, and Jose Luis Pinto-Prades. "The Predictive Validity of Prospect Theory Versus Expected Utility in Health Utility Measurement." *Journal of Health Economics* 28, no. 6 (12, 2009): 1039–1047.

Abraham, Kenneth S. *The Forms and Functions of Tort Law.* Concepts and Insights Series. 2nd ed. New York: Foundation Press, 2002.

Adams, Michael. "Warum Kein Ersatz Von Nichtvermögensschäden?" In *Allokationseffizienz in Der Rechtsordnung,* edited by Ott, Claus and Hans-Bernd Schäfer. Berlin: Springer Verlag, 1989.

Adler, Matthew D. "QALY's and Policy Evaluation: A New Perspective." *Yale Journal of Health Policy, Law, and Ethics* 6 (2006): 1.

Adler, Matthew and Eric A Posner. "Happiness Research and Cost-Benefit Analysis." *The Journal of Legal Studies* 37, no. S2, Legal Implications of the New Research on Happiness. A Conference Sponsored by the John M. Olin Program in Law and Economics at the University of Chicago Law School (2008): S253–S292.

Aiken, Deborah V. and William W. Zamula. "Valuation of Quality of Life Losses Associated with Nonfatal Injury: Insights from Jury Verdict Data." *Review of Law & Economics* 5, no. 1 (2009): 287–310.

Antiretroviral Therapy Cohort Collaboration. "Life expectancy of individuals on combination antiretroviral therapy in high-income countries: a collaborative analysis of 14 cohort studies." *The Lancet* 372 (9635, 2008): 293–299.

Antonak, Richard F. and Hanoch Livneh. "Psychosocial Adaptation to Disability and its Investigation among Persons with Multiple Sclerosis." *Social Science & Medicine* 40, no. 8 (4, 1995): 1099–1108.

ANWB. *Verkeersrecht: Smartengeld.* The Haag: ANWB, 2014.

Arcuri, Alessandra. "Risk Regulation." In *Regulation and Economics,* edited by Pacces, Alessio M. and Roger J. Van den Bergh, 302–338. Cheltenham: Edward Elgar, 2012.

Arlen, Jennifer H. "Tort Damages." In *Encyclopedia of Law and Economics, Volume II. Civil Law and Economics,* edited by Bouckaert, Boudewijn and Gerrit De Geest, 682–734. Cheltenham: Edward Elgar, 2000.

—. "Compensation Systems and Efficient Deterrence." *Maryland Law Review* 52 (1993): 1093–1136.

—. "Liability for Physical Injury when Injurers as Well as Victims Suffer Losses." *Journal of Law, Economics, & Organization* 8, no. 2 (1992): 411–426.

—. "Re-Examining Liability Rules when Injurers as Well as Victims Suffer Losses." *International Review of Law and Economics* 10, no. 3 (12, 1990): 233–239.

Ashenfelter, Orley. "Measuring the Value of a Statistical Life: Problems and Prospects." *The Economic Journal* 116, no. 510 (2006): C10–C23.

Atkinson, Scott E. and Robert Halvorsen. "The Valuation of Risks to Life: Evidence from the Market for Automobiles." *Review of Economics and Statistics* 72, no. 1 (1990): 133–136.

Avraham, Ronen. "Putting a Price on Pain-and-Suffering Damages: A Critique of the Current Approaches and a Preliminary Proposal for Change." *Northwestern University Law Review* 100, no. 1 (2006): 87–120.

—. "Should Pain-and-Suffering Damages be Abolished from Tort Law? More Experimental Evidence." *University of Toronto Law Journal* 55 (2005): 941–979.

Bagenstos, Samuel R. and Margo Schlanger. "Hedonic Damages, Hedonic Adaptation, and Disability." *Vanderbilt Law Review* 60, no. 3 (2007): 745–797.

Baker, Tom and Peter Siegelman, "The Law and Economics of Liability Insurance: A Theoretical and Empirical Review." In *Research Handbook on the Economics of Torts,* edited by Arlen, Jennifer, 169–196. Cheltenham: Edward Elgar Publishing Ltd, 2013.

Bala, M. V., L. L. Wood, G. A. Zarkin, E. C. Norton, A. Gafni, and B. O'Brien. "Valuing Outcomes in Health Care: A Comparison of Willingness to Pay and Quality-Adjusted Life-Years." *Journal of Clinical Epidemiology* 51, no. 8 (1998): 667–676.

Baron, Jonathan, David A. Asch, Angela Fagerlin, Christopher Jepson, George Loewenstein, Jason Riis, Margaret G. Stineman, and Peter A. Ubel. "Effect of Assessment Method on the Discrepancy between Judgments of Health Disorders People have and do Not have: A Web Study." *Medical Decision Making* 23, (2003): 422–434.

Bayoumi, Ahmed M. and Donald A. Redelmeier. "Economic Methods for Measuring the Quality of Life Associated with HIV Infection." *Quality of Life Research* 8, no. 6 (1999): 471–480.

Berridge, Virginia. *AIDS in the UK, the Making of Policy, 1981–1994.* Oxford: Oxford University Press, 1996.

Birch, Stephen and Cam Donaldson. "Valuing the Benefits and Costs of Health Care Programmes: Where's the 'extra' in Extra-Welfarism?" *Social Science & Medicine* 56 (2003): 1121–1133.

Blackmore, C. Craig, Scott D. Ramsey, Frederick A. Mann, and Richard A. Deyo. "Cervical Spine Screening with CT in Trauma Patients: A Cost-Effectiveness Analysis." *Radiology* 212, no. 1 (1999): 117–125.

Bleichrodt, Han. "QALYs and HYEs: Under what Conditions are they Equivalent?" *Journal of Health Economics* 14 (1995): 17–37.

Bleichrodt, Han and Magnus Johannesson. "An Experimental Test of a Theoretical Foundation for Rating-Scale Valuations." *Medical Decision Making* 17, no. 2 (1997): 208–216.

—. "Standard Gamble, Time Trade-Off and Rating Scale: Experimental Results on the Ranking Properties of QALYs." *Journal of Health Economics* 16 (1997): 155–175.

Bleichrodt, Han and John Quiggin. "Life-Cycle Preferences Over Consumption and Health: When is Cost-Effectiveness Analysis Equivalent to Cost-Benefit Analysis?" *Journal of Health Economics* 18 (1999): 681–708.

Bleichrodt, Han, Jose Luis Pinto, and Peter P. Wakker. "Making Descriptive use of Prospect Theory to Improve the Prescriptive use of Expected Utility." *Management Science* 47, no. 11 (2001): 1498–1514.

Blumenschein, Karen and Magnus Johannesson. "Incorporating Quality of Life Changes into Economic Evaluations of Health Care: An Overview." *Health Policy* 36 (1996): 155–166.

—. "Relationship between Quality of Life Instruments, Health State Utilities, and Willingness to Pay in Patients with Asthma." *Annals of Allergy, Asthma & Immunology* 80, no. 2 (1998): 189–194.

Bobinac, Ana, Job A. van Exel, Frans F. H. Rutten, and Werner B. F. Brouwer. "Willingness to Pay for a Quality-Adjusted Life-Year: The Individual Perspective." *Value in Health* 13, no. 8 (2010): 1046–1055.

Bobinac, Ana. *Economic Evaluations of Health Technologies: Insights into the measurement and valuation of benefits.* Dissertation, Erasmus University Rotterdam: The Netherlands, 2012.

Bona, Marco. "Personal Injury Compensation in Italy." In *Personal Injury Compensation in Europe*, edited by Bona, Marco and Philip Mead. Deventer: Kluwer, 2003.

Bovbjerg, Randall R., Frank A. Sloan, and James F. Blumstein. "Valuing Life and Limb in Tort: Scheduling 'Pain and Suffering'." *Northwestern University Law Review* 83, no. 4 (1989): 908–976.

Brazier, John, Mark Deverill, Colin Green, R. Harper, and Andrew Booth. "A Review of the Use of Health Status Measures in Economic Evaluation." *Health Technology Assessment* 3, no. 9 (1999): 1–164.

Brazier, John, Julie Ratcliffe, Joshua A. Salomon, and Aki Tsuchiya. *Measuring and Valuing Health Benefits for Economic Evaluation.* Oxford; New York: Oxford University Press, 2007.

Brazier, John, Tim Usherwood, Rosemary Harper, and Kate Thomas. "Deriving a Preference-Based Single Index from the UK SF-36 Health Survey." *Journal of Clinical Epidemiology* 51, no. 11 (1998): 1115–1128.

Brazier, John, Jennifer Roberts, Aki Tsuchiya, and Jan Busschbach. "A Comparison of the EQ-5D and SF-6D Across Seven Patient Groups." *Health Economics* 13, no. 9 (2004): 873–884.

Brazier, John, Jennifer Roberts, and Mark Deverill. "The Estimation of a Preference-Based Measure of Health from the SF-36." *Journal of Health Economics* 21, no. 2 (2002): 271–292.

Brickman, Philip, Dan Coates, and Ronnie Janoff-Bulman. "Lottery Winners and Accident Victims: Is Happiness Relative?" *Journal of Personality and Social Psychology* 36, no. 8 (8, 1978): 917–927.

Brisson, Mark and John Edmunds. *Valuing the Benefit of Varicella Vaccination: Comparison of Willingness to Pay and Quality-Adjusted Life Years.* Discussion Paper 04–02. City University Department of Economics, 2002.

Bronsteen, John, Christopher Buccafusco, and Jonathan C. Masur. "Hedonic Adaptation and the Settlement of Civil Lawsuits." *Columbia Law Review* 108 (2008): 1516–1550.

Broome, John. "Qalys." *Journal of Public Economics* 50 (1993): 149–167.

Brothers, T. E., G. A. Rios, J. G. Robison, and B. M. Elliott. "Justification of Intervention for Limb-Threatening Ischemia: A Surgical Decision Analysis." *Cardiovascular Surgery* 7, no. 1 (1999): 62–69.

Brouwer, Werner B. F., Louis W. Niessen, Maarten J. Postma, and Frans F. H. Rutten. "Need for Differential Discounting of Costs and Health Effects in Cost Effectiveness Analyses." *British Medical Journal* 331 (2005): 446–448.

Brouwer, Werner B. F., Anthony J. Culyer, N. Job A. van Exel, and Frans F. H. Rutten. "Welfarism Vs. Extra-Welfarism." *Journal of Health Economics* 27, no. 2 (3, 2008): 325–338.

Brouwer, Werner B. F. and Marc A. Koopmanschap. "On the Economic Foundations of CEA. Ladies and Gentlemen, Take Your Positions!" *Journal of Health Economics* 19, no. 4 (7, 2000): 439–459.

Brouwer, Werner B. F., Job A. van Exel, Rachel Baker, and Cam Donaldson. "The New Myth: The Social Value of the QALY." *PharmacoEconomics* 26, no. 1 (2008): 1–4.

Brown, Craig. "Deterrence in Tort and No-Fault: The New Zealand Experience." *California Law Review* 73 (1985): 976–1002.

Brown, John Prather. "Toward an Economic Theory of Liability." *The Journal of Legal Studies* 2, no. 2 (Jun., 1973): 323–349.

Brown, Melissa M., Gary C. Brown, Sanjay Sharma, Brandon Busbee, and Heidi Brown. "Quality of Life Associated with Unilateral and Bilateral Good Vision." *Ophthalmology* 108, no. 4 (2001): 643–647.

Bruce, Christopher. "Selecting the Discount Rate." *Expert Witness* 1, no. 3 (1996): 7 March 2012.

Busbee, Brandon G., Melissa M. Brown, Gary C. Brown, and Sanjay Sharma. "Incremental Cost-Effectiveness of Initial Cataract Surgery." *Ophthalmology* 109, no. 3 (2002): 606–612.

—. "Cost-Utility Analysis of Cataract Surgery in the Second Eye." *Ophthalmology* 110, no. 12 (12, 2003): 2310–2317.

Bush, J. W., S. Fanshel, and M. M. Chen. "Analysis of a Tuberculin Testing Program using a Health Status Index." *Socio-Economic Planning Sciences* 6, no. 1 (2, 1972): 49–68.

Busnelli, Francesco D. and Giovanni Comandé. "Italy." In *Compensation for Personal Injury in a Comparative Perspective*, edited by Koch, Bernhard A. and Helmut Koziol. Vienna; New York: Springer, 2003.

—. "Italy." In *Damages for Non-Pecuniary Loss in a Comparative Perspective*, edited by Rogers, W. V. Horton. Vienna; New York: Springer, 2001.

Calabresi, Guido. *The Costs of Accidents. A Legal and Economic Analysis.* 5th ed. New Haven: Yale University Press, 1977.

Calfee, John E. and Paul H. Rubin. "Some Implications of Damage Payments for Nonpecuniary Losses." *The Journal of Legal Studies* 21, no. 2 (1992): 371–411.

Cane, Peter and Patrick Atiyah. *Atiyah's Accidents, Compensation and the Law.* 7th ed. Cambridge: Cambridge University Press, 2006.

Carr-Hill, R. A. "Background Material for the Workshop on QALYs. Assumptions on the QALY Procedure." *Social Science and Medicine* 29, no. 3 (1989): 469–477.

CDA Cost-Effectiveness Group. "Cost-Effectiveness of Intensive Glycemic Control, Intensified Hypertension Control, and Serum Cholesterol Level Reduction for Type 2 Diabetes." *Journal of the American Medical Association* 287, no. 19 (2002): 2542–2551.

Center for the Evaluation of Value and Risk in Health. "Cost-Effectiveness Analysis Registry." Institute for Clinical Research and Health Policy Studies, Tufts Medical Center, accessed 31 March 2014, www.cearegistry.org.

Cheng, André K. and John K. Niparko. "Cost-Utility of the Cochlear Implant in Adults. A Meta-Analysis." *Archives of Otolaryngology – Head & Neck Surgery* 125 (1999): 1214–1218.

Cheng, André K., Haya R. Rubin, Neil R. Powe, Nancy K. Mellon, Howard W. Francis, and John K. Niparko. "Cost-Utility Analysis of Cochlear Implant in Children." *Journal of the American Medical Association* 284, no. 7 (2000): 850–856.

Clarke, Philip, Alastair Gray, and Rury Holman. "Estimating Utility Values for Health States of Type 2 Diabetic Patients using the EQ-5D (UKPDS 62)." *Medical Decision Making* 22, no. 4 (2002): 340–349.

Claxton, Karl, Mike Paulden, Hugh Gravelle, Werner Brouwer, and Anthony J. Culyer. "Discounting and decision making in the economic evaluation of health-care technologies." *Health Economics* 20, no. 1 (2011): 2–15.

Claxton, Karl, Steve Martin, Marta Soares, Nigel Rice, Eldon Spackman, Sebastian Hinde, Nancy Devlin, Peter C Smith and Mark Sculpher. "Methods for the Estimation of the NICE Cost Effectiveness Threshold. Revised Report Following Referees Comments." Centre for Health Economics, University of York (2013): 1–100.

Coco, Andrew. "The Cost-Effectiveness of Expanded Testing for Primary HIV Infection." *Annals of Family Medicine* 3, no. 5 (2005): 391–399.

College voor Zorgverzekeringen (CVZ). *Richtlijnen voor Farmacoeconomisch Onderzoek; geactualiseerde versie.* Dieman: CVZ 2006.

Comandé, Giovanni. "Doing Away with Inequality in Loss of Enjoyment of Life." In *Personal Injury and Wrongful Death Damages Calculations: Transatlantic Dialogue*, edited by Ward, John O. and Robert J. Thornton. Vol. 91, 255: Emerald Group Publishing, 2009.

Concise Medical Dictionary. 8th ed. Oxford University Press: 2010, accessed 31 March 2014. www.oxfordreference.com/view/10.1093/acref/9780199557141.001.0001/acref-9780199557141.

Cook, Philip J. and Daniel A. Graham. "The Demand for Insurance and Protection: The Case of Irreplaceable Commodities." *The Quarterly Journal of Economics* 91, no. 1 (1977): 143–156.

Cookson, Richard and Paul Dolan. "Public Views on Health Care Rationing: A Group Discussion Study." *Health Policy* 49, no. 1–2 (9, 1999): 63–74.

Cooter, Robert. "Towards a Market in Unmatured Tort Claims." *Virginia Law Review* 75 (1989): 383–412.

Cooter, Robert and Ariel Porat. "Liability for Lapses: First or Second Order Negligence?" *American Law and Economics Association Annual Meetings Working Paper 70* (2008): 1–39.

Cooter, Robert and Thomas Ulen. *Law and Economics.* 5th ed. USA: Pearson Addison Wesley, 2008.

Cousy, Herman and Dimitri Droshout. "Belgium." In *Damages for Non-Pecuniary Loss in a Comparative Perspective*, edited by Rogers, W. V. Horton. Vienna; New York: Springer, 2001.

—. "Belgium." In *Compensation for Personal Injury in a Comparative Perspective*, edited by Koch, Bernhard A. and Helmut Koziol. Vienna; New York: Springer, 2003.

Craig, Benjamin M., A. Simon Pickard, Elly Stolk and John E. Brazier. "US Valuation of the SF-6D." *Medical Decision Making* 33, no. 6 (2013): 793–803.

Croley, Steven P. and Jon D. Hanson. "The Nonpecuniary Costs of Accidents: Pain-and-Suffering Damages in Tort Law." *Harvard Law Review* 108, no. 8 (1995): 1785–1917.

Culyer, Anthony J. "The Normative Economics of Health Care Finance and Provision." *Oxford Review of Economic Policy* 5, no. 1 (1989): 34–58.

Cummins, J. David, Richard D. Phillips, and Mary A. Weiss. "The Incentive Effects of No-Fault Automobile Insurance." *Journal of Law and Economics* 44, no. 2 (2001): 427–464.

Damschroder, Laura J., Brian J. Zikmund-Fisher, and Peter A. Ubel. "Considering Adaptation in Preference Elicitations." *Health Psychology* 27, no. 3 (2008): 394–399.

Danzon, Patricia M. "Tort Reform and the Role of Government in Private Insurance Markets." *The Journal of Legal Studies* 13 (1984): 517–550.

Dardis, Rachel. "The Value of a Life: New Evidence from the Marketplace." *American Economic Review* 70, no. 5 (1980): 1077–1082.

de Pianto, David. "Tort Damages and the (Misunderstood) Money-Happiness Connection." *Arizona State Law Journal* 44, no 4. (2012): 1385–1430.

de Vroom, Bert. "The Dutch Reaction to Contaminated Blood: An Example of Cooperative Governance." In *Success and Failure in Public Governance: A Comparative Analysis*, edited by Bovens, Mark, Paul 't Hart and B. Guy Peters, 508–532. Cheltenham, UK: Edward Elgar, 2001.

Delwart, E. L., N. D. Kalmin, T. S. Jones, D. J. Ladd, B. Foley, L. H. Tobler, R. C. Tsui, and M. P. Busch. "First Report of Human Immunodeficiency Virus Transmission Via an RNA-Screened Blood Donation." *Vox Sang* 86, no. 3 (2004): 171–177.

den Uyl, Debby, van der Horst-Bruinsma, Irene E., and Michiel van Agtmael. "Progression of HIV to AIDS: A Protective Role for HLA-B27." *AIDS Reviews* 6, (2004): 80–96.

Department for Work and Pensions. "Recovery of benefits and lump sum payments and NHS charges: technical guidance." (2013).

Devlin, Nancy and David Parkin. "Does NICE have a Cost Effectiveness Threshold and what Other Factors Influence its Decisions? A Discrete Choice Analysis." *Health Economics* 13, no. 5 (2004): 437–452.

Devlin, Rose Anne. "Some Welfare Implications of No-Fault Automobile Insurance." *International Review of Law and Economics* 10, no. 2 (9, 1990): 193–205.

Dewees, Don, David Duff, and Michael Trebilcock. *Exploring the Domain of Accident Law. Taking the Facts Seriously.* New York, Oxford: Oxford University Press, 1996.

Dewees, Don and Michael Trebilcock. "The Efficacy of the Tort System and its Alternatives: A Review of Empirical Evidence." *Osgoode Hall Law Journal* 30, no. 1 (1992): 57.

Dolan, Paul. "Developing Methods that really do Value the 'Q' in the QALY." *Health Economics, Policy and Law* 3, no. 1 (2008): 69–77.

Dolan, Paul and Richard Edlin. "Is it really Possible to Built a Bridge between Cost-Benefit Analysis and Cost-Effectiveness Analysis?" *Journal of Health Economics* 21, no. 5 (2002): 827–843.

Dolan, Paul. "The Measurement of Health-Related Quality of Life for Use in Resource Allocation Decisions in Health Care." In *Handbook of Health Economics*, edited by Anthony J. Culyer and Joseph P. Newhouse. Vol. 1, Part 2, 1723–1760: Elsevier, 2000.

Dolan, Paul and Daniel Kahneman. "Interpretations of Utility and their Implications for the Valuation of Health." *The Economic Journal* 118, no. 525 (2008): 215–234.

Dolan, Paul, Rebecca Shaw, Aki Tsuchiya, and Alan Williams. "QALY Maximisation and People's Preferences: A Methodological Review of the Literature." *Health Economics* 14, no. 2 (2005): 197–208.

Drummond, Michael F., Mark Sculpher, George W. Torrance, Bernie J. O'Brien, and Greg L. Stoddart. *Methods for the Economic Evaluation of Health Care Programmes.* 3rd ed. Oxford, New York: Oxford University Press, 2005.

Drummond, Michael, Diana Brixner, Marthe Gold R., Paul Kind, Alistair McGuire, and Erik Nord. "Toward a Consensus on the QALY." *Value in Health* 12, no. s1 (2009): S31–S35.

Edelaar-Peeters, Yvette and Anne M. Stiggelbout. "Anticipated adaptation or scale recalibration?" *Health and Quality of Life Outcomes* 11 (2013): 171–180.

Elbert, Thomas, Annette Sterr, Brigitte Rockstroh, Christo Pantev, Matthias M. Müller, and Edward Taub. "Expansion of the Tonotopic Area in the Auditory Cortex of the Blind." *The Journal of Neuroscience* 22, (2002): 9941–9944.

Epstein, Richard A. "Products Liability as an Insurance Market." *The Journal of Legal Studies* 14, no. 3, Critical Issues in Tort Law Reform: A Search for Principles (Dec., 1985): 645–669.

Etchason, Jeff, Lawrence Petz, Emmett Keeler, Loni Calhoun, Steven Kleinman, Cynthia Snider, Arlene Fink, and Robert Brook. "The Cost Effectiveness of Preoperative Autologous Blood Donations." *The New England Journal of Medicine* 332, no. 11 (1995): 719–724.

European Central Bank. "Annual Average Exchange Rate UK Pound Sterling to Euro." European Central Bank, accessed 31 March 2014. http://sdw.ecb.europa.eu/quickview.do;jsessionid=3B7684CC6E9FC6A5CC6643B99E2E596C?node=2018794&SERIES_KEY=120.EXR.A.GBP.EUR.SP00.A.

European Commission Directorate-General Regional Policy. *Guide to Cost-Benefit Analysis of Investment Project*s. European Commission, 2008.

European Commission, Mobility and Transport, "Statistics – Accidents Data." Accessed 31 March 2014. http://ec.europa.eu/transport/road_safety/specialist/statistics/index_en.htm.

European Road Safety Observatory. *Annual Statistical Report 2011*: European Road Safety Observatory, 2011.

EuroQol Group. "EuroQol: A New Facility for the Measurement of Health-Related Quality of Life." *Health Policy* 16, no. 3 (1990).

Eurostat. "Annual Average Inflation Rates 2000–2012." Eurostat, accessed 31 March 2014. http://epp.eurostat.ec.europa.eu/statistics_explained/index.php/Consumer_prices_-_inflation_and_comparative_price_levels.

—. "Health and Safety at Work Statistics." European Commission, accessed 31 March 2014. http://epp.eurostat.ec.europa.eu/statistics_explained/index.php/Health_and_safety_at_work_statistics.

EuroVaQ, *European Value of a Quality Adjusted Life Year Final Publishable Report*, 2010. http://research.ncl.ac.uk/eurovaq/EuroVaQ_Final_Publishable_Report_and_ Appendices.pdf.

Evans, Christopher, Manouche Tavakoli, and Bruce Crawford. "Use of Quality Adjusted Life Years and Life Years Gained as Benchmarks in Economic Evaluations: A Critical Appraisal." *Health Care Management Science* 7, no. 1 (2004): 43–49.

Evans, William N. and W. Kip Viscusi. "Estimation of State-Dependent Utility Functions using Survey Data." *The Review of Economics and Statistics* 73, no. 1 (1991): 94–104.

Fanshel, S. and J. W. Bush. "A Health-Status Index and its Application to Health-Services Outcomes." *Operations Research* 18, no. 6 (1970): pp. 1021–1066.

Faure, Michael G. "Compensation of Non-Pecuniary Loss: An Economic Perspective." In *European Tort Law, Liber Amicorum for Helmut Koziol*, edited by Magnus, Ulrich and Jaap Spier, 143–159. Frankfurt am Main: Peter Lang, 2000.

Faure, Michael G. and Ton Hartlief. "The Netherlands." In *European Tort Law 2002*, edited by Koziol, Helmut and Barbara C. Steiniger, 305–328. Vienna; New York: Springer, 2003.

Federaal Kenniscentrum voor de Gezondheidszorg (KCE). *Richtlijnen voor Farmacoeconomische Evaluaties in Belgie*. Brussels: KCE 2008.

Feeny, David, William Furlong, George W. Torrance, Charles H. Goldsmith, Zenglong Zhu, Sonja DePauw, Margaret Denton, and Michael Boyle. "Multiattribute and Single-Attribute Utility Functions for the Health Utilities Index Mark 3 System." *Medical Care* 40, no. 2 (2002): 113–128.

Folland, Sherman, Allen C. Goodman, and Miron Stano. *The Economics of Health and Health Care*. 5th ed. Upper Saddler River (NJ): Prentice Hall, 2007.

Francis, Howard W., Nelson Chee, Jennifer Yeagle, André K. Cheng, and John K. Niparko. "Impact of Cochlear Implants on the Functional Health Status of Older Adults." *The Laryngoscope* 112, no. 8 (2002): 1482–1488.

Frederick, Shane and George Loewenstein. "Hedonic Adaptation." In *Well-being: The Foundations of Hedonic Psychology*, edited by Kahneman, Daniel, Ed Diener and Norbert Schwarz. New York: Russell Sage Foundation, 1999.

Frederick, Shane, George Loewenstein, and Ted O'Donoghue. "Time Discounting and Time Preference: A Critical Review." *Journal of Economic Literature* 40, no. 2 (2002): 351–401.

Friedman, David. "What is 'Fair Compensation' for Death Or Injury?" *International Review of Law and Economics* 2, no. 1 (6, 1982): 81–93.

Galand-Carval, Suzanne. "France." In *Damages for Non-Pecuniary Loss in a Comparative Perspective*, edited by Rogers, W. V. Horton. Vienna; New York: Springer, 2001.

Garber, Alan M. "Advances in Cost-Effectiveness Analysis of Health Interventions." In *Handbook of Health Economics*, edited by Culyer, Anthony J. and J. P. Newhouse. 1st ed. Vol. 1, 181–221: Elsevier, 2000.

Garber, Alan M., Milton C. Weinstein, George W. Torrance, and Mark S. Kamlet. "Theoretical Foundations of Cost-Effectiveness Analysis." In *Cost-Effectiveness in Health and Medicine*, edited by Gold, Marthe R., Joanna E. Siegel, Louise B. Russel and Milton C. Weinstein, 25–53. New York, Oxford: Oxford University Press, 1996.

Garber, Alan M. and Charles E. Phelps. "Economic Foundations of Cost-Effectiveness Analysis." *Journal of Health Economics* 16, no. 1 (1997): 1–31.

Garner, Clive, Katherine Allen, Alida Coates, Philip Edwards, John Melville Williams, Philip Mead, Emma Smith, and Stuart Brittenden. "Personal Injury Compensation in England and Wales." In *Personal Injury Compensation in Europe*. Deventer: Kluwer, 2003.

Gaudry, Marc. "The Effects on Road Safety of the Compulsory Insurance, Flat Premium Rating and No-Fault Features of the 1978 Quebec Automobile Act " In *Report of Inquiry into Motor Vehicle Accident Compensation in Ontario*, edited by Osborne, Coulter A. Vol. II, 1–28. Ontario, Toronto: Queen's Printer, 1988.

Geistfeld, Mark. "Placing a Price on Pain and Suffering: A Method for Helping Juries Determine Tort Damages for Nonmonetary Injuries." *California Law Review* 83 (1995): 773–852.

Gerdtham, Ulf-G. and Magnus Johannesson. "Income-Related Inequality in Life-Years and Quality-Adjusted Life-Years." *Journal of Health Economics* 19, no. 6 (2000): 1007–1026.

Gill, Carol J. "Health Professionals, Disability, and Assisted Suicide: An Examination of Relevant Empirical Evidence and Reply to Batavia." *Psychology, Public Policy, and Law* 6, no. 2 (6, 2000): 526–545.

Gold, Marthe R., Donald L. Patrick, George W. Torrance, Dennis Fryback G., David C. Hadorn, Mark S. Kamlet, Norman Daniels, and Milton C. Weinstein. "Identifying and Valuing Outcomes." In *Cost-Effectiveness in Health and Medicine*, edited by Gold, Marthe R., Joanna E. Siegel, Louise B. Russel and Milton C. Weinstein. New York; Oxford: Oxford University Press, 1996.

Gold, Marthe R., Joanna E. Siegel, Louise B. Russel, and Milton C. Weinstein. *Cost-Effectiveness in Health and Medicine*. New York; Oxford: Oxford University Press, 1996.

Gold, Marthe, R., David Stevenson, and Dennis Fryback G. "HALYS and QALYS and DALYS, Oh My: Similarities and Differences in Summary Measures of Population Health." *Annual Review of Public Health* 23 (2002): 115–134.

Gotanda, John Y. "Punitive Damages: A Comparative Analysis." *Columbia Journal of Transnational Law* 42, no. 2 (2004): 391–444.

Gougoux, Frédéric, Pascal Belin, Patrice Voss, Franco Lepore, Maryse Lassonde, and Robert J. Zatorre. "Voice Perception in Blind Persons: A Functional Magnetic Resonance Imaging Study." *Neuropsychologia* 47, no. 13 (11, 2009): 2967–2974.

Gravelle, Hugh and Dave Smith. "Discounting for Health Effects in Cost-Benefit and Cost-Effectiveness Analysis." *Health Economics* 10 (2001): 587–599.

Groot, Wim. "Adaptation and Scale of Reference Bias in Self-Assessments of Quality of Life." *Journal of Health Economics* 19, no. 3 (5, 2000): 403–420.

Gyrd-Hansen, Dorte. "Willingness to Pay for a QALY." *Health Economics* 12, no. 12 (2003): 1049–1060.

Hacks, Susanne, Ameli Ring, and Peter Böhm. *Schmerzensgeldbeträge 2009*. Bonn: Deutscher Anwaltverlag, 2009.

Hammitt, James K. "QALYs Versus WTP." *Risk Analysis* 22, no. 5 (2002): 985–1001.

Hammitt, James K. and Jin-Tan Liu. "Effects of Disease Type and Latency on the Value of Mortality Risk." *Journal of Risk and Uncertainty* 28, no. 1 (2004): 73–95.

Hansen, B. O., J. L. Hougaard, H. Keiding, and L. P. Osterdal. "On the Possibility of a Bridge between CBA and CEA: Comments on a Paper by Dolan and Edlin." *Journal of Health Economics* 23, no. 5 (2004): 887–898.

Harker, Judy. "Wound Healing Complications Associated with Lower Limb Amputation." *World Wide Wounds* (2006): 1 May 2012.

Harris, John. "Qalyfying the Value of Life." *Journal of Medical Ethics* 13, no. 3 (1987): 117–123.

—. "Unprincipled Qalys – a Response to Cubbon." *Journal of Medical Ethics* 17, no. 4 (1991): 185–188.

—. *The Value of Life. an Introduction to Medical Ethics.* 5th ed. London, New York: Routledge, 1985.

Hartlief, Ton. "Privaatrecht actueel. Smartengeld bij bewusteloosheid." WPNR (2003): 111–112.

Hatoum, Hind T., John E. Brazier, and Kasem S. Akhras. "Comparison of the HUI3 with the SF-36 Preference Based SF-6D in a Clinical Trial Setting." *Value in Health* 7, no. 5 (2004): 602–609.

Hirth, Richard A., Michael E. Chernew, Edward Miller, A. Mark Fendrick, and William G. Weissert. "Willingness to Pay for a Quality-Adjusted Life Year: In Search of a Standard." *Medical Decision Making* 20, no. 3 (7, 2000): 332–342.

Hofstetter, Patrick and James K. Hammitt. *Human Health Metrics for Environmental Decision Support Tools: Lessons from Health Economics and Decision Analysis.* Washington: U.S. EPA, Office of Research and Development, 2001. www.epa.gov/nrmrl/pubs/600r01104/600R01104.pdf.

Honiden, Shyoko S., Vandana Sundaram, Robert F. Nease, Mark Holodniy, Laura C. Lazzeroni, Andrew Zolopa, and Douglas K. Owens. "The Effect of Diagnosis with HIV Infection on Health-Related Quality of Life." *Quality of Life Research* 15, no. 1 (2006): 69–82.

Horsman, John, William Furlong, David Feeny, and George Torrance. "The Health Utilities Index (HUI®): Concepts, Measurement Properties and Application." *Health and Quality of Life Outcomes* 1, (2003): 30 Sep. 2011. www.hqlo.com/content/pdf/1477-7525-1-54.pdf.

Huang, Elbert S., Morgan Shook, Lei Jin, Marshall H. Chin, and David O. Meltzer. "The Impact of Patient Preferences on the Cost-Effectiveness of Intensive Glucose Control in Older Patients with New-Onset Diabetes." *Diabetes Care* 29, no. 2 (2006): 259–264.

Hugdahl, Kenneth, Maria Ek, Fiia Takio, Taija Rintee, Jyrki Tuomainen, Christian Haarala, and Heikki Hämäläinen. "Blind Individuals show Enhanced Perceptual and Attentional Sensitivity for Identification of Speech Sounds." *Cognitive Brain Research* 19, no. 1 (3, 2004): 28–32.

Ian McEwin, R. "No-Fault and Road Accidents: Some Australasian Evidence." *International Review of Law and Economics* 9, no. 1 (1989): 13–24.

Inflation EU, Worldwide inflation data. "Historic Harmonized Inflation. the Netherlands." Inflation EU, Worldwide inflation data, accessed 31 March 2014. www.inflation.eu/inflation-rates/the-netherlands/historic-inflation/hicp-inflation-the-netherlands.aspx.

Ingber, Stanley. "Rethinking Intangible Injuries: A Focus on Remedy." *California Law Review* 73, no. 3, Symposium: Alternative Compensation Schemes and Tort Theory (1985): 772–856.

Institute for Health Metrics and Evaluation. *The Global Burden of Disease: Generating Evidence, Guiding Policy*. Seattle, WA: IHME, 2013.

Jaeger, Lothar and Jan Luckey. *Schmerzensgeld*. 4th ed. Münster: ZAP Verlag, 2008.

Jenkins, Robin R., Nicole Owens, and Lanelle Bembenek Wiggins. "Valuing Reduced Risks to Children: The Case of Bicycle Safety Helmets." *Contemporary Economic Policy* 19, no. 4 (2001): 397–408.

Johannesson, Magnus M. "On Aggregating QALYs: A Comment on Dolan." *Journal of Health Economics* 18, (1999): 381–386.

Johannesson, Magnus M. and Richard M. O'Conor. "Cost-Utility Analysis from a Societal Perspective." *Health Policy* 39, (1997): 241–253.

Johannesson, Magnus M. *Theory and Methods of Economic Evaluation of Health Care*. Dordrecht, the Netherlands: Kluwer, 1996.

—. "The Relationship between Cost-Effectiveness Analysis and Cost-Benefit Analysis." *Social Science and Medicine* 41, no. 4 (1995): 483–489.

Johannesson, Magnus M., Bengt Jönsson, and Göran Karlsson. "Outcome Measurement in Economic Evaluation." *Health Economics* 5, no. 4 (1996): 279–296.

Johannesson, Magnus M. and David Meltzer. "Some Reflections on Cost-Effectiveness Analysis." *Health Economics* 7, no. 1 (-02, 1998): 1–7.

Johannesson, Magnus M. and Per-Olov Johansson. "Is the Valuation of a QALY Gained Independent of Age? Some Empirical Evidence." *Journal of Health Economics* 16, no. 5 (1997): 589–599.

Johannesson, Magnus M. and Milton C. Weinstein. "On the Decision Rules of Cost-Effectiveness Analysis." *Journal of Health Economics* 12, no. 4 (1993): 459–467.

Judicial College. *Guidelines for the Assessment of General Damages in Personal Injury Cases*. 12th ed. Oxford: Oxford University Press, 2013.

Kahn, Richard, Peter Alperin, David Eddy, Knut Borch-Johnsen, John Buse, Justin Feigelman, Edward Gregg, et al. "Age at Initiation and Frequency of Screening to Detect Type 2 Diabetes: A Cost-Effectiveness Analysis." *The Lancet* 375, no. 9723 (2010): 1365–1374.

Kahneman, Daniel and Amos Tversky. "Prospect Theory: An Analysis of Decision Under Risk." *Econometrica* 47, no. 2 (1979): pp. 263–292.

Kaplan, Robert M. and James W. Bush. "Health-Related Quality of Life Measurement for Evaluation Research and Policy Analysis." *Health Psychology* 1, no. 1 (1982): 61–80.

Kaplan, Robert M. and John P. Anderson. "A General Health Policy Model: Update and Applications." *Health Services Research* 23, no. 2 (1988): 203–235.

Kaplow, Louis. "The Value of Accuracy in Adjudication: An Economic Analysis." *The Journal of Legal Studies* 23, no. 1, Economic Analysis of Civil Procedure (1994): pp. 307–401.

Kaplow, Louis and Steven Shavell. "Accuracy in the Assessment of Damages." *Journal of Law and Economics* 39, no. 1 (1996): 191–210.

Kappel, Klemens and Peter Sandøe. "Qalys, Age and Fairness." *Bioethics* 6, no. 4 (1992): 297–316.

Karapanou, Vaia and Louis Visscher. "Towards a Better Assessment of Pain and Suffering Damages." *Journal of European Tort Law* 1, no. 1 (2010): 48–74.

—. "The Magnitude of Pain and Suffering Damages from a Law and Economics and Health Economics Point of View." *Rotterdam Institute of Law and Economics Working Paper Series* (2009).

Karner, Ernst and Helmut Koziol. "Austria." In *Damages for Non-Pecuniary Loss in a Comparative Perspective*, edited by Rogers, W. V. Horton. Vienna; New York: Springer, 2001.

Kawachi, Ichiro. "QALYs and Justice." *Health Policy* 13 (1989): 115–120.

Keeler, Emmett B. and Shan Cretin. "Discounting of Life-Saving and Other Nonmonetary Effects." *Management Science* 29, no. 3 (1983): 300–306.

Keeton, W. Page, Dan B. Dobbs, Robert E. Keeton, and David G. Owen. *Prosser and Keeton on Torts.* 5th student ed. St. Paul, Minnesota: West Publishing Co., 1984.

Kenkel, Don. "WTP- and QALY- Based Approaches to Valuing Health for Policy: Common Ground and Disputed Territory." *Environmental & Resource Economics* 34, (2006): 419–437.

Kerameus, Konstantinos D. "Greece. Damages Under Greek Law." In *Unification of Tort Law: Damages*, edited by Magnus, U. The Hague: Kluwer Law International, 2001.

—. "Greece." In *Damages for Non-Pecuniary Loss in a Comparative Perspective*, edited by Rogers, W. V. Horton, 129–134. Vienna; New York: Springer, 2001.

Kerkmeester, Heico. "Methodology: General." In *Encyclopedia of Law and Economics: The History and Methodology of Law and Economics*, edited by Bouckaert, Boudewijn and Gerrit de Geest. Vol. 1, 383–401. Cheltenham: Edward Elgar, 2000.

Kind, Paul, Rachel Rosser, and Alan Williams, eds. *Valuation of Quality of Life: Some Psychometric Evidence.* The Value of Life and Safety, edited by Jones-Lee, Michael. Amsterdam; New York; Oxford: Holland Publishing Company, 1982.

King, Joseph H., Jr. "Pain and Suffering, Noneconomic Damages, and the Goals of Tort Law." *SMU Law Review* 57 (2004): 163–209.

Klarman, Herbert E., John O'S. Francis, and Gerald D. Rosenthal. "Cost Effectiveness Analysis Applied to the Treatment of Chronic Renal Disease." *Medical Care* 6, no. 1 (1968): 48–54.

Klose, Thomas. "A Utility-Theoretic Model for QALYs and Willingness to Pay." *Health Economics* 12 (2003): 17–31.

Kochanowski, Paul S. and Madelyn V. Young. "Deterrent Aspects of no-Fault Automobile Insurance: Some Empirical Findings." *Journal of Risk and Insurance* 52, no. 2 (1985): 269–288.

Kötz, Hein. *Deliktsrecht.* 9th ed. Neuwied: Luchterhand, 2001.

Kritikos, Athanasios. *Αποζημίωση από αυτοκινητικά ατυχήματα (Compensation for Traffic Accidents).* 4th ed. Athens: 2004.

Lacey, Heather, Angela Fagerlin, George Loewenstein, Dylan M. Smith, Jason Riis, and Peter A. Ubel. "Are they really that Happy? Exploring Scale Recalibration in Estimates of Well-being." *Health Psychology* 27, no. 6 (2008): 669–675.

Landes, Elisabeth M. "Insurance, Liability, and Accidents: A Theoretical and Empirical Investigation of the Effect of No-Fault Accidents." *Journal of Law and Economics* 25 (1982): 49–66.

Landes, William M. and Richard A. Posner. *The Economic Structure of Tort Law*. Cambridge, MA; London, UK: Harvard University Press, 1987.

Laupacis, Andreas, David Feeny, Alan S. Detsky, and Peter X. Tugwell. "How Attractive does a New Technology have to be to Warrant Adoption and Utilization? Tentative Guidelines for using Clinical and Economic Evaluations." *Canadian Medical Association Journal* 146, no. 4 (1992): 473–481.

Le Galès, Catherine, Catherine Buron, Nathalie Costet, Sophia Rosman, and Pr. Gérard Slama. "Development of a Preference-Weighted Health Status Classification System in France: The Health Utilities Index 3." *Health Care Management Science* 5, no. 1 (2002): 41–51.

Lee, Bruce Y., Ann E. Wiringa, Rachel R. Bailey, Vishal Goyal, Becky Tsui, G. Jonathan Lewis, Robert R. Muder, and Lee M. Harrison. "The Economic Effect of Screening Orthopedic Surgery Patients Preoperatively for Methicillin-Resistant Staphylococcus Aureus." *Infection Control and Hospital Epidemiology* 31, no. 11 (2010): 1130–1138.

Leebron, David W. "Final Moments: Damages for Pain and Suffering Prior to Death." *New York University Law Review* 64, no. 2 (1989): 256–363.

Levin, Frederick S. "Pain and Suffering Guidelines: A Cure for Damages Measurement Anomie Note." *University of Michigan Journal of Law Reform* 22 (1989): 303–332.

Lieu, Tracy A., G. Thomas Ray, Ismael R. Ortega-Sanchez, Ken Kleinman, Donna Rusinak, and Lisa A. Prosser. "Willingness to Pay for a QALY Based on Community Member and Patient Preferences for Temporary Health States Associated with Herpes Zoster." *PharmacoEconomics* 27, no. 12 (2009): 1005–1016.

Lindenbergh, Siewert D. *Smartengeld*. Deventer: Kluwer, 1998.

—. *Smartengeld 10 jaar later*. Deventer: Kluwer, 2008.

Lindenbergh, Siewert D. and Peter P. M. van Kippersluis. "Non Pecuniary Losses." In *Tort Law and Economics, Encyclopedia of Law and Economics*, edited by Faure, Michael. Vol. 1, 215–227. Cheltenham, UK: Edward Elgar, 2009.

Lindenbergh, Siewert D. and Robert Verburg. "Personal Injury Compensation in the Netherlands." In *Personal Injury Compensation in Europe*, edited by Bona, Marco and Philip Mead. Deventer: Kluwer, 2003.

Lipscomb, Joseph, Milton C. Weinstein, and George W. Torrance. "Time Preference." In *Cost-Effectiveness in Health and Medicine*, edited by Gold, Marthe R., Louise B. Russell, Joanna E. Siegel and Milton C. Weinstein, 214–235. Oxford; New York: Oxford University Press, 1996.

Loewenstein, George, Ted O'Donoghue, and Matthew Rabin. "Projection Bias in Prediction Future Utility." *The Quarterly Journal of Economics* 113, no. 4 (2003): 1209–1248.

Loewenstein, George and Peter A. Ubel. "Hedonic Adaptation and the Role of Decision and Experience Utility in Public Policy." *Journal of Public Economics* 92 (8, 2008): 1795–1810.

—. "Hedonic Adaptation and the Role of Decision and Experience Utility in Public Policy." *Journal of Public Economics* 92 (8, 2008): 1795–1810.

Loomes, Graham. "Evidence of a New Violation of the Independence Axiom." *Journal of Risk and Uncertainty* 4, no. 1 (1991): 91–108.

Loomes, Graham and Lynda McKenzie. "The Use of QALYs in Health Care Decision Making." *Social Science & Medicine* 28, no. 4 (1989): 299–308.

Losina, Elena and Kenneth A. Freedberg. "Life expectancy in HIV. Better but not good enough." *British Medical Journal* 343 (2011).

Lucas, Richard E. "Long Term Disability is Associated with Lasting Changes in Subjective Well-being: Evidence from Two Nationally Representative Longitudinal Studies." *Journal of Personality and Social Psychology* 92 (2007): 717–730.

Luce, R. Duncan. "Where does Subjective Expected Utility Fail Descriptively?" *Journal of Risk and Uncertainty* 5, no. 1 (1992): 5–27.

Lundqvist, Christofer, Agneta Siösteen, Christian C. Blomstrand, B. Lind, and M. Sullivan. "Spinal Cord Injuries: Clinical, Functional, and Emotional Status." *Spine* 16, no. 1 (1991): 78–83.

MacKeigan, Linda D., Amiram Gafni, and Bernie J. O'Brien. "Double Discounting of QALYs." *Health Economics* 12 (2003): 165–169.

MacLaren, Robert and Patrick W. Sullivan. "Cost-Effectiveness of Recombinant Human Erythropoietin for Reducing Red Blood Cells Transfusions in Critically Ill Patients." *Value in Health* 8, no. 2 (2005): 105–116.

Maclean, Courtney C. and Jeffrey S. A. Stringer. "Potential Cost-Effectiveness of Maternal and Infant Antiretroviral Interventions to Prevent Mother-to-Child Transmission during Breast-Feeding." *Journal of Acquired Immune Deficiency Syndromes* 28, no. 5 (2005): 570–577.

Magnus, Ulrich and Jörg Fedtke. "Germany." In *Damages for Non-Pecuniary Loss in a Comparative Perspective*, edited by Rogers, W. V. Horton. Vienna; New York: Springer, 2001.

Manolkidis, Sotirios. "Personal Injury Compensation in Greece." In *Personal Injury Compensation in Europe*, edited by Bona, Marco and Philip Mead, 247–260. Deventer: Kluwer, 2003.

Mark, Daniel B., Mark A. Hlatky, Robert M. Califf, C. David Naylor, Kerry L. Lee, Paul W. Armstrong, Gabriel Barbash, et al. "Cost Effectiveness of Thrombolytic Therapy with Tissue Plasminogen Activator as Compared with Streptokinase for Acute Myocardial Infarction." *The New England Journal of Medicine* 332, no. 21 (1995): 1418–1424.

Markesinis, Basil S. and Simon F. Deakin. *Tort Law*. 4th ed. Oxford; New York: Oxford University Press, 1999.

Markesinis, Basil S. and Hannes Unberath. *The German Law of Torts. A Comparative Treatise*. 4th ed. Oxford; Portland: Hart Publishing, 2002.

Markesinis, Basil, Michael Coester, Guido Alpa, and Augustus Ullstein. *Compensation for Personal Injury in English, German and Italian Law*. Cambridge: Cambridge University Press, 2005.

Martín-Casals, Miguel, Jordi Ribot, and Josep Solé. "Spain." In *Damages for Non-Pecuniary Loss in a Comparative Perspective*, edited by Rogers, W. V. Horton. Vienna; New York: Springer, 2001.

Mattei, Ugo. *Comparative Law and Economics*. Ann Arbor, MI: University of Michigan Press, 1997.

McGuire, Alistair. "Theoretical Concepts in the Economic Evaluation of Health Care." In *Economic Evaluation in Health Care: Merging Theory with Practice*, edited by

Drummond, Michael and Alistair McGuire, 1–21. Oxford; New York: Oxford University Press, 2001.

Medley, G. F., R. M. Anderson, D. R. Cox, and L. Billard. "Incubation Period of AIDS in Patients Infected Via Blood Transfusion." *Nature* 328 (1987): 719–721.

Medoff, Marshall H. and Joseph P. Magaddino. "An Empirical Analysis of No-Fault Insurance." *Evaluation Review* 6, no. 3 (1982): 373–392.

Mellors, John W., Charles R. Rinaldo Jr., Phalguni Gupta, Roseanne M. White, John A. Todd, and Lawrence A. Kingsley. "Prognosis in HIV-1 Infection Predicted by the Quantity of Virus in Plasma." *Science* 272, no. 5265 (1996): 1167–1170.

Menzel, Paul, Paul Dolan, Jeff Richardson, and Jan Abel Olsen. "The Role of Adaptation to Disability and Disease in Health State Valuation: A Preliminary Normative Analysis." *Social Science & Medicine* 55, no. 12 (12, 2002): 2149–2158.

Miller, Ted R. "Valuing Nonfatal Quality of Life Losses with Quality-Adjusted Life Years: The Health Economist's Meow." *Journal of Forensic Economics* 13, no. 2 (2000): 145–167.

—. "Willingness to Pay Comes of Age: Will the System Survive." *Northwestern University Law Review* 83, no. 4 (1989): 876–907.

Ministry of Justice Scottish Government and Department of Justice Northern Ireland. "Damages Act 1996: The Discount Rate. Review of the Legal Framework." Consultation Paper 3/2013 (2013): 1–47.

Mishan, Ezra J. "Evaluation of Life and Limb: A Theoretical Approach." *Journal of Political Economy* 79, no. 4 (1971): 687–705.

Miyamoto, John M. and Stephen A. Eraker. "A Multiplicative Model of the Utility of Survival Duration and Health Quality." *Journal of Experimental Psychology* 117, no. 1 (1988): 3–20.

Miyamoto, John M., Peter P. Wakker, Han Bleichrodt, and Hans J. M. Peters. "The Zero-Condition: A Simplifying Assumption in QALY Measurement and Multiattribute Utility." *Management Science* 44, no. 6 (1 June 1998): 839–849.

Morral, John F. III. "An Assessment of the US Regulatory Impact Analysis Program." In *Regulatory Impact Analysis, Best Practices in OECD Countries*, edited by OECD, 71–87. Paris: OECD, 1997.

Morris, Clarence. "Liability for Pain and Suffering." *Columbia Law Review* 59 (1959): 476–485.

Moss, Andrew R. and Peter Bacchetti. "Natural History of HIV Infection." *AIDS* 3, no. 2 (1989): 55–62.

Müller, Gerda. "Zum Ausgleich Des Immateriellen Schadens Nach §847 BGB." *Versicherungsrecht* (1993).

Muñoz, Alvaro, Caroline A. Sabin, and Andrew A. Phillips. "The Incubation Period of AIDS." *AIDS* 11 (1997): S69-S76.

Murray, Christopher J. L. and Arnab K. Acharya. "Understanding DALYs." *Journal of Health Economics* 16, no. 6 (1997): 703–730.

National Institute for Health and Clinical Excellence. *Guide to the Methods of Technology Appraisal.* London, UK: National Institute for Health and Clinical Excellence, 2013.

National Spinal Cord Injury Statistical Center. "The Annual Statistical Report for the Spinal Cord Injury Model Systems." Birmingham, Alabama: 2011, accessed

31 March 2014. https://www.nscisc.uab.edu/PublicDocuments/reports/pdf/2011 %20NSCISC%20Annual%20Statistical%20Report%20-%20Complete%20Public% 20Version.pdf.

Niemeyer, Paul V. "Awards for Pain and Suffering: The Irrational Centerpiece of our Tort System Essay." *Virginia Law Review* 90 (2004): 1401–1422.

Noah, Lars. "Comfortably numb: medicalizing (and mitigating pain and suffering damages)." *University of Michigan Journal of Law Reform* 42, no. 2 (2008): 431–480.

Nord, Erik. *Cost-Value Analysis in Health Care*. New York: Cambridge University Press, 1999.

—. "Methods for Quality Adjustment of Life Years." *Social Science and Medicine* 34, no. 5 (1992): 559–569.

—. "The Person-Trade-Off Approach to Valuing Health Care Programs." *Medical Decision Making* 15, no. 3 (1995): 201–208.

Nord, Erik, Norman Daniels, and Mark Kamlet. "QALYs: Some Challenges." *Value in Health* 12, no. s1 (2009): S10-S15.

OECD. "Life expectancy." In *OECD Factbook 2013: Economic, Environmental and Social Statistics.* OECD Publishing: 2013.

Oemar, Mandy and Mark Oppe. *EQ-5D-3L User Guide: Basic Information on how to use the EQ-5D-3L Instrument*: EuroQol Group, 2013. www.euroqol.org/fileadmin/ user_upload/Documenten/PDF/Folders_Flyers/EQ-5D-3L_UserGuide_2013_ v5.0_October_2013.pdf.

Oemar, Mandy and Bas Janssen. *EQ-5D-5L User Guide: Basic Information on how to use the EQ-5D-5L Instrument*: EuroQol Group, 2013. www.euroqol.org/fileadmin/ user_upload/Documenten/PDF/Folders_Flyers/UserGuide_EQ-5D-5L_v2.0_ October_2013.pdf.

Ogus, Anthony I. "Damages for Lost Amenities: For a Foot, a Feeling Or a Function?" *Modern Law Review* 35, no. 1 (1972): 1–17.

—. *The Law of Damages*. London: Butterworths, 1973.

Oostenbrink, Rianne, Jan B. Oostenbrink, Karel G. M. Moons, Gerarda Derksen-Lubsen, Marie-Louise Essink-Bot, Diederick E. Grobbee, Ken Redekop, and Henriëtte A. Moll. "Cost-Utility Analysis of Patient Care in Children with Meningeal Signs." *International Journal of Technology Assessment in Health Care* 18, no. 03 (2002): 485.

Oswald, Andrew J. and Nattavudh Powdthavee. "Does Happiness Adapt? A Longitudinal Study of Disability with Implications for Economists and Judges." *Journal of Public Economics* 92, no. 5–6 (6, 2008): 1061–1077.

Ott, Claus and Hans-Bernd Schäfer. "Schmerzensgeld Bei Körperverletzungen. Eine Ökonomische Analyse." *Juristenzeitung* (1990): 563–573.

Palmer, Cynthia S., John K. Niparko, J. Robert Wyatt, Margaret Rothman, and Gregory de Lissovoy. "A Prospective Study of the Cost-Utility of the Multichannel Cochlear Implant." *Archives of Otolaryngology – Head & Neck Surgery* 125, no. 11 (1999): 1221–1228.

Papatheofanis, Frank J., Erin Williams, and Steven D. Chang. "Cost-Utility Analysis of the Cyberknife System for Metastatic Spinal Tumors." *Neurosurgery* 64, no. 2 (2009): A73–A83.

Parkin, David and Nancy Devlin. "Is there a Case for using Visual Analogue Scale Valuations in Cost-Utility Analysis?" *Health Economics* 15, no. 7 (2006): 653–664.

Parouty, Mehraj B.Y., Daan Krooshof and Maarten J. Postma, "Differential Time Preferences for Money and Quality of Life," *PharmacoEconomics* (2014).

Patel, Sheela T., Paul B. Haser, Harry L. Bush, and K. Craig Kent. "Is Thrombolysis of Lower Extremity Acute Arterial Occlusion Cost-Effective?" *Journal of Surgical Research* 83, no. 2 (5/15, 1999): 106–112.

Pauker, Stephen G. "Coronary Artery Surgery: The Use of Decision Analysis." *Annals of Internal Medicine* 85, no. 1 (1976): 8–18.

Pezzotti, Patrizio, Pier Angela Napoli, Serenella Acciai, Stefano Boros, Roberta Urciuoli, Vera Lazzeri, and Giovanni Rezza. "Increasing Survival Time After AIDS in Italy: The Role of New Combination Antiretroviral Therapies." *AIDS* 13, no. 2 (1999): 249–255.

Phelps, Charles E. and Alvin I. Mushlin. "On the (Near) Equivalence of Cost-Effectiveness and Cost-Benefit Analyses." *International Journal of Technology Assessment in Health Care* 7, no. 1 (1991): 12–21.

Phelps, Ruby, Kenneth Robbins, Thomas Liberti, Ana Machuca, German Leparc, Mary Chamberland, Marcia Kalish, et al. "Window-Period Human Immunodeficiency Virus Transmission to Two Recipients by an Adolescent Blood Donor." *Transfusion* 44, no. 6 (2004): 929–933.

Pindyck, Robert S. and Daniel Rubinfeld. *Microeconomics.* 6th ed. Upper Sadle River, New Jersey: Pearson Prentice Hall, 2005.

Plant, Marcus L. "Damages for Pain and Suffering." *Ohio State Law Journal* 19, (1958): 200–211.

Pliskin, Joseph S., Donald S. Shepard, and Milton C. Weinstein. "Utility Functions for Life Years and Health Status." *Operations Research* 28, no. 1 (1980): 206–224.

Polinsky, Mitchell A. and Yeon-Koo Che. "Decoupling Liability: Optimal Incentives for Care and Litigation." *RAND Journal of Economics* 22, no. 4 (1991): 562–570.

Pomp, Marc, Werner Brouwer, and Frans Rutten. *QALY-Tijd Nieuwe Medische Technologie, Kosteneffectiviteit En Richtlijnen (QALY-Ty. New Medical Technology, Cost-Effectiveness and Guidelines).* The Hague: Centraal Planbureau, 2007. www.cpb.nl/publicatie/qaly-tijd-nieuwe-medische-technologie-kosteneffectiviteit-en-richtlijnen.

Poser, Susan, Brian H. Bornstein, and E. Kiernan McGorty. "Measuring Damages for Lost Enjoyment of Life: The View from the Bench and the Jury Box." *Law and Human Behavior* 27, no. 1 (2003): 53–68.

Posner, Eric A. and Cass R. Sunstein. "Dollars and Death." *University of Chicago Law Review* 72, no. 2 (2005): 537–598.

Posner, Richard A. *Economic Analysis of Law.* 6th ed. New York, NY: Aspen Publishers, 2003.

—. "A Theory of Negligence." *The Journal of Legal Studies* 1, no. 1 (1972): 29–96.

Powdthavee, Nattavudh. "What Happens to People before and After Disability? Focusing Effects, Lead Effects, and Adaptation in Different Areas of Life." *Social Science & Medicine* 69, no. 12 (12, 2009): 1834–1844.

Powdthavee, Nattavudh. "What Happens to People before and After Disability? Focusing Effects, Lead Effects, and Adaptation in Different Areas of Life." *Social Science & Medicine* 69, no. 12 (12, 2009): 1834–1844.

Pratt, John W. and Richard J. Zeckhauser. "Willingness to Pay and the Distribution of Risk and Wealth." *The Journal of Political Economy* 104, no. 4 (1996): 747–763.

Priest, George L. "The Current Insurance Crisis and Modern Tort Law." *Yale Law Journal* 96, no. 7 (1987): 1521–1590.

Radin, Margaret Jane. "Market-Inalienability." *Harvard Law Review* 100, no. 8 (1987): 1849–1937.

Raftery, James. "Should NICE's threshold range for cost per QALY be raised? Yes." *British Medical Journal* 338 (2009): 268–269.

Ragnarson Tennvall, Gunnel and Jan Apelqvist. "Prevention of Diabetes-Related Foot Ulcers and Amputations: A Cost-Utility Analysis Based on Markov Model Simulations." *Diabetologia* 44, no. 11 (2001): 2077–2087.

—. "Health-Related Quality of Life in Patients with Diabetes Mellitus and Foot Ulcers." *Journal of Diabetes and its Complications* 14, no. 5 (10, 2000): 235–241.

Renda, Andrea. *Impact Assessment in the EU: The State of the Art and the Art of the State.* Brussels: Centre for European Policy Studies, 2006.

Rice, Dorothy P. and Barbara S. Cooper. "The Economic Value of Human Life." *American Journal of Public Health* 57, no. 11 (1967): 1954–1966.

Riis, Jason, George Loewenstein, Jonathan Baron, Christopher Jepson, Angela Fagerlin, and Peter A. Ubel. "Ignorance of Hedonic Adaptation to Hemodialysis: A Study using Ecological Momentary Assessment." *Journal of Experimental Psychology* 134, no. 1 (2005): 3–9.

Robinson, Angela, Dorte Gyrd-Hansen, Philomena Bacon, Rachel Baker, Mark Pennington and Cam Donaldson, EuroVaQ Team. "Estimating a WTP-based value of a QALY: The 'chained' approach." *Social Science & Medicine* 92 (2013): 92–104.

Robinson, Angela, Graham Loomes, and Michael Jones-Lee. "Visual Analog Scales, Standard Gambles, and Relative Risk Aversion." *Medical Decision Making* 21, no. 1 (2001): 17–27.

Robinson, Angela, Paul Dolan, and Alan Williams. "Valuing Health Status using VAS and TTO: What Lies Behind the Numbers?" *Social Science & Medicine* 45, no. 8 (10, 1997): 1289–1297.

Rodgers, Gregory B. "Estimating Jury Compensation for Pain and Suffering in Product Liability Cases Involving Nonfatal Personal Injury." *Journal of Forensic Economics* 6, no. 3 (1993): 251–262.

Rogers, W. V. Horton, ed. *Damages for Non-Pecuniary Loss in a Comparative Perspective.* Vienna; New York: Springer, 2001.

—. "England." In *Compensation for Personal Injury in a Comparative Perspective*, edited by Koch, Bernhard A. and Helmut Koziol. Vienna; New York: Springer, 2003.

—. "England." In *Damages for Non-Pecuniary Losses in a Comparative PerspeViennactive*, edited by Rogers, W. V. Horton. Vienna; New York: Springer, 2001a.

—. "England. Damages Under English Law." In *Unification of Tort Law: Damages*, edited by Magnus, Ulrich. The Hague: Kluwer Law International, 2001b.

—. *The Law of Tort.* 2nd ed. London: Sweet & Maxwell, 1994.

Rollman, Gary B. "Culture and Pain." In *Cultural Clinical Psychology. Theory, Research and Practice*, edited by Kazarian, Shahé and David R. Evans. New York; Oxford: Oxford University Press, 1998.

Rosser, Rachel M. and Vincent C. Watts. "The Measurement of Hospital Output." *International Journal of Epidemiology* 1, no. 4 (1972): 361–368.

Rosser, Rachel R. and Paul Kind. "A Scale of Valuations of States of Illness: Is there a Social Consensus?" *International Journal of Epidemiology* 7, no. 4 (1978): 347–358.

Rothberg, Michael B., Anunta Virapongse, and Kenneth J. Smith. "Cost-Effectiveness of a Vaccine to Prevent Herpes Zoster and Postherpetic Neuralgia in Older Adults." *Clinical Infectious Diseases* 44, no. 10 (2007): 1280–1288.

Rozenbaum, Mark H., Albert Jan van Hoek, Douglas Fleming, Caroline L. Trotter, Elizabeth Miller, and W. John Edmunds. "Vaccination of risk groups in England using the 13 valent pneumococcal conjugate vaccine: economic analysis." *British Medical Journal* 345 (2012): 1–17.

Rubin, Paul H. and John E. Calfee. "Consequences of Damage Awards for Hedonic and Other Nonpecuniary Losses." *Journal of Forensic Economics* 5, no. 3 (1992): 249–260.

Russell, Louise B., Joanna E. Siegel, Norman Daniels, Marthe R. Gold, Bryan R. Luce, and Jeanne S. Mandelblatt. "Cost-Effectiveness Analysis as a Guide to Resource Allocation in Health: Roles and Limitations." In *Cost-Effectiveness in Health and Medicine*, edited by Gold, Marthe R., Joanna E. Siegel, Louise B. Russell and Milton C. Weinstein, 3–24. Oxford; New York: Oxford University Press, 1996.

Russo, Paolo. *I Danni Esistenziali*. Utet Giuridica, 2014.

Sanders, Gillian D., Ahmed M. Bayoumi, Mark Holodniy, and Douglas K. Owens. "Cost-Effectiveness in HIV Screening in Patients Older than 55 Years of Age." *Annals of Internal Medicine* 148, no. 12 (2008): 889–903.

Sanders, Gillian D., Ahmed M. Bayoumi, Vandana Sundaram, S. Pinar Bilir, Christopher P. Neukermans, Chara E. Rydzak, Lena R. Douglass, Laura C. Lazzeroni, Mark Holodniy, and Douglas K. Owens. "Cost-Effectiveness of Screening for HIV in the Era of Highly Active Antiretroviral Therapy." *The New England Journal of Medicine* 352, no. 6 (2005): 570–585.

Schackman, Bruce R., Sue J. Goldie, Kenneth A. Freedberg, Elena Losina, John Brazier, and Milton C. Weinstein. "Comparison of Health State Utilities using Community and Patient Preference Weights Derived from a Survey of Patients with HIV/AIDS." *Medical Decision Making* 22, no. 1 (2002): 27–38.

Schäfer, Hans-Bernd and Frank Müller-Langer, "Strict Liabilty Versus Negligence," in *Tort Law and Economics*, edited by Faure, Michael. Cheltenham, UK: Edward Elgar, 2009.

Schäfer, Hans-Bernd and Claus Ott. *The Economic Analysis of Civil Law* [Lehrbuch der ökonomischen Analyse des Zivilrechts]. Translated by Braham, Matthew. Cheltenham, UK: Edward Elgar, 2004.

—. *Lehrbuch Der Ökonomischen Analyse Des Zivilrechts*. 4th ed. Berlin: Springer, 2005.

Schkade, David A. and Daniel Kahneman. "Does Living in California make People Happy? A Focusing Illusion in Judgments of Life Satisfaction." *Psychological Science* 9, no. 5 (1998): 340–346.

Schwappach, David L. B. "Resource Allocation, Social Values and the QALY: A Review of the Debate and Empirical Evidence." *Health Expectations* 5, no. 3 (2002): 210–222.

Schwartz, Alan. "Proposals for Products Liability Reform: A Theoretical Synthesis." *Yale Law Journal* 97, no. 3 (1988): 353–415.

Schwartz, Gary T. "Reality in the Economic Analysis of Tort Law: Does Tort Law really Deter?" *UCLA Law Review* 42, (1994): 377–444.

Schwarz, Bernhard, M. Gouveia, J. Chen, G. Nocea, K. Jameson, J. Cook, Girishanthy Krishnarajah, Evo Alemao, D. Yin, and Harri Sintonen. "Cost-Effectiveness of Sitagliptin-Based Treatment Regimens in European Patients with Type 2 Diabetes and Haemoglobin A1c Above Target on Metformin Monotherapy." *Diabetes, Obesity & Metabolism* 10, no. s1 (2008): 43–55.

Schweitzer, Eugene J., Eli N. Perencevich, Benjamin Philosophe, and Stephen T. Bartlett. "Estimated Benefits of Transplantation of Kidneys from Donors at Increased Risk for HIV Or Hepatitis C Infection." *American Journal of Transplantation* 7, no. 6 (2007): 1515–1525.

Sculpher, Mark. "The Role and Estimation of Productivity Costs in Economic Evaluation." In *Economic Evaluation in Health Care: Merging Theory with Practice*, edited by Drummond, Michael and Alistair McGuire, 94–112. Oxford, New York: Oxford University Press, 2001.

Sculpher, Mark J. and Martin J. Buxton. "The Episode-Free Day as a Composite Measure of Effectiveness: An Illustrative Economic Evaluation of Formoterol Versus Salbutamol in Asthma Therapy." *PharmacoEconomics* 4, no. 5 (1993): 345–352.

Sculpher, Mark J. and Bernie J. O'Brien. "Income Effects of Reduced Health and Health Effects of Reduced Income: Implications for Health State Valuation." *Medical Decision Making* 20, no. 2 (2000): 207–215.

Sebok, Anthony J. "Translating the Immeasurable: Thinking about Pain and Suffering Comparatively." *DePaul Law Review* 55 (2005–2006): 379–398.

Sen, Amartya. *Commodities and Capabilities.* New Delhi: Oxford University Press, 1999.

—. "Equality of what?" Stanford University, 22 May 1979.

—. *Resources, Values and Development.* Oxford: Basil Blackwell, 1984.

Sharma, Rajiv, Miron Stano, and Mitchell Haas. "Adjusting to Changes in Health: Implications for Cost-Effectiveness Analysis." *Journal of Health Economics* 23, no. 2 (3, 2004): 335–351.

Shavell, Steven. *Economic Analysis of Accident Law.* Cambridge, MA: Harvard University Press, 1987.

—. *Foundations of Economic Analysis of Law.* Cambridge, MA: The Belknap Press of Harvard University Press, 2004.

—. "Strict Liability Versus Negligence." *The Journal of Legal Studies* 9, no. 1 (1980): pp. 1–25.

Shaw, James W., Jeffrey A. Johnson, and Stephen Joel Coons. "US Valuation of the EQ-5D Health States: Development and Testing of the D1 Valuation Model." *Medical Care* 43, no. 3 (2005): 203–220.

Sintonen, Harri. "An Approach to Measuring and Valuing Health States." *Social Science & Medicine* 15, no. 2 (1981): 55–65.

Sintonen, Harri and Markku Pekurinen. "A Fifteen Dimensional Measure of Health-Related Quality of Life (15D) and its Applications." In *Quality of Life Assessment:*

Key Issues in the 1990s, edited by Walker, Stuart R. and Rachel M. Rosser, 185–195. Dordrecht, the Netherlands: Kluwer Academic Publishers, 1993.

Sloan, Frank A., Bridget A. Reilly, and Christoph M. Schenzler. "Tort Liability Versus Other Approaches for Deterring Careless Driving." *International Review of Law and Economics* 14, no. 1 (1994): 53–71.

Smith Pryor, Ellen. "The Tort Law Debate, Efficiency, and the Kingdom of the Ill: A Critique of the Insurance Theory of Compensation." *Virginia Law Review* 79 (1993): 91–151.

Smith, Alwyn. "Qualms about QALYs." *The Lancet* 329, no. 8542 (1987): 1134–1136.

Smith, Craig A. and Kenneth A. Wallston. "Adaptation in Patients with Chronic Rheumatoid Arthritis: Application of a General Model." *Health Psychology* 11, no. 3 (1992): 151–162.

Smith, Dylan M., Norbert Schwarz, Todd R. Roberts, and Peter A. Ubel. "Why are You Calling Me? how Study Introductions Change Response Patterns." *Quality of Life Research* 15, no. 4 (2006): 621–630.

Smith, Dylan M., Ryan L. Sherriff, Laura Damschroder, George Loewenstein, and Peter A. Ubel. "Misremembering Colostomies? Former Patients Give Lower Utility Ratings than do Current Patients." *Health Psychology* 25, no. 6 (11, 2006): 688–695.

Smith, Marilyn Dix, Michael Drummond, and Diana Brixner. "Moving the QALY Forward: Rationale for Change." *Value in Health* 12, no. 1 (2009): S1–S4.

Smith, Stan V. "Hedonic Damages in Personal Injury and Wrongful Death Litigation." In *Litigation Economics*, edited by Gaughan, Patrick A. and Robert J. Thornton, 39. Greenwich, CT; London: JAI Press Inc., 1993.

Spence, Michael. "Consumer Misperceptions, Product Failure and Producer Liability." *The Review of Economic Studies* 44, no. 3 (1977): 561–572.

Sprangers, Mirjam A.G. and Carolyn E. Schwartz. "Do not throw out the baby with the bath water: build on current approaches to realize conceptual clarity. Response to Ubel, Peeters, and Smith." *Quality of Life Research* 19 (2010): 477–479.

Statistisches Bundesamt. "Statistisches Jahrbuch Deutschland und Internationales." Wiesbaden, 2013.

Studdert, David M., Allen Kachalia, Joshua A. Salomon, and Michelle M. Mello. "Rationalizing Noneconomic Damages: A Health-Utilities Approach." *Law and Contemporary Problems* 74 (2011): 57–101.

Sugarman, Stephen D. "Doing Away with Tort Law." *California Law Review* 73 (1985): 558–664.

Sugden, Robert and Alan Williams. *The Principles of Practical Cost-Benefit Analysis.* Oxford: Oxford University Press, 1978.

Suligoi, Barbara, Mariangela Raimondo, Vincenza Regine, Maria-Cristina Salfa, and Laura Camoni. "Epidemiology of Human Immunodeficiency Virus Infection in Blood Donations in Europe and Italy." *Blood Transfusion* 8, no. 3 (2010): 178–185.

Summerfield, A. Quentin, David H. Marshall, Garry R. Barton, and Karen E. Bloor. "A Cost-Utility Scenario Analysis of Bilateral Cochlear Implantation." *Archives of Otolaryngology – Head & Neck Surgery* 128, no. 11 (2002): 1255–1262.

Sunstein, Cass R. "Lives, Life-Years and Willingness to Pay." *Columbia Law Review* 104, no. 205 (2004): 205–252.

—. *The Cost-Benefit State: The Future of Regulatory Protection.* Chicago: American Bar Association, 2002.

—. "Illusory Losses." *The Journal of Legal Studies* 37, (2008): S157-S194.

Sutherland, Heather J., Hilary Llewellyn-Thomas, and James E. Till. "Attitudes Toward Quality of Survival – the Concept of 'Maximal Endurable Time'." *Medical Decision Making* 2 (1982): 299–309.

Swedloff, Rick and Peter H. Huang. "Tort Damages and the New Science of Happiness." *Indiana Law Journal* 85 (2010): 553.

Tengs, Tammy O. and Ting H. Lin. "A Meta-Analysis of Utility Estimates for HIV/AIDS." *Medical Decision Making* 22 (2002): 475–481.

Tjittes, R-J. "Smartengeld Voor Bewustelozen (Pain and Suffering Damages for the Unconscious)." *Nederlands Tijdschrift Voor Burgerlijk Recht* (2003).

Tole, Swati P., A. M. Bayoumi, M. L. Brandeau, C. M. Galvin, D. K. Owens, G. D. Sanders, and T. N. Vinichenko. "Cost-Effectiveness of Voluntary HIV Screening in Russia." *International Journal of STD & AIDS* 20, no. 1 (2009): 46–51.

Torgerson, David J. and James Raftery. "Discounting." *British Medical Journal* 319 (1999): 914–915.

Torrance, George W., Warren H. Thomas, and David L. Sackett. "A Utility Maximization Model for Evaluation of Health Care Programs." *Health Services Research* 7 (1972): 118–133.

Torrance, George W. "Measurement of Health State Utilities for Economic Appraisal: A Review." *Journal of Health Economics* 5, no. 1 (3, 1986): 1–30.

Torrance, George W., David Feeny, and William Furlong. "Visual Analog Scales: Do they have a Role in the Measurement of Preferences for Health States?" *Medical Decision Making* 21, no. 4 (2001): 329–334.

Torrance, George W., David H. Feeny, William J. Furlong, Ronald D. Barr, Yueming Zhang, and Qinan Wang. "Multiattribute Utility Function for a Comprehensive Health Status Classification System: Health Utilities Index Mark 2." *Medical Care* 34, no. 7 (1996): 702–722.

Towse, Andrian. "Should NICE's threshold range for cost per QALY be raised? Yes." *British Medical Journal* 338 (2009): 268–269.

Tribunale di Milano, *Liquidazione del Danno Non Patrimoniale,* Tabelle 2013.

Tribunale di Roma, *Tabella Danno Biologico*, 2013.

Tsevat, Joel, Jenny G. Solzan, Karen M. Kuntz, Julia Ragland, Judith S. Currier, Randall L. Sell, and Milton C. Weinstein. "Health Values of Patients Infected with Human Immunodeficiency Virus: Relationship to Mental Health and Physical Functioning." *Medical Care* 34, no. 1 (1996): 44–57.

Tsuchiya, Aki and Alan Williams. "Welfare Economics and Economic Evaluation." In *Economic Evaluation in Health Care: Mearging Theory with Practice*, edited by Drummond, Michael F. and Alistair McGuire. Oxford, New York: Oxford University Press, 2001.

Tversky, Amos and Daniel Kahneman. "Advances in Prospect Theory: Cumulative Representation of Uncertainty." *Journal of Risk and Uncertainty* 5, no. 4 (1992): 297–323.

—. "The Framing of Decisions and the Psychology of Choice." *Science* 211 (1981): 453–458.

Tyc, Vida L. "Psychosocial Adaptation of Children and Adolescents with Limb Deficiencies: A Review." *Clinical Psychology Review* 12, no. 3 (1992): 275–291.

Ubel, Peter A., Aleksandra Jankovic, Dylan Smith, Kenneth M. Langa, and Angela Fagerlin. "What Is Perfect Health to an 85-Year-Old? Evidence for Scale Recalibration in Subjective Health Ratings." *Medical Care* 43 (2005): 1054–1057.

Ubel, Peter A., George Loewenstein, John Hershey, Jonathan Baron, Tara Mohr, David A. Asch, and Christopher Jepson. "Do Nonpatients Underestimate the Quality of Life Associated with Chronic Health Conditions because of a Focusing Illusion?" *Medical Decision Making* 21, (2001): 190–199.

Ubel, Peter A., George Loewenstein, and Christopher Jepson. "Disability and Sunshine: Can Hedonic Predictions be Improved by Drawing Attention to Focusing Illusions Or Emotional Adaptation?" *Journal of Experimental Psychology: Applied* 11, no. 2 (2005): 111–123.

—. "Whose Quality of Life? A Commentary Exploring Discrepancies between Health State Evaluations of Patients and the General Public." *Quality of Life Research* 12, no. 6 (2003): 599–607.

Ubel, Peter A., George Loewenstein, Norbert Schwarz, and Dylan Smith. "Misimagining the Unimaginable: The Disability Paradox and Health Care Decision Making." *Health Psychology* 24, no. 4 (2005): S57–S62.

Ubel, Peter A and George Loewenstein. "Pain and Suffering Awards: They Shouldn't be (just) about Pain and Suffering." *The Journal of Legal Studies* 37 (06/01, 2008): S195–S216.

UK Cochlear Implant Study Group. "Criteria of Candidacy for Unilateral Cochlear Implantation in Postlingually Deafened Adults II: Cost-Effectiveness Analysis." *Ear & Hearing* 25, no. 4 (2004): 336–360.

van Boom, Willem H. "The Netherlands." In *Compensation for Personal Injury in a Comparative Perspective*, edited by Koch, Bernhard A. and Helmut Koziol. Vienna; New York: Springer, 2003.

—. "Structurele fouten in het aansprakelijkheidsrecht." Inaugural address Tilburg University. The Hague: BJU, 2003.

van Dam, Cees. *European Tort Law.* Oxford, New York: Oxford University Press, 2006.

—. "Een effectief rechtsmiddel voor een bewusteloos slachtoffer." *Verkeersrecht* 143 (2013): 442–448.

van Gerven, Walter, Jeremy Lever, and Pierre Larouche. *Tort Law.* Oxford; Portland, OR: Hart Publishing, 2000.

van Velthoven, Ben C. J. "Empirics of Tort." In *Tort Law and Economics*, edited by Faure, Michael. 2nd ed., 453–498. Cheltenham, UK; Northampton, MA, USA: Edward Elgar, 2009.

Viscusi, W. Kip. "Empirical Analysis of Tort Damages." In *Research Handbook on the Economics of Torts,* edited by Arlen, Jennifer, 460–485. Cheltenham, UK: Edward Elgar, 2013.

—. "The Flawed Hedonic Damages Measure of Compensation for Wrongful Death and Personal Injury." *Journal of Forensic Economics* 20, no. 2 (2008): 113–135.

—. "Pain and Suffering in Product Liability Cases: Systematic Compensation Or Capricious Awards?" *International Review of Law and Economics* 8, no. 2 (12, 1988): 203–220.

—. "The Value of Life: Has Voodoo Economics Come to the Courts?" *Journal of Forensic Economics* 3, no. 3 (1990): 1–15.

Viscusi, W. Kip and Joseph E. Aldy. "The Value of a Statistical Life: A Critical Review of Market Estimates Throughout the World." *Journal of Risk and Uncertainty* 27, no. 1 (2003): 5–76.

Viscusi, W. Kip and William N. Evans. "Utility Functions that Depend on Health Status: Estimates and Economic Implications." *American Economic Review* 80, (1990): 353–374.

Visscher, Louis T. "Tort Damages." In *Tort Law and Economics*, edited by Faure, Michael. 2nd ed. Vol. 1, 153–200. Cheltenham, UK: Edward Elgar, 2009.

Visser, K., S. O. de Vries, P. J. E. H. M. Kitslaar, J. M. A. van Engelshoven, and M. G. M. Hunink. "Cost-Effectiveness of Diagnostic Imaging Work-Up and Treatment for Patients with Intermittent Claudication in the Netherlands." *European Journal of Vascular and Endovascular Surgery* 25, no. 3 (3, 2003): 213–223.

Von Neumann, John and Oskar Morgenstern. *Theory of Games and Economic Behavior.* Princeton: Princeton University Press, 1944.

Wagstaff, Adam. "QALYs and the Equity-Efficiency Trade-Off." *Journal of Health Economics* 10, (1991): 21–41.

Wailoo, Alan, Sarah Davis, and Jonathan Tosh. *The Incorporation of Health Benefits in Cost-Utility Analysis using the EQ-5D*: National Institute for Health and Clinical Excellence Decision Support Unit, 2010.

Weinstein, Milton C. and William B. Stason. "Foundations of Cost-Effectiveness Analysis for Health and Medical Practices." *The New England Journal of Medicine* 296, no. 13 (1977): 716–721.

—. *Hypertension: A Policy Perspective*. Cambridge, MA: Harvard University Press, 1976.

Weinstein, Milton C., George Torrance, and Alistair McGuire. "QALYs: The Basics." *Value in Health* 12, no. s1 (2009): S5–S9.

Weir, Laura, Derek Aldridge, Kelly Rathje, and Christopher Bruce. "The Discount Rate Revisited." *Expert Witness* no. 1 (2008): 6 March 2012.

Weir, Tony. "Damages." In *Tort Law*, edited by Weir, Tony, 185–202. Oxford, New York: Oxford University Press, 2002.

Williams, Alan. "Economics of Coronary Artery Bypass Grafting." *British Medical Journal* 291, no. 6491 (8, 1985): 326–329.

Williams, Alan, Roger W. Evans, and Michael F. Drummont. "Quality-Adjusted Life-Years." *The Lancet* 329, no. 8546 (1987): 1372–1373.

Williams, Alan. "Intergenerational Equity: An Exploration of the 'Fair Innings' Argument." *Health Economics* 6, no. 2 (1997): 117–132.

Williams, Alan and Richard Cookson. "Equity in Health." *Handbook of Health Economics* 1 (2000): 1863–1910.

Wilson, Timothy D., Thalia Wheatley, Jonathan M. Meyers, Daniel T. Gilbert, and Danny Axsom. "Focalism: A Source of Durability Bias in Affective Forecasting." *Journal Personality & Social Psychology* 78, no. 5 (2000): 821–836.

Wilson, Timothy D. and Daniel T. Gilbert. "Affective Forecasting." *Advances in Experimental Social Psychology* 35 (2003): 345–411.

Wissink, Mark H. and Willem H. van Boom. "The Netherlands." In *Unification of Tort Law: Damages*, edited by Magnus, U. The Hague: Kluwer Law International, 2001.

—. "The Netherlands." In *Damages for Non-Pecuniary Loss in a Comparative Perspective*, edited by Rogers, W. V. Horton. Vienna; New York: Springer, 2001.

Wittman, Donald. "Optimal Pricing of Sequential Inputs: Last Clear Chance, Mitigation of Damages, and Related Doctrines in the Law." *The Journal of Legal Studies* 10, no. 1 (1981): 65–91.

Wolff, B. Berthold. "Ethnocultural Factors Influencing Pain and Illness Behavior." *Clinical Journal of Pain* 1, no. 1 (1985): 23–30.

Wolff, B. Berthold and Sarah Langley. "Cultural Factors and the Response to Pain: A Review." *American Anthropologist* 70, no. 3 (1968): 494–501.

World Bank. "GNI Per Capita, Atlas Method." World Bank, accessed 31 March 2014. http://data.worldbank.org/indicator/NY.GNP.PCAP.CD.

World Health Organization. *The Global Burden of Disease. 2004 Update*. Geneva, Switzerland: World Health Organization, 2008.

Wyatt, J. Robert, John K. Niparko, Margaret Rothman, and Gregory de Lissovoy. "Cost Utility of the Multichannel Cochlear Implant in 258 Profoundly Deaf Individuals." *Laryngoscope* 106, no. 7 (1996): 816–821.

Zador, Paul and Adrian Lund. "Re-Analyses of the Effects of No-Fault Auto Insurance on Fatal Crashes." *Journal of Risk and Insurance* 53, no. 2 (1986): 226–241.

Zeckhauser, Richard and Donald Shepard. "Where Now for Saving Lives?" *Law and Contemporary Problems* 40, no. 4 (1976): 5–45.

Zethraeus, Niklas. "Willingness to Pay for Hormone Replacement Therapy." *Health Economics* 7, no. 1 (1998): 31–38.

Zwahlen, Marcel and Matthias Egger. *UNAIDS Obligation no. HQ/05/422204. Progression and Mortality of Untreated HIV-Positive Individuals Living in Resource-Limited Settings: Update of Literature Review and Evidence Synthesis*. Bern: University of Bern, Division of International and Environmental Health, 2006.

ABOUT THE AUTHOR

Vaia Karapanou is a lawyer and a law and economics scholar specializing in economic analysis of tort law and insurance, regulation and law enforcement, comparative law and economics, health economics and regulatory impact assessment. She holds a Bachelor of Laws (University of Athens, Greece), an LLM in Law and Economics (Erasmus University Rotterdam, the Netherlands – University of Hamburg, Germany – University of California, Berkeley, USA) and a PhD in Law and Economics (Erasmus University Rotterdam, the Netherlands – University of Bologna, Italy). She won the Greek Law and Economics Association's Dimitris Karantonis Award in 2013 and the Latin American and Caribbean Law and Economics Association's Robert D. Cooter Microsoft Award in 2009. Dr Karapanou has published in accredited journals and edited volumes.